ADVANCE PRAISE FOR
Childhoods in More Just Worlds:
An International Handbook

"This is a timely and important book. The contributions take up the critical task of inquiring into what it might look like to centre justice in the worlds and worldings of young children in current times of intensified and unevenly distributed precarity. Rather than working with an already-known and universalized meaning of justice, the book powerfully illustrates how confronting the impacts of neoliberal capitalism, colonialism and human exceptionalism on 21st Century childhoods can occur through situated, socio-culturally attuned accounts that attend closely to the places and spaces of childhood becomings."
—*Fikile Nxumalo, Ph.D., Assistant Professor,*
Department of Curriculum, Teaching and Learning,
Ontario Institute for the Studies in Education,
University of Toronto

"This timely and evocative volume traces how historical, political, and developmental discourses continue to influence how we mobilize justice, equity, and care in the lives of young children across the globe. Through its analysis of research, policy, and practice, I was reminded that we (as adults) limit children's capacity to act on their world(s), even in contemporary activist movements. In our effort to advocate *for* children's rights, we potentially diminish their capacity to move along and with us as collaborators and contributors to a more just world. As authors argue, without new and expanded thinking on the most pressing social issues—(im)migration, emotional well-being, colonization, sustainability, neoliberal politics—we potentially reify the conditions that create inequitable systems and boundaries. That is, *caring* for children is not about protecting children or using them as *props* for our own political agendas, but deeply understanding their entanglement with adults, the material world, nonhuman creatures, and our global communities."
—*Haeny S. Yoon, Ph.D., Associate Professor,*
Early Childhood Education,
Teachers College, Columbia University

CHILDHOODS IN MORE JUST WORLDS

Early Years & Youth Studies:
Gaile S. Cannella, Editor

The Early Years & Youth Studies series is a set of volumes designed to focus on the multiple life experiences, forms of representation, relations, changes, and issues facing those who are identified (usually by those who are older in years) as child or youth in the 21st Century. The content is cross-disciplinary, but unique in that each volume always folds back to direct applications for care and/or education. Further, while lived experience, cultural studies, and research in the social sciences have demonstrated that there is no universal childhood or human development, diversity and multiplicity remain to a large extent unrecognized. Authors are encouraged to consider one or more of the following: children and youth as diverse beings and becomings in the 21st Century (e.g., childhood and youth studies after 50 years of the critique of human development, hybrid and indigenous childhoods, youth as refugee and immigrant entanglements, transgendered childhoods); complexities of being young in the digital age (e.g., bullying, digital identities, use of media by those who are younger); critical pedagogies (e.g., of affect; of collective activism, social justice, environmental justice; with/of the more-than-human like forest pedagogies, youth and critical animal studies, educational practices that avoid human/nonhuman and curricular dualisms); and/or activist movements and public policy (e.g., youth activism, parent activism to counter neoliberal education, research methods and practices directly employed to impact childhood public policy).

Books in the Series

Nurture, Care, Respect, and Trust: Transformative Pedagogy Inspired by Janusz Korczak
Edited by Tatyana Tsyrlina-Spady and Peter C. Renn (2020)
Childhoods in More Just Worlds: An International Handbook
Edited by Timothy Kinard and Gaile S. Cannella (2021)
Introducing Critical Childhood Perspectives: Reconceptualist Thought, Diversity, and Social Justice Expectations
Edited by Ashley Lauren Sullivan(Forthcoming)
Childhood, Justice, and Critical Inquiry
by Gaile S. Cannella (Forthcoming)
Critical Literacy Approaches to Children's Literature in the Primary Grades
by Nadine Bryce (Forthcoming)

Authors interested in having their manuscripts considered for publication in Early Years & Youth Studies are encouraged to send a prospectus, sample chapter, and CV to the series editor, Gaile Cannella (gaile.cannella@gmail.com). For instructions and advice on preparing a prospectus, please refer to the Myers Education Press website at http://myersedpress.com/sites/stylus/MEP/Docs/Prospectus%20Guidelines%20MEP.pdf. Gaile S. Cannella (EdD, University of Georgia) is an independent scholar who has served as a tenured full professor at Texas A&M University–College Station and at Arizona State University–Tempe, as well as the Velma Schmidt Endowed Chair of Education at the University of North Texas.

Childhoods in More Just Worlds

An International Handbook

EDITED BY

Tim Kinard and Gaile S. Cannella

Myers Education Press

GORHAM, MAINE

Myers Education Press

Copyright © 2021 | Myers Education Press, LLC

Published by Myers Education Press, LLC
P.O. Box 424
Gorham, ME 04038

All rights reserved. No part of this book may be reprinted or reproduced in any form or by any electronic, mechanical, or other means, now known or hereafter invented, including photocopying, recording, and information storage and retrieval, without permission in writing from the publisher.

> **Myers Education Press** is an academic publisher specializing in books, e-books, and digital content in the field of education. All of our books are subjected to a rigorous peer review process and produced in compliance with the standards of the Council on Library and Information Resources.

LIBRARY OF CONGRESS CATALOGING-IN-PUBLICATION DATA AVAILABLE FROM LIBRARY OF CONGRESS.

13-digit ISBN 978-1-9755-0410-6 (hard cover)
13-digit ISBN 978-1-9755-0411-3 (paperback)
13-digit ISBN 978-1-9755-0412-0 (library networkable e-edition)
13-digit ISBN 978-1-9755-0413-7 (consumer e-edition)

Printed in the United States of America.

All first editions printed on acid-free paper that meets the American National Standards Institute Z39-48 standard.

Books published by Myers Education Press may be purchased at special quantity discount rates for groups, workshops, training organizations, and classroom usage. Please call our customer service department at 1-800-232-0223 for details.

Cover design by Teresa Lagrange.

Visit us on the web at **www.myersedpress.com** to browse our complete list of titles.

Contents

Preface: Childhoods in More Just Worlds: An International Handbook   ix
Gaile S. Cannella and Tim Kinard

Bodies, Beings, and Relations in More Just Worlds

1. The Reduction of Children to "Bare Life": The Case of Child Migration   3
 Michael O'Loughlin and Renata de Assis

2. "Forward to No Place at All": Forceful Migration and Child Welfare   21
 Mlado Ivanovic

3. A Romani Analysis of English Preschool Education   39
 Mandy Pierlejewski and Gyula Vamosi

4. The Shadows and Silences of Colonialism: Resisting Eroding Realities for Māori Children Through Language Re-Vernacularisation in Antipodean New Zealand   55
 Mere Skerrett

5. Staying with the Troubles of Colonised Emotional Well-Being of Young Children in Aotearoa (New Zealand)   71
 Jenny Ritchie

6. Competing Discourses about Immigrant Children: Metaphors of the Right and Left   87
 Theodora Lightfoot

Care and Education: Performing Just Childhood Worlds

7. Refusing Policymakers' Manufactured Crisis: Countering Conceptions of School Readiness   103
 Christopher P. Brown, David P. Barry, and Da Hei Ku

8. Politics of Childhoods: Paradoxical Moments of Be(com)ing — 121
   I-Fang Lee

9. Sitting With the Agency Paradox to Stand for Childhood Liberation: The Case of Critical Mathematics Education — 137
   José Martínez Hinestroza

10. "Your Children Are Having Too Much Fun": Teaching Literacy With Radical Hope — 155
    Luz A. Murillo

11. Justice Mapping: Making Theoretical Kin With/in Childhood Studies — 175
    Tim Kinard

12. Becoming-with Water: Collaboration, Ethico-onto-epistemologies, Experimentations, and Creativity — 191
    Mindy Blaise and Claire O'Callaghan

13. Entanglements of Neoliberalism, Childhoods and Environmental Justice — 207
    Kylie Smith, Casey Myers, and Marek Tesar

Stir of Echoes: 20th-Century Childhoods in the 21st

14. Figurations of the Child in Swedish Early Childhood Education — 223
    Therese Lindgren

15. Innocence and Parenting in Difficult Times — 243
    Emily L. Murphy and Hannah Dyer

16. Playing With the Politics of Play — 259
    Sue Grieshaber and Sally Barnes

17. Becoming Convivial With Child: Dismantling the Race/Child/Learning/Human Assemblage — 279
    Maria Kromidas

    About the Authors — 295

    Index — 303

PREFACE

Childhoods in More Just Worlds: An International Handbook

Gaile S. Cannella and Tim Kinard

THOSE WHO ARE younger continue to be objects of injustice and inequity, injustices that are played out in forms of human exceptionalism that construct specific groups of human beings as superior to others (with the so-called exceptional ones usually those who are White, male, adult, and beneficiaries of economic privilege and/or other forms of hierarchal power). Those who are younger, people of color, females, and human beings living in poverty have never been included in equitable performances of justice, care, respect, and fairness. Furthermore, nonhuman creatures and materialities have also been excluded and harmed by this human exceptionalism that privileges certain so-called humans (and not all). Actively remembering the intersections of *all* these worlds as we attempt to create broader forms of justice is necessary.

Because we are here concerned about younger human beings and are embedded in practices of support, care, and education, we must throughout our imaginings, intra-actions, and becoming(s)-with engage with ways to entangle childhood with movement toward increased justice for these multiple, even pluriversal worlds. We could generate many related questions. Perhaps the main are, How do we acknowledge and enable transformative entanglements toward justice in multiple worlds while recognizing that justice and equity are themselves problematic, emergent, and never definable? and What does that mean for the ways we facilitate relations and become-with those who are younger so their/our/together focus becomes justice and equity in multiple worlds? As critical scholars whose values (and ethics) are, we hope, always embedded in concern for justice and equity (and acknowledging those constructs as multiple, complex, conditional, emergent, and human constructions), we want to avoid approaching theories or philosophical perspectives as universal truths, with some defined as more accurate or newer than others.

The contributors to this volume therefore hope to use the imaginaries and strengths of various perspectives to aid in addressing justice in particular circumstances in ways that have not previously been considered to create more just worlds for those who are young, and for all of us. The first set of chapters, "Bodies, Beings, and Relations in More Just Worlds," place at the forefront the lives of those who are younger who are commonly relegated to positions of invisibility, disqualification, and even erasure. We hope this positioning demonstrates not a form of objectification but, rather, our concern that the physical bodies and lives of children who continue to be disqualified within the colonialist past present, along with those who are displaced through violence, inequities, and other forms of injustice, are disregarded. Even in most of our discussions and debates within fields that are concerned with those who are younger, debates regarding issues like development, care, schooling/learning, and even policy overlook the daily lives of millions of children and their families. In the second section, "Performances of Care and Education for More Just Worlds," the chapter authors acknowledge that conceptualizations of those who are younger, along with an appreciation for human diversity and entanglements between the so-called human and nonhuman worlds, are the foundations for more just care and education environments. From the construction of neoliberal reform discourses to reconceptualizing human relations with nonhuman animals and material worlds, care and learning environments are rethought. The set of chapters in the final section, "Stir of Echoes: 20th-Century Childhoods in the 21st Century," take up the 20th-century critical concerns with constructions of "child" that have dominated and continue to govern perspectives imposed on those who are younger. Ranging from examinations of the perpetual views of "child" as needing saving and "child" as innocent to suggestions for becomings-with those who are younger through resources like reconceptualist scholarship, Black and Indigenous studies, and various posthuman perspectives, the possibilities for more just worlds are generated.

Whatever the emphasis or focus of a section or chapter, throughout the volume is the recognition that dominant discourses (e.g., neoliberal capitalism, conservativism, progressivism, human exceptionalism) and the policies they create (and that facilitate them), influence possibilities for, and limitations to, more just childhood worlds. Therefore, each section includes chapters that address these complex discourses and policy issues. The reader is invited to engage with these complexities, to become-with the various texts, and to generate unthought possibilities for childhoods in more just worlds.

BODIES, BEINGS, AND RELATIONS IN MORE JUST WORLDS

CHAPTER 1

The Reduction of Children to "Bare Life": The Case of Child Migration

Michael O'Loughlin and Renata de Assis

> *These ghosts—men, women, children—walked along rural roads between the border towns of Europe with plastic bags and eyes that locals didn't want to look into for fear of seeing all the world's trouble. And while they waited for their papers to be processed, their past lives lay behind them in ruins. But they couldn't afford to mourn because of a more pressing problem: their new lives couldn't begin.*
>
> —KASSABOVA (2017, P. 191)

IN OUR INEQUITABLE world, many children live lives of great precarity. Endemic poverty, exploitation of child labor, a lack of preventive health care, and access to substandard, if any, schooling are risk factors for many of the world's children. The greatest suffering, however, is reserved for those children who experience displacements from their family and community that layer an additional level of trauma on top of those other deprivations: children who are trafficked; children who are coerced into soldiering; children who are displaced internally or externally by wars, genocides, or natural disasters; and children in families forced to relocate due to loss of livelihood caused by climate change or other factors suffer additional trauma. Children in refugee or asylum-seeking families and children who flee alone are obviously at extreme risk due to the constellation of comorbid vulnerabilities that constitute their life circumstances. Kai Erikson (1976) has documented the long-term psychic damage to individuals when the communal bonds that hold extended families and local communities together are ruptured. Erikson summarized the effects of *collective trauma* this way:

> By collective trauma, I mean a blow to the tissues of social life that damages the bonds linking people together and impairs the prevailing sense of communality. The collective trauma works its way slowly and even insidiously into the awareness of those who suffer from it: thus it does not have the quality of suddenness usually associated with the word "trauma." It is however a form of shock—a gradual realization that the community no longer exists as a source of nurturance and that a part of the self has disappeared. (1976, p. 302)

The trauma induced by a rupture of social bonds is compounded further if children and families experience dislocations caused by forceful erasure of language and culture that accompany many forced migrations and displacements. O'Loughlin (2012, in press), for example, discusses generations of psychic damage resulting from the erasure of the Irish language around 1800 by British colonial powers and the catastrophic mass death and displacements resulting from the Great Famine of the 1840s, while Walsh (2016) has documented epigenetic changes resulting from the Great Famine, an event in which the population was reduced almost by half in a very brief period. Likewise, aboriginal scholar Judy Atkinson (2002) has documented what she refers to as intergenerational *trauma trails* emanating from the physical and cultural genocide of Aboriginal Australians. Strenuous efforts at cultural annihilation were carried out, particularly through the forced extraction of 30,000 children from families and their placement in harsh residential school settings where a systemic effort was made to rupture familial and cultural bonds, resulting in *the stolen generations* of Aboriginal families. Similar scholarship exists around the displacement of Indigenous communities in the United States and Canada. There is extensive documentation on the profound cultural, relational, and psychic damage caused by forced residential schooling in North America. In Canada, this damage has earned the sobriquet *residential school syndrome*.[1] Historically, colonialism and its accompanying capitalist resource extraction have left their mark in terms of the intergenerational trauma sequelae resulting from displacement from ancestral lands. The use of divide-and-conquer policies that uprooted people and severed tribal bonds, what Davoine and Gaudillière (2004) refer to as *rupturing of social links*, have sown the seeds of much of the world's territorial conflicts. The arrival of what are characterized as hordes of former colonial subjects at the doorsteps of their White former colonial masters no doubt produces complex emotions of guilt, fear, and disavowal in the latter.

Freud's concept of *Nachträglichkeit* and Lacan's concept of *après coup*,[2] as well as Winnicott's (1974) notion of the *fear of breakdown* are apposite here, particularly in relation to the suffering of children. These concepts refer to a trauma that is so overwhelming that at the time of its occurrence it does not register. A trauma could be suspended or frozen simply because of the survival imperative of the moment, such as the urgent need to flee war, genocide, or a natural disaster. In children, the risk of petrification from trauma is exacerbated because the relatively immature psychic structure of the child risks being overwhelmed by the trauma. Entering a frozen or dissociated state is the only means of preventing breakdown. At a later time, when the danger has passed, such a person is vulnerable to (re)traumatization with the full force of the original event (Herman, 1997). Work with children of Holocaust survivors (Auerhahn & Prelinger, 1983; Kaplan, 1996), as well as clinical accounts of therapy with child trauma survivors (Rogers, 2006), point to how failure to process such trauma can cause intergenerational sequelae to be transmitted through the child-rearing process thereby leaving future generations burdened with unspoken, unnamable ancestral suffering.

This kind of trauma-based framework is of value in understanding the suffering of refugee and asylum-seeking children, and it does point the way to local work that can be done to assist migrant and refugee children (cf. Bragin, 2019; Drożdek & Wilson, 2007). Important humanitarian work can and must be done to alleviate children's suffering, and indeed, Michael O'Loughlin and doctoral students at Adelphi University participate in this work through the Adelphi Asylum Project run in partnership with the Human Rights Clinic of Healthright International in New York, providing asylum services to children and families.[3] Local work matters. However, as child advocates in Europe and the United States learned the hard way in recent years, such local efforts are seriously challenged by government policies on policing hard borders that cause a migrant toddler to end up facedown, dead on a beach in Bodrum, Turkey; a migrant father and daughter to drown in the Rio Grande; and children to end up in cages, separated from caregivers supposedly in the "care" of U.S. Customs and Border Protection agents.[4] What if the prosperity and privilege of Western neoliberal societies depend on the production of migrants, refugees, and other displaced persons?

Refugee and Asylum Status as a State of Exception

What are we as human beings if we allow our governments to create what Agamben (1998) calls *states of exception* in which some people take on the status of *homo sacer*—unwanted ones, rejects, vermin people?[5] Once they leave or are expelled from their countries of origins, refugees and asylum seekers enter a nether world, a place with no rules, no rights, and often no hope. Existing outside of established governmental systems, refugees have no recognizable being and are apparently not worthy of protection. The situation is further compounded for children because they have no legal or political rights in any sovereign state.

Agamben's notion of *bare life* and *state of exception*, as discussed in *Homo Sacer* (1998), *Remnants of Auschwitz* (2002), and *State of Exception* (2005), although subjected to critique (e.g., Fassin, 2010; Khanna, 2009a), has been adopted by many critical writers on refugee lives[6] because of Agamben's capacity to offer a political explanation for the way in which ostensibly progressive, humanitarian, and democratic countries create conditions of abjection for persons who are refugees or asylum seekers. Agamben's singular contribution is to tie an analysis of the existential condition of the suffering and indeed *disposable* (Khanna, 2009b) refugee to the workings of sovereign power. Agamben thereby questions individual liberty as a foundational assumption of Western democracy—a system that permits citizens to benefit from its freedoms only because it can invoke autocratic powers of extrajudicial regulation to control and manage its Others. Agamben's thesis, then, is that we only enjoy the freedoms that we, citizens of progressive democracies in the West, enjoy because we simultaneously invest our sovereigns with the power to create *homo sacer* or *bare life*:

> The body of *homo sacer*, which is to say bare life . . . is modern democracy's strength and, at the same time, its inner contradiction: modern democracy does not abolish sacred life but rather shatters and disseminates it into every individual body, making it into what is at stake in political conflict. (1998, p. 124)

Turning specifically to refugees, Agamben (1998) begins with Hannah Arendt's remark that the presence of refugees creates a crisis for our conception of human rights:

> The conception of human rights based upon the assumed existence of a human being, as such, broke down at the very moment when those who professed to believe in it were for the first time confronted with people who had indeed lost all other qualities and specific relationships—except that they were still human." (quoted from Arendt, 1966, p. 299, cited in Agamben, 1998, p. 125)

Declarations of rights, Agamben (1998, p. 127) notes, apply only to persons within the normal juridico-political order. The state is not constructed on a natural order based on being human. One becomes a sovereign subject by virtue of birth. Refugees, "by breaking the continuity between *nativity* and *nationality*[,] . . . put the originary fiction of modern sovereignty in crisis" (1998, p. 130, emphasis in original). The case of people placed outside the normal order is readily illustrated by the status of Jews during the Third Reich. The Nazi sovereign took care to strip them of their citizenship, to render them nonpersons, to pave the way for their disposal through death camps, gas vans, and the like. Even in death, the dehumanization of Jews continued: Their bodies were referred to as *Figuren* (puppets) or *Schmattes* (rags).

In a discussion of necropolitics, Mbembe (2003) states that "the ultimate sovereignty resides in the power and the capacity to dictate who may live and who may die" (p. 11). The mechanism by which such life-and-death decisions are made, Mbembe (2003) claims, is through racial dehumanization: "Race has been the ever present shadow in Western political thought and practice, especially when it comes to imagining the inhumanity of, or rule over, foreign peoples" (p. 17). Thus, the heritage of colonial conquest, with its attendant racial dehumanization, and the treatment of contemporary refugees by Western powers are inextricably linked. The state of exception, Mbembe states, was a necessary condition of the "civilizing" mission of the colonies. Mbembe's image of the plantation slave, who experiences social death, serves as a precursor to the more contemporary dehumanization and social death of persons who are designated refugees:

> First, in the context of the plantation, the humanity of the slave appears as the perfect figure of a shadow. Indeed, the slave condition results from a triple loss: loss of a "home," loss of rights over his or her body, and loss of political status. This triple loss is identical with absolute domination, natal alienation, and social death (expulsion from humanity altogether). (2003, p. 21)

"Sovereignty," Mbembe notes, "means the capacity to define who matters and who does not, who is *disposable* and who is not" (2003, p. 27).

Following a similar line of argument, Limbu (2009) suggests that how we come to an understanding of *refugeeness* depends on our ethical stance on the nature of humanity. If, as Kant (1996) suggests in *Perpetual Peace*, hospitality is a human right, persons in need should not be reduced to abject beggarhood and political silencing in order to receive assistance. Drawing on Derrida (1993) and Arendt (1966), Limbu notes that difficulty has arisen because basic human status is tied to the question of citizenship, thereby defining stateless persons as (non)persons without rights. *The refugee*, therefore, is a bureaucratic formulation designed to exclude and to permit actions on the body of the refugee that would never be permitted on persons with full human rights. As Limbu notes, it is useless to seek to reconceptualize the treatment of *the refugee*, without probing the discursive contexts within which the political world has chosen to delimit the human status of *the refugee*. Is it possible to conceptualize humanitarian relief efforts or interventions, absent an understanding of the historicized or politicized contexts within which *refugeeness* is constructed?

Papastergiadis (2006) refers to refugee camps as a form of limbo, and he points out that moral outrage or horror is unlikely to have any influence on the presence of such camps precisely because the construction of the camps "is consistent with modern democratic definitions of executive power" (p. 437) and furthermore that "the normalization of the state of exception is also embedded in a deeper process of depoliticization" in which refugees are nonpersons, people without rights or voices. (p. 437).

The Legal Precarity of Child Migrants and Refugees

In the introduction to *Child Migration and Human Rights in a Global Age*, Jacqueline Bhabha (2014) argues that despite a push toward developing more child-centered migration policies, the outlook for children worldwide is grim:

> Current child-centered policies in the migration field end up targeting children for infantilizing, harsh, and punitive measures that reduce their autonomy and their scope for self-development and self-sufficiency . . . by denying children the family reunion rights that their adult relatives have, by restricting the access to self-sufficiency and autonomy for children escaping situations of gross exploitation, and by misconstruing the alternatives available to child migrants moving for survival, our current interventions are at best ineffective, often counterproductive. (2014, p. 15)

There is a deep tension, Jacqueline Bhabha (2014) notes, in national policies between "the sovereign state's prerogative to exercise border control and the human being's right to respect for family life" (p. 4). She quotes Judith Butler's stark declaration: "The exemplary moment of sovereignty is the act of deportation" (Butler & Spivak, quoted in J. Bhabha, 2014, p. 62). Jacqueline Bhabha also underlines the precarity of migrant children:

> Refugee children and their female caregivers are much *less* likely than adult men to reach a wealthy destination state where they can make an application for permanent refugee protection. Though, as I have just noted, children constitute almost half of the world's refugees, they amount to less than a third of asylum seekers in developed states. Among the majority of children who do not make it to a developed state to claim asylum, some 1–4 million live in impoverished and overcrowded refugee camps and settlements. . . . Tragically, more than two thirds of today's refugees have spent five or more years "warehoused" in such camps where the average length of stay is close to twenty years. These refugees include millions of children trapped in a limbo of *temporary permanence*, dependence and despair, where only periodic aid handouts from international organizations or intracamp fights interrupt the endless flow of boredom and depression induced by the lack of prospects. (2014, p. 209)

According to Jacqueline Bhabha (2011), the lack of legal identity affects an individual's capacity to claim on the state and the state's ability to plan and provide for individuals. Refugee children may fall into two legal categories: de facto statelessness and de jure statelessness. In the de facto category, children have a nationality, but because they are irregular or undocumented migrants, they do not have legal status in their current location. In the de jure category of stateless people, children do not have a nationality of any state; they are literally stateless.

Children are especially affected by statelessness, Jacqueline Bhabha notes, as they are dependent on states for essential services (education, primary care, shelter), and, in the case of refugees, access to legal migration routes. Children born to undocumented migrants are at a higher risk of statelessness. When parents do not have a legal residency permit, the frequency of violations of children's rights increases tremendously, most notably the children's right to family unity. In many instances, children are rendered social orphans and depend even further on the beneficence of the state. Especially concerning, Bhabha states, is that children might be used by governments to punish parents. It is common in such situations that citizen children are separated from their undocumented parents, or they are pressed to forego their legal status to stay close to their parents. In these cases, the government fails to protect the child from harm and provokes hardship in the child's life. Children who are stateless end up in this situation because they are considered dispensable, undeserving, and dangerous.

At best, states have a contradictory mandate, seeking to protect the vulnerable while simultaneously policing its borders. Jacqueline Bhabha (2011) notes that states have developed a bureaucratic apparatus around migrant control which is designed to hinder migrant and refugee access to documentation and citizenship fulfillment. Governments, therefore, are the main dispenser of rights or of repression. She notes that "children do not *in the main* end up without a state by accident or oversight." (2011, p. 21). To complicate matters even more, she notes that rendering children more visible may generate more surveillance and persecution of both children and families. Visibility does not guarantee enfranchised citizenship and may produce its opposite.

Governments have the power to justify how different children are captured by the bureaucratic apparatus and states have the supereminent power of producing harm and hiding it through silencing, exclusion, and broadcasting their role as protectors of children (Humphris & Sigona, 2019, p. 6). Unfortunately, visibility does not equate with empowerment and defense of children's rights. The relation between visibility and invisibility must be treated with great caution in the context of understanding which ulterior motives may be in play when the government assesses migrant children's best interests as they seek to help migrant children achieve personhood in the host country.

The Journey of an "Illegal" Traveler

Shahram Khosravi left his homeland, Iran, as a teenager in 1987, eventually journeying to Sweden. In *'Illegal' Traveller* (2010), Khosravi describes taking that first step across a gravel road and adopting the mantle of "illegality." He notes that dwelling inside borders naturalizes identity, and those who cross borders are seen as polluters. Drawing on Agamben's notion of a state of exception, he states that, by definition, in defining its citizens, a nation-state also identifies "a politically unidentifiable 'leftover', a 'no-longer human being'" (Khosravi, 2010, p. 3). While the term *refugee* implies seeker of refuge, the discourse of illegality naturalizes criminalization and punishment of border crossers. This places the "illegal" traveler in "a space of lawlessness, outside the protection of the law" (Khosravi, 2010, p. 27) and hence vulnerable to all kinds of danger, including death. For children, this passive necropolitical stance is perilous indeed:

> The vulnerability of border transgressors is best demonstrated by their 'animalization'. The terminology in this field is full of the names of animals designating smugglers and their clients: *coyote* for the human smuggler and *pollos* (chickens) for Mexican border crossers ... *shethou* (snakehead) for Chinese human smugglers and *renseh* (human snakes) for smuggled Chinese.... Iranians usually use the term *gosfund* (sheep) or *dar post gosfund* (in the skin of sheep) to refer to illegal border crossers. Dehumanized and represented in terms of chickens and sheep—two animals traditionally sacrificed in rituals—the border crossers are sacrificial creatures of the border ritual. (Khosravi, 2010, p. 27)

Speaking of deaths in the Mediterranean Sea, Khosravi observes how Western nations enact a theater of death:

> The Mediterranean Sea has turned into a cemetery for transgressive travelers, and the floating dead bodies washing up on the shores of European tourist islands are evidence of broader necropolitics. The broader regimen exercises its power not only through 'the right to live and die' but pre-eminently through 'the right to expose to death'. (2010, p. 28)

We can recognize the explicit cruelty of separating children at the U.S. border or the locking of children in cages at U.S. detention facilities. However, despite the media clucking piously about the death of a father and daughter in the Rio Grande and the body of a toddler washed up on the beach near Bodrum as tragic events, these too, are examples of necropolitical intent—migrants are simply allowed to die or to be killed. Our privilege, as members of nation-states is predicated on the establishment of borders policed with conscious necropolitical vigilance. Kurdish Iranian journalist Behrouz Boochani's (2018) description of his journey to Australia and detention on Manus Island is full of such moments of personal suffering and death, and it is also filled with vicarious suffering as Boochani served as witness to death, despair, and suffering among his peers. Hassan Fazili's (2019) video documentary of his family's two-year odyssey from Afghanistan to an uncertain fate in Germany was filmed undercover using a mobile phone. While documenting the crushing uncertainty and ever-present danger in this undocumented family's life, the portrait of the struggles of his two daughters, Nargis and Zahra, is particularly harrowing. Fazili documents the children living in zones of nonexistence, as they seek to grow while discombobulated by placelessness, purposelessness, and nonidentity, as well as by the vicarious traumatization they experienced from witnessing violence and being witness to their parents' reactions to violence, threat, and uncertainty.

Even refugee and migrant relief agencies contribute to this construction of non-personhood. Khosravi (2010) soon learned that to be accepted as a refugee he had to perform the abjection of refugeeness in order to satisfy the noblesse oblige of the United Nations High Commissioner for Refugees (UNHCR), which might deem him abject enough to be worthy of a helping hand:

> To have a chance of getting refugee status, one must have the ability to translate one's life story into Eurocentric juridical language and to perform the role expected of a refugee. Like other newcomers to Cantt station, I was advised to wear dirty clothes when going to the UNHCR and to look 'sad' and 'profound'. (p. 33)

Khosravi (2010) also reminds us of the ever-present shame that is inherent in the nonperson of the refugee:

> I was struck by the shame of my migrant illegality. Nowhere else had I experienced the border so tangibly, powerfully, and distressingly. Shame is part of the punishment for transgressing nation-state sovereignty. Many of my friends told me later how humiliated they felt saying 'I am a refugee' when they arrived at the destination country. The worst was that I internalized shame and for many years lied about my route to Sweden . . . there is a risk that the 'illegal' migrant, subjected to a gaze and treatment that divest him or her of humanity, will internalize the shame—as I did—and understand the lack of travel documents and documentation as personal deficiencies and inadequacies. (p. 67)

A challenge, therefore, in seeking to meet the needs of refugee and migrant children, is that while reaching out a helping hand and offering resettlement and educational and support services, sovereign governments simultaneously practice necropolitical border control management. Unconditional hospitality is a chimera and those of us who seek to extend the hand of hospitality have an obligation to understand the complex implications of these mixed messages about refuge and death directed at migrant and refugee children to whose trust we lay claim.

Refugee Children: Subjectivities in Danger, Challenges in Care

An infinite juxtaposition of factors related to the child's place in society, their place in a family constellation, and their age influences how a child creates a life narrative and thereby constructs his or her subjectivity (Hatem, 2017). Trauma hinders the ability of the child to create a narrative and construct meaning: to narrate a life history and find a place in the world. As the child's mental abilities are overwhelmed, the symbolic capacity of the child can come under attack, and the child may enter a state of defensive disintegration and fragmentation (Alvarez, 2006; Urwin, 2006). Foster (2005) explains that during the turbulent migration process for children forced to flee, traumatogenic events may happen at four different moments. There is the trauma of origin, the trauma of the journey, the trauma of transit camps, and potential traumas related to reception and the demands of assimilation in a host country. The trauma of origin refers to the child's exposure to social rupture and the loss of a social envelope due to violence, natural disaster, war, starvation, and the severance of family and community bonds. Sometimes, born into such upheaval, refugee children may have never known a period of stability and peace. In these situations, schooling and everyday lives are disrupted, and parents cannot provide children with a sense of safety. As Lachal (2020) notes and as the case studies documented in Drožek and Wilson's (2007) book substantiate, parental distress and general insecurity are prevalent. As mentioned earlier and as Hoffman's (1990) autobiography so poignantly illustrates, the assimilative pressure of language and cultural adjustments greatly exacerbates these transitions. In addition to the dehumanization, the lack of place, and the anxiety about an indeterminate future discussed earlier, children may be exposed to extreme danger throughout their travels and risk, for example, being placed in the hands of smugglers, as Khosravi (2010) described, or separated from their parents (Foster, 2005; Lachal, 2020). The third moment starts when children seek asylum but experience continued legal rejection and hardship and endure anomie, deprivation, and violence in refugee camps and resettlement centers (Foster, 2005). Finally, during the final stage of settlement in a new country, children face additional difficulties with adjustment to the host culture, chronic substandard living conditions due to a lack of income, the risk of racial and religious persecution, and an uncertainty for the future (Antony & Thomas, 2017; Foster, 2005; Lachal, 2020; Suárez-Orozco & Suárez-Orozco, 2002).

Traumatic events at any of these moments hinder the ability of the child to create a narrative of their experiences, and the child may have increasing difficulty in symbolizing the past, the present, and the future (Rosenbaum & Varvin, 2007). The trauma will affect the child's relationship to the world in three different dimensions: the body–world dimension, the subject–group dimension, and the subject–discourse dimension. In the body–world dimension, Rosenbaum and Varvin (2007) conceptualize a human being as linked to other human beings by means of unconscious bodily feedback and mirroring responses. Thus, the child's experience of the world is emotive and psychophysiological (p. 1531). The subject–group dimension corresponds to the human being's capacity to link affectively to group formations and identify with others. In normal development, a child will experience their self as, at the same time, unique and similar to others. A healthy child will be able to develop intersubjectivity and inter-intentionality with time. The subject–discourse dimension describes a person's capacity to develop a cultural understanding of politics, ideology, education, ethics, moral conduct, and religion. In states of extreme instability and trauma, Rosenbaum and Varvin (2007) note that the subject may be limited in the ability to concretize or symbolize bodily sensations:

> Self-support and self-soothing may be transformed into greedy dependence, adhesion or fusion with the other, or it may adversely be transformed into fierce rejection, unempathic distancing or total isolation and coldness. (p. 1534)

Additionally, they note, due to trauma, the person may experience the group as either "a devalued or idealized part of the self and the trust in the group is lost" (Rosenbaum & Varvin, 2007, p. 1534). As a consequence, the child will experience a deep sense of loss of personal identity in relation to the group. This dimension is particularly important in cultures in which group affiliation is critical. And finally, when the relationship between child and society is unstable, the child will experience being surrounded by a fragmented environment that induces states of polarity and disintegration, whereby meaning has been shattered, rendering it difficult for the traumatized child to symbolize and make meaning (Rosenbaum & Varvin, 2007, pp. 1534–1535).

When faced with chronically traumatic events it is adaptive for children to enter states of unawareness, psychological splitting,[7] denial, and dissociation (Goldsmith, Barlow & Freyd, 2004). A child that experiences a traumatic event becomes vulnerable, therefore, to both immediate effects and later psychological consequences and repercussions (Hatem, 2017). Such ruptures in symbolic abilities raise the specter of intergenerational transmission unless children are offered therapeutic experiences to restore their metabolic capacities for receiving, processing, and expressing emotion.

The family of a refugee child is placed in a bind. It cannot organize itself using its traditions and customs of origin but is faced with suddenly being organized instead by the sovereign, by state law (Maminachvili, 2014). The original social institutions that allowed for the existence of alterity may have been destroyed in the country of origin. Children may experience the loss of this cultural and familial envelope, with the vanishing of places and routines that were part of the child's life. Clinical work with refugee children should help them reestablish the capacity for symbolization, integrating the life period previous to the traumatic experiences with the fragmented experiences of the refugee life without overlooking the conflicts that the host culture will trigger in the child (Drożdek & Wilson, 2007; Morantz, Rousseau & Heyman, 2011; Ní Raghallaigh, 2013; Rosenbaum & Varvin, 2007).

Toward a Psychoanalytic Understanding of Subaltern Subjectivity: The Case of the Child Refugee

What is called for then, perhaps, is a greater awareness of the sociohistorical and sociopolitical genealogy of subaltern subjectivity. We have some sympathy with Abdul JanMohamed's (1995) doubts about the capacity of any person or discursive system to engage in the kind of critical self-reflection required to lift the veil of ideological interpellation:

> Genuine and thorough comprehension of Otherness is possible only if the self can somehow negate or at least severely bracket the values, assumptions, and ideology of his [sic] culture ... this entails in practice the virtually impossible task of negating one's very being, precisely because one's culture is what formed that being. Moreover, the colonizer's invariable assumption about his moral superiority means that he will rarely question the validity of his own or his society's formation and that he will not be inclined to expend any energy in understanding the worthless alterity of the colonized. (p. 18)

While acknowledging this human limitation, self-reflexive and critical uses of psychoanalysis by postcolonial and feminist theorists[8] illustrate ways in which intellectuals have grappled productively with the complexity of subaltern subjectivity. Because of evident exclusion by the sovereign, the one deemed *the refugee* provides the clearest example of the workings of *bare life* as part of the power structure.

The work of scholars who have taken history seriously[9] suggests that a critical receptivity to history and to archaic and ghostly residue allows scholars to trace the genealogy (Apfelbaum, 2002; Khanna, 2009b; O'Loughlin, 2013) of absence and lack through such signifying remnants. Khanna (2009a) draws on the spectral theory of Abraham and Torok (1994) and on Derrida's (1993) writing on spectrality to suggest that the presence of the abject, the excluded, and the spectral provides a potentially useful means of accessing those aspects of our being that are submerged in a palimpsest of political ideology and socialization. Khanna (2006) captures a piece of this process under the rubric of critical melancholia. Speaking of a monument to the uncounted disposable people who died in the conflict in Algeria, she notes:

> But, while the monument tells a tale of necropolitics, a critical melancholia remains, in which the remnants of an ideal leave an irrefutable mark. No map, census, print, or museum can be entirely successful at presenting the nation seamlessly. While the work of mourning may relegate swallowed, disposable bodies to the garbage can of modern nationalism, the work of melancholia, critically attesting to the fact of the lie intrinsic to modern notions of sovereignty, is the only hope for the future. To sustain a people existing in the sovereign state of necropolitics and lost causes, critical melancholia, formulated through the ghosts with ideals, is the only way for democracy to come. (Khanna, 2006, p.10)

Ultimately, therefore, the ways in which societies conceptualize, legislate, and provide for refugees, asylum seekers, and other powerless, disposable potential nonpersons, most particularly displaced migrant children—the human waste products of modern capital (Khanna, 2009a, p. 260)—holds a mirror up to the sociopolitical values a society lives by. Given a neoliberal and sometimes even hard-right shift in the politics of Western societies, the challenge of advocating for the rights of vulnerable displaced children is formidable. But then, if we are not willing to step up, who will take a moral stand and advocate for their rights?

Notes

1. On the effects of the residential school experience see, for example, Churchill (2004), Fournier and Crey (1997), and Milloy (1999). For the origin of the term *residential school syndrome*, see Brasfield, (2001). For the overall psychic effects of colonization on Indigenous peoples, see Atkinson (2002), Brave Heart (2011), and Duran (2006). For testimony to the long-term effects of such displacements, see, for example, *Unseen Tears*, https://vimeo.com/76653540, and *The Lost Children*, https://www.cultureunplugged.com/play/1758/The-Lost-Children.
2. For a detailed explication of the evolution of these two concepts, see House and Slotnick (2015) and Laplanche (2017).
3. For Adelphi Asylum Project, see https://www.adelphi.edu/news/derner-students-as-expert-witnesses-the-adelphi-asylum-project/, and for Healthright Human Rights Clinic, see https://healthright.org/our-work/human-rights-clinic/.
4. For Bodrum, see Smith (2015). For Rio Grande, see Ahmed and Semple (2019). For migrant children in cages, see Long (2019).
5. For related discussion, see Scheper-Hughes (1997) on people who get rubbished: Bauman (2003) and Khanna (2009b) on disposable people. Also see Bauman (2014).
6. See, for example, Edkins (2000), Jerrems (2011), Malkki (2006), Mbembe (2003), Mills (2003), Mummary (2006), and Papastergiadis (2006).
7. Splitting is adopted as a means of psychological defense against severe abuse that can ultimately lead to what psychologists refer to as borderline personality disorder, a psychological condition characterized by emotional volatility and severe difficulty in regulating emotions. For details on splitting, see Burland (1994), and for classic work on this condition, see Kernberg (1975).
8. See, for example, Bhabha (1994), Morley and Chen (1996), Parry (2004), Seshadri-Crooks (1994), and Spivak (1988).
9. See, for example, Abraham and Torok (1994), Davoine and Gaudillière (2004), Faimberg (2005), Frosh (2013), Gordon (2008), O'Loughlin (2015), O'Loughlin and Charles (2015), and Schützenberger (1998).

References

Abraham, N., & Torok, M. (1994). *The shell and the kernel: Vol. 1*. University of Chicago Press.
Agamben, G. (1998). *Homo sacer: Sovereign power and bare life* (D. Heller-Roazen, Trans.). Stanford University Press.
Agamben, G. (2002). *Remnants of Auschwitz: The witness and the archive* (D. Heller-Roazen, Trans.). Zone Books.
Agamben, G. (2005). *State of exception* (K. Attell, Trans.). University of Chicago Press.
Ahmed, A., & Semple, K. (2019, July 25). Photo of drowned migrants captures pathos of those who risk it all. *New York Times*, https://www.nytimes.com/2019/06/25/us/father-daughter-border-drowning-picture-mexico.html.

Alvarez, A. (2006) Some questions concerning states of fragmentation: Unintegration, under-integration, disintegration, and the nature of early integrations. *Journal of Child Psychotherapy*, 32(2), 158–180.

Antony, M. G., & Thomas, R. J. (2017). *Interdisciplinary perspectives on child migrants: Seen but not heard.* Lexington Books.

Apfelbaum, E. (2002). Uprooted communities, silenced cultures and the need for legacy. In V. Walkerine (Ed.), *Challenging subjects: Critical psychology for a new millennium* (pp. 75–87). Palgrave.

Arendt, H. (1966). *The origins of totalitarianism.* Harcourt.

Atkinson, J. (2002). *Trauma trails: Recreating songlines.* Spinifex Press.

Auerhahn, N., & Prelinger, C. (1983). Repetition in the concentration camp survivor and her child. *International Review of Psychoanalysis*, 10(1), 31–46.

Bauman, Z. (2003). *Wasted lives: Modernity and its outcasts.* Polity Press.

Bauman, Z. (2014, March 11). Disposable life: Zygmunt Bauman [Transcript]. Open Transcripts. http://opentranscripts.org/transcript/disposable-life-zygmunt-bauman/

Bhabha, H. (1994). *The location of culture.* Routledge.

Bhabha, J. (2011). From citizen to migrant: The scope of child statelessness in the twenty-first century. In J. Bhabha (Ed.), *Children without a state: A global human rights challenge* (pp. 1–39). MIT Press.

Bhabha, J. (2014). *Child migration and human rights in a global age.* Princeton University Press.

Boochani, B. (2018). *No friend but the mountains: Writings from Manus Prison.* House of Anansi Press.

Bragin, M. (2019). Myth, memory, and meaning: Understanding and treating adolescents experiencing forced migration. *Journal of Infant, Child & Adolescent Psychotherapy*, 18(4), 319–329.

Brasfield, C. (2001). Residential school syndrome. *British Columbia Medical Journal*, 43(2), 78–81.

Brave Heart, M. Y. H. (2011). Historical trauma among Indigenous peoples of the Americas: Concepts, research, and clinical considerations. *Journal of Psychoactive Drugs*, 43(4), 282–290.

Burland, J. A. (1994). Splitting as a consequence of severe abuse in childhood. *Psychiatric Clinics of North America*, 17(4), 731–742.

Churchill, W. (2004). *Kill the Indian, save the man: The genocidal impact of American Indian residential schools.* City Lights Books.

Davoine, F., & Gaudillière, J-M. (2004). *History beyond trauma: Whereof one cannot speak, thereof one cannot stay silent.* Other Press.

Derrida, J. (1993). *Specters of Marx: The state of the debt, the work of mourning & the new international.* Routledge.

Drożdek, B., & Wilson, J. (Eds.). (2007). *Voices of trauma: Treating survivors across cultures.* Springer.

Duran, E. (2006). *Healing the soul wound: Counseling with American Indians and other Native peoples.* Teachers College Press.

Edkins, J. (2000). Sovereign power: Zones of indistinction and the camp. *Alternatives*, 25(1), 3–25.

Erikson, K. (1976). Loss of communality at Buffalo Creek. *American Journal of Psychiatry*, 133(3), 302–305.

Faimberg, H. (2005). *The telescoping of generations: Listening to the narcissistic links between generations.* Routledge.

Fassin, D. (2010, Fall). Ethics of survival: A democratic approach to the politics of life. *Humanity*, 8, 10–95.

Fazili, H. (Director). (2019). *Midnight traveler* [Film]. Old Chilly Pictures. https://www.imdb.com/title/tt8923500/

Foster, R. M. P. (2005). The new faces of childhood perimigration trauma in the United States. *Journal of Infant, Child, and Adolescent Psychotherapy, 4*(1), 21–41.

Fournier, S., & Crey, E. (1997). *Stolen from our embrace: The abduction of first nations children and the restoration of Aboriginal communities*. Douglas & McIntyre.

Frosh, S. (2013). *Hauntings: Psychoanalysis and ghostly transmissions*. Palgrave Macmillan.

Goldsmith, R. E., Barlow, M. R., & Freyd, J. J. (2004). Knowing and not knowing about trauma: Implications for therapy. *Psychotherapy: Theory, Research, Practice, Training, 41*(4), 448–463.

Gordon, A. (2008). *Ghostly matters: Haunting and the sociological imagination*. University of Minnesota Press.

Hatem, N. (2017). Fractales d'enfance dans la guerre du Liban [Childhood fractals in the Lebanon War]. *NAQD, 35*(1), 185–213. https://doi.org/10.3917/naqd.035.0185

Herman, J. (1997). *Trauma and recovery*. Basic Books.

Hoffman, E. (1990). *Lost in translation*. Penguin Books.

House, J., & Slotnick, J. (2015). Après-Coup in French psychoanalysis: The long afterlife of Nachträglichkeit: The first hundred years, 1893 to 1993. *The Psychoanalytic Review, 102*(5), 683–708.

Humphris, R., & Sigona, N. (2019). The bureaucratic capture of child migrants: Effects of in/visibility on children on the move. *Antipode, 51*(5), 1495–1514.

JanMohamed, A. (1995). The economy of Manichean allegory. In B. Ashcroft, G. Griffith, & H. Tiffin (Eds.), *The postcolonial studies reader* (pp. 18–33). Routledge.

Jerrems, A. (2011). Book review: Bordering beyond state boundaries. *Borderlands, e-journal, 10*(1). https://webarchive.nla.gov.au/awa/20110726123021/http://pandora.nla.gov.au/pan/30280/20120729-0013/www.borderlands.net.au/vol10no1_2011/jerrems_borders.htm

Kant, I. (1996). Toward perpetual peace. In M. J. Gregor (Ed. & Trans.), *Practical philosophy* (pp. 311–351). Cambridge University Press.

Kaplan, L. (1996). *No voice is ever wholly lost: An exploration of the everlasting attachment between parent and child*. Simon & Schuster.

Kassabova, K. (2017). *Border: A journey to the edge of Europe*. Graywolf Press.

Kernberg, O. (1975). *Borderline conditions and pathological narcissism*. Jason Aronson.

Khanna, R. (2006). Post-palliative: Coloniality's affective dissonance. *Postcolonial Text, 2*(1). https://www.postcolonial.org/pct/article/viewArticle/385/815

Khanna, R. (2009a). *Dark continents: Psychoanalysis and colonialism*. Duke University Press.

Khanna, R. (2009b). Disposability. *Differences: A Journal of Feminist Cultural Studies, 20*(1), 181–198.

Khosravi, S. (2010). *'Illegal traveller': An ethnography of borders*. Palgrave Macmillan.

Lachal, C. (2020). L'enfant Mort. L'enfant Vie: Donner la parole aux enfants dans les guerres [The death child. The life child: Giving a voice to children in wars]. *L'Autre, 21*(2), 163–176. https://doi.org/10.3917/lautr.062.0163

Laplanche, J. (2017). *Après coup*. (J. House & L. Thurston, Trans.). Unconscious in Translation.

Limbu, B. (2009). Illegible humanity: The refugee, human rights, and the question of representation. *Journal of Refugee Studies, 22*(3), 257–282.

Long, C. (2019, July 11). Written testimony: "Kids in cages: Inhumane treatment at the border." Human Rights Watch. https://www.hrw.org/news/2019/07/11/written-testimony-kids-cages-inhumane-treatment-border

Malkki, L. (2006). Speechless emissaries: Refugees, humanitarianism and dehistoricization. *Cultural Anthropology, 11*(3), 377–404.

Maminachvili, C. (2014). L'enfant réfugié: L'inscription psychique du statut politique [The refugee child: The psychic inscription of political status]. *Psychologie Clinique, 38*(2), 63–74. https://doi.org/10.1051/psyc/201438063

Mbembe, A. (2003). Necropolitics. *Public Culture, 15*(1), 11–40.

Milloy, J. S. (1999). *"A national crime": The Canadian government and the residential school system, 1879 to 1986*. University of Manitoba Press.

Mills, C. (2003). An ethics of bare life: Agamben on witnessing. *Borderlands, e-journal, 2*(1). https://webarchive.nla.gov.au/awa/20031027120811/http://www.borderlandsejournal.adelaide.edu.au/vol2no1_2003/mills_agamben.html

Morantz, G., Rousseau, C., & Heyman, J. (2011). The divergent experiences of children and adults in the relocation process: Perspectives of child and parent refugee claimants in Montreal. *Journal of Refugee Studies, 25*(1), 71–93.

Morley, D., & Chen, K. (Eds.). (1996). *Stuart Hall: Critical dialogues in cultural studies*. Routledge.

Mummary, J. (2006). States of exception. *Borderlands, e-journal, 5*(2). https://webarchive.nla.gov.au/awa/20070830081650/http://www.borderlandsejournal.adelaide.edu.au/vol5no2_2006/mummery_states.htm

Ní Raghallaigh, M. (2013). The causes of mistrust among asylum seekers: Insights from research with unaccompanied asylum-seeking minors living in the Republic of Ireland. *Journal of Refugee Studies, 27*(1), 82–101.

O'Loughlin, M. (2012). Trauma trails from Ireland's Great Hunger: A psychoanalytic inquiry. In L. Bohm, R. Curtis, & B. Willock (Eds.), *Loneliness & yearnings* (pp. 233–250). Routledge.

O'Loughlin, M. (2013). Reclaiming genealogy, memory and history: The psychodynamic potential for reparative therapy in contemporary South Africa. In C. Smith, G. Lobban, & M. O'Loughlin (Eds.), *Psychodynamic psychotherapy in contemporary South Africa: Contexts, theories, practices* (pp. 242–272). Wits University Press.

O'Loughlin, M. (Ed.). (2015). *The ethics of remembering and the consequences of forgetting: Trauma, history and memory*. Rowman & Littlefield.

O'Loughlin, M. (In press). Cultural ruptures and their consequences for mental health across generations: The case of Ireland. In I. Lambrecht & A. Lavis (Eds.), *Culture and psychosis*. Routledge.

O'Loughlin, M., & Charles, M. (Eds.). (2015). *Fragments of trauma and the social production of suffering: Trauma, history and memory*. Rowman & Littlefield.

Papastergiadis, N. (2006). The invasion complex: The abject other and spaces of violence. *Geografiska Annaler, 88B*(4), 429–442.

Parry, B. (2004). *Postcolonial studies: A materialist critique*. Routledge.

Rogers, A. (2006). *The unsayable: The hidden language of trauma*. Random House.

Rosenbaum, B., & Varvin, S. (2007). The influence of extreme traumatization on body, mind and social relations. *International Journal of Psychoanalysis, 88*(Pt. 6), 1527–1542.

Scheper-Hughes, N. (1997). People who get rubbished. *New Internationalist, 295*. https://newint.org/features/1997/10/05/people/

Schützenberger, A. A. (1998). *The ancestor syndrome: Transgenerational psychotherapy and the hidden links in the family tree*. Routledge.

Seshadri-Crooks, K. (1994, Autumn). The primitive as analyst: Postcolonial feminism's access to psychoanalysis. *Cultural Critique, 28*, 175–218.

Smith, H. (2015, September 2). Shocking images of drowned Syrian boy show tragic plight of refugees. *The Guardian*. https://www.theguardian.com/world/2015/sep/02/shocking-image-of-drowned-syrian-boy-shows-tragic-plight-of-refugees

Spivak, G. S. (1988). Can the subaltern speak? In C. Nelson & L. Grossberg (Eds.), *Marxism and the interpretation of culture* (pp. 271–316). University of Illinois Press.

Suárez-Orozco, C., & Suárez-Orozco, M. (2002). *Children of immigration.* Harvard University Press.

Urwin, C. (2006). Notes on unintegration and disintegration from historical and developmental perspectives. *Journal of Child Psychotherapy, 32*(2), 193–213.

Walsh, O. (2016). "An invisible but inescapable trauma": Epigenetics and the Great Famine. In C. Kinealy, J. King, & C. Reilly, (Eds.), *Women and the Great Hunger* (pp. 173–184). Ireland's Great Hunger Institute.

Winnicott, D. W. (1974). Fear of breakdown. *International Review of Psycho-Analysis, 1*(1–2), 103–107.

CHAPTER 2

"Forward to No Place at All": Foreceful Migration and Child Welfare

Mlado Ivanovic

Where will we go? I don't know, everything is changing all the time. Where would I like to live? Uh, I don't know what to tell you, I haven't thought about it a lot because nobody asks me. Now that I think about it. . . . Well, I would like that all of us lives together again, it's all the same for me where. My Dad and my brother are in Germany. I am here in the camp with my sister and two brothers. And stepmother, but she has her own kids. They are a family for themselves. My Dad says we will soon join him and I can't wait. I'm just not sure how we will get there. I am not afraid that much, my sister is the one who's scared. She is 19 years old and I think she is afraid because we will travel alone with boys.

—LAYLA, A CHILD REFUGEE[1]

WHEN WE CONSIDER the scope of forceful migration today—almost 80 million displaced individuals worldwide—people who have been forced to flee their homes represent one of the most precarious aspects of humanity (United Nations High Commissioner for Refugees [UNHCR], 2020). Children make up to 50% of this number, yet these numbers tell us very little about the underlying dynamics of forceful displacement and the vulnerabilities that it entails (UNICEF, 2021). As I considered writing this chapter on the youngest refugees, I was immediately confronted with the disheartening context of issues affecting them. While many children escape poverty, involuntary military recruitment, child labor, environmental degradation, conflict zones, or generalized human rights abuses, some also run from more intimate forms of violence—namely, sexual and domestic abuse perpetrated by their family members and relatives, community-based oppression due to sexual orientation, inhumane cultural practices, or a lack of access to education. Faced with such predicaments, forcefully displaced children are a highly vulnerable social group susceptible to some of the most extreme forms of harm. Subsequently, one would assume that children are at the forefront of the refugee law and refugee discourse, considering the specific nature of their needs and vulnerabilities. Unfortunately, that is not the case. In addition to dangers children face from armed groups, once on the move, they are also at risk of being brutalized by human traffickers, other migrants, border security forces, asylum officers, and even nongovernmental organization (NGO) workers themselves. This, in turn, further determines their experiences as most of these traumas bleed into social and cultural environments, wherein these children often face stigmatization and isolation. Sadly, the list of vulnerabilities that migrant and refugee children face is further aggravated by institutional settings and oppressive deterrence policies that many countries, including the European Union and the United States, practice today.

Taking these predicaments as a starting point, the main focus of this chapter is not only to disclose the present difficulties of the increasing number of displaced youth and children but also to reevaluate the ethical and political commitments that affluent societies embody in their culture, sentiments, institutions and asylum/immigration policies and practices. I hope that my analysis will encourage and promote a better understanding of the different contexts of humanitarian, political, and legal problems and solutions that displaced children face. In the following pages, I approach these tasks from two different, yet interrelated, perspectives. The *first* takes violence, oppression, and various forms of exclusion faced by refugee and migrant children to demonstrate the structural limits of the present refugee and asylum system. Here I take the international community and their humanitarian practices under critical scrutiny. Most of my work in this chapter focuses on the failures and omissions of an outdated and overwhelmed system of humanitarian governance. The *second* closely related perspective refers to legal and administrative contexts in which the notion of "child refugee" operates. Sadly, the specific status of children is largely unaddressed in historical and contemporary refugee law, which exacerbates their vulnerabilities. This is mostly a consequence of the dissonance between two relevant conventions, the 1951 Refugee Convention (UNHCR) and the 1989 Convention on the Rights of the Child (OHCRC), but the discord that exists between them has a dire impact on the status and understanding of children in terms of obligations that the international community has. In spite of the progress made regarding children's rights in recent decades, the child rights framework has made a fleeting impact on the status and conditions of children in refugee law and humanitarian spaces. Ultimately, by drawing attention to the social realities of forcefully displaced children and by disclosing the gap between justice on one side and political rhetoric and unfulfilled humanitarian obligations on the other, I hope to create analytical space wherein there is a growing concern to understand the pressing moral and political failures that can lead toward a transformation of present humanitarian practices in regard to refugee children.

Children on the Move: Between Precariousness and Autonomy

Notwithstanding the prevailing belief among the public in the Western world, the vast majority of forcefully displaced children seek and find refuge mostly in historically impoverished countries (UNHCR, 2020). Often, they have no resources or the capacity to reach sanctuary in affluent societies of Europe, North America, and Australia. The recent focus of media on issues tied with the management of forcefully displaced children in the Western industrialized world is a consequence of the uncommon geographical proximity of the phenomena that is a sadly historical trend for most of the "developing" world. Based on the recent UNHCR data, 85% of the world's displaced people are hosted in developing societies (i.e., Turkey, Pakistan, Uganda, Sudan, Colombia, Iran, and Lebanon), and 40% of them are children (UNHCR, 2020). As media outlets sufficiently illustrate, forcefully displaced children may be found throughout most of the world: in historically unstable regions of Central America (i.e., Honduras, Guatemala, El Salvador, etc.) from where thousands of unaccompanied minors are attempting to reach the "safety" of the United States; in the asylum processing and detention centers in several affluent countries (e.g., Italy, Greece, United States, Australia, etc.); in the vast refugee camps sprawling in the Middle East and remote areas of Africa; and in Southeast Asia and Oceania, where countless individuals have been embarking on dangerous sea voyages in pursuit of a better life in Australia and New Zealand. Thanks to the media and humanitarian imagery the dominant image of refugees and displaced children is one of need and precariousness. Public portrayals that fuel social media activism, and humanitarian governance, in general, show people often with no autonomy or agency.[2] Despite this deeply rooted image, one should avoid a common tendency to consider children in historically unstable parts of the world solely in terms of victims, as powerful political and socioeconomic forces of our globalized epoch often mobilize their agency and resistance. Sadly, in the face of overwhelming circumstances that they must endure there is, of course, a considerable degree of truth in prevailing analyses of the impact of global poverty and violence; thus, it would be naïve to place an overriding emphasis on children's agency in face of such overarching destitution. Yet, it is of vital importance to realize that in light of the malign impacts of globalization, one should not ignore the way in which refugee and migrant children make sense of their reality and act on it. While it may be true that external economic, ecological, political, and cultural circumstances define the environments in which children live and often define their destitution and limited access to opportunities, at the same time, children are always interpreters of that environment regardless of how coercive it may be. Ignoring this fact prevents us from understanding an important aspect of the ongoing migratory flow of young people across the globe.

Despite the fact that the total number of displaced children remains unknown, it is evident that this is a phenomenon of enormous proportions. For children and youth, the search for viable alternatives to appalling conditions at home reflects the transient nature of their age, and these often significantly differ from those of their parents or other adults. Additional difficulties arise by the inconsistent articulation and uneven implementation of policies and regulations on the part of the international refugee regime, diverse national governments, and humanitarian assistance agencies (i.e., solutions such as voluntary repatriation, local integration, and resettlement to a third country). Today, a very small number of young individuals want to return to their countries of origin, and less than one percent of forcefully displaced people have access to other humanitarian and legal mechanisms. The international community has struggled to effectively and humanely respond to the sudden growth in forced displacement and has failed to find effective solutions to the overwhelming immediate humanitarian needs of affected children and youth. Gendered and intergenerational differences regarding the impact and perceived desirability of alternatives are rarely considered. Hence, such alternatives remain insufficiently understood and largely unexplored, impeding the morally urgent and politically necessary transition from humanitarian aid to human development.

Global Structures of Vulnerability and Injustice

Theoretically, the normative status of refugee individuals encompasses a commitment for protecting the essential interests of displaced people and a commitment to respect the dignity of individuals who are uprooted from their homes. In reality, the precarious position of asylum seekers and refugees is increasingly one in which such commitments are not only ignored or denied, but rather, their vulnerabilities are exacerbated by increasingly dehumanizing institutional framework and policies that the international community relies on in managing humanitarian challenges and their political obligations. Many authors have recently drawn attention to this point by analyzing the pathological character of the global refugee and humanitarian regime as one that combines neoliberal dehumanizing logic of humanitarianism together with surveillance, management, and control (Betts & Collier, 2017; Oliver, 2017; Owen, 2019; Parekh, 2017; Weizeman, 2011; among others). Despite the fact that my target here is more limited (i.e., my focus is on the impact of global humanitarian and refugee regimes on migrant and refugee children), I echo their concerns, and I extend their attempt to understand the implications of this current trend by disclosing the moral and political implications that international humanitarian and refugee laws have on the most vulnerable layers of humanity. In order to make this state of affairs clear, my analysis focuses on observable social realities that are embodied in the experiences of children on the move. Rather than being led by prevailing legal definitions, I use the terms *migrant* and *refugee children* in a capacious way to refer to children who are seeking refuge in affluent Western countries owing to adverse circumstances in their countries of origin.[3]

Consequently, when we consider the legal and administrative context of the category "refugee" and apply it to lives of migrant and refugee children, it immediately becomes obvious that its narrowly defined scope fails to address the shifting moral and political terrains of our globalized epoch. According to the convention relating to the status of refugees agreed on by the United Nations in 1951, the term has a very specific meaning applying to any displaced person who is faced with "well-founded fear of being persecuted for reasons of race, religion, nationality, membership of a particular social group or political opinion" (UNHCR, 1951, Article 1). Many of the children whose turmoil is considered here often do not make normative requirements to fit the definition of a refugee as present articulation ignores many essential factors that force children to leave their homes.[4] Often, reasons behind their displacement are rooted in harmful socioeconomic contexts of their home communities and not direct persecution or war. That in itself limits their access to refugee and asylum systems, as a substantial number of them cannot apply for specific legal status owing to various constraints arising from the nature of harms that they experienced back home, their age, and, more frequently, diverse policies of deterrence pursued by potential host countries. In order to make these realities evident, I would like to sketch an image of refugeehood that is embodied in the lives of forcefully displaced children and some of their experiences that too often point at failures of international humanitarian regimes and undermined political legitimacy of the international and national political systems.[5] Sadly, the list of difficulties and failures does not end there, as recent years have shown limited reach of international solidarity and an increasing inability of public culture in industrialized societies to come in terms with the complex nature of responsibilities that exist in face of such unwarranted suffering and indignity on a global level.

We can start introducing this image by focusing on underlying contexts that constitute refugee children as some of the most vulnerable. At this point, it makes sense to begin with the sociopolitical, economic, and ecological aspects of forceful migration and then move toward pathologies of the current international asylum and refugee regime. This will allow us to better understand the complex dynamics of this phenomenon that ground and further intensify vulnerabilities of migrant and refugee children. As I have argued in more detail elsewhere, each year, countless children flee difficult living conditions, harm, and violence at home and take an uncertain journey in the hope of finding safety somewhere else.[6] Despite evidently local causes, the growing number of children on the move (i.e., refugee, internally displaced, stateless, trafficked, immigrant, and street youth) reflects global relations of power that result in worldwide political, social, and environmental instability. When we reflect on different axes of vulnerabilities and harms that follow from such a state of affairs, the issues affecting refugee and migrant children must be placed in a broader context. This broader context requires us to be attentive toward a wide range of causes that uproot children and their families from their homes. Solely focusing on obvious factors such as violence and persecution may be insufficient in the face of towering economic inequalities and increasing ecological degradation. Today, most of the migration is forceful, as the movement of people is initiated by unsustainable living conditions that can be traced to impacts of global politics and economy. Historical and present structural aspects of inequalities (e.g., colonialism, neocolonialism, poverty, climate change, etc.) form an important backdrop for understanding forces that result in the movement of refugee and migrant children, as it allows us to see that forceful migration takes place at the intersection of many different factors. This intersectional character of forceful migration is manifested in overlapping and interdependent systems of harm, discrimination, or disadvantage. Thus, when we consider reasons why a child from Afghanistan has decided to leave their home and embark on a dangerous journey, we have to be clear that in an attempt to understand causes and motives we cannot focus solely on violence or cultural persecution or low standards of living and poverty but, rather, on all these factors combined as they allow us insight into a complex and disheartening image of globalization and the neoliberal world in which we live and perpetuate.

This brings us to another point that is relevant to understanding the primary drivers of forceful migration, namely, structural aspects of both global and local states of affairs. What I have in mind here refers to a reality that people in developing societies are more likely to live in unstable environments than privileged people in the affluent Western world. These environments are defined by pervasive political, economic, and ecological issues that make a sustainable existence impossible, as their impact not only lowers the quality of living standards but rather diminishes access to more essential aspects of human existence, such as food, water, health, education, employment, and so on. Being surrounded by conditions that make a normal life unsustainable highlights structural nuisances and harms that are primarily caused by states of affairs for which global and local institutions bear the main responsibility—either in their failures and omissions to distribute equitably or to strive to lessen and, if possible, eliminate excruciating inequity.[7] In the case of refugee and migrant children, the negative impact of these structures have twofold character: They (a) initiate displacement as global inequalities result in unsustainable living conditions at home, and (b) during the migration (and within humanitarian spaces), they face obstacles imposed on them by ways in which international humanitarian (and refugee) regimes operate. The harm these structures produce is a product of historical and present human choices and not natural occurrences; thus, they raise important questions of justice and responsibility in the face of suffering that they ultimately cause. In terms of relevance for analyzing conditions of child refugees, recognizing structural harm helps us understand the hazardous nature of humanitarian practices and policies relied on by the international community as deterrence and aid.[8] In other words, these policies and practices ultimately create conditions of exclusion and disenfranchisement for children on the move.

How are, then, exclusion and disenfranchisement manifested? How can we understand this in terms of the experiences that child refugees face? To address these questions, we need to examine more closely the harm that refugee children are exposed to. Children are thrust into positions of disadvantage in an overall array of vulnerabilities that embody their experiences, from their immediate living circumstances that they are trying to escape, the traumatic events during the transit, and, of course, issues that plague humanitarian spaces such as transit, refugee, and/or asylum camps. Children often occupy vulnerable social positions, and the surrounding state of affairs does not merely enable and constrain action; rather, these discursive and material structures exist only in the action and interaction between individuals, institutions, and practices. In terms of the lives of migrant and refugee children, this has multifaceted implications. *First*, policies and practices of Western societies implemented to deter and completely discourage potential arrivals are directly exacerbating the suffering of affected individuals, especially children and youth who are already the most vulnerable group among migrants and refugees. *Second*, accompanying pathological developments follow such constraining conditions—human trafficking, human smuggling, international crime rings, forced labor, debt bondage, and so on. *Third*, humanitarian spaces that are designed and organized to provide shelter and assistance have turned into sites wherein most of the exclusion, violence, and abuse take place. I will leave some of these concerns aside as my intention here is not to repeat criticism levied against national policies of many affluent societies; rather, for the purpose of this chapter, I focus on how these clusters of failures and omissions are translated into vulnerabilities and deprivation of children on the move. Despite the fact that "refugee status" is usually characterized by its transient nature (i.e., an event of relatively short duration), for many forced migrants, especially children languishing in refugee camps, detention centers, or transit zones, their liminal state takes on a new type of being, an ongoing, lasting state of uncertainty and exclusion.

Humanitarian Spaces and Their Discontents

The best way to understand the limits of the current asylum and refugee system is to understand the implications of how humanitarian discourses and practices operate today. I wanted to start this task by sharing additional fragments of Layla's testimony that was brought to my attention during a recent interview with Sara Ristić and Ivana Anđelković, activists in a local humanitarian NGO Info Park from Belgrade, Serbia:

> Since my mom is not with us, my sister takes care of us—she looks after my younger brother, she cleans our room and sometimes she goes to work. I also help a lot with our younger brother and with the cleaning.... We are all together in one room, all the other rooms are full, outside there is boys and I can't listen to them. All the time they are saying bad words to us.... [T]he other boys who

are in the camp without parents keep following us and saying things. I don't know what to do about it really, I just keep quiet and try to walk quickly, what else? This is why I prefer not to leave my room. They say things to my sister too, even worse things! When we go to the market together, she walks quickly and holds me strongly by the arm and looks straight ahead and doesn't say a word. I told her that my hand hurts when she squeezes it like that and that I am angry that we cannot talk back to the boys. She didn't respond to me.

She used to be the best sister in the world, seriously! We went to school together, and watched Bollywood movies, and I told her my secrets. Now all she does is clean our room, or look after our brother, or lying down in bed. I think she felt bad when our Dad didn't allow her to continue to go to school. He said that people will tell bad things about her because she is going with boys to school, and he is not here with us to defend her, so it is better that she stays in room. She didn't respond to him. A little while after that I stopped going to school too. The transportation was abolished, and all my female friends' parents said they cannot go by regular bus with boys, so my Dad said I can't go either. Because he is not here. I tried to argue with him and explain, but he wouldn't listen to me.[9]

The earlier-mentioned experiences are of one of the many unaccompanied minors that my correspondents are working with in recent years. Today, the reality of refugees is often synonymous with encampment—as camps have become the predominant humanitarian spaces of "refuge." Some of the essential aspects of a camp are its authoritarian and constraining character. This is manifested in ways in which humanitarian spaces share essential features with other similar institutions, such as prisons or mental hospitals. Considering the essential restrictions that it enforces, the nature of a refugee camp is also manifested in its dehumanizing character and persistent shortage of basic necessities such as food and a lack of access to satisfactory education or health care. Acute malnutrition is common in various African countries that host some of the most dreadful refugee camps in the world, and according to UNHCR (2000) data, malnutrition among children in camps varies between 20% and 70%. Frequently located in remote, arid, and insecure border areas, refugee camps facilitate the disheartening reduction of what is distinctively human to merely biological.[10] As people begin to settle into their new life in the camp, they quickly realize that there is no future for them. Refugees are given food and shelter but not the freedom to pursue their individual aspirations. They are usually not permitted to work legally, and there is little they are allowed to do to improve their own situation. What at first was intended to be emergency relief turned into long-term containment and the denial of basic human rights and dignity. The impacts are, of course, disheartening.

So are refugee camps good for children? It seems difficult for anyone to pursue a normal life in such an artificial environment where everyone is restricted in their autonomy and opportunities. As the most vulnerable group of displaced people, children have specific needs that place them at heightened risk. The reason for the deplorable situation of increased vulnerability of child refugees and unaccompanied minors is not simply inadequate policies aimed at protecting and preventing children from further harm, or their absence (or weak implementation). From the perspective of a child refugee, the reason for the deplorable situation of increased vulnerability are material constraints within camps—such as the lack of essential resources—and because of the gendered political and power structures that exist within them. Once in the camp, women and children can experience a lack of protection and security due to the spatial organization and social structure of the predominantly male-governed environment. Female child refugees may be forced to sleep alongside male refugees, even if they are traveling alone. Camps often lack gender designated toilet facilities that would allow women and children necessary privacy. Thus, violence, sexual abuse, and forced relationships are frequent occurrences. Many families are separated, and children either rely on the support of one parent, or they are alone like in case of Layla and her sister. This in itself has multifaceted implications for children. In a camp environment, children lose role models who are essential for their healthy upbringing. Even in situations in which both parents are present, families are amid abnormal conditions that, in turn, deteriorate bonds and constitutive dependencies among family members. In order to provide for their children, parents rely on foreign aid or handouts from local NGOs, depriving them of their authority. Their role as caregivers is undermined by their own dependence on a humanitarian system over which they have no control. According to Barbara Harrell-Bond's (2000) addition to a UNHCR report, the main issue is

> parents become degraded in the eyes of their children. Parents suffer the further humiliation of standing in queues to get food, being forced to manipulate the system to get extra ration cards in order to have enough food. They may also suffer from enforced idleness which contributes to the loss of self-esteem, particularly that of men due to overwhelmingly patriarchal cultural norms that operate within such spaces. Domestic violence always increases in refugee situations and family breakdown is common. Both men and women may be suffering anxiety and depression as a consequence of the hopeless situation in which they are living. Substance abuse is a common problem among men, but women refugees also abuse alcohol as a means of forgetting. Whatever is happening at home, children in camps are growing up in conditions which do not permit their socialization according to the values of their own culture. (p. 7)

Given the ongoing refugee camp conditions I briefly outline earlier, it probably will not be surprising to learn that many young individuals avoid them or refuse to be confined in them for long. Many flee for large urban areas in neighboring countries (e.g., Beirut, Nairobi, Istanbul, etc.) where they maintain freedom of movement and can make a living in the informal sector. They may also attempt to reach affluent European welfare states such as Germany, Austria, or Sweden, in order to request asylum. Of course, there are some disadvantages to these choices. The biggest drawback in urban areas is that child refugees cannot receive material assistance from the UNHCR for housing, food, health care, or education. For example, only 1% of the 8 million Syrian refugees in Turkey, Lebanon, and Jordan receive any material support from the United Nations or its partners (Betts & Collier, 2017). In the case of urban refugee children, there is a range of risks confronting them as they seek to provide for themselves in settings where there is almost no institutional assistance. In many contexts, access to housing brings greater protection against sexual harassment and/or abuse present in encampments. But for urban refugee children, employment in informal sectors increases vulnerability to gender-based harm, arrest, detention, and extortion. Because of their precarious position, many young refugees also experience insecurities and exploitation at their workplaces: wages unfairly withheld, arbitrary firing, sexual harassment, unsafe working conditions, and so on. What is worse, survival and the urgency to work excludes youth from access to necessary education. According to the recent UNHCR (2016) study, about half of 6 million school-aged children today do not attend any school at all.

During my conversation with Sara and Ivana, it was frequently reiterated that children who decide to reach affluent European countries and request asylum face another set of challenges. The biggest one is the dangerous passage to European countries. Continuous efforts of European states to halt the movement of refugees through administrative measures (locking land borders, building walls and fences, warehousing refugees in controlled environments, etc.) has, for the most part, proved, unsuccessful in preventing them from trying to reach the safety of the Western world.[11] However, such measures have made their efforts increasingly unsafe. Unable to reach refuge by land, children resort to dangerous routes where they become easy prey to smugglers that control illegal pathways to European countries, mostly sea routes in the Aegean and Mediterranean and land routes from transit countries such as Serbia (Tinti & Reitano, 2017). The harm to refugees who must employ smugglers to get to Europe is great. The rising numbers of young boys and girls making the journey to Europe in recent years also face many of the same risks endured by children confined in camps and in urban areas. A significant number experience sexual or physical abuse by smugglers, other migrants, local population, or even government officials and NGO workers. Between 60% and 80% of female migrants traveling through Africa and the Balkans are harassed or sexually assaulted along the way, and even when refugee children have been successfully "smuggled" into Europe, the ordeal does not end immediately.[12] Reaching their destination ultimately may not provide relief as they may end up experiencing sexual exploitation due to fraudulent arrangements with smugglers or forced marriages, or they end up caught in criminal networks of begging and petty crime such as pickpocketing.

Reception centers and asylum-seeking processes unleash a new set of traumas. Detention is routine in many European coastal countries that border on the Mediterranean (e.g., Greece, Malta, Italy), and conditions in transit reception centers are terrible. As Sara Ristić described,

> a lot of challenges depend on the fact that many of these children are locked in a transit context, so they want to continue their trip either on their own volition or due to ongoing pressure from their families who stayed back home. This makes it difficult for the government or local Non-governmental organizations to provide social and psychological support for them.[13]

Among those who are passing through Serbia, almost a third of registered unaccompanied children have experienced violence, either physical, psychological, or sexual. Sara's colleague Ivana says that "minors are under continuous pressure by their adult peers, what frequently results in manipulation, physical violence or rape, mostly during the transit but also within humanitarian spaces organized within transit countries such as Serbia." The increasing number of the children Ristić and Anđelković worked with had developed issues like anxiety, depression, substance abuse, and behavioral problems, such as suicide attempts and self-harm. State- and UN-funded refugee camps can be dangerous too. Most of the children that Sara and Ivana talked to described both physical and verbal violence as a common practice by both employees and other members of the camp. "Insults based on ethnic and religious basis are common and that ultimately adds to the dehumanizing treatment of those children." Ivana adds, "Sexual violence toward minors is present in the government-run refugee centers, especially in those where no separation between minors and their older peers exists." This type of violence is unrecognized and underreported, and often the victims themselves are not aware of what is going on and what actually constitutes assault, which, in turn, makes it difficult for support agencies to address it and prevent it from further occurrence.

Leaving the humanitarian spaces aside, increased police violence in urban areas, attacks from diverse right-wing groups, forced pushbacks, and expulsions without the chance to apply for asylum at borders, are common deterrence practices among Balkan countries. For Sara, Ivana, and others who work with unaccompanied minors, the well-being and rights of children on the move is not only threatened by inhumane conditions back at home or during the migration—the hazard continues with humanitarian governance and the dissolute nature of the dehumanizing treatment in the international asylum and refugee system. This leaves us with an important, and yet disheartening image of the inadequate responses of "Western" countries, in protecting refugee children and ensuring their access to humane conditions. Everything considered, I would like to end this modest analysis in the same way I began, namely, with the words of a child who wrestles with circumstances that were never her choice alone. I hope that her experiences and her aspirations may serve as an everlasting testimony of our omissions and an important reminder to change ways in which the international community articulates, feels, and acts on pressing issues of less fortunate others:

I haven't seen my Dad in five months. I don't know how our journey will be. But that also has to end sometime, right? I decided to be a humanitarian worker or a social worker when I grow up. I mean, at first I wanted to be a doctor. But then I changed my mind. Because I want to help people who are poor and who are in difficult situations and who are alone. I know how it is and when I go to school I will learn how to help and find a job. I don't care in what country, I just care that I spend my time helping others.[14]

Conclusion: Moral Erasure, a Lack of Solidarity, and Necessary Reforms

In closing, I would like to end this chapter by turning the critical lens toward us, the public in the West. Namely, in face of major institutional omissions, much of it depends on us, people, to understand, organize, and redefine what solidarity and justice actually mean in the face of such circumstances as I have outlined earlier. Nothing Western governments are doing in response to the suffering of children will actually make deprivation less likely for millions of others across the globe. If anything, history teaches us the opposite. In the wake of present issues, affluent societies have not only failed to understand the extent of tragedy that displaced individuals must endure but have rather created absurd restrictions levied against people on the move. Western audiences seem to feel far greater sympathy for refugees than for migrants; the former are seen as victims without real choice, while the latter are not forced to move out of desperation for their lives. But how can we justify these distinctions? Are they really valid or is this, again, mere euphemism? Most of our humanitarian efforts unfold as a polarization between those people whom we humanize and are willing to sympathize with and those whom we decide are not worthy of our solidarity and empathy. In such an unjust world, one can ask a disheartened question: Who is eligible for Western tears? If it is only people from Syria, what about those who are coming from Eritrea, El Salvador, and Afghanistan? If we focus our attention only on the children who somehow drown at our doorstep, what about those who are still alive but trapped in provisional camps at the outskirts of the "developed" West?[15] If we focus our attention only on children, what about their parents and other family members? Can we really define what makes a meaningful environment for a child, determining what family members are worthy enough to be present from those who are seemingly expendable in a child's life? What gives us the power to make such a choice in the first place? If we owe our compassion and support only to people who are fleeing from violence, what about those who are desperately trying to escape poverty or issues related to climate change? What is, then, the threshold of pain and vulnerability that we will acknowledge as a valid justification for people to leave their homes or relevant conditions for us to acknowledge our responsibilities? Identifying the structural features that account for these humanitarian and legal selections is more disheartening than noting the humanitarian failures themselves. What the current situation with migrant and refugee children and their treatment by the international community show is that political and administrative spheres of the liberal West are not only unable to respond adequately but are increasingly part of the problem.

All things considered, just as this chapter and experiences that it refers to cannot tell us much beyond overall circumstances of the unjust and unfair globalized world, it also cannot instruct us how to ignite the fleeting moment of compassion and mobilize it into a political impulse capable of changing horrifying conditions that children like Layla experience on a daily basis. If the parts of testimony and the life it captures change anything, what is now different? The fate of Layla, or any other child that receives media attention or ends up as content in academic publications is one of those tragic, entrenched, and seemingly common processes that often surround us. The ongoing lurch on social media and news outlets draw public attention to the specific instances of human vulnerability and suffering, and although such attention is very welcome, in the end, it has limited reach and longevity. There are layers of experience invoked by the perception of such tragic events, and it not only emphasizes selectivism in ways in which the migration crisis has been handled up to this point but also further discloses a deeply entrenched evaluative framework that regulates whose lives are deemed valuable and whose are rendered invisible. There is suffering among children all over the world—children whose faces and bodies we (by commission or omission) do not see—and since we allegedly do not *see* them, their suffering has no impact on us. To understand this paradox, one has to disclose the ways in which the public pendulum shifts between humanizing and dehumanizing the other. That is not an easy task, as if we fail to understand the implications of our present moral and political choices, lives of Layla, and millions of other children lost in the humanitarian and legal limbo of the "civilized" West, will remain a painful statistic and a testimony of failures of a world that is morally immature and drowned in its own hypocrisy.

In the end, not to give in to resignation and apathy, I want to ask: What is necessary to take such conditions seriously? What is actually required to think conscientiously about the fate of millions of forcefully displaced children who represent the most vulnerable group of people? In an era of towering inequalities and in an era of obvious affluence, doing nothing about pressing conditions would not only undermine the very legitimacy of our core values and moral commitments but would also render worthless all the effort that has been made to create a world that is not plagued by injustice, indifference, and omissions. With this said, how do we begin to tackle these issues and pave the way for genuine moral and political engagement amid so many injustices and vulnerabilities that child refugees face today? We could see from previous pages that structural failures of international institutions and affluent governments constitute a grim humanitarian present for millions of forcefully displaced people. Yet, in light of shifting social and cultural contexts, highlighting limits and disclosing these exclusionary relations also entail a possibility to break out of oppressive contexts and chart new venues for humanitarian practices and solidarity with people in need. In the case of refugee children and the exclusion they experience, it is urgent to react properly and enable access to remedies and their further development. This can ultimately happen in at least two ways, through (1) legal means, complementing the 1951 Convention Relating to the Status of Refugees with the Convention on the Rights of the Child (CRC), which would then serve as a guiding framework for the interpretation of child rights and freedoms, and (2) change in ways in which we understand aims and methods of international humanitarian actions (and our role in it), what will ultimately allow a transformation of the nature of our moral and political commitments.

Regarding the first, children in humanitarian spaces have fewer chances to access justice than adults, especially in cultures where a child's status is subjected or tied to constraining patriarchies. It is obvious that forced migration can increase discrimination against children and worsen the opportunities for satisfying their legal claims, leaving victims with no access to justice. The rights contained in the CRC are rights that are directly attributed to children "irrespective of the child's or their parent's or legal guardian's race, color, sex, language, religion, political or other opinion, national, ethnic, or social origin, property, disability, birth or other status" (OHCRC 1989, Article 2). As Samantha Arnold (2018) has recently argued on this specific topic,

> due to the comprehensive nature of the CRC, which includes both civil and political and social and economic rights, there is arguably a scope for even further development of the interpretation of persecution considering children's rights . . . including those rights where a child's development is affected. (p. 93)

Hence, there is an ignored potential for the refugee convention and international asylum system to expand and incorporate a children's rights approach that would allow us to avoid many of the pathologies that I have highlighted throughout this chapter. What would follow from this is that international conventions and agreements, once adopted by the individual countries become part of their legal system and often have a priority compared to national laws. Thus, formally, there would be no legal obstacles for the successful assessment and implementation of these norms worldwide, which would put the necessary pressure on countries to meet their obligations and provide services and care that children essentially require. With clear international rules, UNHCR together with the CRC, UNICEF, and other international NGOs can fill in the gaps and provide guidelines for addressing the issues of exclusion and increased vulnerability of the youngest among migrants and refugees in ways that would avoid further marginalization and suffering.

Regarding the second, in order to ensure that refugee children thrive rather than merely survive, every feasible change in ways how the international humanitarian community works today needs to focus on fostering the autonomy of forcefully displaced children and youth. Empowering young individuals will allow them to engage in rebuilding their lives and making an impact on social circumstances that surround them. As I wrote in more details elsewhere, it is also necessary to realize that a humanitarian response is never a humanitarian response alone and that the success of humanitarian practices often depends on the institutional capacity to creatively interact with different normative policy fields, namely, development, human rights, gender justice, gender equality, children rights, community and environmental sustainability, economic and ecological resilience, and so on.[16] In the case of refugee children and unaccompanied youth, the success of this process will ultimately rely on how well we implement the protection of their essential needs and how efficiently we nurture their aspirations. Improvements are necessary in at least five areas: access to education, protection from sexual and gender-based violence, inclusion into the decision-making processes, fostering of economic self-reliance, and easier access to empowerment programs within UN-governed spaces and host societies. Through such reforms, child refugees would receive culturally and linguistically appropriate inclusion, which, in turn, would allow them to thrive and achieve self-sufficiency in the new environment. These goals can only be achieved by improving the integration of humanitarian assistance with development practices.[17] The first step toward this goal is to find the right balance between the need for standardized approaches and the need to adapt to unique contexts and challenges for each specific aspect of the humanitarian crisis. A reimagined humanitarian regime must work for everyone, not just for the fortunate few who reach the "civilized West." Hence, in the case of forcefully displaced children whose increased vulnerability invokes additional responsibilities on the international community, it is necessary to focus on fostering their *humanitarian sustainability*. As the nature of humanitarian crises changes, we are witnessing not only the increase in the number of those affected but also a change in the nature of the harm that they are exposed to. Focus on improving sustainability and resilience of afflicted communities and individuals means that international assemblage of humanitarian assistance and governance aims at restoring the autonomy of individuals who are the target of humanitarian efforts. After immediate relief, humanitarian policies and institutions should focus on enabling an environment that promotes self-sufficiency and growth. Of course, the empowering nature of these development projects will depend on the specific social contexts and requires certain creativity (and flexibility) in improving the conditions of those affected. The precise models of humanitarian development will vary across different contexts that will take into consideration the specific nature of stakeholders' needs and vulnerabilities (in this case, needs of forcefully displaced children and youth).

Taking everything into account that has been said, for the international community and humanitarianism to fulfill this role, they have to rethink the foundations of their ethics, change their normative commitments from charity to justice, detach from universalizing Eurocentric patriarchal discursive hegemonies, reimagine its methodology and reconstruct institutional organization in order to strive towards a more inclusive approach toward afflicted individuals. In practical terms, building the capacity of the staff members and government partners, educating the public, ensuring training opportunities, and providing updated guidance on how to further strengthen the inclusion of the most vulnerable sectors of humanity must be a priority in a world plagued by exclusion, violence, and injustice. Otherwise, the lives of children like Layla will remain an uncontested scar on Western political values and moral commitments.

Notes

1. I would like to thank a local nongovernmental organization from Serbia, Info Park, and especially two of their activists, Sara Ristić and Ivana Anđelković, for all their support in terms of writing this chapter. Info Park is a refugee/migrant information center based in Belgrade, Serbia, specializing in providing services to newly arrived beneficiaries from Syria, Iraq, Afghanistan, Pakistan, and other countries. Info Park offers protection services, referrals, information sharing and provides helps with accommodation in and transport to state-run camps. The interview with them has given much-needed personal perspectives on issues that many displaced children face today. Thanks to them, I am able to share testimony of one of their stakeholders—Layla. This is not her real name, and we have decided to hide it in order to provide protection and privacy for the affected minor. The interview with Sara and Ivana was conducted on October 22, 2020. The conversation was in Serbian language and was translated by M. Ivanovic for the purpose of this chapter. Sara and Ivana provided written permission to use their actual names.
2. I have written on this theme on several occasions. For further information, see Ivanovic (2015, 2016, 2018, 2019) and Ivanovic and Malavisi (2019).
3. I have adopted the term *Western* following its common usage in academic milieu and literature to encompass the industrialized affluent societies of the European Union, North America, Japan, Australia, and New Zealand.
4. Within the UNHCR context, a distinctive category of separated children defined as "children under 18 years of age who are outside their country of origin and separated from both parents, or their previous legal/customary primary caregiver" (UNHCR, 2004, 2). Refugee children may be seen as representing a distinct group within a broader category of displaced children. Strictly speaking, becoming a refugee child depends on a process according to a specific legal status to a child who has crossed an international border and is deemed individually, or as part of the family, as having a well-founded fear of prosecution.
5. As a former child refugee and a humanitarian activist who works with forcefully displaced people, I heavily rely on my personal experiences, both as an affected individual and as a person in a position to observe and witness the hardships of others. I do not argue that there is "one size fits all" approach to such complex circumstances that plague vulnerable individuals, and I am aware that experiences differ from person to person. Sadly, something that has become evident in recent decades is that institutional and policy framework echoes repeating patterns of exclusion and vulnerability. This is easily traceable observing circumstances and impacts on people on the move. Paying attention to that allows me to carefully generalize some of the issues that are common for the majority of people who are targets of humanitarian efforts in regard to forceful displacement and migration.
6. For further information, see Ivanovic and Malavisi (2019).
7. Institutions that I am referring to here are monetary and development agencies, legislative and executive branches of government, NGOs, humanitarian organizations, UN humanitarian spaces, international law, and enforcement processes, among others. Understanding their failures and omissions means understanding systematic ways in which social and political structures both locally and globally harm or otherwise disadvantage groups of individuals.

8. Structural injustice, in fact, is a subtle, invisible state of affairs that, due to its normalization in social relations and institutions, serves as a norm of behavior and as such are rarely challenged (especially by social groups that benefit from such state of affairs). Injustice in our example is rooted in ways in which international and humanitarian institutions are structured and operationalized, wherein consequences favor and protect privileged sectors of humanity. These same people, in turn, influence the structures and operations of international institutions in ways that protect their own interests without taking responsibility for disproportionate burdens on other people and communities.
9. Testimony shared during a recent interview. "Layla" is not the real name of the affected child, and we have decided to hide it in order to provide protection and privacy to the affected minor. Interview with Sara and Ivana was conducted on October 22, 2020. The conversation was in Serbian language and was translated by M. Ivanovic for the purpose of this chapter.
10. In other words, camps do offer access to basic necessities, yet this access is insufficient and does not meet any other need beyond mere subsistence. There seems to be a focus on sustaining "life," but the quality of that life remains irrelevant.
11. The sheer number of refugees moving through transit countries has overwhelmed the capacity of states to provide for basic needs (e.g., accommodations, food, and water). One of the common issues in countries such as Macedonia, Serbia, and/or Bosnia is that there is an evident lack of specialized services for children, children with disabilities, or children with special needs. Considering the chaotic nature of the journey, many recent reports indicate that children often get separated from their parents or other guardians during difficult crossings of EU borders (e.g., European Network of Ombudspersons for Children, 2020. In light of such a state of affairs, there is a legal obligation for EU states to take necessary measures to prevent the separation of children from their families. See Articles 12, 23(5), and 24 of the European Reception Conditions Directive (2013).
12. For more details, Amnesty International (2016).
13. This testimony was shared during the interview conducted via Zoom on October 22, 2020, by M. Ivanovic. The goal of the interview was to acquire testimonial data on the personal experiences of NGO workers and unaccompanied minors who were currently warehoused in Serbia as one of the main transit countries for migrant and refugee children.
14. This testimony was shared during the interview conducted via Zoom on October 22 by M. Ivanovic. The goal of the interview was to acquire testimonial data on personal experiences of NGO workers and unaccompanied minors who were currently warehoused in Serbia as one of the main transit countries for migrant and refugee children.
15. I am referring here to the tragic fate of Alan Kurdi, a 3-year-old Syrian boy who drowned as his family tried to reach the Greek island of Kos.
16. For more details, Ivanovic (2019) and Ivanovic and Malavisi (2019).
17. The UNICEF with its "No Lost Generation" initiative already provides a meaningful set of instructions for how to tackle some of these issues. For more details, see https://www.unicef.org/appeals/syrianrefugees.html#16.

References

Amnesty International. (2016, January 18). *Female refugees face physical assault, exploitation and sexual harassment on their journey through Europe.* https://www.amnesty.org/en/latest/news/2016/01/female-refugees-face-physical-assault-exploitation-and-sexual-harassment-on-their-journey-through-europe/

Arnold, S. (2018). *Children's rights and refugee law conceptualizing children within the Refugee Convention*. Routledge.
Betts, A., & Collier, P. (2017). *Refuge: Rethinking refugee policy in a changing world*. Oxford University Press.
European Reception Conditions Directive. (2013). https://eur-lex.europa.eu/legal-content/EN/TXT/?uri=celex%3A32013L0033
European Network of Ombudspersons for Children. (2020). https://www.europarl.europa.eu/cmsdata/234594/ENOC-2020-Position-Statement-on-CRIA-FV-1.pdf
Harrell-Bond, B. (2000). *New issues in refugee research* (Working Paper No. 29). UNHCR. https://www.unhcr.org/3ae6a0c64.pdf
Ivanovic, M. (2015). Lives rendered invisible: Bearing witness to human suffering. *Etikk I Praksis - Nordic Journal of Applied Ethics, 10*(2), 59–74. https://doi.org/10.5324/eip.v10i2.1919
Ivanovic, M. (2016). Holding hands with death: The dark side of our humanitarian present. *Radical Philosophy Review, 19*(2), 359–379.
Ivanovic, M. (2018). The European grammar of inclusion: Integrating epistemic and social inclusion of refugees in host societies. *Radical Philosophy Review, 21*(1), 103–127.
Ivanovic, M. (2019). Stubborn realities, shared humanity: The state of humanitarian ethics today. *Ethics and Economics, 16*(1), 71–87.
Ivanovic, M., & Malavisi, A. (2019). Tales of abuse and negligence: Current humanitarian practices and refugee children. *Journal of Global Ethics, 15*(3), 1–17.
Office of the High Commissioner for Human Rights. (1989). *Convention on the rights of the child*. https://www.ohchr.org/EN/ProfessionalInterest/Pages/CRC.aspx
Oliver, K. (2017). *Carceral humanitarianism: Logics of refugee detention*. University of Minnesota Press.
Owen, D. (2019). Refugees and politics of indignity. In K. Oliver, L. M. Madura, & S. Ahmed (Eds.), *Refugees now: Rethinking borders, hospitality and citizenship* (pp. 13–27). Rowman & Littlefield.
Parekh, S. (2017). *Refugees and the ethics of forced displacement*. Routledge.
Tinti, P., & Reitano, T. (2017). *Migrant, refugee, smuggler, savior*. Oxford University Press.
UNICEF. (2021). *Child migration*. https://data.unicef.org/topic/child-migration-and-displacement/migration/
United Nations High Commissioner for Refugees. (1951). *The 1951 Refugee Convention*. https://www.unhcr.org/en-us/1951-refugee-convention.html
United Nations High Commissioner for Refugees. (2000). *New issues in refugee research*. https://www.unhcr.org/3ae6a0c64.pdf
United Nations High Commissioner for Refugees. (2004). *Statement of Good Practice*. https://www.unhcr.org/4d9474399.pdf
United Nations High Commissioner for Refugees. (2016). *UNCHR reports crisis in refugee education*. https://www.unhcr.org/en-us/news/press/2016/9/57d7d6f34/unhcr-reports-crisis-refugee-education.html
United Nations High Commissioner for Refugees. (2020). *Figures at a glance*. https://www.unhcr.org/en-us/figures-at-a-glance.html
Weizman, E. (2011). *The least of all possible evils*. Verso.

CHAPTER 3

A Romani Analysis of English Preschool Education

Mandy Pierlejewski and Gyula Vamosi

THIS CHAPTER HAS been written by Mandy, a *gadji*, or non-Roma academic, and Gyula, a *rom* (adult Roma male). It uses a sociocultural approach to explore the education of Roma children in an English setting, focusing on the case study of a 4-year-old child. Themes of transition, cultural expectations and play are analysed. For each theme, an excerpt from an ethnographic study is used as a basis for reflection by both Gyula and Mandy. Gyula gives a unique Roma interpretation of the data, relating it to his personal, insider understanding of Roma culture. He does not claim to represent all Roma people but presents his personal experience of being a member of this ethnic group. Mandy reflects on this as a teacher, considering the implications of the knowledge shared for her understanding of the case study child and future practice with Roma children. The process of writing this chapter was impacted by the COVID-19 epidemic as the authors were unable to meet in person. To overcome this, matters were discussed in online meetings and social media was used to facilitate writing. A method emerged in which Mandy would send excerpts of her field notes to Gyula in a digital chat form. He would then write a response, using a social media app. These WhatsApp conversations have become the main body of the chapter. Digital chat writing created a non-threatening space, in which both authors could communicate. The use of mobile phones, rather than the computer, to write also contributed to a more relaxed writing environment, reducing the power imbalance between the authors. A decision was made to preserve the voice of both writers through the use of excerpts from field notes followed by voiced responses, written in the first person. Writing in the third person throughout would have detracted from the Roma voice, a voice which we felt was missing from educational literature. We did not want to confer a voice on the 'other' but, rather, privilege the subaltern voice (Cannella & Viruru, 2004).

Gyula: History of Roma in the United Kingdom

Roma, often referred to by the non-Roma population as 'Gypsies', originate from various parts of the northwest of India. The base of our language is Sanskrit; therefore, it is similar to Urdu, Punjabi and Gujarati. This group migrated from India between 1000 and 1068 and then stayed in Byzantium for about 200 years before moving towards the Balkans (Hancock, 2002; Matras, 2014). In what is present-day Romania, Roma people were enslaved for about 500 years. During the Second World War, along with Jews and other groups, Roma people were selected for elimination. It is impossible to establish definite numbers, but Hancock estimates that 1.5 million Roma were killed in what is now known as the 'Gypsy Holocaust' (Fonseca, 1996; Hancock, 2002; Matras, 2014). Following this, during a period of communist rule in Eastern Europe, attempts were made to assimilate the Roma into mainstream culture (Scheffel, 2005). Since the collapse of the former Soviet Union and the enlargement of the European Union in 2004, large numbers of Eastern European Roma have moved to settle in the United Kingdom. Estimates of numbers vary but range between 80,000 and 300,000 (Morris, 2016). These have added to the numbers of people classed as Gypsy, Roma and Travellers (GRT), with estimates of at least 500,000 GRT people in the United Kingdom, Eastern European Roma make up an estimated 50% of the GRT population. These groups are not travelling people but live in settled communities in the cities of the United Kingdom.

The influx of Eastern European Roma people into UK cities has been a relatively recent event: Schools in some parts of the country now have large populations of Roma children. Having no past experiences with Eastern European Roma, these schools have struggled to adapt as their existing knowledge of Roma culture is very limited. The new communities have often experienced issues with communication as schools have little knowledge of the Romani language. When non-Roma Eastern European bilingual support staff have been used, there have been examples of racism and prejudice (Penfold, 2015) as well as a lack of understanding that for many children, the Eastern European language is not their mother tongue. Schools therefore experience problems such as poor attendance, a lack of parental engagement and low achievement but have little or no understanding of the reasons behind these issues (Penfold, 2016).

Mandy: Literature Focusing on Roma Education

There is a wealth of literature focusing on the education of Roma children in Europe and beyond. This literature can be categorised into two main groups: literature which focuses on interventions to enable Roma children to integrate into mainstream school culture and literature which focuses on developing intercultural understanding. Intervention-focused literature starts from an assumption that children are a homogeneous group. It sees children as developing along predetermined pathways based on developmental psychology, irrespective of culture. Roma culture and child development are looked at from the perspective of the mainstream White middle-class culture, creating an ethnocentric deficit model. Roma parenting is thus pathologised in a similar way to other practices which do not conform to normative expectations (Phoenix, 1997). Bennett's (2012) report into Roma early childhood inclusion exemplifies this view. The key messages are that barriers to learning must be torn down, enabling children to perform at the same level as their non-Roma counterparts. Roma children are seen as a problem which must be fixed. Questions arise about why Roma behave in the way they do are not asked, which means that their culture is not valued or understood. Most policy-based literature represents this deficit discourse, proposing evidence-based strategies to improve outcomes (Klaus & Marsh, 2014; Wilkin, Derrington and Foster, 2009).

Literature which focuses on intercultural understanding, however, tells a different story. Some of this is written by members of the Roma community, with notable examples being Smith (1997) and Kyuchukov (2000). These examples give detailed information about Roma culture, explaining from an insider's perspective, the behaviours identified as 'problematic' for mainstream educators and researchers. Smith explores Romani child socialisation processes, exploring the development of the Roma child and their education within the family. The values of autonomy, responsibility and the active participation of children in society are contrasted with mainstream middle-class views of children as dependent and regulated by the school regime. Similarly, Kyuchukov focuses on the beliefs of teachers that all children start school with the same level of knowledge and that they should know how to cope with the school rules.

Non-Roma researchers who have taken an intercultural approach to educating Roma children have identified that working closely with the community to try to gain an understanding of Roma and mainstream values and beliefs can be very successful. Schools and organisations that are willing to adapt and change based on this developing awareness tend to find approaches and strategies which are amenable to both the Roma families and the schools. An example of this is Lalueza, Martinez-Lozano, and Macias-Gomez-Estern's (2019) work with Roma children in Spain. The projects discussed demonstrate a deep understanding of Roma culture and attempt to make school learning meaningful to Roma children by relating it directly to their lives and values. We wanted to build on this intercultural model of work with Roma children by working as a team to gain a better understanding of Roma culture.

Research Project

The research we undertook was a participatory ethnographic action research project. In this approach, the researcher and participants work together for change (Tedmanson & Banerjee, 2012). The work is emancipatory in purpose and involves the people involved experiencing and formulating the problem being investigated (Cohen, Manion & Morrison, 2011; Montero, 2000). All members of the research team were insiders, albeit in different positions of authority, researching their own practice and experience (Mills & Morton, 2013). The project took place in a preschool (ages 4–5) class in the north of England for a year, starting in June 2018 and ending in July 2019. The research team consisted of a number of school staff. Mandy worked as an additional staff member, and Gyula, who was a Roma advisor for the project, joined the team halfway through the year. The team worked together to try to devise new ways of assessing and teaching children, with a specific focus on six Roma children in the class. The research took place in Pinetree School (pseudonym), a very large primary school in the northern English city of Bradford. The school is located in one of the most deprived wards in the region as defined by national measures of deprivation (Ministry of Housing & Local Government, 2019). The population is mixed, with about half of the children from Pakistani heritage and one quarter of Eastern European Roma origin, mainly from the Czech and Slovak regions. The remaining population represents a broad range of ethnicities. A focus for the school was to improve the educational outcomes of Roma children, as this group has been shown to be the lowest performing group nationally in the key performance measures (Department for Education, 2019).

The work for this chapter was completed by two members of the research team: Mandy and Gyula. Mandy has focused on the experience of teaching, and Gyula has contributed his knowledge of the Romani people and their history, characteristics and values. Both Mandy and Gyula have been involved in the analysis of field notes with Gyula offering a Roma interpretation and Mandy responding to this with reflections on practice. Gyula's wife, Maria, has also been involved in this analysis to give a female Roma perspective. Matras and Leggio (2018) note that many Roma advisers have not been included in the writing of academic papers, despite the fact that their contribution in terms of insider knowledge has been significant. This chapter starts from the acknowledgement of this omission and aims to go some way to address it.

Following on from the research project, both Mandy and Gyula have continued to be involved with the school. Mandy has taken a post as a school governor, and Gyula is now employed as a Roma liaison worker. Gyula supports Roma children with home learning activities and helps the well-being of Roma families via establishing a secure and safe home environment. He also introduces the school community to Roma culture through music and artistic projects.

The main focus of the analysis is a case study of a Roma child with whom Mandy worked during the research project. An outline of the case is included, followed by excerpts from Mandy's field notes which are analysed by both Gyula and Mandy.

Focusing on Celina: A 4-Year-Old Roma Child

'Celina' is a 4-year-old Roma girl. She arrived at Pinetree School without registering beforehand and so was not already in the school system. She had not attended the school nursery (ages 3–4) class as most of her classmates had. She arrived speaking no English, using her own language for the first week or two. She was very distressed during the first week of school and cried for long periods. The school knew virtually nothing about Celina upon her arrival. They were unclear about who her carer was, what language she spoke and who her immediate family were. At first, the sister was thought, by staff, to be her cousin, and her grandmother was thought to be her mother. As the year progressed, staff made enquiries with Celina's family and, by halfway through the school year, had discovered that Celina's parents had been deported to Slovakia and her grandmother was the main carer. Celina lives in a very deprived part of the city, within a Roma community. She spends time out of school with other Roma children and families. She was very slow to learn English, but by the end of the year she could speak in short sentences and phrases. Gyula deduced that of the many disparate Roma communities, Celina was from the Vlax group through assessing her dialect.

Transition

This excerpt from Mandy's field notes is taken from the first week of the school term in September. Mandy reflects on Celina's transition to school.

> Celina was very upset and crying for about an hour this morning. This child has virtually no English and has no previous experience of education. She has been in school since Wednesday and started full time on the first day. The child was clearly very distressed. I tried to distract the child and comfort her. She responded briefly to a teddy but then became distressed again. The staff said that this was her worst day but that on previous days, she had calmed down when left to her own devices. They said that attention seemed to make her more distressed. Later the child did calm down and played with the other children and adults.

Gyula Writes

Parenthood in the Roma community is considered to be the most important obligation in life. The community will do everything possible to keep a family together and children's well-being overrides parents' individual goals. With a long history of persecution, every day in the life of a large proportion of Roma families is a matter of survival. Members of a Roma household and the extended family are expected to make a contribution to meet the physiological and safety needs of every member of the family support network in terms of food, shelter, generating income, health and housing. Individual ambitions to gain status or recognition in the 'gadjo' (non-Roma) world or desires to fully achieve one's own potential without an actual benefit to the Roma family and/or wider community will be perceived as 'gadjikano' (belonging to the non-Roma world). Therefore, children also have their role to play in looking after younger siblings, keeping their home tidy and, following the Roma rules, engaging with adults not belonging to the household. The mini adult-child (as the gadjo would see it) may also help with cooking and gathering or chopping firewood. They are also responsible for passing on gadjikano knowledge such as school lessons or digital skills such as using YouTube, Facebook and TikTok (often the only social media platforms known by Roma) to younger children.

Housing and homelessness have been an issue for the Roma community since the abolition of the 'Gypsy Laws' in Romania in the second half of the 19th century (Achim, 1998). Roma communities often need help navigating emergency situations such as evictions and police raids, and in such distressing situations, children normally have an important role to play. Most members of the Roma community rarely nurture relationships or friendships in the gadjo world, and their only opportunity for direct contact with the gadje are emergency situations. As a result of this, being left in the gadjo world without any member of the family support network, would be perceived as the most heartbreaking situation for a Roma child. However, if a Roma child is exposed long enough to the gadjo environment, their beliefs about the gadjo adults will change, and they will learn ways of connecting to the non-Roma world. This leads to children becoming the mediators for adult members of the family support network whenever they need to connect to the gadjo world, which is a phenomenon often seen with immigrant children mediators (Chu, 1999).

I believe that the most important lesson children receive not only from the parents but also from all members of the extended family, which includes grandparents, uncles, aunts and their children, is that absolute honesty in the family support network is at the core of any interaction. Showing love and giving support to other family members in hard situations are more important than individual feelings or developmental goals and even goes beyond individual freedom. Family goals will override individual financial needs or career aspirations. Among all family roles, however, motherhood is perceived as sacred by the Roma.

The strongest bond one develops in the Roma Gypsy community is traditionally with the mother. The physical connection is established via breastfeeding that may last several years. A Roma mother will teach her child to stand out in the Roma community and will also pass on the defence mechanisms against anti-Gypsyism that many Roma come across upon engaging with the non-Roma world. The expectation to act as mini adults is a hard burden on children, which is constantly counterbalanced by a strong emotional connection with all family members.

Mandy Responds

Gyula's response to the excerpt from my field notes explores three aspects of the role of the child in the Roma community. These are the bond between the mother and the child, the role of the child in supporting the family unit and the isolation of the community from the gadjo world. These aspects largely stem from an important Roma value, which is the importance and closeness of the family unit. Although this will vary from family to family, Gyula feels that this value is shared by most Roma people. His reflection contrasts starkly with the deficit picture painted by reports into Roma inclusion such as Bennett's (2012). Here, the focus is on urgent intervention to ensure 'developmental readiness' of Roma children. These interventions focus on "pre- and postnatal health, parenting and adult education" (Bennett, 2012, p. 14). Bennett (2012) is explicit later in the study, stating that "many factors interfere with the Roma child's readiness for school" (p. 37). The measure of successful parenting here is "readiness for school"—a measure which is based on the developmental expectations of mainstream middle-class culture. In this measure, Roma parents, like many other groups whose parenting approach is different from mainstream expectations, are perceived to fall short (Phoenix, 1997). It also ignores the communal nature of childcare, a form of *othermothering* (Wane, 1996) in which many members of the community are involved in caring for children. The solutions suggested focus on the education of Roma mothers in mainstream approaches to parenting. They do not take into account the different understandings of the role of the parent and child discussed by Gyula in his reflection. They also ignore the fact that, for Roma mothers, as for many mothers in Indigenous populations and the global majority world, the aim of parenting is to support the child in their ongoing participatory role within the family. It is not to prepare the child for later life in the gadjo world. As in other cultures, children learn tasks such as caring for younger siblings, supporting older relatives and helping parents with cooking and cleaning (Katz, 2004). Children participate in the mature activities of the community, learning by participation, rather than being separated from the adult world and treated as different. These skills, however, are not seen or measured and as a result, do not count.

Contextualising Educator Expectations

The next extract from Mandy's field notes explores Celina's struggles to engage with books. Written in February 2019, it focuses on Mandy's concerns about Celina's lack of focus. By this time, Celina had been in school for 5 months, about half of the school year.

> Celina and I sat in the foyer to look at the book. Celina wanted to start at the back of the book and found it very difficult to cope with working through the story in order. She continually took the book from me and looked at random pages. When we were looking at a particular page, she would not actually look

at the pictures, but rather looked all around the foyer. She was unable to focus on the book. She holds books upside down, starts at the back and does not treat them with respect. Her lack of focus is starting to concern me. Her behaviour is very different to the other children, but it is unclear at this stage if this is just a lack of school readiness and experience or if it is Attention Deficit Hyperactivity Disorder (ADHD) It is very difficult to have a conversation with Celina as she is constantly being distracted.

Gyula Writes

Tools such as toys for improving fine-motor skills or books for either parents or children are completely lacking in many Roma households. Roma children will be trained to engage with objects used in cleaning and maintaining the home environment or with items and/or animals belonging to the traditional trade of the family network such as violins, wood, horses, spoons, nails and the like. Learning activities are social in nature with activities being carried out in collaboration as part of a team normally formed between siblings and cousins. One-to-one teaching only rarely occurs in Roma families and even then, it will focus on human engagement. Learning to use an item which does not contribute to the daily survival or growth of the family is normally considered insignificant.

I feel that the key aim of education in a Roma family is to develop children's human engagement skills. Being highly skilled at social interactions at a young age is perceived as highly valuable. With Roma children, the focus is on learning and instantly applying social engagement rules as per the internal code of conduct which is called 'Pachiv', or more widely referred to as 'Romanipen/Romanipe'. Children are often judged on their ability to engage with adults while following Pachiv.

Pachiv is the code of respect: the thousands of unwritten civil laws of the Roma that have been passed down from one generation to another for centuries. The strict rules apply to every individual in the community and impose strict obligations. Breaking the code will risk the survival of the community and could result in someone becoming ostracised by their own family support network. Pachiv defines how one is supposed to behave in certain situations. Members of the community learn these roles by growing up and living with the community and the obligations will change throughout the various stages of life. A 'sòrri' (a young unmarried girl) is expected to look after younger siblings as soon she is strong and sensible enough to copy the adult behaviour patterns. Both a sòrri and a 'savorro' (young unmarried male) are expected to follow the code and act as (what gadjo would see as) mini adults. The Vlax Romany Gypsy communities, with the highest concentration in Central and Eastern Europe and the North American continent, consciously maintain the thousands of rules and would also verbally educate their children about the rules of Pachiv. However, many other Roma communities would also follow the code even though they are not familiar with its actual name or origins. As a śòrri in a non-Roma context, a girl would be expected to engage with a non-Roma person, such as the teacher, and show the same level of respect as to a Roma adult. According to the Roma code of conduct, Celina was fulfilling her role by trying to engage with the teacher. However, the subject of their engagement contributed no value to Pachiv or to the survival or growth of her family network.

Mandy Responds

The code of conduct outlined by Gyula was completely hidden from me as a teacher. Although I knew something about the Roma community from reading, I had no real concept of what it meant to be a Roma person. I based all my assumptions about Celina on my White middle-class academic understanding of children's development and learning. Although this included knowledge of other minority cultures, the culture of the Roma people was not something I had experienced prior to this. In this sense, I was typical of most British teachers. My knowledge of Pachiv began to develop when I visited Gyula's family and was given the opportunity to build relationships with members of the Roma community. Over time, through many conversations, Gyula helped me to understand more about the code, which, in turn, has enabled me to reflect on the experiences of Celina and the other Roma children in the class.

At the time, my observations focused on Celina's inability to meet my expectations of a 4-year-old child. I expected her to be able to look at a book, talk about the pictures, start at the front and work systematically through the book and to focus on a task with me, the teacher. I found that Celina could do none of these things. She entered the class with no concept of what a book was. She had no interest in books, apart from as a device to gain my attention. At the time, I was concerned that this lack of interest in books was an indication of a neurological condition such as ADHD. My only explanation for her inability to meet my developmental expectations was that she must have a special educational need (SEN), thus pathologising her behaviour. Very high levels of SEN within the Roma community at the school were noted by other members of staff, indicating that this was a frequent misunderstanding, contributing to an "overrepresentation" of Roma students being identified as requiring special education interventions (Artiles, 2003, p. 165).

My developing knowledge of Pachiv and Roma culture gives a very different perspective. To Celina, her primary role was to develop social interactions with others. Her education at home would have focused on learning the skills of human interaction, developing social intelligence. Technical intelligence—the skills of relating to and manipulating objects such as toys and books—would not have been highly valued and therefore not encouraged. This could be seen in how Celina used books. She perceived quite early in her relationship with me that I valued books. For me, the opportunity to look at a book had the purpose of developing early literacy skills. For Celina, however, the opportunity to look at a book meant that she could be alone with me in a quiet place and we could have uninterrupted social interaction. Celina used these opportunities to ask questions and talk. The book itself was a distraction from this valuable learning experience. Book sessions were a useful stimulus for conversation, and in my field notes, I recorded many examples of such fruitful conversations. My comment in this excerpt about the difficulty I experienced in having a conversation with Celina was based on my assumption that the conversation must be about the book. As the book did not interest Celina and had no value to her, she did not want to have a conversation about it. I overlooked her social intelligence by looking for the literary intelligence valued by the school culture.

My evaluation of Celina's struggles to focus on the book also belies my assumption that Celina had an understanding of written language. For British teachers, the notion of 'school readiness' includes a knowledge of written English as a means of communication (Peckham, 2017). We expect children to have read books at home and be familiar with text. This is reflected in the non-statutory guidance used in many English early-years settings, *Development Matters* (Early Education, 2012). This document outlines developmental expectations in terms of age bands. From the earliest age band, birth to 11 months, children should enjoy "looking at books and other printed material with familiar people" (Early Education, 2012, p. 28). This document is presented as a value-free, factual account of a universalist child development. It takes no account of the cultural nature of development and the varying expectations for change experienced in different communities. This view of child development and learning has been challenged for many years (Burman, 1994/2017; Cannella, 1997). Far from value-free, it is a raced, classed and gendered version of the child which is presented as a norm. *Development Matters* can also be compared to a kind of child development manual. By the dominant British culture, it is seen as 'common sense', but to other cultures, it is anything but common, a point made by DeLoache and Gottlieb (2000) in their imagined childcare guides.

For Roma children, looking at books written in their home language of Romani is not a possibility as Romani is largely a verbal language. Roma children would not have access to children's books written in Romani. They may also have very little experience of the spoken word being written down as symbols. This symbol system, for many, may be relatively unknown. The exception to this is the use of mobile phones as a communication medium. This is becoming increasingly popular with Roma people and may offer the opportunity for Roma children to develop an awareness of text. The language of school, however, is not Romani. For children such as Celina, learning to read involves first learning the new language, then learning that speech can be represented as symbols and following on from that mastering the symbol system to be able to decode text.

The child-led approach practised at her school that allowed for collaborative, social learning helped Celina to gain an understanding of literacy. She had the freedom to spend time observing both adults and children engaged in writing and reading. She often watched me intently as I made my field notes in the classroom. Sometimes she would mark-make on my notes, and as the year progressed, she began to engage in writing herself. She was excited to recognise her name in my notes, showing that she was beginning to develop some reading skills despite the fact that she did not particularly enjoy books.

The Construct of Play

This final excerpt focuses on Celina's play. It formed part of a long observation, recorded in January 2019, during which Mandy spent an entire morning playing with Celina.

> We played with Luke in the house for a sustained period of time. Celina was fascinated with the real lamp in the house. She switched it on and off at the plug lots of times. I said "on off". I asked if she wanted it on or off and she said *on*. She is learning these words. Celina and I made a shopping list. I instigated this when Celina got a shopping list sheet. I said that I needed to go to the shops. We played a game where I phoned Celina and said "Ahoy Celina, can you go to the shop and get some bread?" She was on the other phone and said "yes". Then she used mainly emergent writing to write her shopping list. We did bread, eggs, coffee and milk.

Gyula Writes

Many Roma families live in extreme poverty in which the daily food acquisition, heating provision and helping others in the family support network are the main focus of everyday life. Buying educational toys for children and reading books are an uncommon practice in Roma families. Therefore, Roma children use whatever is available in play. Roma children will turn anything they have access to into play. Beds and light switches can be found in even the poorest households. Switching the light on and off and jumping on beds in the house are exciting games for many Roma children. Due to the lack of constant energy supply in some Roma households, switching the light on and off can be rather 'electrifying' for Roma children. From time to time, they may also access run-down toys found on the streets or in bins and may introduce them into their play. However, the focus normally is on playing together with siblings and cousins. Role-playing is probably the most popular game with Roma children, where they copy the behaviour patterns of adults in the family support network, such as parents, grandparents, uncles, aunts and elderly cousins, and act out scenes they find funny in everyday life. These scenes are normally taken from negative experiences and crisis situations such as playing out evictions, quarrels and fights between family and with non-Roma.

Mandy Responds

Gyula's reflection contrasts the learning environment at home with that of the school. To Celina, the classroom and its contents were a completely alien environment. The focus on playing with objects is not a part of her culture, so she has little understanding of how to play with objects such as toys. The most familiar aspects of the school environment were the outdoor learning space and the real objects. She would spend time engaged in physical play outside, digging, climbing, jumping and sometimes engaging in boisterous play with other children. Inside, she used the junk modelling area, experimenting with recycled materials such as boxes and tubes.

Reflecting on Celina's play over the year, one of her primary objectives was to participate in shared endeavours with adults. To do this, she needed to gain the attention of the adults who were often involved with other children. She tried various strategies, including asking the adult to do things for her and performing actions which she knew would gain attention, such as taking other children's toys and finding objects like books which she knew adults valued. She also spent a lot of time observing other children and adults playing but did not play with the resources herself. When holding a toy or making something, she often looked around the classroom. She was focused on the other people rather than the objects. This links to Gyula's earlier explanation of the importance of developing social intelligence in Roma education. Toys can be seen as a distraction from this learning rather than a tool for learning themselves. Celina was following the Roma code, focusing on developing relationships with the adults in the setting through gaining their attention.

Conclusion

Rogoff's (2003) exploration of the cultural nature of child development divides approaches to the education of children into two broad categories. The categorising of cultural practices into two groups can polarise them. It can also present groups as homogeneous, which they clearly are not. Despite this danger of reification, Rogoff's categorisation is useful in explaining the difficulties the two groups find in understanding each other. She proposes that in some systems, children are involved with adult activities as soon as they are able. They are seen as full members of the community from birth and have responsibilities within the community which change as they master the various practices valued by the group. All learning occurs within the context of the activity and children are motivated by a desire to participate. The other main cultural system separates children from the adult population. Rather than participating from birth, they are not seen as full members of the community until they reach adulthood. Childhood is seen as a preparatory phase during which lessons are learnt which will prepare the child for later adult life. Gyula's description of Roma children as "mini adults" who have responsibilities within the community aligns with the first cultural system of children as participants. The approach of the school, and of the wider community, is based on the second system, in which children are segregated and educated together in schools. Although Roma children attend schools in the United Kingdom, they have retained the values of children as participants. While varying within themselves, their cultural systems, ways childhood is constructed and the purposes of learning, are fundamentally different from the dominant cultures within the United Kingdom.

In order for education to be relevant to Roma families, both the Roma community and the school community must work together to develop intercultural understanding. This needs to go beyond seeing Roma culture as a resource to facilitate learning. It is useful to celebrate International Roma Day, sing Roma songs and tell Roma stories, but such activities are not enough. If schooling is to make sense to Roma families, pedagogy must be shaped to build on Roma cultural systems. Examples could be to move away from individualistic approaches to learning and work towards collaborative, collective learning. Involving children in real tasks in which groups can work together would echo home learning in which children participate in adult activities. Early-years settings could provide opportunities for children to use recycled materials and open-ended resources such as pieces of material, boxes, and crates, which will be more familiar to the children than toys. Roma staff could tell and read stories in Romani to children, modelling literacy in the home language. Liaison workers who are Roma, whenever possible, are essential in providing this bridge between the two communities, supporting each to learn from the other. These developments are only possible if real connections are made with members of the Roma community. Finally, these connections will be realised only if Roma culture, intelligence, communication, and involvement is genuinely valued, encouraged and supported.

References

Achim, V. (1998). *The Roma in Romanian history*. Central European University Press.
Artiles, A. J. (2003). Special education's changing identity: Paradoxes and dilemmas in views of culture and space. *Harvard Educational Review*, 73(2), 164–202.
Bennett, J. (2012). *Roma early childhood inclusion: Overview report*. Open Society Foundations.
Brown, P., Scullion, L., & Martin, P. (2013). *Migrant Roma in the United Kingdom*. University of Salford.
Burman, E. (2017). *Deconstructing developmental psychology* (3rd ed.). Routledge. (Original work published 1994)
Cannella, G. S. (1997). *Deconstructing early childhood education: Social justice and revolution*. Peter Lang.
Cannella, G., & Viruru, R. (2004). *Childhood and postcolonization: Power, education, and contemporary practice*. Routledge.

Chu, C. M. (1999). Immigrant children mediators (ICM): Bridging the literacy gap in immigrant communities. *New Review of Children's Literature and Librarianship, 5*(1), 85–94. https://doi.org/10.1080/13614549909510616

Cohen, L., Manion, L., & Morrison, K. (2011). *Research methods in education* (7th ed.) Routledge.

DeLoache, J., & Gottlieb, A. (2000). *A world of babies: Imagined childcare guides for seven societies*. Cambridge University Press.

Department for Education. (2019). *National curriculum assessments: Key Stage 2, 2019. Key Stage 2 revised tables 2019*. Crown. https://assets.publishing.service.gov.uk/government/uploads/system/uploads/attachment_data/file/851798/KS2_Revised_publication_text_2019_v3.pdf

Early Education. (2012). *Development matters in the Early Years Foundation Stage*. Crown.

European Union, Agency for Fundamental Rights. (2016). *Poverty and employment the situation of Roma in 11 EU Member States: Roma survey: Data in focus*. https://doi.org/10.2811/413303

Fonseca, I. (1996). *Bury me standing: The Gypsies and their journey*. Vintage.

Hancock, I. F. (2002). We are the Romani people. Ame sam e Rromane džene. University of Hertfordshire Press.

Katz, C. (2004). *Growing up global: Economic restructuring and children's everyday lives*. University of Minnesota Press.

Klaus, S., & Marsh, A. (2014). A special challenge for Europe: The inclusion of Roma children in early years education and care. *European Early Childhood Education Research Journal, 22*(3), 336–346. https://doi.org/10.1080/1350293X.2014.912896

Kyuchukov, H. (2000). Transformative education for Roma (Gypsy) children: An insider's view. *Intercultural Education, 11*(3), 273–280.

Lalueza, J., Martinez-Lozano, V., & Macias-Gomez-Estern, B. (2019). The transition of Roma children into school: Working relationally, across cultural boundaries in Spain. In M. Hedegaard (Ed.), *Supporting difficult transitions children, young people and their carers* (pp. 153–174). Bloomsbury Academic.

Matras, Y. (2014). *I met lucky people: The story of the Romani Gypsies*. Penguin.

Matras, Y., & Leggio, D. V. (2017). *Open borders, unlocked cultures: Romanian Roma migrants in Western Europe*. Routledge.

Ministry of Housing & Local Government. (2019). National Statistics English indices of deprivation 2019. In *The English indices of deprivation 2019*. https://www.gov.uk/government/statistics/english-indices-of-deprivation-2019

Mills, D., & Morton, M. (2013). *Ethnography in education*. Sage Publications.

Montero, M. (2000). Participation in participatory action research. *Annual Review of Critical Psychology, 2*, 131–143. https://discourseunit.com/annual-review/2-2000/

Morris, M. (2016). *Roma communities & Brexit: Integrating & empowering Roma in the UK*. Institute for Public Policy Research. https://www.ippr.org/publications/roma-communities-and-brexit

Peckham, K. (2017). *Developing school readiness*. Sage Publications.

Penfold, M. (2016). *Improving education outcomes for pupils from the new Roma communities*. British Council. https://www.romasupportgroup.org.uk/uploads/9/3/6/8/93687016/improving_education_outcomes_for_roma_pupils.pdf

Phoenix, A. (1997). Theories of gender and Black families. In H. S. Mirza (Ed.), *Black British feminism: A reader* (pp. 63–66). Routledge.

Rogoff, B. (2003). *The cultural nature of human development*. Oxford University Press.

Scheffel, D. (2010). *Svinia in black and white: Slovak Roma and their neighbours*. University of Toronto Press.

Smith, T. (1997). Recognising difference: The Romani "Gypsy" child socialisation and education process. *British Journal of Sociology of Education, 18*(2), 243–256. https://doi.org/10.1080/0142569970180207

Tedmanson, D., & Banerjee, S. B. (2012). Participatory action research. In A. J. Mills, G. Durepos, & E. Wiebe (Eds.), *Encyclopedia of case study research* (pp. 656–658). Sage Publications. https://doi.org/http://dx.doi.org/10.4135/9781412957397

Wane, N. N. (1996). Reflections on the mutuality of mothering women, children and othermothering. *Journal of the Association for Research on Mothering, 2*(2), 105–116. https://jarm.journals.yorku.ca/index.php/jarm/article/view/2143

Wilkin, A., Derrington, C., & Foster, B. (2009). *Improving the outcomes for Gypsy, Roma and Traveller pupils: Literature review* (Research Report DCSF-RR077). National Foundation for Educational Research, Department for Children, Schools and Families.

CHAPTER 4

The Shadows and Silences of Colonialism: Resisting Eroding Realities for Māori Children Through Language Re-Vernacularisation in Antipodean New Zealand

Mere Skerrett

NEW ZEALAND (NZ), as a colony of Britain, is still marginalising and colonising Indigenous peoples, NZ society, and its education systems. The Māori are the Indigenous people of NZ. Staying with our racist colonialist past is important in order to deconstruct it and recognise ourselves as Indigenous peoples in our neocolonial/neoliberal present, especially if we want to transform it. Davies et al. (2013) discuss the construct of *recognition*, in the sense that acts of recognition (i.e., acts that are recognised and rewarded) simply serve, paradoxically, to reinforce the status quo or what is valued in society. Following in the behaviourist tradition, recognition assists in increasing the conformity of the collective by rewarding individuals according to the values of the norm, simultaneously shaping those values of the norm. The process acts as a unifying force, a powerful standardising force. The system of recognition then, as a system of societal/neocolonial control, is an authoritative regulating force resulting in the oxymoron of the rational autonomous/repressed subject, subjected to norms yet longing to escape the terms of subjection. It is this guise of the rational autonomous, yet regulated, individual which leads to cognitive dissonance and tensions between the colonizers/

colonized of colonialism. These tensions highlight the need to critically deconstruct how recognition operates, for example through the media, through schools and other societal constructs, whilst at the same time resisting those power constructs.

Failure to locate our Indigenous lives in colonial relations 'past' and neocolonial relations 'now' operationalises the status quo of White supremacy or presumptions of power whilst simultaneously silencing Indigenous voices and erasing Indigenous histories. The loss of a past through colonialism always leads to tensions through the loss of a present and presence, with the stress and trauma of not knowing and forced becomings being passed down through the generations. The dominant settler view continues to structurally mask the sometimes subtle, sometimes not, yet always harmful ways colonialism happens in the now. That explains why racism (Bonilla-Silva, 2012), through its racial grammar, and linguicism (Skutnabb-Kangas, 2015), through language hierarchies, are so difficult to eradicate and, importantly, why we must stay with our colonial past. Bonilla-Silva (2012) argues that racial domination "works best when it becomes hegemonic, that is, when it accomplishes its goal without much fanfare" (p. 173). Skutnabb-Kangas (2015) argues that language domination provides the ideologies, structures and practices to discriminate between peoples based on the language(s) they speak.

In colonial NZ, racial domination was obtained through a hegemonic system of governance used by the British through an effective device known as *indirect rule*. This system controlled the colony through utilising the pre-existing Indigenous power structures (Simon, 1998) whilst entrenching Britain's common law system. In NZ, the indirect rule of colonialism led to societal relations of *Pākehā* domination and Māori subordination in all aspects of living, speaking, being and becoming. Furthermore, Bonilla-Silva (2012) adds, racial domination generates a grammar that maintains the racial order as 'just the way things are,' without question. Maintenance of the status quo or hegemonic normalising discourses shape how we see, or don't see, the 'world' (as if that is real), how we frame, think and feel about matters of 'race' in a world now dominated by racial ideologies. He coined the term 'racial grammar,' a distillate of racial ideology and, hence, of White supremacy. Moreover, he proposed that if racial ideologies furnish the material that is spoken, argued and transacted, then it is racial grammar that "provides the 'deep structure', the 'logic' and 'rules' of proper composition of racial statements and, more importantly, of what can be seen, understood, [recognised] and even felt about racial matters" (Bonilla-Silva, 2012, p. 174). The grammar of racial discourse is acquired through social interaction and communication in the same way that we acquire the grammar of language/s which change over time. This grammar construct is helpful because it gives us a tool to question and rethink the histories and colonialist practices that create and maintain racist institutions and, of import to this chapter, education institutions. Schools and early childhood settings are not some universal, sacrosanct institutions that exist because 'that is the way they are'. They are carefully designed constructs, with structures, histories, curriculum, signs, symbols, words, songs, dances, drama, arts, routines, and so on which, in NZ, signify and reproduce Pākehā (British)

Whiteness. To move backward into our futures, we must face forward into our pasts. This chapter stays with our colonialist past, the silences and erasures which cemented European Pākehā racial dominance, forcing Indigenous Māori subordination to live in the shadows of our lands. It argues that as Māori lands shifted to European freehold ownership title, Māori language/s shifted to a written English alphabet grammar. The accompanying racial grammar adapted to, and embedded in, the structures of NZ society lead to Māori subjugation, forcing us to live in the shadows and echoes of our language/s. Finally, this chapter traverses the struggles to shift Māori children from the margins of society through the early years' language revitalization movement which is Te Kōhanga Reo (Māori language nests).

Colonial Positionings

NZ's colonial history is replete with the hallmarks of colonial violence. Mutu (2010) chronicles how NZ was annexed to New South Wales, then under British rule, in 1839. Annexation meant some form of British governance and policy had to be established, ostensibly in order to control the lawlessness of British settlers and offer protections to Māori, the Indigenous people. But, as with all 'protectorates' or 'trucial states' (states where treaties are signed), there is always a far more sinister agenda of invasion through settler colonialism. The guise of protection was a cover for ushering in land-hungry settler immigrants. As the balance of power gradually swung from Māori social structures to the advancing numbers of British immigrants, the British property (privatising land), political (common law) and sociolinguistic (monolingual English) systems were also ushered in. This property system regulated by common law principles facilitated the alienation of Māori lands and resources, away from the *Mana Whenua* (local tribal peoples with jurisdiction over lands) to the farming British immigrants, forever altering Māori people's lives. As Banner (1999) puts it,

> the centrality of property within the thought of both peoples, however, meant that the transformation of Māori into English property rights involved much more than land. Religious belief, engagement with the market economy, political organization—all were bound up in the systems by which both peoples organized property rights in land. To anglicize the Māori property system was to revolutionize Māori life. (p. 807)

The transformation, initially by stealth, was all too soon to become all about wealth for Britain and its settlers. As Mutu (2010) documents, in March 1834, Aotearoa's first flag, the flag of the United Tribes was designed. The following year, James Busby, the British Resident in NZ, called a hui on 28 October at Waitangi, and by the end of that day, 34 chiefs had signed *He Whakaputanga o te Rangatiratanga o Nu Tireni* (known in

English as the *Declaration of Independence of the United Tribes of New Zealand*) formally acknowledged by King William IV of England in May 1836. That declaration asserted that mana (authority) and sovereign power in New Zealand resided *fully* with Māori through their Confederation of United Tribes. There were three other elements:

1. Foreigners (the British or French mainly) would **not** be allowed to make laws;
2. Te Whakaminenga, the Confederation of United Tribes, was to meet at Waitangi each autumn to frame laws; and
3. in return for their protection, of British subjects in their territory the chiefs sought King William's protection against threats to their mana.

At that time, in 1835, Māori also thanked the king for acknowledging their flag, symbolic of Māori sovereignty. However, the king died in 1837, leaving his teenage niece, Victoria, to succeed him. Still, Māori continued signing the declaration. By July 1839, 52 chiefs had signed it, including Te Wherowhero, who was to become New Zealand's first Māori king.[1]

As the declaration was officially acknowledged by the British government, Busby saw it as a significant mark of Māori national identity and believed it would prevent other countries from making formal deals with Māori or claims on Māori lands. The laws of England then applied as in January 1840 (Webb, Sanders & Scott, 2010). The next critical move was the creation of a treaty between Māori and the British Crown, signed in February 1840, and meant to deliver us (Māori) from evil. But the reverse happened. We came under the hammer of the hierarchical British rule both classist and racist. Māori have been challenging the system that resulted from signing Te Tiriti o Waitangi (the Treaty of Waitangi) ever since. Māori customary rights were systematically eroded, despite King William's acknowledgement of Māori sovereignty, and Queen Victoria's treaty, leading Māori to often ask, 'Trick or treat/y?'

Abbas (2020) discusses how royal families were implicated in the subjugation of Indigenous peoples for economic gain. He cites the example of a documentary series *Britain's Forgotten Slave Owners*. This tells the untold history of British involvement in the slave trade which permeated more sections of society than the British were led to believe, cutting across the British royal family, the aristocracy and the banking and industrial classes. The British continued to own slaves up until 1833 when owning slaves became illegal. The spoils of slavery, however, persisted. Slavery gave Britain and British people great wealth, having fuelled its economic development including the industrial revolution and key socio-political infrastructures that still benefit them today.

But by the mid-19th century, when the slave trade was no longer the pillar of the colonial economies of Europe, other wealth-creating and exploitative projects were embarked upon. Centuries of plunder with the still extant slavery mindset led to British Europeans setting their sights on the lands and resources of the Pacific. The race was on between the Europeans to gain a foothold in the vast Māori lands and resources of Aotearoa, culminating in the British signing a treaty with Māori (before the French). The act of 'treaty-ing', implicated in the same long-standing wealth-creating tactics and undergirding ideologies of slavery, was met with considerable debate, scepticism, and concern on the part of the Māori chieftainship in 1840.

One of the prominent chiefs at the time of signing Te Tiriti, Nōpera Panakareao, an influential leader of the north, supported its signing. According to Salmond (2017), he was essential to the Kaitāia signings of 28 April 1840 alongside his wife, Eleanora. During the meeting at Kaitāia, he was the last speaker before signing when he asked his people to accept Governor William Hobson. He then spoke the now-famous words, "The shadow of the land will go to Queen, but the substance remains with us" (Orange, 2004, p. 38). Only a year later, in 1841, the missionary Richard Taylor noted that Panakareao reversed his statement, that he feared the substance of the land would go to the British and the shadow only be left for Māori (Department of Internal Affairs, 1991). Panakareao's prediction foreshadowed the dark ages of colonialism to come.

Evison (1997), in his book *The Long Dispute: Māori Land Rights and European Colonisation in Southern New Zealand*, documents how mounting pressure for Māori lands in the 1800s, in the face of much Māori resistance, left Māori the shadow portions. Skulduggery was rife. Many land deals through dodgy land deeds and forced land sales left all the southern tribal groupings landless and without the means to eke out an existence. Any hint of resistance often led to the threat of government troops being sent in against them. Contract/s were regularly breached as the land continued to be alienated through unlawful confiscations, illegal land sales, continuous dodgy deeds, deliberately misprinted maps with makeshift boundaries, immigrant settler/squatter thefts and racist settler-government political and legislative processes.

Evison argues that with the transformation and colonisation of Aotearoa, a new ethic crept into NZ affairs: deliberate lying by prominent Crown public servants like Kemp and Mantell through to the top echelons of Crown representation, the British queen's representative Governor Grey. It is the primary role of the governor to grant royal assent to legislation and to summon and dissolve *elected* parliaments. But our settler government was never elected into power. In fact, it took nearly three decades for Māori men to gain the vote and even longer for Māori women. Legislation from Britain was imported holus-bolus, one case in point being the land privatising schedules of the Enclosure Acts of Britain. These land acts eroded Māori customary rights (the rights to sustain livelihoods through land use) in precisely the same way that it alienated land in support of the British 'class' society. The series of Enclosure Acts caused people in Britain to become homeless as their land was stripped through the law itself. Karl Marx observed:

> The law itself becomes the instrument of the theft of the people's land. . . . The parliamentary form of the robbery is that of Acts for enclosures of Commons, in

> other words, decrees by which the landlords grant themselves the people's land as private property, decrees of expropriation of the people. (Sharman, 1989, p. 45)

Between 1600 and 1900, there were more than 5,000 parliamentary acts which transformed land use for more than one fifth of England (Sharman, 1989), so by the time the British annexed Aotearoa, they were well versed in alienating customary lands in support of the newly landed gentry.

In a common law[2] country where *customary rights* are grounded, Indigenous customary rights are meant to be protected. In international law, a settled country must also recognise the **customary rights** of the Indigenous people. But Māori customary rights and protections offered under the newly established NZ parliamentary system did not last long. The test was first put to the courts in 1847, which found that, under the treaty, Māori customary rights were protected. But after that initial case, mounting pressure by settler immigrants led to a retrenchment of that ruling and the entrenchment of illegal land transfers, land wars and land confiscations. It was to take approximately 140 years for any real traction to occur within NZ's judiciary and legislative system in terms of honouring the treaty. The establishment of a NZ parliamentary system (and its developing administrative, political, legal and provincial ruling systems) based on the British system became the mechanism via which Māori customary rights were systematically legislated into the shadows as foretold by Panakareao.

Imperialism and Its Colonial Powers

Evison (1997) discusses how Governor Grey, a British soldier, explorer and colonial administrator in NZ, Australia and South Africa and governor of NZ twice at pivotal times (1845–1853[3] and 1861–1868), was instrumental in leading the wars which spanned nearly three decades from 1845 to 1872. Grey was a key figure in the shaping of NZ war history, shaping societal discourse and introducing a racial grammar. He secured the Wellington area in 1846 as the future 'capital' and the seat of power. He prevented Ngāti Toa's prominent chief Te Rauparaha from any political activity by stealthily landing his ship, the HMS *Driver*, at Te Rauparaha's peacetime village, his *Taupō*,[4] in the middle of the night. At daybreak, he sent in a landing party of 200 armed men to surround the peacetime dwelling and added, "Without warning, the great chief was seized in his bed, naked and struggling" (Evison, 1997, p. 163). This idea of a 'naked' chief provides the racial grammar which plays nicely into the 'naked savage' myth. Te Rauparaha was abducted aboard the warship without warrant and imprisoned for 10 months without trial, eventually being released to Auckland (an area in the north, outside of his tribal area, effectively neutralising his chieftainship). This act alone was to have a crippling effect on the ability of Māori in both the North and South Islands to exercise *rangatiratanga*, or sovereignty over their own lands and lives, whilst simultaneously contributing greatly to Grey's political advantage.

Following the wars, the colonising agenda was heightened. The landmark case in 1877 heard by Judge Prendergast led to his well-known finding that the Treaty of Waitangi was a *nullity*, again playing into the racial grammar discourse of Māori as 'savages' and the legal argument used based on the doctrine of discovery of 'vacant lands' and the false premise that there were no humans in Aotearoa when Cook arrived. Ngāti Toa leader Wi Parata had taken a case against the Bishop of Wellington (Williams, 2013) for misuse of lands initially gifted in 1848 for the establishment of school for young Ngāti Toa people. But the intervening land wars meant that the school never eventuated. In 1877, Judge Prendergast found that the British Crown 'owned' all the land by virtue of discovery and occupation and the doctrine of terra nullius (vacant lands), so no possible gift could have been made. Prendergast's finding that NZ was a territory inhabited only by 'savages', and the treaty was signed by primitive 'barbarians'. This was to have far-reaching consequences invoking precedential land law which continues to shift Māori land away from Māori customary rights and ownership. The racial grammar, replete with utterances of the treaty being 'worthless' because it was signed between a 'civilised' (British) nation and a 'savage' (Māori) nation, continues to 'savage-ise' Māori today. The more recent Foreshore and Seabed Act 2004 (Charters, Erueti & Erueti, 2007), in which there was a Crown 'presumption of power' and 'right' to take ownership of the foreshore and seabed, is testament to the ongoing shift of Māori customary lands. The racial grammar of the doctrine of 'discovery' (Miller, 2008) is still evident in the history books forming part of the curriculum in schools which are implicated in Māori language shift to English as successive governments manoeuvre to complete the colonial assimilation agenda.

Māori Language Shift Through Colonisation

According to Anaru (2018), te reo Māori has Austronesian ancestry with its origins somewhere in China. Successive migrations and migration pauses saw the Māori people and their language travel through Taiwan, the Philippines and eventually to Aotearoa/NZ. This migration pattern happened over thousands of years. Once settling in Aotearoa, the migrations stopped, and the Māori language and culture emerged from within the contours and contexts of Aotearoa for many centuries. It became a new fluid language and culture as it melded and moulded to these lands whilst still holding much of its historical and genealogical remnants, its beliefs and the values of its ancient Polynesian past. The natural linguistic and cultural change was an environmental, physical and spiritual adaptation. Māori culture in Aotearoa is a millennias-old culture (Walker, 2004). It slowly settled into life in Aotearoa for more than 1,000 years before the arrival of the first Europeans in the late 18th century. In the past 150 years, it has undergone a rapid shift to English in a very unnatural process of change through colonisation. The one constant, it is argued by Anaru, is that Aotearoa/New Zealand shall forever remain the birthplace of te reo Māori, and forever part of the *whakapapa* or genealogy of this land. However, the impact of decades of wars, introduced European diseases, increasing numbers of British settlers aided by successive corrupt settler parliaments, was to take its toll on Māori society. The Māori population decline was unavoidable. The shift of Māori lands into Crown/privatised British hands resulted in a phenomenon I have coined 'linguafaction' (see Skerrett, 2017), a condition which continues to facilitate Māori language shift to English, shrinking Māori language vernaculars and threatening language death. That we currently have a Māori language week is testimony to that. What other country in the world has a language week for its official language? Do the British have an English-language week in Britain?

Silences and Erasures

Many colonialists fighting against Māori in the NZ wars became parliamentarians, public servants, historians, and the writers of texts underpinning the curriculum in the education system. They were the reframers of history and reshapers of society. In that way, colonial histories become the 'officially recognised' sources of 'truth,' while Māori histories, world views, ways of being, knowing, thinking, and speaking are systematically erased. Ngũgĩ Wa Thiong'o (2005), researching and writing from a Kenyan (also colonised by the British) position, talks about the cultural bomb as a mechanism "to annihilate a people's belief in their names, in their languages, in their environment, in their heritage, in their unity, in their capacities and ultimately in themselves" (p. 3). He argues that when you opt for the colonizing language, you accept the fatalistic logic, to a greater or lesser degree, of its social norms, attitudes and values. He also illuminates how the colonial land wars shift into the classroom when he asserts that

> the night of the sword and the bullet was followed by the morning of the chalk and the blackboard. The physical violence of the battlefield was followed by the psychological violence of the classroom. But where the former was visibly brutal, the latter was visibly gentle ... one began to understand that their real power resided not at all in the cannons of the first morning but in what followed ... the new school. The new school had the nature of both the cannon and the magnet. From the cannon it took the efficiency of a fighting weapon. But better than the cannon it made the conquest permanent. The cannon forces the body and the school fascinates the soul. (Thiong'o, 2005, p. 9)

Social structures and language/s built around those structures are important vehicles through which power is both erased and fascinated. The bullet was the means of the physical subjugation, the pen the means of sociocultural dislocation. Colonisation and the colonial wars left many Māori silenced and impoverished, "living as outcasts on meagre, isolated reserves" (Evison, 1997, p. 231). Many Māori were forced into subsistence living, whilst more died of starvation. Governor Grey's presence in Wellington encouraged the formation of NZ's first scientific society, founded in July 1851 (Evison, 1997). As the first president of that society, Grey's opening address portended doom and gloom for Māori:

> We who stand in this country occupy an historical position of extraordinary interest. Before us lies a future already brilliant with the light of a glorious morn. Behind us lies a night of fearful gloom, unilluminated by the light of written records, of picture memorials, of aught which can give a certain idea of the past. A few stray streaks of light in the form of tradition, of oral poetry, of carved records, are the only guides we have. (Evison, 1997, p. 236)

In one foul discourse, he silenced and erased *mātauranga Māori*, Māori knowledge, language and, even more sinister, established a racial discourse of invisibilising people. Allegedly all that was left were carvings and poetry. According to Evison, Governor Grey's scientific society's successor is the Royal Society of New Zealand, a leading research network connected to NZ's very powerful research communities. One of its early proponents, James Hector came from another royal society in Edinburgh in 1862 to do geological surveys. He became an indispensable advisor to the government on science, technology, medicine and commerce. He also founded the colonial museum to which the 'carvings and poetry' were enslaved as artefacts and exhibits. In the same year that Governor Grey founded the scientific society in the North Island, the *Lyttleton Times* in the South Island published a resolution from a public meeting in the capital city of Wellington:

> The Native race is fast becoming extinct, and there is no prospect of their becoming as a body sufficiently enlightened for the exercise of political privileges before the period of their extinction shall arrive. Nevertheless, some participation may be allowed provided sufficient guarantees be given against the possibility of the superior intelligence of the Europeans being over-balanced by the ignorance of the uncivilized race. (Evison, 1997, p. 229)

Whilst the abolition of slavery in England in the 1830s meant British colonial activities in NZ prohibited the enslavement of Māori people it did not apply to Māori lands, lives and resources. The racial grammar discourses of NZ colonialism privatising Māori lands and shifting Māori people from invisible to uncivilized savages to extinct people and into museum curiosities was another form of enslavement as Māori human rights and lives were relentlessly eroded leading to silences and erasures.

Shadows and Echoes

Forced language shift in colonial societies is an effective means of silencing Indigenous voices. The spiritual and psychological subjugation in the formation of a new 'national' (English) identity through a cultural particularism that is British is testimony to that. Nōpera Panakareao, who raised the notion of Māori living in the shadow of the land within a short time of signing the treaty, is also credited with saying in 1840, "Our sayings will sink to the bottom like a stone, but your sayings will float light, like the wood of the whau-tree, and always remain to be seen" (Salmond, 2017, p. 147). Perceptively, he recognised the threat not only to Māori lands but also to Māori language and knowledge.

Anaru (2018) uses Plato's allegory of the prisoner in a cave as a theoretical application to the Māori context. He argues the Cave is about the mind ascending from a realm of images (in the cave) to that of visible real tangible objects (outside of the cave). Furthermore, that the people in the cave are shackled in the darkness of the cave and only able to see shadows on the wall in front of them, radiated by a fire behind them. None of the radiated shadows has any substance or 'truth' so long as they remain distorted shadows on the wall. Striving for knowledge within a shadow world thus is seemingly futile.

Likewise, sayings that sink to the bottom of the water are no longer audible. The further down they go, the more they become muffled echoes of gurgling and then deathly silence. To the extent that they are no longer spoken nor heard, their ability to generate meaning, understanding, knowledge and growth are extinguished. Like the shadows on the cave wall divorced from realities, distortions and echoes of silence become divorced from meaning-making authenticities which define and enrich human lives.

He reo e kōrerotia ana, he reo ka ora (A Spoken Language Is a Living Language)

Pojman and Vaughn (2011) argue in favour of Plato's claim that the sight and seeing realms are deficient if one rests on the argument that for senses to be used, all that is needed is the sense itself and that which can be sensed by it. For example, to taste sweetness, one needs the sense of a sweet taste as well as something that tastes sweet. They explain that if a person's eyes are capable of sight and that person is trying to look at something that is coloured, the sight will not see the coloured thing, unless there is also present an extra element which is made specifically for this purpose. That element is light. In line with Plato's argument, sight (in the visible realm) and hearing (in the audible realm) are deficient without light and sound. In tandem with that, for an oral language to be audible, it requires not only ears, but it must also be spoken; that is, it must have speakers to be a thriving living language. To draw on Panakareao's allegory, a sinking language becomes inaudible, a silenced language. He foreshadowed language shift, hastened by the English-language encroachment he witnessed. Subsequent English-only education language policies accelerated it. The rich, exuberant Māori culture with unique world views, sights and sounds swiftly shifted to the shadows and echoes of society, carefully controlled through societal structural mechanisms and institutions, especially schools. Throughout the world, Indigenous languages living in the shadows of dominant colonial languages, cultures and ideologies face constant challenge and the threat of language loss through linguafaction, institutional racism and their racial grammars. The apprehensions and ideas portended by the likes of Panakareao and successive Māori chieftainship have led to the unremitting pushback by Māoridom over the last 200 years of the colonial experience in NZ. The establishment of a Māori King movement, called the Kīngitanga, in 1858 and the formation of the Kōhanga Reo movement in 1982 were critical and strategic manoeuvres in that push-back.

Te Hua Kawariki: Māori Political Independence and Kōhanga Reo

> Māku anō e hanga i tōku nei whare. Ko te tāhuhu he hīnau, ko ngā poupou he māhoe, patatē. Me whakatupu ki te hua o te rengarenga, me whakapakari ki te hua o te kawariki. Nā Kīngi Tāwhiao. (Māhuta, 1993/2011, para. 13)

The first Māori King, Pōtatau Te Wherowhero, was quickly succeeded by his son, King Tāwhiao, in 1860. As we have seen, the first years of Tāwhiao's reign were dominated by land wars. King Tāwhiao and his followers were declared rebels and forced into exile and some 1.2 million acres of their fertile lands were confiscated, severely incapacitating Māori socio-political and economic advancement. But his quest for *mana motuhake* (Māori political independence) was ceaseless. King Tāwhiao is famous for the prophetic saying that opens this section, which speaks to Māori political independence, holding on to Māori land and ways of doing things and continuing to strengthen the people. Translated, it reads:

> I will build my house, its ridge pole will be made of hīnau [a native lowland forest tree], its posts will be made of māhoe [whiteywood, a tree found in abundance in coastal regions] and patatē [seven-finger, again easily utilised as a resource]. Raise the generations with the fruit of the rengarenga [an abundant spinach-like native plant] and strengthen them with the fruit of the kawariki [coprosma]. (Author's translation of Māhuta, 1993/2011, para. 13)

The *kawariki* is a bitter plant that was given to children to make them stronger. I have titled this section 'Te Hua Kawariki' after King Tāwhiao's saying which I would argue speaks to the importance of utilising natural resources and specifically references the importance of strengthening children. Over his time, King Tāwhiao witnessed the increasing impoverishment among his people in the North and the impact on children.

Similarly, in the South, Evison (1997) argues, "loss of ancestral lands brought spiritual anguish, as well as deprivation and disgrace" (p. 24). I belong to both northern and southern tribes and was nurtured in the importance of fighting injustices and strengthening children. In Tawhiao's proverbial saying, the reference is to sustain the body through natural resources like the fruit of the kawariki. In this chapter, of equal importance is to sustain the mind using words and language. The two are intricately entangled.

Children of the Land

Prior to the impact of colonialism and the NZ land wars, many early colonial eyewitness accounts from Europeans observed shared parental roles in small family groupings. Children were cared for and treated with love and affection, and the children were independent thinkers, courageous, expressive, robust, and lively; possessed, in general, pleasing countenances; and were incredibly free and very intelligent (Salmond, 2017). John Walton, in 1863, wrote:

> The unbounded freedom in which the children are indulged, seems very favourable to their growth, which is much more rapid than that of European children, who are less strong and active at ten years of age than those in New Zealand are at six. The tuition of the children begins at an early period, for the development of their mental powers is as rapid as that of their physical.... One effect of the excessive fondness of parents for their children is, that they are very rarely punished for any impropriety of conduct whatever. (Salmond, 2017, p. 459)

Children were situated within wider family groupings, not merely to their own nuclear family. Māori very commonly enacted this collective system of parenting called *whāngai* which literally means 'to feed or nurture.' This customary practice meant that grandparents or closely related blood relatives would foster child/ren, especially from large families. As William Colenso in 1868 stated,

> their love and attachment to children was very great, and that not merely to their own immediate offspring. They very commonly adopted children; indeed no man having a large family was ever allowed to bring them all up himself— uncles and aunts and cousins claimed and took them.... They certainly took every physical care of them ... petted and spoiled them. The father, or uncle, often carried or nursed his infant on his back for hours at a time and might often be seen quietly at work with the little one there snugly ensconced. (Salmond, 2017, p. 460)

The historic dismantling the Māori collectives of whānau, hapū and iwi and Māori communal ways of living came hand in hand with land loss and exacerbated language loss which impacted the intergenerational transmission of knowledge to children. The reinstatement of these land and language structures is what underpins the political movement of the Kīngitanga and the self-help radical movement of Kōhanga Reo (Māori language nests). Kōhanga Reo is as much a political resistance movement to the prevailing racism and linguicism endemic in the colonial education system as it is a Māori-language regeneration movement. I have been instrumental in the establishment of Kōhanga Reo and birthed my five children into the movement. The aims of the Māori-language nests are to provide the hua kawariki, the fruit that cultivates our *tamariki* (descendants of the gods) to strengthen them, to shape their minds, to nurture their inner beings and to fortify their identities. Kōhanga Reo has been the marae (courtyard) of revolutionary action needed to rebuild, to revitalise the Māori language, dismantle racialized discourses, displace settler colonialism and move children out of the silences and shadows and into becoming more informed, more articulate, liberated children of the land.

Discussion

This chapter has argued that the colonial agenda continues to promote the transition from 'substance' to 'shadow' by creating commodities, privatising lands and individualising responsibilities rendering structural and material (systemic) racism and linguicism invisible whilst simultaneously, paradoxically, masking and entrenching it. Colonial-settler racism and the apparatus of the colonial nation state works effectively through colonial processes through systematically stripping Indigenous nations of their collective power structures and voices to repressed individuals, easily regulated and controlled. Staying with our colonialist past ensures that we remain historically located. As argued by Abbas (2020), not to do so is to continue the colonial project of invisibilising our histories, erasing our perspectives and engulfing us within unquestioned, colonialist practices intellectually, physically, socially and spiritually.

The colonial history of NZ has shown how critical theories of racial hierarchy promoted, in the first instance, the massive land grab of the 19th century and resulted in linguafaction. Whilst the abolition of slave ownership in England not long before signing the treaty may have prohibited the physical enslavement of Māori bodies its legacy of cultural annihilation remained in the minds, ideologies, structures and practices of the colonisers. As Ngũgĩ Wa Thiong'o (2005) asserted, the 'cultural bomb' annihilated people's beliefs in their names, languages, lands, histories, capacities, realities and ultimately in themselves. And the establishment of a British parliamentary system which privatised Māori lands simply locked Māori into an oppositional relationality of the Crown versus the people, quite the opposite of what a treaty is meant to do and be. Instead, it pitted the Pākehā Crown, with the assumption of parliamentary power and competitive individualism, against Māori collectivities and Pākehā immigrants, with the presumptions of White supremacy, against Māori Indigenes struggling to assert rangatiratanga or Māori sovereignty.

The colonial propaganda disseminated by colonial media gave recognition to racial grammar discourses. The construct of racial grammar provides for a way of analysing the discourses of racism and linguicism which permeate into the heartwood of society. These became and remain the dominant societal pillars of NZ hegemony, reflected in current media disseminations, pathologizing socio-educational discourses and practices. First there are the myriad of discourses surrounding the doctrine of 'discovery.' Then the discourses soon turned into ones of civilised versus savage predicted in the reversal of the shadow of the land going to the Crown discourse, silencing and erasing aeons of Māori perspective, history, language, being and becoming. It led to a myriad of education discourses based around failure/s leading to deficit policies and thinking such as Māori being the lagging 'tail,' 'priority' learners 'at risk' with 'warrior genes,' systemic linguicism, streaming and racial profiling in schools.

Media and education institutions play out as powerful structural mechanisms of surveillance to reward and recognise, on one hand, and objectify, dehumanise, discipline, silence and erase, on the other. The guise of rational automaton yet controlled automaton leads to the cognitive dissonance and tension between both the colonizers and colonized, the former's inability to recognise different humanities and the latter losing a sense of who they are to recognise themselves. Davies et al. (2013) in discussing this construct of 'recognition' note the importance of recognising 'difference.' They argue that the move from difference as categorical difference to difference as emergent, continuous difference and recognition as mutually constitutive intra-active acts of becoming, through which 'being' is made to make sense (Davies et al., 2013, p. 681), not to lose one's sensibilities in who and what they are. But therein lies a tension or the potential for loss without careful articulation of the forces that work in anti-colonising endeavours.

It was argued that the initial observations of Māori prosperity in the early 19th century based on common land rights was eroded in successive land privatisation acts into settler-European hands. As had happened in Britain, "communal well-being was replaced by communal poverty and private wealth" (Evison, p. 231). It was also argued that Māori language was also heavily impacted, being marginalised in the shadows and echoes of schools and centres in NZ society. In line with the theorising around languages being inaudible, without sound, it is clear for a language to be audible it requires not only ears; it must be spoken. Panakareao's allegory of our (Māori) sayings sinking like stones has emerged through English-only language policies first introduced in 1847 but still prevalent in NZ. Throughout the world, Indigenous languages living in the shadows of dominant cultures and ideologies face constant challenge and threat of language-in-culture death referred to as linguafaction. Systemic racism will always exist when structural policies and practices run deep into the fabric of society.

Conclusion

This chapter has overviewed the struggle for resistance, survival, and revival. It illuminates the need for liberatory pedagogies that support our young people to sustain their own languages and cultures, to be courageous enough to shape their own identities, to live in their own skins and minds while simultaneously resisting capture in the tensions of new transformed realities.

Notes

1. A Māori King movement, headed by Te Wherowhero, was established in the mid-19th century to counter the dominance of the British King movement, an act which precipitated the NZ land wars and land confiscations.
2. Common law is derived from custom and judicial precedent or case law in contrast with statute law.
3. Governor Grey left NZ in 1853 to become governor of Cape Colony, South Africa.
4. So named a 'night-time haven,' Māori protocol dictated no fighting at night.

References

Abbas, M. S. (2020). The promise of political Blackness? Contesting Blackness, challenging Whiteness and the silencing of racism: A review article. *Ethnicities, 20*(1), 202–222.

Anaru, N. A. (2018). *A critical analysis of Indigenous Māori language revitalisation and the development of an ontological data base* [Doctoral Dissertation, Auckland University of Technology]. https://openrepository.aut.ac.nz/handle/10292/11469.

Banner, S. (1999). Two properties, one land: Law and space in nineteenth-century New Zealand. *Law & Social Inquiry, 24*(4), 807–852.

Bonilla-Silva, E. (2012). The invisible weight of Whiteness: The racial grammar of everyday life in contemporary America. *Ethnic and Racial Studies, 35*(2), 173–194.

Charters, C., Erueti, A., & Erueti, A. K. (Eds.). (2007). *Māori property rights and the foreshore and seabed: The last frontier.* Victoria University Press.

Davies, B., De Schauwer, E., Claes, L., De Munck, K., Van De Putte, I., & Verstichele, M. (2013). Recognition and difference: A collective biography. *International Journal of Qualitative Studies in Education, 26*(6), 680–691.

Department of Internal Affairs. (1991). *The people of many peaks: The Māori biographies from the Dictionary of New Zealand biography, Volume 1. Volumes 1769–1869.* Bridget Williams Books.

Evison, H. (1997). *The long dispute: Maori land rights and European colonisation in southern New Zealand.* Canterbury University Press.

Māhuta, R. T. (2011). *Tāwhiao, Tūkāroto Matutaera Pōtatau Te Wherowhero: Dictionary of New Zealand Biography.* Te Ara – the Encyclopedia of New Zealand. https://teara.govt.nz/mi/biographies/2t14/tawhiao-tukaroto-matutaera-potatau-te-wherowhero (Original work published 1993)

Miller, R. J. (2008). *Native America discovered and conquered: Thomas Jefferson, Lewis and Clark, and Manifest Destiny*. University of Nebraska Press.

Mutu, M. (2010). Constitutional Intentions: The Treaty of Waitangi texts. In M. Mulholland & V. Tawhai (Eds.), *Weeping waters: The Treaty of Waitangi and constitutional change*. Huia Publishers.

Orange, C. (2004). *An illustrated history of the Treaty of Waitangi*. Bridget Williams Books.

Pojman, L., & Vaughn, L. (2011). *Classics of philosophy*. Oxford University Press, Inc.

Salmond, A. (2017). *Tears of Rangi: Experiments across worlds*. Auckland University Press.

Sharman, F. A. (1989). An introduction to the enclosure acts. *The Journal of Legal History, 10*(1), 45–70.

Simon, J. A. (1998). Anthropology, 'native schooling' and Māori: The politics of 'cultural adaptation' policies. *Oceania, 69*(1), 61–78.

Skerrett, M. (2017). Te Kōhanga Reo: Early childhood education and the politics of language and cultural maintenance in Aotearoa, New Zealand—A personal–political story. In L. Miller, C. Cameron, C. Dalli, and N. Barbour (Eds.), *The SAGE handbook of early childhood policy* (pp. 433–451). Sage Publications.

Skutnabb-Kangas, T. (2015). Language rights. In W.E. Wright, S. Boun, & O. García (Eds.), *The handbook of bilingual and multilingual education* (pp. 185–202). Malden, MA: Wiley-Blackwell.

Thiong'o, N. W. (2005) *Decolonizing the mind: the politics of language in African literature*. Cambridge University Press.

Walker, R. (2004). *Ka Whawhai Tonu Mātou: Struggle without end* (Rev. ed.). Penguin.

Webb, D., Sanders, K., & Scott, P. (2010). *The New Zealand legal system: Structures and processes*. LexisNexis.

Williams, D. V. (2013). *A simple nullity?: The Wi Parata Case in New Zealand law and history*. Auckland University Press.

CHAPTER 5

Staying with the Troubles of Colonised Emotional Well-Being of Young Children in Aotearoa (New Zealand)

Jenny Ritchie

Introduction

Denial and suppression of emotion and of repertoires and vocabularies of emotional expression are a particular characteristic of societies with colonialist histories such as Aotearoa (New Zealand), Australia, the United States, the United Kingdom, and Canada (Came & da Silva, 2011; Matias & Zembylas, 2014). Colonising nations impose their regimes of truth, including their own 'emotional rules' onto others (Zembylas, 2006, p. 254). To date, our dominant, modernist, and currently hyper-neoliberal Western culture has not placed a great deal of emphasis on understanding the historical, cultural, social, political, and economic contexts of the meanings and expression of emotions. Some contexts for consideration include power effects, historical and cultural influences, social class, social media (Zembylas, 2006) and, currently, the increasingly serious impacts of climate change and the COVID-19 pandemic.

This chapter provides a brief series of historico-cultural snapshots of emotions as recognised and expressed within early-years pedagogies in Aotearoa. Beginning with a glimpse into traditional Māori child-rearing (Jenkins & Harte, 2011; Makareti, 1986), it then problematises the suppression of emotional expression imposed through British colonisation, which inflicted both emotional, spiritual, and physical pain on Māori

(Pihama et al., 2014), notably via schooling (Walker, 2004). Next it chronicles the introduction to Aotearoa (New Zealand) of progressive educational ideals via the New Education Foundation/Fellowship, which included recognition of children's emotional lives through the insights of Susan Isaacs, who addressed New Zealand teachers in 1937 (Campbell, 1938). These ideas are reflected in the writing of Sylvia Ashton-Warner, an infant teacher in this era who developed a pedagogy that affirmed Māori children's emotional expression (Ashton-Warner, 1980; Jones & Middleton, 2009). The chapter concludes with a consideration of the current status of emotions within early childhood care and education curriculum and pedagogy in Aotearoa and a call for supporting a post-colonial re-visibilisation of the emotional worlds of young children.

Traditional Māori Child-Rearing

Te ao Māori, the Māori world/world view, is infused with emotional and spiritual resonance (Pihama et al., 2004). Both spiritual and emotional wellbeing are integral elements of wellbeing from a Māori perspective (Ahuriri-Driscoll, 2014). This is despite the impact of Western Cartesian and cognitivist paradigms inflicted through the colonisation process. In traditional Māori child-rearing, the respect for the child's intrinsic mana (spiritual power, esteem) prevented adults from inflicting on children punishment of any kind (neither verbal, emotional or physical). Thus, early Western observers considered Māori children to be 'indulged' or 'spoilt' due to this lack of the authoritarian and often harsh discipline that was characteristic of Western child-rearing practice at that time (Jenkins & Harte, 2011; Salmond, 1991; Smith, 1995). For Māori, it was important to protect the child's mana from the potential damage caused by *whakamā*, an extreme sense of feeling ashamed or embarrassed (Metge, 1986). This contrasts with Western societies in which shame whilst ubiquitous, tends to be suppressed and hidden (Scheff, 2014). Children were also taught how to protect themselves from the spiritual dis-ease that would result from breaches of tapu, spiritual protections. Emotional and spiritual wellbeing was integrally dependent on connectedness with whānau (extended family), *whenua* (ancestral lands), and ancestral knowledges, including knowledge of the *Atua* (gods).

In te ao Māori (the Māori world), mutual respect and bonds between children and elders are valued and fostered (Makareti, 1986; Pere, 1982). Boys, youth and adult men participate fully in the emotional lives of their communities, including sharing the nurturing of infants and young children (Rua, 2015). Emotional expression is culturally sanctioned through myriad ritual practices, many of which deliberately invoke collective emotional expression and responses. Emotion is powerfully expressed in *tangihanga* (funeral) rituals, which involve the metaphorical and actual sharing of *roimata* and *hupe* (tears and mucous) over an extended time. Emotional expression is also vividly portrayed in other aspects of the Māori world, such as the performing arts of *kapa haka*.

Colonisation of Emotion

The 1840 treaty Te Tiriti o Waitangi allowed for British settlement in exchange for promising Māori the retention of their *tino rangatiratanga* (absolute authority) over their *taonga katoa* (everything of value to Māori; Kawharu, 1989; Orange, 1988). In 1852, Britain established the settler government, whereby they proceeded to operate from a position of White supremacy that denigrated Māori language, beliefs and practices and stripped them of lands and resources. The breadth and depth of the historical, traumatic and ongoing impacts of British colonisation on Māori have been well documented (Orange, 1987; Pihama et al., 2014; Waitangi Tribunal, 1986, 2011a, 2011b; Walker, 2004). These impacts are reflected in a broad range of negative social statistics in which Māori are disproportionately over-represented (New Zealand Ministry of Social Development, 2016).[1] The recursive cycle of historical and ongoing trauma is reflected in the fact that

> Māori are substantially more likely to experience the sudden loss of loved ones through hospitalization and premature death from a wide range of causes including cardiovascular disease, cancer, diabetes, asthma, infant mortality, self-harm, suicide, motor vehicle accidents, and unintentional and intentional injuries. (Pihama et al., 2014, p. 256)

In the context of this legacy of trauma, an aspect of colonisation that is not often recognised or discussed is the colonisation of Māori emotions. Missionary and settler regimes imposed considerable repression of emotional and spiritual expression and wellbeing, for both Māori and *Pākehā* (White) settler children. The most obvious signifier of this repression for Māori children was the prohibition imposed in state schools for many generations that resulted in Māori children being beaten for speaking their own language, te reo Māori (Walker, 2004). The Māori language contains a wide vocabulary of terms that describe spiritual and emotional states and feelings, such as *ihi, wehi* and *wana*, for which there are no direct English translations.[2] Proscribing the use of this emotional vocabulary is a further level of emotional colonisation. Moreover, colonisation has impacted on traditional patterns of gender roles and relations, with the imposition of patriarchal settler expectations having inhibited Māori men's expression of subtler emotions and roles such as nurturing (Rua, 2015). High levels of child abuse in Māori families are another impact of the violence of colonisation. Horrifically, as of this year, 2020, Māori infants are still being removed from their families at birth, contributing to devastating ongoing intergenerational trauma (Office of the Children's Commissioner, 2020).

Not only did Māori, through colonial/state schooling, suffer the colonisation of their language and ways of knowing, being, doing and relating, but they also suffered the suppression and denial of the indignation, anger and grief aroused by the imposition of colonial policies of dispossession and the ongoing intergenerational trauma that has emanated from this history (Pihama et al., 2014). This denial is in itself re-traumatising.

Since Māori consider geographical features and flora and fauna to be relations, connected through ancestry to Papatūānuku (the Earth Mother) and Ranginui (the Sky Father), a further layering of trauma is the grief felt by both Māori and other Indigenous peoples regarding the despoliation and desecration of their traditional lands, mountains, rivers and oceans and the biodiversity that these sustain (Pihama et al., 2014; Rose, 2008).

Emotion in Progressive Education in Aotearoa: Two Examples

New Zealand education in the 1930s and 1940s was influenced by progressive ideals which facilitated 'a time of great excitement, experimentation and unprecedented freedom' (Middleton, 2009, p. 65). These progressive ideals reflected a commitment to democracy and active citizenship. In education, this translated to 'child-centredness,' meaning that even young children should be listened to and encouraged in pursuit of their talents and interests through explorative experiential learning (Bar-Haim, 2017).

In 1937, the New Zealand Department of Education hosted a conference featuring an international range of speakers from the arena of progressive education, closing the nation's schools for a week in order that teachers might attend (Campbell, 1938). One of the speakers at this 'New Education Fellowship (NEF) Conference' was Dr Susan Isaacs (1885–1948), then head of the Department of Development at the London University's Institute of Education. Her previous role from 1924 to 1927 had been as a manager of Malting House, an experimental school in Cambridge, United Kingdom. Here, Isaacs had followed ideals of progressive education, including the belief that creativity allowed for the expression of emotions, including fiercer emotions that could otherwise lead to aggressive acts (Bar-Haim, 2017).

In her presentations to the NEF Conference, Isaacs (1938) noted the predicament of the young child whose intense emotions and strong immediate impulses were not yet tempered by self-control, or recognition of the consequences of these actions. She recognised that the primary needs for children were security, patient adult support and play and that if these needs are unmet, a child's frustrations may result in anger as well as anxiety. Security, Isaacs believed, is achieved through adults providing rhythmic patterns in daily routines, along with demonstrating firm, stable and caring attitudes. She highlighted the importance of children experiencing the expression of 'warm, generous love' (Isaacs, 1938, p. 91). Isaacs (1938) viewed play as an important medium for the child's emotional wellbeing:

> In the emotional field as in the intellectual, the child's free spontaneous play is the best help to his [sic] attaining mental balance and harmony, learning to trust himself, to measure the strength of his own impulses, to work out the consequences of his own actions, to feel powers of control grow within himself, to believe in his own love and constructive wishes, to identify himself with

others and incorporate their needs within his own nature – and so to become a social being. Throughout the early years, play is his chief means of maintaining health and ensuring normal social growth. (p. 92)

In a previously published book, Isaacs (1929) had also emphasised the value of play, stating that 'play is indeed the child's work, and the means whereby he [*sic*] grows and develops' (p. 9). In her talks to the NEF Conference, she clearly outlined to the teachers attending that children's needs for emotional support should be provided by patient adults who were skilled in offering children security, affection and opportunities for expressive play (Isaacs, 1938). She considered the role of educators as being 'to help the child become an 'independent moral being' and to encourage the child to find her or his 'private inner voice' (as cited in Bar-Haim, 2017, p. 110). The eminent New Zealand early childhood scholar, Dr Geraldine McDonald (2002), wrote that

> among the outstanding people brought to New Zealand, Susan Isaacs made perhaps the greatest impact. In England, she had established a school for young children using child centred and free play methods, and had written two books based on analysis of the thinking processes and the social and emotional behaviour of young children. She had studied psychoanalysis and believed in allowing children to express their feelings. She believed Jean Piaget had underestimated the reasoning powers of young children. (pp. 25–26)

Given the government mandate and encouragement of teachers to attend the weeklong conference, the influence and uptake of these progressive ideas is likely to have been far-reaching. Influenced by the progressive ideals of this era, such as those of Susan Isaacs briefly described earlier, the New Zealand teacher and writer Sylvia Ashton-Warner, was at the forefront of implementing and documenting her teaching practices with young Māori children in her infant classrooms. Her teaching philosophy also valued play, creativity and daily rhythms, which included walks exploring the outdoors, which were in keeping with progressive education practices of the day. Her work was innovative, however, in its respectful and responsive application in Māori rural school settings. Ashton-Warner wrote, in her publication 'Teacher', of the sensitivities required by European teachers in respecting the 'organic life' of young Māori children:

> It's not beauty to abruptly halt the growth of a young mind and to overlay it with the frame of an imposed culture. There are ways of training and grafting young growth. The true conception of beauty is the shape of organic life and that is the very thing at stake in the transition from one culture to another. If this transition took place at a later age when the security of a person was already established there would not be the same need for care. But in this country it

happens that the transition takes place at a tender and vulnerable age, which is the reason why we all try to work delicately. (Ashton-Warner, 1980, p. 34)

Ashton-Warner encouraged children to 'caption' their own lives, and then formed from these captions an 'organic' 'Key Vocabulary' that was meaningful to the children, expressive of their experiences, interests and emotional lives, their creative and destructive aspects. She wrote:

> Out press these words, grouping themselves in their own wild order. All boys wanting words of locomotion, aeroplane, tractor, jet, and the girls the words of domesticity, house, Mummy, doll. Then the fear words, ghost, tiger, skellington, alligator, bulldog, wild piggy, police. The sex words, kiss, love, touch, haka. The key words carrying their own illustrations in the mind, vivid and powerful pictures which none of us could possibly draw for them—since in the first place we can't see them and in the second because they are so alive with an organic life that the external pictorial representation of them is beyond the frontier of possibility. We can do no more than supply the captions. (Ashton-Warner, 1980, p. 39)

In Ashton-Warner's (1956/2009b) pedagogy of 'organic reading' she elicited the young Māori children's own words and stories, based on the realities of their daily lives: "Words following intimately from day to day the classroom mood; echoing the tangi [funeral] in the district, recounting the pictures [movies] in the hall the night before or revealing the drama behind the closed doors of the pa [village]" (p. 38).

> Out follow these captions. It's a lovely flowing. I see the creative channel swelling and undulating like an artery with blood pumping through. And as it settles, just like any other organic arrangement of nature it spreads out into an harmonious pattern; the fear words dominating the design, a few sex words, the person interest and the temper of the century. Daddy, Mummy, ghost, bomb, kiss, brothers, butcher knife, gaol, love, dance, cry, fight, hat, bulldog, touch, wild piggy . . . if you were a child, which vocabulary would you prefer? Your own or the one at present in the New Zealand infant rooms? Come John come. Look John look. Come and look. See the boats? The vocabulary of the English upper middle class, two-dimensional and respectable?' (Ashton-Warner, 1980, pp. 40–41)

Creativity was valued as a form of emotional expression within Sylvia Ashton-Warner's (1955/2009) pedagogy: "I see the mind of a five-year-old as a volcano with two vents; destructiveness and creativeness. And I see that to the extent that we widen the creative channel we atrophy the destructive one" (p. 21). Sylvia advocated a non-judgemental stance whereby the teacher engaged the child in conversation about the child's writing: "You never want to say that it's good or bad.... You've got no right to criticise the content of another's mind.... Your job is to see what's in it" (Ashton-Warner, 1956/2009a, p. 36). The only comments about a child's writing should be ones that demonstrate respectful interest: "From the teacher's end it boils down to whether or not she [sic] is a good conversationalist; whether or not she has the gift or the wisdom to listen to another; the ability to draw out and preserve that other's line of thought" (Ashton-Warner, 1956/2009a, p. 36).

Ashton-Warner (1980) recognised the importance of including Māori culture and understandings in the classroom, writing "In all matters in a Maori infant room there is a Maori standard as well as a European one" (p. 42). A prominent national leader of the Kōhanga Reo movement, Dame Iritana Tawhiwhirangi, had spent time as a young teacher in Ashton-Warner's infant classroom at Waiomatatini in 1948. She later drew on this experience as one of the founders of the Kōhanga Reo Māori language and *whānau* (family) development movement. Aspects of Ashton-Warner's class that were noted by Tawhiwhirangi (2009) were the welcoming of whānau, including Elders, to spend time in her classroom alongside the children, the pedagogical focus on learning rather than teaching, and the way in which Sylvia Ashton-Warner "made learning joyful" (p. 175).

That Ashton-Warner engaged children's emotions, recognising and validating the full spectrum of these as expressed, for example, through the powerful 'organic' words of the Māori children in her classroom, is a powerful contribution of her pedagogy. She was visionary in recognising the power of emotions in relation to learning and creativity and that all these aspects operate within cultural contexts. The work of Sylvia Ashton-Warner has resonance with that of the acclaimed critical pedagogue Paulo Freire (1970/2005), whose literacy approach also required learners to name their worlds in order to articulate their own cultural meanings and thus reclaim power over their destinies. Freire's work was grounded in a deep love for people and for the world. He wrote that

> if it is in speaking their word that people, by naming the world, transform it, dialogue imposes itself as the way by which they achieve significance as human beings.... Dialogue cannot exist, however, in the absence of a profound love for the world and for people. The naming of the world, which is an act of creation and re-creation, is not possible if it is not infused with love.... If I do not love the world—if I do not love life—if I do not love people—I cannot enter into dialogue. (Freire, 1970/2005, p. 71)

The emotional connection of love expressed through mutual respectful dialogue is thus positioned at the heart of both educational and social transformation.

Emotion in Current Early Childhood Pedagogies in Aotearoa

The field of early childhood care and education is one which, theoretically at least, validates emotional realms and an ethic of care. The Aotearoa (New Zealand) early childhood curriculum, *Te Whāriki* (New Zealand Ministry of Education, 1996, 2017), is notable in that it is both 'bicultural' and holistic. The term *bicultural* is used in the curriculum document to reflect the recognition of both Māori and European/Pākehā peoples' cultural perspectives. By way of acknowledging the colonialist history of education in Aotearoa, the original (1996) curriculum stated that

> particular care should be given to bicultural issues in relation to empowerment. Adults working with children should understand and be willing to discuss bicultural issues, actively seek Māori contributions to decision making, and ensure that Māori children develop a strong sense of self-worth. (New Zealand Ministry of Education, 1996, p. 41)

The core principles and interwoven strands of *Te Whāriki* recognise the inter-relatedness and interconnectedness of children's holistic development, emotional, cultural and spiritual wellbeing and that this wellbeing is dependent on that of their families. It advocates for a climate of emotional support, and recognition of the spiritual dimension by teachers, particularly in relation to Māori and Pacific Islands' children and families. The spiritual dimension of children's holistic wellbeing is integrally positioned within the 2017 version of *Te Whāriki*:

> Human development can be thought of in terms of cognitive (hinengaro), physical (tinana), emotional (whatumanawa), spiritual (wairua), and social and cultural dimensions, but these dimensions need to be viewed holistically, as closely interwoven and interdependent. For Māori the spiritual dimension is fundamental to holistic development because it connects the other dimensions across time and space. (New Zealand Ministry of Education, 2017, p. 19)

Te Whāriki 2017 further outlines, in the Mana Whenua | Wellbeing strand, the goal that children should experience an environment where their "emotional wellbeing is nurtured" and includes the learning outcome that children "become increasingly capable" of "[m]anaging themselves and expressing their feelings and needs" (p. 24). It should be noted, however, that the non-prescriptive nature of the curriculum means that individual teachers and early childhood settings vary considerably in the way in which they weave together the principles and strands to enact their own particular version of the curriculum (Ritchie, 2003).

Unfortunately, the intent of *Te Whāriki* regarding empowerment, the expectation that children's mana will be upheld, is undermined by the New Zealand Ministry of

Education of 'Incredible Years', promotion of a U.S. behaviourist programme. This programme includes emotionally suppressive strategies such as 'planned ignoring' of children's feelings and actions which have been deemed unacceptable by teachers (Ritchie, 2016). In such programmes, there is a problematic imposition of judgement, from a monocultural stance, with regard to the expression of feelings and behaviours which are deemed to be acceptable versus unacceptable by the authority figure such as the teacher. One manifestation of this is the privileging of those emotions and behaviours defined as 'positive' over those viewed as 'negative'. A report from the Education Review Office (2011), the official body that evaluates education settings in Aotearoa (New Zealand), is titled *Positive Foundations for Learning: Confident and Competent Children in Early Childhood Services*. The report positions children's emotional wellbeing alongside expectations of their 'appropriate behaviour', stating that "educators have a key role in nurturing children's emotional wellbeing and helping children to develop an understanding of appropriate behaviour" (Education Review Office, 2011, p. 1). The title of the report and the previously quoted sentence expose the tensions in Western discourse created by delineating and reifying binaries of 'positive' and 'negative' emotions and/or behaviour, raising questions as to the culturally determined nature of what is deemed 'positive' and 'appropriate'. The same discursive emphasis is seen in the more recent Ministry of Education document *He Māpuna Te Tamaiti*, which describes itself as a resource of "strategies for promoting wellbeing and positive behaviour" (Rohan, 2019, p. 8).

Emotional regulation and suppression, particularly regarding those emotions deemed 'negative', might be considered a characteristic of many Western cultures. The dominance of Western cultural values in education in Aotearoa can therefore lead to misinterpretation and denunciation of demonstration of emotional expression that sits outside of these 'norms'. For example, in European/Pākehā contexts, to poke out one's tongue is seen as a rude or derogatory gesture. For Māori, the *pūkana*, which can involve protruding both eyes and tongue (*whētero*), is a much-admired gesture often performed during a haka (performing art form) that demonstrates an intense excitement, commitment, and passion. Similarly, the defiance and boundary-pushing of the archetypal demigod Māui has been validated in Māori early childhood education documents as representing an embodiment of a *whakapapa* (genealogy) possessing potentiality and demonstrating a disposition of confidence, self-reliance, cheekiness, cunning, trickery, challenging, leadership, questioning, lateral thinking, and risk-taking (New Zealand Ministry of Education, 2009). During my kindergarten teaching years, I frequently observed defiant Māori boys being chastised having been adjudged 'naughty' and 'disrespectful' by fellow teachers who lacked a te ao Māori (Māori world-view) lens, when these same qualities might be admired in a Māori context. Teachers' responses often involved suppressing children's expression of emotions, invoking feelings of shame or *whakamā* which can have long-lasting impacts on children and constitute a colonising of their emotions and emotional wellbeing (Metge, 1986; Röttger-Rössler et al., 2015; Scheff, 2014).

Post-Colonial Possibilities for Revalidating and Re-Visibilising Emotion

This final section builds on some of the threads that are interwoven in this paper with a view to considering possibilities for post-colonial re-visibilising of emotions in early childhood pedagogies in Aotearoa. The first thread was the colonialist suppression of Māori expression, including the Māori language and emotional repertoires and resonances. The second was the recognition that despite inheriting the British education system and its oppressive structures, we do have here in Aotearoa a history of recognising progressive education philosophies that validate the emotions such as those expressed by Susan Isaacs and Sylvia Ashton-Warner. Third, we have an early childhood curriculum that with its holistic, socio-cultural and 'bicultural' approach contains encouragement for teachers to focus on validating children's emotional and spiritual wellbeing.

Education policies in Aotearoa had for the decade of the previous National-led government (2008–2017) been concerned with the 'schoolification' of early childhood care and education (Alcock & Haggerty, 2013) via a turn to behaviourist and cognitivist educational approaches. In current Ministry of Education discourse, the child is now 'the learner' and early childhood care and education is now described as 'early learning'. A generation of primary/elementary school children has endured the imposition of a narrowing of curriculum to focus primarily on literacy and numeracy and equally narrow forms of assessment via 'national standards' (Thrupp, 2014; Thrupp & Easter, 2013). Such modernist, rationalist, cognitivist 'level playing field' approaches fail on a number of levels. First, they are counterproductive even on technicist terms, since recent international comparisons have demonstrated a drop in the highly desired literacy achievement of New Zealand school children (RNZ, 2017). More important, they ignore the historical inequities and intergenerational trauma of colonialist histories that are a burden carried even by very young children into their educational experience. They fail to recognise and value the benefits of a broad-based holistic curriculum that offers children opportunities to express their feelings and creativity. Furthermore, in furthering the artificial binary of the cognitive versus emotional realms, they ignore the integral engagement of emotion in children's learning.

From infancy, young children utilise "sophisticated emotional strategies to actively engage adults" in noticing and responding to their needs (Salamon, Sumsion & Harrison, 2017, p. 363). Emotions are increasingly being given recognition as intrinsic to learning rather than being viewed as an obstacle to it (Cliffe & Solvason, 2020). Validating the centrality of emotions to children's wellbeing along with the richness of their cultural expression across different ethnic groups is fundamental to challenging the damaging dogmatic dominance of technicist behaviourist and cognitivist discourses. A revalidating of the centrality of emotions in education can be promoted through teachers modelling and fostering deliberative processes of reflection, of sitting with one's emotions and allowing them to be felt and acknowledged, through empathy, discussion and critical thinking. This involves teachers demonstrating and encouraging the capacity to listen to and consider the viewpoints and feelings of others and to collaboratively problem-solve, thus providing children with opportunities to develop emotional regulation and coping strategies (Ojala, 2013). Suppression of those emotions judged to be 'negative', such as anxiety or anger, is not only a form of oppression but also denies children the opportunity to draw on the full spectrum of emotions as sources of deliberation that if recognised, validated and supported, can enhance reflective capacity and motivate action for change (Ojala, 2013).

This chapter argues that emotions should be recognised as political, as sites for the enactment of social justice, as highlighted by Cliffe and Solvason (2020). Relationships with families and with members of different cultural communities are key to teachers gaining in-depth understandings of cultural nuances regarding emotional expression and culturally determined aspirations and dispositions. In re-envisioning pedagogies that value, recognise and respond to multiple and culturally diverse forms of emotional expression, teachers can support children in their recognition of self-empathy and their capacity to mirror empathy towards others (Rosenberg, 2003a, 2003b). A wide spectrum of emotions can thus be validated rather than imposing an artificial binary of Western-defined 'positive' and 'negative' emotions and emotional expression and the suppression of those judged to be 'negative'. The fostering of a culturally informed vocabulary of emotions can be the focus for education settings, moving beyond a narrow Western-determined set of desirable dispositions and behaviours. In this re-envisioned pedagogy, an "ongoing consciousness of emotions" of both adults and children is key to understanding and respecting different responses and that feelings arise when our values are being impinged upon or needs left unmet (Salamon et al., 2017, p. 371). In this view, conflict is also not judged as 'negative' behaviour and is instead viewed as a learning opportunity for children to recognise the feelings and needs of others using an increasingly nuanced vocabulary of emotions, and to co-construct solutions that can meet everyone's needs. This indeed is a foundational set of competencies for operating in democratic ways, and in service of social justice (Arnott, 2018).

It should be noted that cultural understandings and practices are fluid. Traditional values and expectations are influenced by national and international political discourses (such as the United Nations Convention on the Rights of the Child) as well as globalised Western capitalist and neoliberal effects (Bialostok & Aronson, 2016; Hsueh & Tobin, 2003). These may constitute subtle and hegemonic forms of emotional and cultural colonisation through, for example, the constant bombardment of social media manifestations. As educators committed to social justice it is important that we illuminate this ongoing neo-colonisation within educational policy and practice that serves to perpetuate the colonisation of young children and, in particular, their emotional and cultural worlds.

Notes

1. Many Pacific Islands have histories of colonisation, and Pacific Islands' peoples living in Aotearoa also experience racism and the lack of having their cultural patterns and languages validated and supported within the wider New Zealand society. They are similarly over-represented in negative social statistics such as health outcomes and educational achievement.
2. *Ihi* may be translated as 'psychic force'; *wehi* may be translated as 'a response of awe'; *wana* may be translated as 'excitement'.

References

Ahuriri-Driscoll, A. (2014). He kōrero wairua. Indigenous spiritual inquiry in rongoā research. *MAI Journal, 3*(1), 33–44. http://www.journal.mai.ac.nz/content/he-k%C5%8Drero-wairua-indigenous-spiritual-inquiry-rongo%C4%81-research-0

Alcock, S., & Haggerty, M. (2013). Recent policy developments and the "schoolification" of early childhood care and education in Aotearoa New Zealand. *Early Childhood Folio, 17*(2), 21–26. https://doi.org/10.18296/ecf.0117

Arnott, L. (2018). Children's negotiation tactics and socio-emotional self-regulation in child-led play experiences: The influence of the preschool pedagogic culture. *Early Child Development and Care, 188*(7), 951–965. https://doi.org/10.1080/03004430.2018.1443919

Ashton-Warner, S. (1980). *Teacher. The testament of an inspired teacher*. Virago.

Ashton-Warner, S. (2009). The Māori infant room: Organic reading and the key vocabulary, National Education. In A. Jones & S. Middleton (Eds.), *The kiss and the ghost. Sylvia Ashton-Warner and New Zealand* (pp. 19–26). NZCER Press. (Original work published 1955)

Ashton-Warner, S. (2009a). The Māori infant room: No. 3: Organic Writing. National Education 1. In A. Jones & S. Middleton (Eds.), *The kiss and the ghost. Sylvia Ashton-Warner and New Zealand* (pp. 32–37). NZCER Press. (Original work published 1956)

Ashton-Warner, S. (2009b). The Māori infant room: No. 4: Organic Reading, National Education 3. In A. Jones & S. Middleton (Eds.), *The kiss and the ghost. Sylvia Ashton-Warner and New Zealand* (pp. 37–42). NZCER Press. (Original work pubulished 1956)

Bar-Haim, S. (2017). The liberal playground: Susan Isaacs, psychoanalysis and progressive education in the interwar era. *History of the Human Sciences, 30*(1), 94–117. https://doi.org/10.1177/0952695116668123

Bialostok, S. M., & Aronson, M. (2016). Making emotional connections in the age of neoliberalism. *Ethos, 44*(2), 96–117. https://doi.org/10.1111/etho.12118

Came, H. A., & da Silva, S. (2011). Building political competencies for the transformation of racism in Aotearoa. *Kōtuitui: New Zealand Journal of Social Sciences Online, 6*(1–2), 113–123. https://doi.org/10.1080/1177083X.2011.615332

Campbell, A. E. (1938). *Modern trends in education: The proceedings of the New Education Fellowship Conference held in July, 1937*. Whitcombe and Tombs.

Cliffe, J., & Solvason, C. (2020). The role of emotions in building new knowledge and developing young children's understanding. *Power and Education, 12*(2), 189–203. https://doi.org/10.1177/1757743820930724

Education Review Office. (2011). *Positive foundations for learning: Confident and competent children in early childhood services*. https://www.ero.govt.nz/publications/positive-foundations-for-learning-confident-and-competent-children-in-early-childhood-services/

Freire, P. (2005). *Pedagogy of the oppressed*. Continuum. (Original work published 1970)

Hsueh, Y., & Tobin, J. (2003). Chinese early childhood educators' perspectives: On dealing with a crying child. *Journal of Early Childhood Research*, 1(1), 73–94. https://doi.org/10.1177/1476718X030011004

Isaacs, S. (1929). *The nursery years. The mind of the child from birth to six years*. Routledge & Kegan Paul.

Isaacs, S. (1938). Emotional difficulties and nursery training. In A. E. Campbell (Ed.), *Modern trends in education. The proceedings of the New Education Fellowship Conference held in New Zealand in July 1937* (pp. 90–92). Whitcombe & Tombs.

Jackson, M. (2009). Mana tāne, mana wāhine, mana motuhake. *Māori Health Review*, 21, 1.

Jenkins, K., & Harte, H. M. (2011). *Traditional Maori parenting. An historical review of literature of traditional Maori child rearing practices in pre-European times*. Te Kahui Mana Ririki. http://www.ririki.org.nz/research/our-research

Jones, A., & Middleton, S. (Eds.). (2009). *The kiss and the ghost: Sylvia Ashton-Warner and New Zealand*. NZCER Press.

Kawharu, I. (Ed.). (1989). *Waitangi: Māori and Pākehā perspectives of the Treaty of Waitangi*. Oxford University Press.

Makareti. (1986). *The old time Mäori*. New Women's Press. (Original work published 1938)

Matias, C. E., & Zembylas, M. (2014). 'When saying you care is not really caring': Emotions of disgust, Whiteness ideology, and teacher education. *Critical Studies in Education*, 55(3), 319–337. https://doi.org/10.1080/17508487.2014.922489

McDonald, G. (2002). Dr CE Beeby. The quality of education. *Set*, 2, 25–27.

Metge, J. (1986). *In and out of touch: Whakamaa in cross-cultural context*. Victoria University Press.

Middleton, S. (2009). Sylvia's place: Ashton-Warner as New Zealand educational theorist. In A. Jones & S. Middleton (Eds.), *The kiss and the ghost. Sylvia Ashton-Warner and New Zealand* (pp. 61–84). NZCER Press.

New Zealand Ministry of Education. (1996). *Te Whāriki. He whāriki mātauranga mō ngā mokopuna o Aotearoa: Early childhood curriculum*. Learning Media. https://education.govt.nz/assets/Documents/Early-Childhood/Te-Whariki-1996.pdf.

New Zealand Ministry of Education. (2009). *Te Whatu Pōkeka. Kaupapa Māori assessment for learning. Early childhood exemplars*. Learning Media. https://www.education.govt.nz/early-childhood/teaching-and-learning/assessment-for-learning/te-whatu-pokeka-english/

New Zealand Ministry of Education. (2017). *Te Whāriki. He whāriki mātauranga mō ngā mokopuna o Aotearoa. Early childhood curriculum*. https://www.education.govt.nz/earlychildhood/teaching-and-learning/te-whariki/

New Zealand Ministry of Social Development. (2016). *The social report*. https://www.msd.govt.nz/about-msd-and-our-work/publications-resources/monitoring/social-report/index.html

Office of the Children's Commissioner. (2020). *Te Kuku O Te Manawa - Ka puta te riri, ka momori te ngākau, ka heke ngā roimata mo tōku pēpi. A review of what needs to change to enable pēpi Māori aged 0-3 months to remain in the care of their whānau in situations where Oranga Tamariki-Ministry for Children is notified of care and protection concerns*. https://www.occ.org.nz/publications/reports/te-kuku-o-te-manawa/

Ojala, M. (2013). Emotional awareness: On the importance of including emotional aspects in education for sustainable development (ESD). *Journal of Education for Sustainable Development*, 7(2), 167–182. https://doi.org/10.1177/0973408214526488

Orange, C. (1987). *The Treaty of Waitangi*. Allen and Unwin/Port Nicholson Press.

Orange, C. (1988, September 23–24). *The Treaty of Waitangi – A historical overview* [Paper presentation]. New Zealand Planning Council Seminar: Pakeha Perspectives on the Treaty, Wellington, New Zealand.

Pere, R. R. (1982). *AKO. Concepts and Learning in the Māori Tradition* (Working Paper No 17). University of Waikato.

Pihama, L., Reynolds, P., Smith, C., Reid, J., Smith, L. T., & Te Nana, R. (2014). Positioning historical trauma theory within Aotearoa New Zealand. *AlterNative: An International Journal of Indigenous Peoples, 10*(3), 248–262. https://doi.org/10.1177/117718011401000304

Pihama, L., Smith, K., Taki, M., & Lee, J. (2004). *A literature review on kaupapa Maori and Maori education pedagogy*. Ako Aotearoa.

Ritchie, J. (2003). Te Whāriki as a potential lever for bicultural development In J. Nuttall (Ed.), *Weaving Te Whāriki* (pp. 79–109). NZCER Press.

Ritchie, J. (2016). Creating spaces of empathy in the face of regimes of control. *Global Studies of Childhood, 6*(1), 112–122. doi:110.1177/2043610615627928

RNZ. (2017). *NZ's literacy score drops for first time in 15 years*. https://www.rnz.co.nz/news/national/345567/nz-s-literacy-score-drops-for-first-time-in-15-years

Rohan, T. (2019). *He māpuna te tamaiti. Supporting social and emotional competence in early learning*. Cognition Education for the New Zealand Ministry of Education. https://tewhariki.tki.org.nz/assets/Uploads/files/He-Mapuna-te-Tamaiti-complete-book.pdf.

Rose, D. B. (2008). On history, trees, and ethical proximity. *Postcolonial Studies, 11*(2), 157–167.

Rosenberg, M. (2003a). *Life-enriching education. Help schools improve performance, reduce conflict and enhance relationships*. Puddledancer Press.

Rosenberg, M. (2003b). *Nonviolent communication. A language of life*. Puddledancer Press.

Röttger-Rössler, B., Scheidecker, G., Funk, L., & Holodynski, M. (2015). Learning (by) feeling: A cross-cultural comparison of the socialization and development of emotions. *Ethos, 43*(2), 187–220. https://doi.org/10.1111/etho.12080

Rua, M. R. (2015). *Māori men's positive and interconnected sense of self, being and place*. [Doctoral thesis, University of Waikato]. https://hdl.handle.net/10289/9440

Salmond, A. (1991). *Two worlds: First meetings between Māori and Europeans, 1642–1772*. Viking.

Salamon, A., Sumsion, J., & Harrison, L. (2017). Infants draw on 'emotional capital' in early childhood education contexts: A new paradigm. *Contemporary Issues in Early Childhood, 18*(4), 362–374. https://doi.org/10.1177/1463949117742771

Scheff, T. (2014). The ubiquity of hidden shame in modernity. *Cultural Sociology, 8*(2), 129–141. https://doi.org/10.1177/1749975513507244

Smith, L. T. (1995, August/September/October). The colonisation of Māori children. *Youth Law Review*, 8–11.

Tawhiwhirangi, I. (2009). Learning without teaching: Sylvia Ashton-Warner's classroom as a seed for kōhabnga reo. In A. Jones & S. Middleton (Eds.), *The kiss and the ghost. Sylvia Ashton-Warner and New Zealand* (pp. 171–178). NZCER Press.

Thrupp, M. (2014). At the eye of the storm: Researching schools and their communities enacting National Standards. *New Zealand Journal of Educational Studies, 49*(1), 6–20.

Thrupp, M., & Easter, A. (2013). 'Tell me about your school': Researching local responses to New Zealand's National Standards policy. *Assessment Matters, 5*, 94–115. https://doi.org/10.18296/am.0113

Waitangi Tribunal. (1986). *Report of the Waitangi Tribunal on the Te Reo Maori claim (WAI 11)*. GP Publications. http://www.justice.govt.nz/tribunals/waitangi-tribunal

Waitangi Tribunal. (2011a). *Ko Aotearoa tēnei. A report into claims concerning New Zealand law and policy affecting Māori culture and identity (Wai 262). Te taumata tuarua. Volume 1.* http://www.justice.govt.nz/tribunals/waitangi-tribunal

Waitangi Tribunal. (2011b). *Ko Aotearoa tēnei. A report into claims concerning New Zealand law and policy affecting Māori culture and identity (Wai 262). Te taumata tuarua. Volume 2.* http://www.justice.govt.nz/tribunals/waitangi-tribunal

Walker, R. (2004). *Ka Whawhai Tonu Matou. Struggle without end* (Rev. ed.). Penguin.

Zembylas, M. (2006). Challenges and possibilities in a postmodern culture of emotions in education. *Interchange, 37*(3), 251–275. https://doi.org/10.1007/s10780-006-9003-y

CHAPTER 6

Competing Discourses about Immigrant Children: Metaphors of the Right and Left

Theodora Lightfoot

RIGHT NOW, A lot of the discourse of conservative and right-wing Americans has focused on immigration and the dangers that immigrants and refugees pose to U.S. society. Elsewhere I have written about the logic specific to conservatives concerning immigration (Lightfoot, 2001). Here, instead, I want to write about another phenomenon—that is, our society's general tendency to use deficit language when referring to our immigrant population—or, more precisely, specific elements within our immigrant population. It is obvious how this language comes from the right. However, in trying to help groups that are seen as having problems and deficiencies, many people use language that highlights the problems immigrants bring to society rather than the resources they provide. Most commonly, those who seek to provide "help" to immigrants emphasize that group's neediness in order to ask for help providing for them. Thus, for example, advocates for bilingual education will use predictions that immigrant children, or, most specifically, children from certain immigrant backgrounds—most commonly Mexicans and Central Americans, whom the right likes to vilify—will fail unless they are given extra resources. I am concerned that by doing so, they inadvertently add ammunition to an already contentious debate about immigration. In this chapter, I look at deficit language concerning immigrants as it comes from both the right and the "mainstream," or left. I encourage those who support the immigrants in our population to refer to them in more positive terms. I do not expect that by doing so all the fear of immigration coming from the right will disappear. However, it may help prevent those who support immigrants from adding negative energy to an already contentious situation.

Mainstream educational discourse is generally sympathetic to immigration and immigrant children and tends to be supportive of multiculturalism and bilingualism. However, it has often used threats to get program support. Supporters often claim that children will fail if not given special programs, which often cost money. In contrast, conservative, or right-wing, discourse is generally unsympathetic to immigrants and immigration. Some of their arguments are extremist, and some are untrue—like claims that immigrants are violent and more likely to commit crimes than native-born citizens. For example, Donald Trump, who has referred to Mexicans as "criminals, rapists and murderers" four days before the 2020 election, also declared a "Proclamation on National Day of Remembrance for Americans Killed by Illegal Aliens, 2020" (Motion Law—Immigration, 2020), four days before the election. However, and this is the uncomfortable part, most of the arguments made against immigration are more moderate, and there are some similarities between the language used by anti-immigrant groups and those who welcome immigrants but feel that immigrant children are going to need special help if they are going to be part of our school system. These arguments have, at least superficial, similarities to those made by pro-immigrant groups. In this chapter, I argue that those who are supportive of immigration may want to find different, less deficit-oriented ways to talk about immigrants and immigrant children—emphasizing the resources they bring to the country rather than the resources they need in order to avoid being an economic drag on the country.

Theoretical Orientation

This chapter is oriented in two theoretical areas. The first draws on the assertions from poststructuralist philosophy that truth is not an absolute entity. It is created by culture and politics. It creates the way we see the world and is also created by it. As the philosopher Michel Foucault (1980) wrote,

> truth is a thing of this world: it is produced only by virtue of multiple forms of constraint. And it produces regular effects of power. Each society has its régime of truth, its "general politics" of truth. (p. 131)

Whereas the late 1980s would perhaps add to Foucault to assert that society is not a time and a place—it is a culture. As the linguist/philosopher Alastair Pennycook would add to Foucault's assertions about régimes of truth in light of posthumanist philosophy, not everyone living in the same society is "modern" to the same degree and in the same way. Although I do not go into this in great detail in this chapter, the idea of posthumanism helps explain many of the cultural differences between the right and the left in the 21st-century United States (Pennycook, 2018). As Pennycook (2018) writes, "the universality of humanism has never been universal; [the idea of a universal human] has been blind to difference, culture and diversity" (p. 23). We are living in an era in which there is great cultural difference in the United States—not merely among racial, ethnic, and national groups but also within these groups, based on cultural and religious beliefs. When making decisions about how to frame our discourse, pro-immigration Americans want to take these cultural differences into account.

In understanding the way these cultural differences are formed and play out, one of the most important factors is metaphor. As O'Brien (2003) writes,

> problem setting, or the formation of how societal problems are perceived, may be a more important policy issue than problem solving, and problems are framed, in large part through the employment of metaphors. (p. 33)

Metaphors consist of various levels and types. One level, which I often call "surface metaphors," appears obviously in the text through obvious comparisons, that is, snowy white (metaphor) or white as snow (simile). These are the tropes we learned about in literature class. The other type of metaphor is called "frames" (Kövecses, 2006), whereby words or phrases appearing in the text evoke often hidden links to narratives that often lie outside the text. In addition to surface metaphors, metaphorical framings play an important part in the discourse of the right and, of course, the left. Often when the two groups say things that sound superficially similar, they tie into extremely different "frames."

Methods

The analysis forming the basis of this chapter has come from reading large numbers of texts from both the right and the left and looking for patterns of both surface metaphors and frames that appear in a multitude of examples. Obviously, a metaphor, no matter how striking, that appears in one text and is not repeated is of no interest to someone trying to understand the cultural characteristics of particular societal groups. Metaphors that are repeated, either in identical phrasing or in similar forms, are, in contrast, indictive of cultural patterns, or of ways of understanding the world and forming concepts of truth that characterize various groups within society (Lakoff & Johnson, 1980). This is particularly striking in the "post-truth" society that has existed ever since the election of Donald Trump, meaning a particular assertion is often much more closely tied to its metaphorical relevance to some cultural group in society than to its adherence to external reality.

The Good Side to Immigration

There has been a tradition in the United States of describing immigrants and their languages in positive terms. This was especially prevalent in the immediate postwar years through the early 1960s. During World War II, it had become evident that the United States lacked fluent speakers of other languages. In the days before air travel, the United States was geographically separated from most of the rest of the world. Although there were Spanish speakers in the Southwest and French speakers across the border in Canada, the tradition in the United States was to teach foreign languages by reading and writing. When the United States needed large numbers of foreign language speakers as interpreters, spies, and in other capacities, it became evident that not only did our schools not produce fluent foreign-language speakers but also that many of the children of immigrants had lost their skills in languages other than English (Lightfoot, 2001). For a period following the war, there was priority put on helping the children of immigrants maintain their heritage language skills as assets to their new country. One often-cited example is the Coral Way bilingual school in Miami, which was described as a place where a young person, by maintaining their heritage language, would "have skills, abilities and understandings which will greatly extend his vocational potential and thus increase his usefulness to himself and the world in which he lives" (Mackey & Von Nieda, 1977, p. 68).

Immigrants Need Our Help

However, beginning in the late 1960s, educational programs designed to help immigrant children were increasingly described, not as fostering skills and resources valuable to the country but instead as ways of mitigating the risks posed by the immigrants in our midst. These children began being seen as both poor and at risk of remaining poor unless something was done, but their language skills, which had previously been seen as an advantage to the country, began to be seen as part of a calculus of risk (Lightfoot 2001). You can see the difference between the description of the children in the Coral Way school in the early 1960s and the following description of bilingual people in the late 1960s:

> Unemployment in these slums [is] a matter of personal rather than economic condition.... The problem is less one of inadequate opportunity than of inability to use opportunity.... Fundamental to the problem seem to be the linguistic barriers Mexican-Americans must face. [A lack of proficiency in English] is as much of a handicap socially speaking as a cleft palate, deafness, etc. are in organic or physical terms. (Natalicio & Natalicio, 1969, pp. 263–264)

Metaphorically, if the first quote ties into metaphorical associations with ability, success, and progress, the second ties into narratives of failure, persistent poverty, or an internal third world within the United States. Children coming from these "slums" (i.e., neighborhoods where a lot of Latino immigrants live) need to be changed and remedied before they can contribute to society. Not surprisingly, it was at this point in our country's history that many bilingual programs changed from "maintenance" (i.e., keeping and developing children's first-language skills) to transitional (using the first language as a crutch to learning English and then taking it away; Lightfoot, 2001).

Throughout this period, there has been another distinctive feature to the way advocates of rights for immigrants have talked about bilingualism. Throughout the last several decades, certain groups of immigrants (Latinos and Blacks) have been singled out as being potential societal problems (if not remedied) while other groups, particularly East Asians, have been seen as much less problematic and less likely to cause problems in school or to be poor and "burdens to society" as adults. This is true even when certain groups of Asian students have struggled in school. Again, advocating for extra school funding for Latino students, you can see in this quote from 10 years later the same logic (Lightfoot, 2001):

> Latinos' current social, educational, and economic status must vastly improve if their demographic power is to be translated into economic strength, both for themselves and for the United States.... Hispanics remain the most undereducated major segment of the U.S. population. (Perez & De la Rosa Salazar, 1997, p. 99)

Finally, to show that the same language continues up to the present, I quote at some length from a contemporary publication that uses language strikingly similar to the three quotes earlier:

> Latinos are mostly poor and concentrated in the low-wage service sector—especially if they do not speak English.... Furthermore, twice as many Latino children as African-American children have parents who do not have a high school diploma, and they are more than five times as likely as white children to have parents with less than a high school education.... In many of the nation's largest public school districts, at least one of three students is Latino. ... In cities with AFT [American Federation of Teachers] affiliates—such as Los Angeles, San Antonio, and Miami—Latino students make up the vast majority of the student population. In sum, these demographic trends indicate that the Latino population growth had been inversely proportional to economic progress and, as the next section points out, academic success. Despite some promising signs of progress, educational outcomes for Latinos have not

improved dramatically in the last 30 years. Latinos continue to have low academic achievement and the highest dropout rates in the nation, as well as low college preparatory course enrollment and postsecondary attainment. (AFT, 2019, "Demographic Trends"–"Educational Outcomes")

In all the earlier citations, Latinos and their children are portrayed in strikingly similar terms. All the descriptors refer to a narrative of poverty and failure within an otherwise prosperous nation within which others are succeeding while Latinos are not. The cause of this failure is a lack of education and a lack of familial skills. The writers are all arguing for more investment in the education of Latinos. However, this investment is called for within the narrative—the frame—of human capital theory, in which a nation's prosperity is built on the cumulative educational level of its citizens. In all these quotes, we can see the implied threat of Latinos within the United States. Latinos are the most undereducated segment of the population. As such, they are a threat to national prosperity. If we want to improve the prosperity of our nation—to make good use of the nation's human resources—we need to need to invest in the education of Latinos.

Right-Wing Discourse and Latinos

To understand conservative and right-wing understandings of Latino immigrants, I have been reading right-wing publications such as Breitbart News, the Drudge Report, the Michelle Malkin Blog, and Fox News publications. Some of these publications use relatively polite language to talk about immigrants, while others use rougher language. What ties them together is that all of them have negative viewpoints toward immigrants. What is interesting is that these publications often use language that bears some similarities to what you see from pro-immigrant groups, although they tie into different metaphorical frames or different underlying narratives:

> The cost of meeting the educational needs for the kids who are arriving illegally as part of the surge is the main way that these children put burdens on local governments. . . . These kids will require special Limited English Proficient (LEP) classes conducted in Spanish or in other languages indigenous to Central America, as well as other taxpayer funded services, such as free and reduced school meals. Once again the costs of [the] federal government's failed immigration policies are borne at the local level, and the nation's public school system is where the costs are most visible. (May, 2016, Para. 1)

These children who are costing the local governments a lot of money are also failing to learn English, creating an alien subpopulation within the United States that does not share our language or culture:

> An annual report by the Office of Refugee re-settlement [reveals] the extent to which assimilation to life in America has failed for the refugee population. About 58 percent, or nearly 6-in-ten refugees have "below basic" English skills after living in the US for five years. Less than 20 percent of refugees in the US who have lived in the country for five years have proficient English speaking skills. Since 2008, as Breitbart News reported, the US has permanently resettled more than 1.7 million foreign nationals and refugees.... This is a refugee population larger than Philadelphia Pennsylvania. (Binder, 2018a, para. 4)

Like the pro-immigration educators I quoted earlier, conservatives are also concerned about immigrants being poor. Numerous articles in publications like Breitbart News mention poverty as an issue concerning immigrants and refugees. Although this does not appear in every text, the implication is that most of those bringing poverty into the United States are Central American, that is, Latino.

The following is an example:

> The majority, about 56 percent of refugee households between 2011 and 2015 were on food stamps, a welfare service that is subsidized by the American taxpayer. Nearly 30 percent of refugees received cash welfare of some sort ... while 34 percent of refugees 18 years old or older said they had no health insurance. Of the refugees who said they did have health insurance, about 50 percent said they were either on Medicaid or Refugee Medical Assistance both of which are taxpayer funded. (Binder, 2018a, para. 6)

In addition to refugees, immigrants as a whole are likely to be poor, says Breitbart News. They leave conditions of poverty and bring poverty to the United States:

> New immigrants to the United States are twice as likely to live in poverty as native-born Americans a new study by the Center for Immigration Studies finds.... The median income of new arrivals was $18,402 in 2017. (Binder, 2018b, para. 3)

If people on the right are concerned that immigrants in the United States are bringing poverty to the communities they live in, they are also concerned that the immigrants leaving Central America are fleeing poverty. They leave poverty and bring poverty with them. Numerous articles about migrants tell stories of immigrants who are fleeing poverty and coming to the United States to escape that poverty and send money to relatives who are desperate and unemployed or underemployed. For example, take the description of one immigrant, Ana Leva, who has come to the border trying to cross and find work so she can send money to her family:

>A *TRT World* report profiled a female caravan migrant from El Salvador who is currently in Tijuana, Mexico.... [She is] seeking work to send money home.... Ana Leva just called her mom.... She left El Salvador with the dream of sending money to her grandchildren. (Binder, 2018b, para. 6)

The Same but Different

I have been showcasing similarities between the ways people who are sympathetic to Latino immigrants and those who are afraid of them talk about immigration and foreigners in our midst. Both sides show concern about the fact that many Latinos in the United States do not know English or speak English at a level that is inadequate for getting good educations and professional jobs. Both sides are aware that it may be necessary to make a substantial investment to help Latino students succeed. Both sides are very concerned about high poverty rates among Latinos in the United States. There is another way in which both sides are similar. This again comes down to framing, or to the way apparently neutral descriptions can link to important narratives that are outside of the text, that is, race or ethnicity. Latinos are racially diverse and do not constitute a singular racial group. However, in common discourse in the United States, they are often treated as if they were. (Latinos are not a race in that as a group they are racially diverse, but in U.S. discourse, they are often treated as if they were.) Interestingly, race is very rarely mentioned directly in the discourse of either side. However, the concept of race is implicitly present—in fact, omnipresent in most descriptions of Latino immigrants. Educators concerned about inequality in the schools do mention other races, but there is a fixation on Latinos when talking about a lack of preparedness for school or school failure. This is particularly true when talking about immigrants. There are other groups of immigrants, such as some Southeast Asians who are also struggling in school. However, a disproportionate number of articles about school failure among immigrants focus on Latinos, to the point where there are sometimes fewer resources allocated to members of other immigrant groups who are struggling with English or other issues than to Latinos (Lightfoot, 2001). People on the right are fixated on Latino immigrants to an even larger degree. When reading right-wing publications, one would imagine that almost all the immigrants coming into the United States are Latino.

However, it is important when talking about similarities in discourse between those sympathetic to immigrants and those who are afraid of them, not to overemphasize these similarities. It is obvious that there are major differences in the way the two groups perceive immigration despite real similarities in the texts I have drawn from the two types of publications. Here, again, I refer to metaphorical framing, or the way that language in any given text that appears neutral can link to an outside narrative that tells a different story. In this case, the texts appear similar, but the framing is very different.

In the texts from educators, there are references to difficulties in learning languages. These link to a frame in which (a) immigrants want to learn English but are having difficulty and (b) it is our social responsibility to help them. Immigrants want to learn English, and it is our social responsibility to help them. Learning English is a social issue for which we all bear responsibility.

In right-wing publications, the same references link to a frame of refusal to learn. Immigrants come to the United States. It is their personal responsibility to learn English. If they do not learn, it is their personal failure because they did not try hard enough. There are frequent references to "our ancestors" who came here and learned English. Thus, the failure to learn English is a personal refusal to integrate into the United States linguistically and culturally. To make things worse, we, through our school taxes, are being asked to pay for their failures or their refusals.

The same thing holds true for the issue of poverty. Texts from both pro- and anti-immigration groups make frequent mention of poverty. Lakoff (2002) points out that the issue of poverty is a major difference in framing between the right and the left. For people on the left, poverty is a social issue. People are poor because the system is unfair and disadvantages some people while favoring others. This applies both nationally and internationally. Some countries are richer than others for historical reasons. Because poverty is generally not the "fault" of those who suffer from it, it is the responsibility of everyone to work to end poverty—both within the United States and internationally. Mentions of the fact that a person is poor or that a group suffers disproportionately from poverty invokes both empathy and a desire—or even responsibility to help change the situation. According to Lakoff (2002), people on the right see poverty very differently. Poverty represents personal responsibility and personal failure. Although obviously some people are born poor and others are born rich, we all have the ability and the social responsibility, to work to change our circumstances. Getting out of poverty is our personal duty. Interestingly, most conservatives do not see the desire of people to move out of Central America to look for opportunity as admirable. They may tell sad stories about people leaving Guatemala or Honduras because of extreme poverty and then state that poverty is not an eligible claim for asylum (Binder, 2018a). In other words, it is the responsibility of Central Americans to stay where they were born and work hard to change their circumstances.

Of course, there are other ways in which the discourses of the right and the center or left differ on immigration. For example, those on the left/center end of the political spectrum generally assert that immigrants tend to be less violent than the general population. As the *Washington Post* writes,

> the social-science research on immigration and crime is clear. Undocumented immigrants are considerably less likely to commit crime than native-born citizens with immigrants legally in the United States even less likely to do so. In

contrast, Fox News asserts that immigrants are considerably MORE likely to commit crimes than native-born citizens. (Ingraham, 2018, para. 3)

Violence, crime, and terrorism are integral parts of the way people on the right "frame" or narrate immigrants. References, both direct and indirect, to violence and crime run through a great deal of the literature on immigration from the right. See, for example, the following excerpt from an article printed by Fox News. It is unclear whether their statistics are correct, but if one believes them, crime and immigration are tightly linked:

> Non-citizens constitute only about 7 percent of the U.S. population. Yet data from the Justice Department's Bureau of Justice Statistics reveals that non-citizens accounted for nearly two-thirds (64 percent) of all federal arrests in 2018. (Von Spakovsky, 2019, para. 5)

However, despite these differences, as we have seen, there are a lot of similarities between the arguments made by those who seek support for immigrants—especially Latino immigrants by making them look vulnerable and needy and those who seek to use the needs and vulnerabilities attributed to that group to keep them out of the United States. Why is that problematic?

Framing: The Way Educators Talk Inadvertently Activates the Frames of the Right

Again, we turn to Lakoff and the idea of framing. In his blog post about abortion, for example, Lakoff (2002) points out that when talking about abortion, members of the pro-choice community inadvertently say things that activate the framings or the narratives of those who are opposed to abortion. For example, talk of the morning-after pill evokes images of immoral behavior and irresponsible partying and dating whereby a woman chooses not to say no and later regrets it. The term *partial birth abortion*, which is now used by both sides of the debate was invented by a hired, conservative language professional to evoke grisly scenes of viable, almost-at-term babies being ripped out of their mother's wombs. Those in the pro-choice movement who do not share these narratives—these images—have no idea what imagery they are touching on when they use that terminology. A more neutral term for the other side might be something like *medically necessary abortion*. In other words, people who do not share narratives and are unaware of the narratives that underly the perceptions of others risk inflaming feelings and setting off reactions that are the opposite of what they intended.

As we have seen, then, innocent remarks made about immigrants referring to their possibilities of failing in school unless we help them, of the difficulties they may have learning English unless given extra support, or of the disproportionate number of immigrants who are living in poverty may not elicit the same reaction of sympathy or the desire to help that is felt by the authors. Someone whose narrative about immigration is different from their own may read those articles and think the opposite of what the authors intended. Their reactions may instead be the following: Those Latino immigrants are going to bring down the quality of our schools by failing. Their lack of economic success may create pockets of concentrated poverty in the United States—full of crime, despair, and other problems that accompany those who have allowed themselves to fall into poverty. They were unable to pull themselves out of poverty in their home countries and now they come here asking for our help. Latinos seem unwilling to learn English or to assimilate to our culture. We have large and growing numbers of people in our country who do not know English and do not keep our cultural traditions. They are not like us.

How Could We Talk More Productively About Immigration?

I suggest that in talking about issues that have become flashpoints for conservatives, educators and others who are concerned about the education of immigrant students find a more positive and productive way to talk about the students they want to help. More productive language would carefully and consciously avoid activating the negative narratives that cause conservatives to be afraid of immigration.

There are other ways these arguments could potentially be framed while staying within the realm of possible "truths." Here are some possible ways.

Many people on the right are afraid that Spanish speakers will retain their language and divide the country by forming an alien enclave in our midst. Educators could return to the language of the 1950s about immigrant languages and the need for fluent speakers of other languages in our country. Fewer than 1% of adult Americans are proficient in languages they did not grow up speaking, and alarmingly, in a rapidly globalizing economy, very few Americans study foreign languages compared to students in other parts of the world (Devlin, 2018). Immigrants would not have to be the only ones to profit from bilingualism. More emphasis could be put on using immigrant students as mentors in foreign-language or limited (partial-day) immersion programs. Not only would English-speaking young people profit from the presence of immigrants in their schools, but they would also gain skills in learning languages other than the one they were exposed to. It has been demonstrated that people who were exposed to other languages as children have a superior language-learning ability that lasts through life. As counterintuitive as it may sound, early training in Spanish may lead to people becoming fluent in strategically necessary languages such as Arabic or Mandarin later in life (University of Haifa, 2011).

Perhaps much of the anxiety over language learning and identity can be alleviated by pointing out that immigrant Latinos are learning English and assimilating culturally as fast as earlier European immigrants. (Citrin et al., 2007) point out that Latino immigrants assimilate linguistically as fast or faster than previous generations of European immigrants. In addition, by the third generation, not only do most American Latinos not speak Spanish, but a significant fraction have also intermarried with members of other groups and no longer have a strong identity as Hispanic (Lopez et al., 2017). The perception that Latinos do not speak English is largely driven by the fact that new immigrants who do not yet speak English are continually arriving. The fact that Latinos overall have been successful at learning English does *not* negate the need to provide instruction in English when new immigrants arrive in school. English is necessary to succeed in U.S. schools, and students need to learn it as rapidly as possible on arrival. However, instead of framing the language issue in terms such as "these children may fail to learn English if we do not help them"—a frame that triggers the fears of people on the right—it may be possible to say, "These children will eventually learn English but we need to support them in learning as fast as possible so they do well in school." A subtle change in perspective may make a difference.

Latinos are also stigmatized in right-wing publications for doing low-wage labor. It may be possible to alter perceptions by changing the concept of "low wage," which also occurs in many articles on education, to "hardworking." For example, Latino youth begin working for wages earlier in life than their peers from other ethnic groups do, and they earn more wages while still in school (Echautegui, 2015). This can be framed as a sign of poverty and likely a failure to succeed academically (a trigger to the right) or as having the willingness to work hard and having high motivation and drive that can be channeled into academic success if young people are provided with the right opportunities. Instead of saying, "Latino youth tend to be disengaged from school and are at high risk of academic failure," one could say, "Latino youth are extremely hardworking and often work outside the home to help support their families. This drive can be channeled into academic success if they are given the right opportunities to make this possible."

In fact, most of the negative language used about Latino and other stigmatized immigrants can be turned around and seen in a more positive light. There are several reasons why this narrative can and should shift. In the following, I enumerate a few of the ways this is possible.

Many immigrant children also bring a strong work ethic and desire to succeed to their new country. Because many first-generation Latino immigrants do not attend college, this is at first hard to perceive. However, statistics show that Latino immigrant youth enter the workforce earlier, work harder than other youth, and earn more money. This shows that they have energy and drive. On many levels, they are highly oriented toward success. They merely do not see the means of putting this energy and drive into higher education. If this strong desire for success could be channeled toward education—both by teachers and schools with high expectations more than negative stereotypes and by programs making education more affordable and feeling more attainable to these immigrant youth—their already existing drive could lead to much higher levels of success.

Finally, it is possible to point to many Latinos who have achieved positions of prominence in the United States. Instead of saying, "We need to save Latinos from failure," we could point to well-known Latinos like Supreme Court Justice Sonia Sotomayor or Representatives Joaquin Castro or Alejandra Ocasio Cortez or Nina Vaca, who serves on the boards of three Fortune 500 companies. We could say, "We want to give our Latino students the best education possible to have more highly successful people like these."

While changing the discourse used to talk about Latino students sounds simple, sadly, that is not true. The way we have learned to ask for, and receive, money for programs benefiting immigrant children has depended mainly on calculi of failure. Unfortunately, visions of failure, high expectations, and hope tend to be incompatible.

This tradition of predicting failure to promote success is deeply embedded in our educational traditions. It is, for example, extremely difficult to obtain grant funding for programs targeted to Latino students without demonstrating "need," and need usually translates into a calculus of failure. As an example, the author of this chapter once obtained major grant funding for a limited two-way bilingual program in which Latino immigrants were seen as a benefit to the school. The funders denied access to the money until the grant was rewritten to frame the immigrants in a more deficit-oriented way.

Although these traditions of negative discourse are and will be highly difficult to change, both for structural (political and financial) reasons and because it is difficult to alter the way we are used to framing situations, it is highly important to try. If we are used to talking about certain students in terms of their probability of failure, it is difficult to simultaneously have high expectations for them and envision them as successes. All children need educators to expect success from them, but this need may be particularly strong for immigrant children whose families are escaping from difficult life circumstances and trying to build a better life. These trends will be very difficult to shift, but it is very important to try. We need to expect success from young Latino immigrants, and they need our high expectations. We also need to bolster their chances of success by framing them discursively in ways that are as likely as possible to foster that success.

References

American Federation of Teachers. (2019) *Closing the achievement gap: Focus on Latino students*. https://www.colorincolorado.org/article/closing-achievement-gap-focus-latino-students-0

Binder, J. (2018a, August 16). *The majority of foreign refugees arriving in the United States every year cannot speak English, even after they have lived in the US for five years*. Breitbart News. https://www.breitbart.com/politics/2018/08/16/majority-of-foreign-refugees-cant-speak-english-after-five-years-living-in-u-s/

Binder, J. (2018b, April 20). *New immigrants twice as likely to live in poverty as Americans*. Breitbart News. https://breitbart.com/politics/2018/04/20/study-new-immigrants-twice-as-likely-to-live-in-poverty-as-americans

Citrin, J., Lerman, A., Murakami, M., & Pearson, K. (2007) Testing Huntington: Is Hispanic immigration a threat to American Identity. *Perspectives on Politics*, 5(1), 31–48.

Devlin, K. (2018, August 6). *Most European students are learning a foreign language while Americans lag.* Pew Research Center. https://www.pewresearch.org/fact-tank/2018/08/06/most-european-students-are-learning-a-foreign-language-in-school-while-americans-lag/

Enchautegui, M. (2015, September 14). *Immigrant youth outcomes: Patterns by generations and race and ethnicity.* Urban Institute. https://www.urban.org/sites/default/files/publication/22991/413239-Immigrant-Youth-Outcomes-Patterns-by-Generation-and-Race-and-Ethnicity.PDF

Foucault, M. (1980) *Power/knowledge.* Pantheon Books.

Ingraham, C. (2018, June 19). *Two charts demolish the notion that immigrants illegally here commit more crime.* Washington Post. https://www.washingtonpost.com/news/wonk/wp/2018/06/19/two-charts-demolish-the-notion-that-immigrants-here-illegally-commit-more-crime/

Kövecses, Z. (2006) *Language, mind and culture: A practical introduction.* Oxford University Press.

Lakoff, G. (2002). *Moral politics: How liberals and conservatives think.* University of Chicago Press.

Lakoff, G., & Johnson, M. (2003). *Metaphors we live by.* University of Chicago Press. (Original work published 1980)

Lightfoot, T. (2001). *Education as literature: Tracing our metaphorical understandings of immigrant and language minority students* [Unpublished doctoral dissertation]. University of Wisconsin–Madison.

Lopez, M., Gonzalez-Barrera, P., & Lopez, G. (2017, December 20). *Hispanic identity fades across generations as immigrant connections fade away.* Pew Research Center, Hispanic Trends. https://www.pewreseqaqrch.org/hispanic/2017/12/20/hispanic-identity-fades-across-generations-as-immigrant-connections-fade-away

Mackey, W., & Von Nieda, B. (1977) *Bilingual schools for a bicultural community.* Newbury House Publishers.

May, C. (2016, June 1). *Legal and illegal immigration to US surges over past two years.* Breitbart News. https://www.breitbart.com/politics/2016/06/01/embargoed-5am-tomorrow-wednesday-legal-illegal-immigration-u-s-surges-past-two-years/

Natalicio, L., & Natalicio, D. (1969). The educational problems of atypical student groups: The native speakers of Spanish. *Urban Education, 4*(3), 262–272.

O'Brien, G. (2003). Indigestible food, conquering hordes and waste materials: Metaphors of immigrants and early immigration restriction debate in the United States. *Metaphor and Symbol, 18*(1), 33–47.

Pennycook, A. (2018) *Posthumanist applied linguistics.* Routledge.

Perez, S. & De la Rosa Salazar, D. (1997) Economic, labor force and social implications of Latino educational and populational trends. In A. Darder, R. Torres, & H. Gutierrez (Eds.), *Latinos and education: A critical reader* (pp. 45–79). Routledge.

Von Spakovsky, H. (2019, August 30). *Hans von Spakovsky: Crimes by immigrants widespread across US.* Fox News. https://www.foxnews.com/opinion/hans-von-spakovsky-crimes-by-illegal-immigrants-widespread-across-us-sanctuaries-shouldnt-shield-them

University of Haifa. (2011, February 11). *Bilinguals find it easier to learn a third language.* Science Daily. https://www.sciencedaily.com/releases/2011/02/110201110915.htm

CARE AND EDUCATION: PERFORMING JUST CHILDHOOD WORLDS

CHAPTER 7

Refusing Policymakers' Manufactured Crisis: Countering Conceptions of School Readiness

Christopher P. Brown, David P. Barry, and Da Hei Ku

THE CRISIS OF children not being ready to succeed in elementary school has been a key driver in the expansion of early childhood education (ECE) programs across the United States and the globe (Brown, 2008a; Pérez & Cannella, 2011; World Bank, 2018). The argument is that too many children, particularly children from low-income families, single-parent families, children of color, children of immigrants, and children who do not speak "White dialects of English" (Alim, 2005) enter school not ready to succeed academically (Gullo, 2018; Nxumalo & Adair, 2019). Thus, they and their families should enroll in early education programs so that they can get the head start they need to thrive in and out of school (Brown, 2010).

While such rhetoric has been used to advocate for the expansion of ECE in the United States since the introduction of kindergarten in the 1800s (Beatty, 1995; Dombkowski, 2001), it has only increased with the expansion of publicly funded intervention programs such as Head Start in the 1960s (Zigler & Styfo, 2010) and prekindergarten beginning in the 1980s (Rose, 2010). Adding to this crisis of school readiness was the emergence of policymakers' neoliberal reforms in the 1970s (Brown, 2009). By framing the issue of school readiness through conceptions of individualization, crisis, and recovery (Brown, 2015; Slater, 2015), policymakers and many early education advocates continue to fuel anxiety (De Lissovoy, 2018; Kane, 2016) around this issue while ignoring the historical debt (Ladson-Billings, 2006) and dominant White, Western European policies of colonization, slavery, and capitalism that led to and further amplify the current framing of this construct (Pérez, 2019; Soto & De Moed, 2011; Valencia, 1997).

Our goal in this chapter is to disrupt this dominant neoliberal framing that children's readiness for elementary school is in a state of crisis. To do that, we begin by examining how these risks for school readiness were put upon children and families through ECE policies in the United States and exacerbated by policymakers' neoliberal reforms. We then provide a brief summary of the conceptual and practical responses that emerged alongside these reforms and speak back to such deficit framings of children and families. We then connect this history to the current landscape of policymakers employing the crisis of school readiness to further enact their neoliberal reforms (De Lissovoy et al., 2015; Slater, 2015). We conclude with a discussion of potential opportunities for conceptual change and practical actions that could disrupt the dominant neoliberal framing of the crisis of school readiness.

The Problem of School Readiness and the Rise of Neoliberalism

In the United States, school readiness became a national policy problem with the implementation of Project Head Start in 1965 under the Economic Opportunity Act and the Elementary and Secondary Education Act, which was part of the Johnson administration's War on Poverty (Brown & Barry, 2019). This intervention program was designed to address what was seen as the root cause of poverty: the home environment (Gomez & Rendon, 2019). It did so by providing children from low-income families with a head start for school entry by teaching them a specific set of knowledge and skills and providing their families with training and governance opportunities within the program (Zigler & Styfo, 2010).

Johnson's policies, including Project Head Start, were unpopular among conservative politicians and business organizations (Apple, 2001; Tabb, 2003). As Harvey (2005) noted, "there was a growing sense among the U.S. upper classes that the antibusiness and anti-imperialist climate that had emerged toward the end of the 1960s had gone too far" (p. 30). To respond to these social programs, particular conservative groups, working with and through business organizations (e.g., the American Chamber of Commerce and the Business Roundtable), sought to maintain their privilege by establishing political think tanks (e.g., the Heritage Foundation) and supporting politicians (e.g., Nixon and Regan) to "demonstrate that what was good for business was good for America" (Harvey, 2005, p. 30). Working collectively through varied social, political, and institutional networks (e.g., Demas et al., 2003), these groups put forward a neoliberal vision of governance in which society is to be governed by "the laws of the market, free competition, private ownership, and profitability" (Apple, 2001, p. 30). Policymakers no longer sought "to govern through 'society' but through the regulated choices of individual citizens, now constructed as subjects of choices and aspirations to self-actualization and self-fulfillment" (N. Rose, 1996, p. 41). For citizens to attain such fulfillment, it is necessary for them to make choices that allow them to accrue the credentials and capital needed to participate successfully in the markets that define society (Lemke, 2001; N. Rose, 1996; Wright, 2012).

As Nikolas Rose (1999) pointed out, there is a "strange coupling" of power under neoliberalism (p. 276) in which, as Dahlberg and Moss (2005) noted, the "state remains strong despite appearing to dissolve" (p. 133). The revisions to Project Head Start in an increasingly neoliberal environment are good examples. The program was legislated in the 1960s in the United States for a range of reasons, both positive and negative, that included breaking what was then called the "cycle of poverty." Head Start began as a community-based, parent-governed early education and health care program functioning differently in diverse locations as determined by community members. However, in the increasingly more neoliberal environment, some legislators became concerned that community voices were too strong and that there should be legislatively controlled accountability for such investment. Consequently, studies like the Westinghouse Learning Corporation's (1969) evaluation were conducted. Results suggested that the cognitive gains (as defined by test scores) of students in the program quickly faded by second or third grade and raised concerns over the effectiveness of these government-funded programs (Cuban, 1998).

The strange coupling was further manifested in the Nixon administration's creation of the National Institute of Education, an attempt to ensure that the public programs the Johnson administration implemented provided a return on the investment the federal government made in education.[1] To maintain programs of some type for young children, this strange coupling had forced some members of the early education community to attempt to describe different returns on investment (not something that educators tended to practice). As examples, they argued that while increases in test scores might not be sustainable, students who participated in such programs were more successful academically and socially as they continued through school than were those students who did not receive these services (see as an example Schweinhart & Weikart, 1980). Even for those who might disagree with this form of capitalism that literally interprets human beings (and everything) as capital, the neoliberal argument could not be easily countered. As a result, the definitions for return on investments were thus expanded in the attempt to continue the program as a support for those children and their families.

These types of circumstances and actions reinforced the neoliberal belief that public funding must always provide a "return on investment" (e.g., Reynolds et al., 2002). Nobel laureate economist James Heckman (2000) even opened the Center for the Economics of Human Development using human capital theory, a perspective dominated by the work of Adam Smith and developed by Mincer (1958) and Becker (1964, 1975). Heckman's economic framing of ECE shifts the premise for public support from breaking the cycle of poverty for others to saving the taxpayer money. Of even greater concern for ECE is that the notion of investment also reinforces the neoliberal framing of early learning (Brown, 2007), including issues such as school readiness, around the conception of educators providing children with specific "inputs" so that children can attain particular "outputs" to move through the education system and accrue the capital needed to participate successfully in the markets that define society (Ball, 2007, p. 28).

A Brief Summary of Neoliberal Education Reforms in the United States

Since the Reagan era, there have been a series of neoliberal education reforms that extended the groundwork laid by the Nixon administration in seeking to dismantle public education systems across the United States and privatize the process of educating students (Brown, 2004). Examples of these reforms include the National Commission in Excellence on Education's publication of *A Nation at Risk* (1984); the Clinton administration's Goals 2000 legislation,[2] which made its first goal that every child in the United States would start school ready to learn (National Education Goals Panel, 1991); or George W. Bush's No Child Left Behind Act (NCLB; Harvey, 2008; Hursh, 2007). Across these reforms, policymakers have employed a theory of action (Argyris & Schon, 1974) that each of the stakeholders in the education system is to ensure that all students are taught the mandated knowledge and skills (i.e., content standards), are tested on their mastery of the content (i.e., performance standards), and reach the specified level of achievement they must attain on the tests (i.e., proficiency standards; O'Day, 2002). If students do not meet the proficiency standards, consequences, which are commonly referred to as "high stakes," can be put in place to hold students, their teachers, school, and/or district accountable. While these high-stakes assessments typically do not begin until the third grade, many states and school districts in the United States have put in place instructional expectations on ECE teachers and a series of assessment measures across the early grades to ensure children are on a trajectory for success by the time they take their state's high-stakes assessments (Brown, 2007, 2018).

Framing School Readiness as a Crisis

While each of these larger neoliberal education reforms positions public education within the United States as a failed government enterprise that must be reformed through markets, standardization, and accountability (Brown, 2009, 2015), the field of ECE becomes an increasingly important aspect in the "process of recovery" that serves to ready all children for the "neoliberal lifeworld" (Slater, 2015, p. 1), a lifeworld in which policymakers' "rhetoric of readiness and risk seduce" teachers, families, and children from notions of "subjecthood into markethood" (Sonu & Benson, 2016, p. 243).

"The process of recovery" is a necessary reaction to the crises/disasters policymakers either manufacture through their achievement tests (Berliner & Biddle, 1996) or create (Pérez & Cannella, 2011) through their "free-market ideology" (Klein, 2007a, p. 49) that disregards the impact of human behavior on the earth. This process allows policymakers and their allies "to expand sectors of potential profit accumulation" (see, as an example, Pérez & Cannella's (2011) critical analysis of the impact of disaster capitalism and neoliberal reform on New Orleans post-Katrina); by doing so they increase their "opportunities to actualize their" neoliberal "visions" of governance (Slater, 2015, p. 4).

Slater (2015), and others (e.g., Klein, 2007b), articulated that "recovery" within a neoliberal cycle "is ultimately an empty promise" (p. 12). Rather than address the "crises" with long-term solutions, policymakers' "neoliberal recovery merely stabilizes the circulation and accumulation of capital, and further entrenches the neoliberalization of spaces, capabilities, and potentialities" (Slater, 2015, p.12). Thus, within ECE, this "recovery" to the crisis of risks is emulated through such acts as early educators teaching all children, through technical activities, the same sets of knowledge and skills needed to succeed on academic achievement tests that begin in preschool (e.g., Brown, 2011; Lee, 2017) and in the larger world (Apple, 2001).

To survive in this market of academic achievement and accountability, early educators must become "salespeople for their own pedagogical performances" (De Lissovoy, 2014, p. 428) who can increase children's "readiness in the now" (Brown, 2013, p. 570). Educators are expected to demonstrate skills in increasing children's academic achievement and knowledge not only on a daily basis in their classrooms but also on the "barrage of assessments" that awaits them in the later grades (Brown & Barry, 2019, p. 25). By selling their ability to ready children for the now, early educators must push aside their culturally sustaining pedagogical practices that seek to create "humanizing" learning communities and disrupt the "legacies of educational inequities" (Cheruvu, 2020, p. 116).

Thus, by focusing on the readiness of individuals while destroying public institutions in the name of accountability, the theory of action (Argyris & Schon, 1974) under neoliberalism leads children, families, and the larger society to seek to "self-regulate themselves according to the rules of neoliberal governmentality" (Sonu & Benson, 2016, p. 232). These rules are framed as means of "recovery." The act of recovery within neoliberalism accomplishes two goals. First, any act of recovery (e.g., Pérez & Cannella, 2011) simultaneously fuels these crises in order "to expand sectors of potential profit accumulation" (Slater, 2015, p. 3); as Klein (2007a) noted, "once a market has been created, it needs to be protected" (p. 52). Second, the acts of recovery are framed through "neoliberal subjectivity," which suppress collective action and any "revolutionary potential" (Slater, 2015, p. 12).

For children and families in early learning settings, the crisis of school readiness is to be resolved by their participation in intervention programs or market-based solutions such as for-profit tutoring services that benefit "from parental uncertainties, confusion and unease caused by these public school reforms" (Aurini & Davies, 2004, p. 434). Thus, to refuse these policies (Gillborn, 2015; Slater, 2015) and counter such neoliberal logic is a daunting and almost impossible endeavor (De Lissovoy, 2014), particularly since policymakers continue to put in place an ever-evolving set of reforms that fuel the crisis of school readiness while simultaneously seeking to solve it (Brown & Lan, 2018).

The Current Crisis of School Readiness

Currently, the notion of crisis in children's readiness for elementary school is perpetuated by two 'types' of reforms that policymakers have and continue to fund: Quality Rating and Improvement Systems (QRIS), which focus on ECE programs, and Kindergarten Readiness Tests, which focus on individual children (Brown & Barry, 2019; Pérez & Cahill, 2016).[3] The rise of QRIS came out of the Obama administration's Race to the Top—Early Learning Challenge (RTT-ELC) Grants. The logic behind QRIS was to improve the 'quality' of ECE programs because researchers have consistently shown that high-quality early learning experiences can improve children's language, academic, and social skills (e.g., Burchinal et al., 2011). Yet a substantial number of children attending ECE programs in the United States do not have access to such programs (Gillispie, 2019). QRIS score ECE programs on a range of quality measures, which include such criteria as licensing compliance, staff qualifications, research-based curricula, teacher-to-child ratios, and assessment measures of children's varying developmental domains. These components are then converted into an overall rating of quality at the program level (Zellman & Fiene, 2012). This rating is designed to (a) inform families and the community about the 'quality' of specific ECE programs and (b) provide programs with information relevant to improving their score (i.e., 'quality') in relation to the items evaluated on the QRIS (Zellman & Fiene, 2012). However, these new accountability systems can dictate what early educators should do within their daily practices with young children even though the impact of these programs on children's academic and social development is mixed at best (e.g., Burchinal et al., 2011). In fact, several studies show no correlation between quality and improving children's academic and social readiness for school (Hong et al., 2015; Sabol & Pianta, 2015).

Similar to QRIS, there was an increased use of kindergarten entry assessments with the implementation of the federal government's RTT-ELC and the Enhanced Assessment Grants (Weisenfeld et al., 2020). However, Weisenfeld et al. (2020) noted that currently, 35 states and the District of Columbia implement some type of entry assessment; four states had an entry exam at one point and phased it out, and nine states do not implement such an assessment. Moreover, these exams were originally quite comprehensive and focused on children's physical, social, language, and cognitive development as well as their approaches to learning (see National Education Goals Panel, 1991), but they now primarily "focus on literacy" (Weisenfeld et al., 2020, p. 17).

Both sets of reforms demonstrate how the logic of neoliberal crisis and recovery (Slater, 2015) continues to impact the teaching opportunities for early educators and the learning experiences for children in a negative manner (e.g., Pérez & Cahill, 2016). Instead of focusing on the assets children and their families bring to early learning environments (Moll et al., 1992; Pérez & Saavedra, 2017; Swadener & Lubeck, 1995), these policies continue to push forward the appearance of "the school-as-factory model in a layer of slogans to give a field intellectual and economic legitimacy and a sense of neutrality" (Apple, 2004, p. 106), an education system that is to "solve large-scale economic problems through the production of future workers" (Pérez & Cahill, 2016, p. 23). However, these evaluation tools are espousing a standardized, narrow, universalist conception of school readiness and academic achievement (Brown & Lan, 2015) coupled with a monologic discourse of education in which "each successive stage of the system," be it early childhood or elementary education, is "to make clear to those in the stage below them what they expect and need from children when passed up to them" (Moss, 2012, p. 14).

This neoliberal construct of school readiness and the current systems of education within the US benefit some children and their families more than others (Brown & Lan, 2018). Neoliberal framing of school readiness creates a policy environment in which children and their families are blamed if they are not ready to enter the public education system and are often labeled as "at risk" or "not ready." These labels, as Apple (2004) explained, imposed by "hegemonic structures of dominant groups in American society ... have rather wide ethical, political, and social implications in that they may assist in sorting out individuals according to class, race, and sex quite early in life" (p. 140). Nxumalo (2019), using the work of Melamed (2015), added that the racial capitalism found within these reforms works "to shape subjectivities in service of individualist capitalist relations" (p. 169). These relations within capitalism, as well as within global North onto-epistemologies (Pérez & Saavedra, 2017), are focused on accumulation (De Lissovoy, 2019).

Along with an increasing racial and gender economic gap, policymakers' neoliberal conceptions of school readiness and schooling will tend to discriminate against children of color, children from low-income female-headed households, and an even great number of poor children and their families by labeling them "not ready" for school (Brown, 2008b; Nxumalo & Adair, 2019). Subsequently, these constructs ignore the institutional structures and systemic deficits that continue to repress those who fall outside the monied, male, white image of the ready child (Baldridge, 2014; Pérez, 2019; Valencia, 1997).

Policymakers' neoliberal reforms distract stakeholders from the systemic and structural issues related to socioeconomic level, race, and gender that contribute to children's readiness for or performance in school (Ladson-Billings, 2006), which include access to health care and a consistent/reliable source of food as well as the familial issues of employment, parental leave, and so on (Ma et al., 2016; Towne, 2017). These issues demonstrate the inequities present in current systems of schooling and further perpetuate inequities by "not only reflect[ing] but actually embody[ing] the interests in stratification, unequal power, certainty, and control" (Apple, 2004, p. 142) that continue to be reproduced in policymakers' reforms. For example, policies enforcing accountability measures on children, families, and other school stakeholders, such as NCLB, are, as Leonardo (2009) argued, "guided by an ideology of whiteness" that promotes color-blind racism and maintains white privilege (p. 135). In doing so, policymakers "overtly target[ed] improving four subgroups of student performance: minority children, students with disabilities, poor children, and English language learners" (Leonardo, 2009, p. 135). This masked "act of whiteness" (Leonardo, 2009, p. 127) perpetuates a façade of neutrality and fairness while at the same time "declar[ing] students of color failures under a presumed-to-be fair system" (p. 136).

Moving Forward

Historically, many within the field of early childhood education have responded to the manufactured crisis of school readiness (Berliner & Biddle, 1996) by reframing the rhetoric of readiness (Lakoff, 2004). For example, Swadener and Lubeck (1995) and many others (e.g., Iorio & Parnell, 2015; Miller, 2016) have and continue to advocate for focusing on the promise of children and families. Instead of seeing school readiness as a policy problem, it is "a pedagogical opportunity—an opening to something unpredictable brought about through a relational encounter that expands the space of the possible" (Evans, 2019, p. 73).

Such an understanding of school readiness requires that early educators recognize that all families want their children to succeed in school (Brown & Lan, 2018; Colegrove & Krause, 2017) and that they access the "funds of knowledge" they bring to the classroom (Moll et al., 1992). Moreover, education stakeholders must develop an awareness of how policymakers' neoliberal reforms narrow the understanding of achievement to a limited set of outcomes and a deficit-oriented perspective toward children and their families (Baldridge, 2014; Loh & Hu, 2014). Rather than allow schools to define the readiness of children for school, families should be empowered within this process; this would require a local assurance that school staff and administrators are ready to support the learning and development of all children they serve (Brown, 2010, 2021), and globally, policymakers are enacting reforms that fund policies that adequately fund the "social, personal, economic, and educational resources" required for all communities to flourish (Graue, 2006, p. 51).

While such actions can result in evolutionary change around the construct of school readiness in schools and in the larger policy world (e.g., California Assembly Bill-413[4]), much of the rhetoric and logic of policymakers' neoliberal reforms remains intact. Slater (2015, p. 16) contends that children, families, and educators must engage in a politics of refusal towards this cycle of crisis and recovery that exists within neoliberalism. To do that, De Lissovoy (2015) argues that we must become aware of the "contradiction ... within neoliberalism," the contradiction being "how can a doctrine that argues for equal access to competition and the stripping away of artificial and unfair protections within the marketplace be compatible with the systems privileging of some groups over others" (p. 54).

To illuminate such contradictions and speak back to policymakers' neoliberal reforms, critical ECE researchers such as Cannella and Viruru (2004), Pérez and Saavedra (2017), Souto-Manning (2018), and many others (e.g., Nxumalo & Adair, 2019) within ECE have made clear that dominant, so-called global North onto-epistemologies and methodological processes for change "have not made a difference with regard to the 'outcomes' for the most marginalised children" (Urban, 2015, p. 300). Thus, there needs to be a shift in conceptualizing schooling and early education in general toward multiplicities that include global South perspectives (Spivak, 1988), Indigenous points of view (Bhabha, 1994), and traditionally marginalized ways of thinking and understanding (Rivas, 2010). Doing so refuses to require children "to thrive in competition" or "learn capitalist ways that disregard their own humanity" (Soto & De Moed, 2011, p. 237)

Conceptually, such a shift decenters dominant thinking (Bhabha, 1994; Fregoso Bailón & De Lissovoy, 2019) and recognizes that "social injustices are based on cognitive injustice" (Santos, 2014,[5] p. 189). The construct of school readiness itself needs to be rethought (Brown et al., 2021). If not, as Nxumalo (2016) argued, the "erasures, displacements and exclusions that become normalized in everyday encounters" will remain intact (p. 643). Thus, rethinking school readiness requires "epistemological dialogues and debates" among early education stakeholders at both the policy and practical levels of early education so that the complex realities of children and families from a range of sociocultural identities are brought to the forefront (Santos, 2014, p. 189).

Politically, such change in a nation like the United States requires a complete restructuring, or even the elimination, of such discriminatory policies as QRIS and kindergarten entry exams (Pérez & Cahill, 2006), along with the redistribution of resources and restructuring of governing policies around conceptions of both "promise" (Swadener & Lubeck, 1995) and the brilliance of traditionally marginalized communities (Pérez & Saavedra, 2017; Viruru, 2001). Doing so could support local communities in revitalizing the practices of care and education around the funds of knowledge that exist among them (Moll et al., 1992). While local control is a foundational belief across many states within the United States (e.g., Brown, 2004, 2008b), as De Lissovoy (2015) and others (e.g., Slater, 2015) have pointed out, such policies are only sustained if they benefit the neoliberal agenda. Thus, systemic change also requires a naming of the specific power-oriented practices, places, and discourses that inhabit schools and the construct of school readiness (Brown, 2021; Nxumalo, 2016; Pérez, 2019). Furthermore, political awareness that the "differential impact and asymmetries of violence and harm" that result from the neoliberal framing of schooling are not an "effect" of the so-called crisis but are actually made possible as policymakers construct and impose neoliberal normative reforms (Grande, 2018, p. 169).

Tensions will arise from any such structural change that was to be implemented (Brown, 2008b; Nxumalo & Cedillo, 2017). Educational stakeholders at all levels of governance will have to commit to changes in a system that may disempower them and deny them access to privileges and resources they take for granted (Ladson-Billings, 2006).

Globally, the work of Ritchie and Rau (2010), Ritchie (2013), and Chan and Ritchie (2016) has demonstrated how kindergarten teachers in Aotearoa (New Zealand) employed the Indigenous pedagogies of care and affect to counter "the global technicist, corporatist exploitation of human and natural resources" (Ritchie, 2013, p. 403). Their actions led them to engage in pedagogical practices with their students that were "restorative of an ethic of biocentric relationality" (Ritchie, 2013, p. 404). Such work exemplifies how members of global South communities and others "trouble social issues and normative perceptions in a critically conscious manner" so that they can position themselves as "agents of change in their classrooms and beyond" (Souto-Manning, 2017, p. 96). This work counters the neoliberal logic of schooling and repositions the histories and tellings of Indigenous and marginalized peoples to the frontline of the curriculum (Fregoso Bailón & De Lissovoy, 2019; Lane, 2018). Such a shift opens up the construct of school readiness to "be different and unique to each setting and spatial location in relation to the unique power relations embedded within each space" (Eizadirad, 2019, p. 203).

In brief, these practical changes could "act as a counterweight to the hegemony of capitalist interests and ideas by protecting the frugal, compassionate, curious, and emotionally generous nature" of students and their families, and in doing so, such a pathway might attract members from a range of communities that seek out schools that are "mindful of, value, care for, and preserve the unique culture created by" students and their teachers (Butler et al., 2019, p. 12). Whatever practical changes might emerge from new pathways toward reconceptualizing school readiness can be easily used to reinforce the standardized, neoliberal image of the "ready student" (Yosso, 2002). Nevertheless, as De Lissovoy (2016) reminds us, "resistance means a belief in the possibility that the space of teaching might be governed by different meanings and purposes" (p. 359).

In sum, refusing the neoliberal framing of school readiness and rethinking schooling with/through perspectives found in local communities and/or traditionally marginalized understandings requires "a transformation in our knowledge, standpoint, and practices" (K. Brown, 2016, p. 173). As many have argued (e.g., Cannella & Manuelito, 2008; Pacini-Ketchabaw et al., 2011; Pérez, 2019; Viruru, 2005), taking on global South and other traditionally marginalized perspectives acknowledges the harm that capitalism and other Western perspectives have imposed on children from various groups, as well as families living in poverty; upends the current patriarchal, racial, capitalist framing of education; and offers an opportunity for systemic and practical change. Policymakers should (or be challenged by the electorate to) reevaluate policies that attempt to shroud privilege for particular groups in the neoliberal language of neutrality so that students and families can gain access to and participate in classrooms that reflect their sociocultural conceptions of the learning process (Apple, 2004; Brown, Barry & Ku, 2021; Leonardo, 2009).

Early educators and administrators should also reexamine policies and procedures within their programs/schools that require them to view young children as being "at risk" (e.g., Adair et al., 2018; Brown, 2021). Doing so could assist them in seeing the brilliance of their students (Pérez & Saavedra, 2017), the myriad sources from which their brilliance derives (Moll et al., 1992; Yosso, 2002), and how their brilliance can be expanded on through a range of instructional practices (Blaise & Nuttal, 2011; Paris & Alim, 2017) and programmatic policies that de-center privilege in all forms (De Lissovoy, 2015). As explored in this chapter, to do so will be a challenge. However, such reform could open up space for the creation of reimagined ECE learning spaces in which young children (alongside their families) have the chance to learn in ways that are relevant to their lives (I. Lee, 2016; Freire, 1974; Ladson-Billings, 1995) rather than be positioned as "at risk" or a "crisis" to be intervened upon (Brown et al., 2019; Nxumalo & Adair, 2019).

Notes

1. At this same time, Nixon vetoed the Comprehensive Child Development Act of 1971, which was to expand the federal government's funding of childcare and education while creating a framework for child services (Beaty, 1995, p. 198).
2. Goals 2000 developed out of the President H. W. Bush's failed America 2000 legislation, the reform proposal that emerged from the 1989 Education Summit in Charlottesville, Virginia.
3. See I-Fang Lee (2016) for a critique of international quality rating systems.
4. See http://leginfo.legislature.ca.gov/faces/billStatusClient.xhtml?bill_id=201920200AB413.
5. In using the work of Santos and many others who are advocating for the decolonization of education (e.g., Grande, 2018), we are not seeking to appropriate these decolonial or Indigenous knowledges (Tuck, 2009) that lead to us engage in a new form of colonization (Todd, 2016) or take on the role of being a transmitter of Indigenous knowledges (Calderon, 2014). Rather, we are simply pointing out possible "pathways" (Santos, 2018) that may or may not be taken up by those seeking to counter policymakers' neoliberal reforms.

References

Adair, J. K., Colegrove, K. S. S., & McManus, M. E. (2018). Troubling messages: Agency and learning in the early schooling experiences of children of Latinx immigrants. *Teachers College Record, 120*(6), 1–40.

Alim, H. S. (2005). Critical language awareness in the United States: Revisiting issues and revising pedagogies in a resegregated society. *Educational Researcher, 34*(7), 24–31.

Apple, M. W. (2001). *Educating the "right" way: Markets, standards, God, and inequality.* Routledge.

Apple, M. W. (2004). *Ideology and curriculum* (3rd ed.). RoutledgeFalmer

Argyris, C., & Schon, D. A. (1974). *Theories in practice: Increasing professionalism.* Jossey-Bass.

Aurini, J., & Davies, S. (2004). The transformation of private tutoring: Education in a franchise form. *Canadian Journal of Sociology/Cahiers canadiens de sociologie, 29*(3), 419–438.

Baldridge, B. J. (2014). Relocating the deficit: Reimagining Black youth in neoliberal times. *American Educational Research Journal, 51*(3), 440–472.

Ball, S. J. (2007). *Education PLC: Understanding private sector participation in public sector education*. Routledge.

Beatty, B. (1995). *Preschool education in America: The culture of young children from colonial era to the present*. Yale University Press.

Becker, G. S. (1964). *Human capital: Theoretical and empirical analysis: With special reference to education*. National Bureau of Economics Research.

Becker, G. S. (1975). *Human capital: A theoretical and empirical analysis, with special reference to education* (2nd ed.). National Bureau of Economic Research.

Berliner, D. C., & Biddle, B. J. (1996). The manufactured crisis: Myths, fraud, and the attack on America's public schools. *NASSP Bulletin, 80*(576), 119–121.

Bhabha, H. K. (1994). *The location of culture*. Routledge.

Blaise, M., & Nuttal, J. (2011). *Learning to teach in the early years classroom*. Oxford University Press.

Brown, C. P. (2004). Analyzing discourses of accountability through Wisconsin's 4th and 8th grade promotion statutes [Doctoral dissertation, University of Wisconsin-Madison]. ProQuest Dissertations and Theses Global.

Brown, C. P. (2007). Unpacking standards in early childhood education. *Teachers College Record, 109*(3), 635–668.

Brown, C. P. (2008a). Research in review: Advocating for policies to improve practice. *Young Children, 63*(4), 70–77.

Brown, C. P. (2008b). Examining how the student "determines" the success and/or failure of education reform. *International Critical Childhood Policy Studies, 1*(1), 1–27.

Brown, C. P. (2009). Being accountable for one's own governing: A case study of early educators responding to standards-based early childhood education reform. *Contemporary Issues in Early Childhood, 10*(1), 3–23.

Brown, C. P. (2010). Balancing the readiness equation in early childhood education reform. *Journal of Early Childhood Research, 8*(2), 133–160.

Brown, C. P. (2011). Searching for the norm in a system of absolutes: A case study of standards-based accountability reform in pre-kindergarten. *Early Education and Development, 22*(1), 151–177.

Brown, C. P. (2013). Reforming preschool to ready children for academic achievement: A case study of the impact of Pre-K reform on the issue of school readiness. *Early Education and Development, 24*(4), 554–573.

Brown, C. P. (2015). Conforming to reform: Teaching pre-kindergarten in a neoliberal early education system. *Journal of Early Childhood Research, 13*(3), 236–251.

Brown, C. P. (2018). School readiness. In L. Miller, C. L. Cameron, C. Dalli, & N. Barbour (Eds.), *The SAGE handbook of early childhood policy* (pp. 287–302). Sage Publications.

Brown, C. P. (2021). *Resisting the kinder-race: Restorying joy to early learning*. New York: Teachers College Press.

Brown, C. P., & Barry, D. P. (2019). Public policy and early childhood curriculum in the United States. In J. J. Mueller & N. File (Eds.), *Curriculum in early childhood: Re-examined, reclaimed, and renewed* (2nd ed., pp. 17–33). Routledge.

Brown, C. P., Barry, D., & Ku, D. (2021). How education stakeholders made sense of school readiness in and beyond kindergarten. *Journal of Research in Childhood Education, 35*(1), 122–142.

Brown, C. P., Englehardt, J., Ku, D., & Barry, D. P. (2019). "Where's the joy in the classroom?": Families' sensemaking of the changed kindergarten. *The Elementary School Journal, 120*(2), 319–346.

Brown, C. P., & Lan, Y. (2015). A qualitative metasynthesis comparing U.S. teachers' conceptions of school readiness prior to and after the implementation of NCLB. *Teaching and Teacher Education, 45*(1), 1–13.

Brown, C. P., & Lan, Y. C. (2018). Understanding families' conceptions of school readiness in the United States: A qualitative metasynthesis. *International Journal of Early Years Education, 26*(4), 403–421.

Brown, K. D. (2016). *After the "at-risk" label: Reorienting educational policy and practice*. Teachers College Press.

Burchinal, M., Kainz, K., & Cai, Y. (2011). How well do our measures of quality predict child outcomes? A meta-analysis and coordinated analysis of data from large-scale studies of early childhood settings. In M. Zaslow, I. Martinez-Beck, K. Tout, & T. Halle (Eds.), *Quality measurement in early childhood settings* (pp. 11–31). Paul H. Brookes.

Butler A., Teasley, C., & Sánchez-Blanco, C. (2019). A decolonial, intersectional approach to disrupting Whiteness, neoliberalism, and patriarchy in Western early childhood education and care. In P. Trifonas (Ed.) *Handbook of theory and research in cultural studies and education* (pp. 1–18). Springer International Handbooks of Education.

Calderon, D. (2014). Speaking back to Manifest Destinies: A land education-based approach to critical curriculum inquiry. *Environmental Education Research, 20*(1), 24–36.

Cannella, G. S., & Manuelito, K. D. (2008). Feminisms from unthought locations: Indigenous worldviews, marginalized feminisms, and revisioning an anticolonial social science. In N. K. Denzin, Y. S. Lincoln, & L. T. Smith (Eds.), *Handbook of critical and Indigenous methodologies* (pp. 45–59). Sage Publications.

Cannella, G. S., & Viruru, R. (2004). *Childhood and postcolonization: Power, education, and contemporary practice*. RoutledgeFalmer.

Chan, A., & Ritchie, J. (2016). Parents, participation, partnership: Problematising New Zealand early childhood education. *Contemporary Issues in Early Childhood, 17*(3), 289–303.

Cheruvu, R. (2019). Disrupting standardized early education through culturally sustaining pedagogies with young children. In F. Nxumalo & C. P. Brown (Eds.), *Disrupting and countering deficits in early childhood education and care* (pp. 103–118). Routledge.

Colegrove, K. S. S., & Krause, G. (2017). "Lo hacen tan complicado": Bridging the perspectives and expectations of mathematics instruction of Latino immigrant parents. *Bilingual Research Journal, 40*(2), 187–204.

Cuban, L. (1998). How schools change reforms: Redefining reform success and failure. *Teachers College Record, 99*(3), 453–477.

Dahlberg, G., & Moss, P. (2005). *Ethics and politics in early childhood education*. RoutledgeFalmer.

De Lissovoy, N. (2014). Pedagogy of the impossible: Neoliberalism and the ideology of accountability. *Policy Futures in Education, 11*(4), 423–435.

De Lissovoy, N. (2015). Neoliberalism and the contradictions of freedom: Ideology, subjectivity, and critical pedagogy. *Texas Education Review, 3*(2), 44–54.

De Lissovoy, N. (2016). Race, reason and reasonableness: Toward an "unreasonable" pedagogy. *Educational Studies, 52*(4), 346–362.

De Lissovoy, N. (2018). Pedagogy of the anxious: Rethinking critical pedagogy in the context of neoliberal autonomy and responsibilization. *Journal of Education Policy, 33*(2), 187–205.

De Lissovoy, N. (2019). Decoloniality as inversion: Decentering the West in emancipatory theory and pedagogy. *Globalisation, Societies, and Education, 17*(4), 419–431.

De Lissovoy, N., Means, A. J., & Saltman, K. J. (2015). *Toward a new common school movement*. Routledge.

Demas, E., Cannella, G., & Rivas, A. (2003). Conservative foundations and the construction of public regulatory curriculum: Or methods that use poor children to legislatively reinscribe dominant power. *Journal of Curriculum Theorizing, 19*(3), 107–123.

Dombkowski, K. (2001). Will the real kindergarten please stand up?: Defining and redefining the twentieth-century US kindergarten. *History of Education, 30*(6), 527–545.

Eizadirad, A. (2019). *Decolonizing educational assessment: Ontario elementary students and the EQAO*. Palgrave Macmillan.

Evans, K. (2016). Beyond a logic of quality: Opening space for material-discursive practices of 'readiness' in early years education. *Contemporary Issues in Early Childhood, 17*(1), 65–77.

Fregoso Bailón, R. O., & De Lissovoy, N. (2019). Against coloniality: Toward an epistemically insurgent curriculum. *Policy Futures in Education 17*(3), 355–369.

Freire, P. (1974). *Pedagogy of the oppressed* (M. B. Ramos, Trans.). Seabury Press.

Gillborn, D. (2015). Intersectionality, critical race theory, and the primacy of racism: Race, class, gender, and disability in education. *Qualitative Inquiry, 21*, 277–287.

Gillispie, C. (2019). *Young learners, missed opportunities: Ensuring that Black and Latino children have access to high-quality state-funded preschool*. Education Trust.

Gomez, R. E., & Rendon, T. (2019). Early childhood policy and its impact on the field: Historical and contemporary perspectives. In C. P. Brown, M. B. McMullen, & N. File (Eds.), *The Wiley handbook of early childhood care and education* (pp. 493–514). Wiley Blackwell.

Grande, S. (2018). Aging, precarity, and the struggle for Indigenous elsewhere. *International Journal of Qualitative Studies in Education, 31*(3), 168–176.

Graue, M. E. (2006). The answer is readiness – now what is the question? *Early Education and Development, 17*(1), 43–56.

Gullo, D. F. (2018). A structural model of early indicators of school readiness among children of poverty. *Journal of Children and Poverty, 24*(1), 3–24

Harvey, D. (2005). *A brief history of neoliberalism*. Oxford University Press.

Heckman, J. J. (2000). Policies to foster human capital. *Research in Economics, 54*(1), 3–56.

Hong, S. L. S., Howes, C., Marcella, J., Zucker, E., & Huang, Y. (2015). Quality rating and improvement systems: Validation of a local implementation in LA County and children's school-readiness. *Early Childhood Research Quarterly, 30*(Pt. B), 227–240.

Hursh, D. (2007). Assessing No Child Left Behind and the rise of neoliberal education policies. *American Educational Research Journal, 44*(3), 493–518.

Iorio, J. M., & Parnell, W. (2015). *Rethinking readiness in early childhood education: Implications for policy and practice*. Springer.

Kane, N. (2016). The play-learning binary: US parents' perceptions on preschool play in a neoliberal age. *Children & Society, 30*(4), 290–301.

Klein, N. (2007a, October). Disaster capitalism. *Harper's Magazine, 315*, 47–58.

Klein, N. (2007b). *The shock doctrine: The rise of disaster capitalism*. Macmillan.

Ladson-Billings, G. (1995). Toward a theory of culturally relevant pedagogy. *American Educational Research Journal, 32*(3), 465–491.

Ladson-Billings, G. (2006). From the achievement gap to the education debt: Understanding achievement in US schools. *Educational Researcher, 35*(7), 3–12.

Lakoff, G. (2004). *Don't think of an elephant: Progressive values and the framing wars—A progressive guide to action*. Chelsea Green Publishing.

Lane, T. M. (2018). The frontline of refusal: Indigenous women warriors of standing rock, *International Journal of Qualitative Studies in Education, 31*(3), 197–214.

Lee. I. F. (2016). The dangers of neoliberal imaginary of quality: The making of early childhood education and care as a service industry. In G. S. Cannella, M. S. Pérez, & I. F. Lee (Eds.), *Critical examinations in quality in early education and care: Regulation, disqualification, and erasure* (pp. 105–121). Peter Lang.

Lee, K. (2017). Making the body ready for school: ADHD and early schooling in the age of accountability. *Teachers College Record, 119*, 1–38.

Lemke, T. (2001). "The birth of bio-politics": Michel Foucault's lecture at the Collège de France on neo-liberal governmentality. *Economy and Society, 30*(2), 190–207.

Leonardo, Z. (2009). *Race, Whiteness, and education*. Taylor & Francis.

Loh, J., & Hu, G. (2014). Subdued by the system: neoliberalism and the beginning teacher. *Teaching and Teacher Education, 41*(1), 14–21.

Ma, X., Liese, A. D., Bell, B. A., Martini, L., Hibbert, J., Draper, C., Burke, M. P. & Jones, S. J. (2016). Perceived and geographic food access and food security status among households with children. *Public Health Nutrition, 19*(15), 2781–2788.

Melamed, J. (2015). Racial capitalism. *Critical Ethnic Studies, 1*(1), 76–85.

Miller, L. L. (2016). Power and the framing of quality discourses in early childhood education and care: A case study of Arizona's Proposition 2013. In G. S. Cannella, M. S. Pérez, & I. F. Lee (Eds.), *Critical examinations in quality in early education and care: Regulation, disqualification, and erasure* (pp. 27–40). Peter Lang.

Mincer, J. (1958). Investment in human capital and personal income distribution. *Journal of Political Economy, 66*(4), 281–302.

Moll, L. C., Amanti, C., Neff, D., & González, N. (1992). Funds of knowledge for teaching: Using a qualitative approach to connect homes and classrooms. *Theory Into Practice, 31*(2), 132–141.

Moss, P. (2012). *Early childhood and compulsory education: Reconceptualising the relationship*. Routledge.

National Commission on Excellence in Education. (1984). *A nation at risk: The full account*. USA Research.

National Education Goals Panel. (1991). Goal 1 Technical Planning Group Report on School Readiness. NEGP. https://govinfo.library.unt.edu/negp/reports/goalsrep.pdf

Nxumalo, F. (2016). Towards 'refiguring presences' as an anti-colonial orientation to research in early childhood studies. *International Journal of Qualitative Studies in Education, 29*(5), 640–654.

Nxumalo, F. (2019). Disrupting racial capitalist formations in early childhood education. In F. Nxumalo & C. P. Brown (Eds.), *Disrupting and countering deficits in early childhood education* (pp. 164–178). Routledge.

Nxumalo, F., & Adair, J. K. (2019). Social justice and equity in early childhood education. In C. P. Brown, M. B. McMullen, & N. File (Eds.), *The Wiley handbook of early childhood care and education* (pp. 661–682). Wiley Blackwell.

Nxumalo, F., & Cedillo, S. (2017). Decolonizing place in early childhood studies: Thinking with Indigenous onto-epistemologies and Black feminist geographies. *Global Studies of Childhood, 7*(2), 99–112.

O'Day, J. A. (2002). Complexity, accountability, and school improvement. *Harvard Educational Review, 72*(3), 293–329.

Pacini-Ketchabaw, V., Nxumalo, F., & Rowan, C. (2011). Nomadic research practices in early childhood: Interrupting racisms and colonialisms. *Reconceptualizing Educational Research Methodology, 2*(1), 19–33.

Paris, D., & Alim, H. S. (Eds.). (2017). *Culturally sustaining pedagogies: Teaching and learning for justice in a changing world.* Teachers College Press.

Pérez, M. S. (2019). Dismantling racialized discourses in early childhood education and care: A revolution towards reframing the field. In F. Nxumalo & C. P. Brown (Eds.), *Disrupting and countering deficits in early childhood education* (pp. 20–36). Routledge.

Pérez, M. S., & Cahill, B. (2016). "Readiness" as central to the (re)production of quality discourses in the United States. In G. S. Cannella, M. S. Pérez, & I. F. Lee (Eds.), *Critical examinations in quality in early education and care: Regulation, disqualification, and erasure* (pp. 11–25). Peter Lang.

Pérez, M. S., & Cannella, G. S. (2011). Disaster capitalism as neoliberal instrument for the construction of early childhood education/care policy: Charter schools in post-Katrina New Orleans. *International Critical Childhood Policy Studies, 4*(1), 47–68.

Pérez, M. S., & Saavedra, C. M. (2017). A call for onto-epistemological diversity in early childhood education and care: Centering global South conceptualizations of childhood/s. *Review of Research in Education, 41*(1), 1–29.

Reynolds, A. J., Temple, J. A., Robertson, D. L., & Mann, E. A. (2002). Age 21 cost-benefit analysis of the Title I Chicago child-parent centers. *Educational Evaluation and Policy Analysis, 24*(4), 267–303.

Ritchie, J. (2013). Indigenous onto-epistemologies and pedagogies of care and affect in Aotearoa. *Global Studies of Childhood, 3*(4), 395–406.

Ritchie, J., & Rau, C. (2010). Kia mau ki te wairuatanga: Countercolonial narratives of early childhood education in Aotearoa. In G. S. Cannella & L. D. Soto (Eds.), *Childhoods: A handbook* (pp. 355–373). Peter Lang.

Rivas, A. (2010). Modern research discourses constructing the postcolonial subjectivity of (Mexican) American children. In G. D. Cannella & L. D. Soto (Eds.), *Childhoods: A handbook* (pp. 245–264). Peter Lang.

Rose, E. (2010). *The promise of preschool: From Head Start to universal pre-kindergarten.* Oxford University Press.

Rose, N. (1996). Governing "advanced" liberal democracies. In A. Barry, T. Osborne, & N. Rose (Eds.), *Foucault and political reason: Liberalism, neo-liberalism, and rationalities of government* (pp. 37–64). University of Chicago Press.

Rose, N. (1999). *Powers of freedom: Reframing political thought.* Cambridge University Press.

Sabol, T. J., & Pianta, R. C. (2012). Patterns of school readiness forecast achievement and socioemotional development at the end of elementary school. *Child Development, 83*(1), 282–299.

Santos, B. d. S. (2014). *Epistemologies of the South: Justice against epistemicide.* Routledge.

Santos, B. d. S. (2018). *The end of the cognitive empire: The coming of age of epistemologies of the South.* Duke University Press.

Schweinhart, L. J., & Weikart, D. P. (1980). *Young children grow up: The effects of the Perry Preschool Program on youths through age 15* (Monographs of the High/Scope Educational Research Foundation 7). High/Scope Education Research Foundation.

Slater, G. B. (2015). Education as recovery: Neoliberalism, school reform, and the politics of crisis. *Journal of Education Policy, 30*(1), 1–20.

Sonu, D., & Benson, J. (2016). The quasi-human child: How normative conceptions of childhood enabled neoliberal school reform in the United States. *Curriculum Inquiry, 46*(3), 230–247.

Soto, L. D., & De Moed, S. T. (2011). Toward 'our ways of knowing' in the age of standardization. *Contemporary Issues in Early Childhood, 12*(4), 327–331.

Souto-Manning, M. (2018). Disrupting Eurocentric epistemologies: Re-mediating transitions to centre intersectionally-minoritised immigrant children, families and communities. *European Journal of Education, 53*(4), 456–468.

Spivak, G. C. (1988). Can the subaltern speak? In C. Nelson & L. Grossberg (Eds.), *Marxism and the interpretation of culture* (pp. 280–316). University of Illinois Press.

Swadener, B. B., & Lubeck, S. (Eds.). (1995). *Children and families "at promise": Deconstructing the discourse of risk.* SUNY Press.

Tabb, W. K. (2003). After neoliberalism? *Monthly Review, 55*(2), 25–34.

Todd, Z. (2016). An Indigenous feminist's take on the ontological turn: "Ontology" is just another word for colonialism. *Journal of Historical Sociology, 29*(1), 4–22.

Towne, S. D., Jr. (2017). Socioeconomic, geospatial, and geopolitical disparities in access to health care in the US 2011–2015. *International Journal of Environmental Research and Public Health, 14*(6), 573.

Tuck, E. (2009). Suspending damage: A letter to communities. *Harvard Educational Review, 79*(3), 409–427.

Urban, M. (2015). From 'closing the gap' to an ethics of affirmation: Reconceptualising the role of early childhood services in times of uncertainty. *European Journal of Education, 50*(3), 293–306.

Valencia, R. R. (1997). *The evolution of deficit thinking: Educational thought and practices.* Routledge.

Viruru, R. (2001). *Early childhood education: Postcolonial perspectives from India.* Sage Publications.

Viruru, R. (2005). The impact of postcolonial theory on early childhood education. *Journal of Education, 35*(1), 7–30.

Weisenfeld, G. G., Garver, K., & Hodges, K. (2020). Federal and state efforts in the implementation of kindergarten entry assessments (2011–2018). *Early Education and Development.* Advanced online publication. doi:10.1080/10409289.2020.1720481

Westinghouse Learning Corporation. (1969). *The impact of Head Start: An evaluation of the effects of Head Start on children's cognition and affective development* (ED036321). ERIC. https://eric.ed.gov/?id=ED036321

World Bank. (2018). *World development report 2018: Learning to realize education's promise.*

Wright, A. (2012). Fantasies of empowerment: Mapping neoliberal discourse in the coalition government's schools policy. *Journal of Education Policy, 27*(3), 279–294.

Yosso, T. J. (2002). Toward a critical race curriculum. *Equity & Excellence in Education, 35*(2), 93–107.

Zellman, G. L., & Fiene, R. (2012). *Validation of quality rating and improvement systems for early care and education and school-age care* (Research-to-Policy, Research-to-Practice Brief OPRE 2012-29). Office of Planning, Research and Evaluation, Administration for Children and Families, U.S. Department of Health and Human Services.

Zigler, E., & Styfo, S. J. (2010). *The hidden history of Head Start.* Oxford University Press.

CHAPTER 8

Politics of Childhoods: Paradoxical Moments of Be(com)ing

I-Fang Lee

Childhood: The period of someone's life when they are a child: 'she had a happy childhood'.

—CHILDHOOD (N.D.)

CHILDHOODS IN CONTEMPORARY times are shaped by multiple trajectories of cultural, educational, socio-political, economic, and regional/global climatic changes. Today, children's lifeworlds—their living and learning experiences across multiple socio-cultural settings and networks—are exposed to the full impacts and effects of the COVID-19 global pandemic. Examples of experiencing the global in the local and the local in the global for the formation of "glocal" can be seen across every domain of children's lives. Situated within particular glocal socio-historical events and structural conditions, children today are experiencing different types of childhoods in comparison to their (grand)parents. The landscapes of children's lifeworlds are not only being (re)produced by but are also (re)producing (new) dominant cultural discourses, political-economic reasoning, educational practices, and social policies to perpetuate a dangerous politics of childhoods with a universal experience of childhood.

In this chapter, I grapple with several critical analytical concepts as analytical tools to create a new toolbox to dismantle the dominant and universal construction of children. Coming from a critical perspective with a post-structural sensibility, I seek to reconceptualize, unpack, deconstruct, and reflect on how a dominant Western-centric construction of childhood has been at work to prescribe normality and govern a restrictive way of be(com)ing for children. I position my analysis and discussion within the networks of global and local circulations of discourses with both linear and non-linear ways of understanding time–space–matter to investigate the socio-political constructions of contemporary childhoods. I argue that the concept of *childhood* should be de/reconstructed by recognizing and acknowledging *our* multiple histories and realities, diverse socio-cultural perspectives, and competing socio-political standpoints if we desire to re(con)figure a better social imaginary towards the formation of a more sustainable, just, and inclusive future for all.

The analysis and discussion in this chapter are organized into three major sections. In the first section, I begin by grappling with the analytical tools from the paradigms of poststructuralism and posthumanism to disrupt a simplified, narrowed, and biased construction of childhood. This onto-epistemological positioning enables me to map as well as to untangle the messy knots of multiple dominating systems of reasoning that contribute to the intelligibility and desirability of a single narrative of childhood. In the second section, I highlight several dis/connections of glocal socio-cultural events across the East Asian geopolitical spaces in Taiwan and Hong Kong to discuss how politics of childhoods are constructed while foregrounding the landscapes of the children's lifeworlds in the paradoxes of nationalism and political differences. Connected and situated within my specific socio-cultural and historical localities of networks for work and life across three decades of multicultural experiences, this mapping of children's lifeworlds is based on my socio-cultural and socio-political observations of the contexts to elucidate what it means to be children belonging to Generation Z and Generation Alpha/α in East Asian geopolitical spaces.[1] Additionally, as there is no escape from the widening scope and effects of the global pandemic, I place my mapping of children's lifeworlds within the backdrop of how the global crisis of COVID-19 has exacerbated issues regarding inequity and injustice in childhood while interjecting and acknowledging signs of hope to enable us to challenge as well as to rethink ways of dismantling forms of systematic discrimination and everyday socio-cultural practices of "othering." In the third section, I highlight and problematize multiple threads of socio-cultural discourses that have contributed to the landscapes of children's lifeworlds.

Throughout this chapter, my critical discussions are intended to unsettle the dangerous framing of what an ideal childhood should look like in an effort to carve out an alternative but critical space in which to reconceptualize a more just and inclusive future for all. I assert that it is important to critically reflect on how a narrowed narrative about the child and their ideal childhood has been dangerously at work to perpetuate a classed image of the child/family and to inscribe a popular but problematic socio-cultural imaginary of an "ultimate stage of development" for all children.

Onto-Epistemological Positioning: Creating a New Analytical Toolbox

In this section, I grapple with a mixture of analytical tools to create a new analytical toolbox, placing my onto-epistemological positioning within the paradigms of post-structuralism and posthumanism. This toolbox (re)shapes the ways in which I come to understand and problematize the making of the child and childhoods in contemporary times. Echoing the call for onto-epistemological diversity (see Pérez & Saavedra, 2017), in this chapter, I deploy the following analytical concepts, including Deleuze and Guattari's (1987) notion of *rhizome* and Karen Barad's notion of *timespacemattering* to shape my critical discussion as well as to challenge the conventional ways of understanding children and their childhoods.

A Rhizomatic Childhood: A Philosophical Shift Towards Deleuzoguattarian Thoughts

Deleuze and Guattari's (1987) analytical concept of the *rhizome* has worked to steer me away from being trapped within conventional theories and methods for understanding the making of the child and childhood. This concept of the rhizome has interrupted the typical ways of thinking and talking about the child and childhood in a linear trajectory with hierarchical conceptions about learning, development and progress. Embedded within the dominance of global capitalism and the popular logic of neoliberal reasoning, a common contemporary phenomenon for thinking and talking about the child and childhood has been dangerously centred on the ideas of competition or the race to reach the next desirable state/milestone "to be." For example, in the race to achieve better educational and developmental outcomes, whether it is national or international, development and learning theories inscribe a predictable linear trajectory to reach or to achieve desirable (or better) outcomes while a singular truth about the future competitive economic market is implied.[2]

The concept of the rhizome, as introduced, elaborated and summarized by Deleuze and Guattari (1987):

> Unlike trees or their roots, the rhizome connects any points to any other point, and its traits are not necessarily linked to traits of the same nature; it brings into play very different regimes of signs, and even nonsign states.... It is composed not of units but of dimensions, or rather directions in motion. It has neither beginning nor end, but always a middle (*milieu*) from which it grows and which it overspills. It constitutes linear multiplicities with *n* dimensions having neither subject nor object, which can be laid out on a plane of consistency, and from

> which the One is always subtracted ($n - 1$). When a multiplicity of this kind changes dimension, it necessarily changes in nature as well, undergoes a metamorphosis. Unlike a structure, which is defined by a set of points and positions, with binary relations between the points and biunivocal relationships between the positions, the rhizome is made only of lines: lines of segmentarity and stratification as its dimensions, and the line of flight or deterritorialization as the maximum dimension after which the multiplicity undergoes metamorphosis, changes in nature.... The rhizome is an antigenealogy. It is a short-term memory, or antimemory. The rhizome operates by variation, expansion, conquest, capture, offshoots. Unlike the graphic arts, drawing, or photography, unlike tracings, the rhizome pertains to a map that must be produced, constructed, a map that is always detachable, connectable, reversible, modifiable, and has multiple entryways and exits and its own lines of flight. (p. 21)

Grappling with the concept of the rhizome enables me to reconceptualize the making of the child and childhood beyond a fixed structure that prescribes norms of developmental milestones or indicators for achieving best outcomes across different stages. Applying this concept of the rhizome in the context of learning and development, each child—as an organic being—in the process of learning and developing across different lifeworlds or socio-cultural settings is always transforming and transformative in an ongoing and never-ending process of metamorphosis. In other words, every child is "growing," and the process of growth is never ending, without an imagined "ultimate" developed stage. Therefore, learning outcomes, as much as they have been rationalized to be measurable and quantifiable, should not be understood as linear progress to indicate and imply the "best" or "ultimate" stage(s) of development to classify or sort any children according to their performances or states of development.

In this Deleuzoguattarian conceptual framework, the child is always in the middle of becoming. Therefore, the landscape of childhood is rhizomatic, without a beginning and an end point, as segments or parts of lifeworlds have situated socio-cultural contexts/meanings. The "category" of childhood is not a stage of development in a linear plan of human development. The lifetime trajectory of development and progress should not be conceptualized as a single narrative line from childhood to adulthood. This reconceptualization of the child and childhood has allowed my rethinking to work against the flow of a plethora of conventional modern childhood studies in which the desirable and projected norms of learning outcomes are quantifiable and measurable to determine future success.

A Deleuzoguattarian conceptual framework enables me to see the concept of childhood as a rhizomatic mapping in which multiple lines of dis/connecting thoughts are representing an ensemble of a particular socio-cultural imaginary to inscribe the child and the child to be. The landscape of childhoods and children's lifeworlds are fluid, mapping without a beginning or an ending, that's filled with lines of discourses and events.

Therefore, the concept of a rhizomatic childhood opens up new discursive spaces to interject critical discussions about the politics of childhoods in which the "ideal" child or "best" ways of caring/educating the child have been paradoxically prescribed and perpetuated in contemporary times across geopolitical spaces.

Playing with Space–Time–Matter: Childhood as In/visible Entanglements

Paying critical attention to the nuanced and inter- and intra-connectiveness of time, space, and matter, Karen Barad's theoretical and conceptual framework of the concept of *spacetimemattering* enables me to challenge the limitation of using a logic of dualism to understand childhood. In an interview by Juelskjær and Schwennesen (2012), Karen Barad elaborated her innovative thinking by posing questions about the dis/continuity of inter- and intra-relations of objects, events, and discourses to put forward an argument against a binary logic of reasoning. This view requires a different onto-epistemological home, for it challenges us to rethink the binary and dualistic construction of the child and childhood in relation to space–time–matter. Explaining her theoretical thinking of spacetimemattering, Karen Barad elucidates that everything is entangled together in a messy entanglement as a cartography without a clear cut for a beginning or an end for borders. As shared in an interview, Karen Barad asserts:

> In performing the labor of tracing the entanglements, of making connections visible, you're making our obligations and debts visible, as part of what it might mean to reconfigure relations of spacetimemattering. So spacetimemattering can be reconfigured in a way that reopens the past, in fact it happens all the time whether or not it's something that we directly observe under specific experimental conditions. But what it says then is that what is at issue is not the *erasure of events* but *reconfigurings of spacetimemattering*. (Juelskjær & Schwennesen, 2012, p. 20, italics in the original)

Building on this conception of spacetimemattering, I see the mapping of the past, present, and future for the conception of childhood should not be restricted with a logic of a linear timeline. Rather, the concept of childhood could be thought of as a cartography of a messy entanglement in which the present embodies the hybrid of the memories from the past and the desires and fears about the future. Indeed, fragmented or biased memories about the past and the present are coexisting in the present moments to construct contemporary phenomena. In Barad's onto-epistemological harbour, there is no "return" to the good old days just as the desirable better future can be an illusion. Barad (2014) has elaborated:

> The past is not present. 'Past' and 'future' are iteratively reconfigured and enfolded through the world's ongoing intra-activity.... Phenomena are not located in space and time; rather *phenomena are material entanglements enfolded and threaded through the spacetimemattering of the universe*.... Every gesture, every word involves our past, present, and future.... Time can't be fixed. The past is never closed, never finished once and for all, but there is no taking it back, setting time aright, putting the world back on its axis. There is no erasure finally. The trace of all reconfigurings is written into the enfolded materialisations of what was/is/to-come. (pp. 182–183, italics in the original)

Grappling with Karen Barad's fluid concept of spacetimemattering has led me to re-conceptualize the making of the child and childhood as entanglements of socio-historical events, inter- and intra-actions of multiple discourses as well as trajectories of tensions. What's important about seeing the child and childhoods as entanglements through the concept of spacetimemattering is to make the invisible visible so we can challenge the current status of childhoods with ethical considerations for a more inclusive and just world. Aligning with Barad's ethico-epistem-ontology of agential realism, which denotes that "phenomena do not occur at some particular moment in time; phenomena are specific ongoing reconfigurings of spacetimemattering" (Juelskjær & Schwennesen, p. 12), it helps me to think about the concept of childhood as never-ending and constantly enmeshed within the phenomena of socio-cultural and historical events. The making of the child and the making of childhoods are co-constructed through countless inter- and intra-actions. This view of childhood as entangled and ongoing phenomena enables me to pose critical questions such as, How are particular socio-cultural values and expectations made in/visible, and why? and What constitutes the making of a normal child or who is (or performs like) a good student? Through these questions, it becomes possible to unsettle/unpack what has been deemed and constructed as the *new truth* to bring forth a much-needed discussion on issues relating to the politics of childhoods.

In the making of the child and childhood, social and educational justice issues relating to diversity and inclusion in classrooms/schools have been dangerously (re)configured as *personal/family choices* and *individual responsibility*. To avoid dualism and the binary construction of categories, such as good versus bad, normal versus abnormal, and a simple logic of causality with a narrowed and restrictive way to understand the child and childhood, I need a new toolbox—a new analytical toolbox with flexible and fluid analytical concepts to reshape my onto-epistemology. A Deleuzoguattarian concept of the rhizome and Barad's theoretical concept of spacetimemattering have worked to allow me to pursue multiple rethinkings of what a "good" child/student should look like. Through this different analytical toolbox, I shift to pay nuanced attention to the multiplicity of children's different lived experiences of childhoods and studenthoods in the East Asian contexts to unpack the ongoing challenges of education equality and equity (see Lee & Yelland, 2017, for one example in Hong Kong).

Crafting the Landscape for Childhood: Lifeworlds in the 21st Century

Mapping the socio-historical events in which multiple lines of flight such as political rhetoric, social and educational policies, natural/environmental issues, and the COVID-19 pandemic enables me to critically examine the interplays of power/knowledge in relation to the making of rhizomatic childhoods. I ponder questions such as, How have contemporary childhoods been re(con)figured as multiple sociopolitical events occupying every channel of our daily attention in the landscape of rhizomatic childhoods? What does it look like to be a child growing up in this time within the current spacetimemattering entanglement? What's the glocal politics of childhoods and how have macro and micro politics (re)shaped the making of the child?

While recognizing the conventional definition of (early) childhood as being from birth to 8 years old, I turn to a broader definition and wider view by counting from birth to 18 years old as childhood (e.g., see United Nations, 1989, or UNICEF, n.d.). This extended view of the child and childhood allows for a more comprehensive and fluid understanding of children's living and learning experiences by expanding discussions from early childhood learning environments to K–12 school settings. For the purpose of analysis and discussion, I work between a global (macro) and local (micro) mapping of the landscapes and socio-political circumstances of contemporary childhoods to highlight how the socio-political events and glocal living and learning conditions are scaffolding the intelligibility and desirability of the ideal child and childhood(s) in the 21st century.

Understanding the Lifeworlds of Gen Z and Gen α

Who are today's children and how are they different from previous generations of children? Through a populational reasoning within a positivist research paradigm, people are often categorized and classified into age cohorts as demographic groups (Dolot, 2018; Seemiller & Grace, 2017; Shatto & Erwin, 2016). In this section of the discussion, while I recognize the limits and dangers of using populational reasoning, I tap into the sociological concept of *generation* to identify some of the paradoxical constructions of childhoods of today's two youngest demographic cohorts of children—Generation Z (demographic cohort born during 1997–2010) and Generation Alpha/α (demographic cohort born after 2010 up the mid-2020s). Different from the theoretical concepts of human development in stages in the field of educational and psychological studies, the sociological concept of generations allows me to tap into a relatively more fluid socio-political thread of thoughts to "see" children and their shared, as well as situated, generational experiences of "growing up" through the mapping of socio-political and socio-cultural events.

Politics of Growing Up?

A quick overview across the geopolitical spaces of Pacific Asia shows the landscapes of childhoods for the youngest generations of children/humans are crafted and configured through a variety of shared global and regional (macro), as well as specific local (micro), time–space–mattering networks. For instance, in the sociopolitical context of Taiwan, both Generations Z and α are children and young people who are experiencing their young(er) years through waves of national paradoxical political projects through discourses involving the double tracks of de-Chinesenization and the establishment of a "new" Taiwanese nationalism or ideology, which are rooted within a knotted populism for inscribing a politically correct way of be(com)ing: "Taiwanese-ness." Such a national imaginary has played a key role in shaping educational reform policies and contemporary cultural discourses as political projects to constitute new socio-cultural beliefs and values since the 1990s. For Generations Z and α, their socio-cultural experiences are situated within the entanglement of Taiwanese-ness. The positioning and the making of Us (the Taiwanese) versus Them (the Chinese) for Generations Z and α are perpetuated in contemporary educational reforms as the politics of growing up in Taiwan.

Turning to the socio-political context of Hong Kong, both Generations Z and α are children born after the 1997 political handover to China from being a British colony. Growing up during the post-1997 era under a new "national" identity as a "new Chinese" in Hong Kong entails a different type of experience for childhoods in a post-colonial era. The post-1997 era entails a complex cultural identity project with the double tracks of decolonization and recolonialization to reflect the appropriate Chinese-centric politics of a Chinese identity, which is also reflected in the changing educational policies. For example, the birth of a "Biliterate and Trilingual" language policy, which had been creating new parameters for reshaping education and society as well as governing identities and practices (Lee & Tseng, 2013).[3]

In the following paragraphs, I seek to provide a sketch of mappings for each of the landscapes of lifeworlds in which Generations Z and α are living and experiencing Taiwan and Hong Kong. Drawing from my cultural observations of the two East Asian geopolitical locations and contexts, these mappings are presented in the form of a vignette about a day in the life as a child/student in Taiwan and Hong Kong during the 2019–2020 school year. Lacing through these vignettes are macro and micro politics of childhoods. My mapping of these socio-cultural and socio-political landscapes of lifeworlds is in progress and should not be thought of as a completed work.

Living in Taiwan as a Child: Whose Typical Day in the Life May This Be?

Micro Politics of Growing Up: Like the majority of almost all 6-year-olds in Taiwan, Mei-Mei is a Year 1 student in a public primary school in the 2019–2020 school year.

Mei-Mei's parents are in their early to mid-40s, and she is the only child in her family. Her typical Monday starts with getting ready to school and changing into her school uniform. For Mei-Mei, a Year 1 student, her typical school day is from 8:45 a.m. to noon (except on Wednesdays, when her school day is extended until 3:30 p.m.). As her parents are working parents, Mei-Mei attends an after-school program (contracted care) every day during the school term. After being picked up and bused to the after-school care facility, Mei-Mei has her lunch with her "classmates" there. She usually completes/finishes nearly all her homework at her after-school program under the supervision of a team of carers/teachers. Mei-Mei also attends some extracurricular activities at her after-school program with an additional tuition fee such as a weekly English tutorial group. Around 5:30 p.m., one of her parents will pick her up by car or motorcycle. Mei-Mei's dinner is usually at home (or take-home orders from nearby restaurants) between 6:30 p.m. and 8:00 p.m. with her parents. After dinner, her evening activities at home typically include the following combination: reading a book, playing a video game on her iPad or Nintendo Switch, watching TV with her parents, or FaceTiming with her grandparents, who live in a different city. Mei-Mei usually goes to bed by 9:30 p.m. (or 10:00 p.m.) on school nights.

Macro Politics of Growing Up: The year 2020 has not created too much interruption in Mei-Mei's daily activities in her lifeworlds. Her school days and routine are still the same or at least very much like last year prior to the hit of the COVID-19 pandemic in Taiwan. Mei-Mei had a slightly longer winter holiday for an additional 2 weeks due to the effects of growing numbers of COVID-19 cases in February. This extended national school winter break was at the cost of a shorter summer break in July for Mei-Mei as all students/schools are required to make up the school days missed in February 2020. This same rule/policy about modified school terms is a centralized policy for all children in Taiwan, including all students in preschools, primary schools, secondary schools and universities (regardless of whether they are public or private schools). Mei-Mei wears a facemask to school as a required part of her uniform. News hours on every TV channel are about the growing cases of "Wuhan Virus" in China and how other countries are also closing their borders and/or which global city is experiencing lockdowns. Within the geopolitical space of Taiwan, COVID-19 is referenced as the Wuhan Virus from China. Reflecting the political tensions between China and Taiwan, this was a politically correct way of describing and naming the coronavirus until late January 2021, when U.S. President Biden issued an executive order banning the use of phrases such as "China virus" and "Wuhan virus" when referring to COVID-19. Aside from the political construction and the racial/ethnic discrimination in reference to the virus, amid the global pandemic of COVID-19, Taiwan has been doing well in keeping all citizens safe and healthy, with very low numbers of confirmed cases and deaths. Thus COVID-19 has had a relatively small impact, as Mei-Mei continues her school days with no interruptions.

Living in Hong Kong as a Child: What's the New Normal?

Micro Politics of Growing Up: Kay is a 5-year-old kindergarten student in a local non-profit kindergarten (not an international kindergarten) in Hong Kong. Kay's parents are in their early and mid-30s, and she is is the only child in her family. Kay's parents are both working, and they have hired an in-home domestic helper from the Philippines since Kay was born in 2015. Marietta, like many Filipino domestic helpers in Hong Kong, is the primary but contracted carer for the family's child/ren. Kay's typical Monday starts with getting ready for school and changing into her school uniform. For Kay, as a kindergarten student, her typical school day starts at 8:50 a.m. and ends at 11:50 a.m. (the half-day program is typical for kindergartens in Hong Kong). Kay walks to her kindergarten every morning and gets picked up by her family's Filipino domestic helper, Marietta, by 11:50 a.m. Kay has lunch at home, and her typical after-school activities include the following combination: doing homework from kindergarten (ranging from English, Chinese, and math worksheets), afternoon nap, dance class, online Mandarin Chinese lessons with a private tutor, watching TV, playing on her iPad, playing with toys, and drawing. Kay usually has dinner with her parents at around 7 p.m., and she goes to bed around 10 p.m. on school nights.

Macro Politics of Growing Up: There were multiple significant socio-historical events in Hong Kong in 2019 and 2020. In September 2019, pro-democracy protests, demonstrations, and political tensions were ongoing due to the announcement and proposal of a China Extradition Bill and continued to gain public attention, with increasing numbers of students in secondary schools and universities joining protests, boycotting schools, and getting arrested by the police. Kay's parents would choose to have Kay stay home with Marietta when the protests were projected to escalate and intensify, with tear gas and large crowds of both protesters and police officers in full armour. Due to the location of Kay's kindergarten, the surrounding neighbourhood was affected by the aftermath of the protests and many of the bricks of the footpath/sidewalk were missing, as people used them to create road barriers to stop the police cars/trucks driving through. It got to the point where Kay's kindergarten would need to be closed for a few days after some major protest events. The everyday scenery of shopping malls and streets in Kay's neighbourhood has changed dramatically since late in the summer of 2019.

Around late February to early March 2020, only a few weeks into the new semester, Kay's kindergarten followed the mandatory policy and was closed due to the growing numbers of COVID-19 cases in Hong Kong. Kay has one 1-hour online Zoom session with her kindergarten teachers and classmates on a daily basis. With a vivid memory of SARS from 2003, Kay's parents do not allow her to do any outdoor play activities. As the new routine and the new normal for Kay during the months of March to July 2020, a typical COVID-19 pandemic day would include the following combination: 1-hour Zoom meeting with her kindergarten teacher, TV/video/cartoon, drawing and gaming on her iPad, 1-hour Mandarin Chinese lessons with a private tutor, playing with toys in her bedroom, and working/completing the printed worksheets that her teachers send to parents.

What I have presented here is a quick sketch of the politics of childhoods for each of the geopolitical localities to elucidate a way of mapping the current politics of childhoods. Through micro and macro politics of childhood, we get a glimpse of what children's lifeworlds may look like. Around the world, the ubiquitous effects of the COVID-19 pandemic have been creating different degrees of challenges and stresses while exacerbating the already existing and ongoing problems in every aspect of our lives. The landscapes of our/children's lifeworlds—living conditions, modes of living, and lives—have been reshaped and continue to be shaped. Within the field of education, the affects and effects of the coronavirus have driven all children (and their families) and educators/teachers (and their families) to states of crises. However, the levels of the crises are "felt and experienced" differently, as the material reality in each of the geopolitical regions would be different. Each circumstance is different for each individual, family, community and country/state/nation. Despite these differences in geopolitical locality, every one of us is connected with each other as our lifeworlds are connected and co-constructing one another.

Troubling the Politics of Childhoods

There are multiple ways of "seeing" children, childhoods and their lifeworlds. With an alternative analytical toolbox, I avoid "seeing" the landscapes of children's lifeworlds as fixed or deterministic. In this section of the discussion, in addition to acknowledging the pervasiveness of the COVID-19 pandemic, I highlight two of the multiple lines of thought in the making of rhizomatic childhoods through which the current politics of childhood are configured: (1) neoliberalism and (2) nationalism. Both of these lines of thought contribute to the landscape of childhoods in the form of the politics of be(com)ing to produce dangerous norms and truths about how "good" children/family/parenting should look and should be.

Neoliberalism: Buying and Selling Services of Care

Matters about care for children have been commonly constructed as a private choice/family decision. In many East Asian contexts like Taiwan and Hong Kong where dual-income families are becoming a common socio-economic practice, young families with children are often "left" to make "private" choices/arrangements for care. For example, within the early childhood education and care sector, a typical timetable for kindergartens in Hong Kong is a half-day program. Young children between the ages of 3 and 6 typically attend morning *or* afternoon kindergarten sessions as the availability of the full-day kindergarten program is limited. Furthermore, accessibility to early childhood centres for children younger than 3 years old is very limited. What's at issue here is that the provision of education and care programs has been "left" to be organized primarily by the private sector as a type of business. In Hong Kong, despite the push for universal early childhood education, the sector of pre-primary education is organized through the form of education vouchers to cover families' expenses of the tuition fees for their young children as the focus of public interest about preschool programs has been on education rather than care (Wong & Rao, 2015). "Selling" services of care and education outside of school hours/settings is a problematic neoliberal economic logic in the field of education, for it evokes multiple points calling for critical examination. For example, the problematic of such a logic is treating and conceptualizing care and education as a commodity. What is dangerously at work here is a neoliberal logic which supports the commodification of care and education for children and the making of the field of education a semi-market. This re(con)figuration of care and education as purchasing a commodity perpetuates a market economy through which parents (and their children) are not only consumers but also entrepreneurial persons. Another problematic of the logic of "selling" services of care and education outside of school hours/setting evokes a discussion about who can afford to buy/consume what. Issues of affordability, accessibility, and accountability for quality education and care for all children are shifted to become the individual family's choices. For instance, Kay's family ability in Hong Kong to afford the "free choice" of hiring Marietta, a Filipino domestic helper, and Mei-Mei's family's ability in Taiwan to afford an inclusive but private after-school care program are two examples of the problematics of sugar-coating the classed notion of "privileged choice" as "freedom to choose." Stories and cases of education in a capitalist system raises a significant question of educational and social equity. What is at risk here through a neoliberal logic is how it re(con)figures every aspect of children's lifeworlds with a market model to perpetuate the inequality and inequity, without recognizing the institutionalized disparity (for instance, generational debts in the social structure). "Freedom" to make a choice (to buy) can very well be an illusion of freedom and democracy.

Socio-political conditions and socio-economic circumstances of systematic disparity have been made invisible or "erased" within the neoliberal landscaping of childhoods. What a "good" family that cares for and about their child/ren should look like is narrowly and dangerously prescribed. Take the stories of Mei-Mei in Taiwan and Kay in Hong Kong as examples. Contract care arrangements, whether in the home or at a private after-school service provider, are becoming "typical" contemporary childhood experiences for Generations Z and α in many East Asian contexts.

Evoked through the discussions of how children are spending (more) time and interactions with carers through contracts that are arranged and paid by their parents is another important discussion related to the (re)inscription of (in)visible gendered discourses about parenting and mothering. Caught in the messy knots of meeting the norm of being a productive citizen by participating in paid-labour work, what's at issue here is a new provocation for us to reconsider various layers of discussions such as the ethics of care and gendered constructions of "good" mothering. Having the capacity to arrange quality and socio-culturally appropriate contracted care for children for "outsourcing" the responsibility of parenting has become a dangerous socio-cultural norm of "ideal" mothering practice for middle-class families in Taiwan and Hong Kong.

Nested within a complex entanglement of spacetimemattering, the reconceptualization of childhoods and contracted care in a neoliberal market economy of care cannot be simplified. The definitions of childhood, family, and motherhood, as well as good mothering practices, are narrowly reinvented to suit the logic of a neoliberal market model. Critical discussions that aim to unpack the knotted formation of contract care as a by-product of growing up experiences for the young(er) generations in global neoliberalism are too important to ignore, for care work is intra- and interpersonal and socio-culturally situated. Caring, across the different spaces of children's multiple lifeworlds, happens in a web of relations, and children's positionings (as care receivers and givers) are also in relation to and with one another.

Nationalism: A Socio-Political Project of National Identity—Us Versus Them

When unsettling the entanglements of childhoods, it is possible to sort out traces of socio-political lines of thought. The ensemble of contemporary childhoods embodies a socio-cultural and socio-political imaginary. The making of the child and the re(con)figuring of who "we/the children" are in a nation entails complex processes of othering, cultural assimilation, and governing. Zooming into the geopolitical spaces of East Asian contexts, Mei-Mei's and Kay's childhood memories of growing up are unique. For example, for Kay, growing up as a Generation α in Hong Kong in the post-1997 political era is a very different type of childhood memory from that of her parents, who are Generation X and who experienced their childhoods in the British colonial period. The different socio-political projects of different times are manufacturing different national identities which involve multiple tracks of socio-cultural discourses in a new national imaginary. For Kay's time/era, the "politically" correct socio-cultural imaginary is positioned in the double track of decolonization and recolonization, which involves the dual socio-cultural practices of remembering (to be a Chinese) and forgetting (to be a British National Overseas).[4] For Kay, the dual socio-cultural practices are infused in segments of her everyday lifeworlds such as school, homework, educational policies and reforms as well as what's being broadcast during news hours on TV. More specifically, Kay is growing up in an era of a Biliterate and Trilingual language policy in Hong Kong, which is not just an educational policy that has a direct impact on Kay's learning in school but is also a significant change for Kay's parents for reprioritizing what's important for their everyday parenting practices (i.e., the hiring of a Filipino domestic helper who is fluent in English and Kay's taking up of additional Mandarin Chinese lessons outside of school hours).

Turning to Mei-Mei's experience in Taiwan, the nationalism at work is nested within the political tensions, with a similar socio-political logic of dual socio-cultural practices of remembering (to be a Taiwanese) and forgetting (to be a Chinese). The socio-political context of Taiwan is unique, as the national imaginary in the spacetimemattering configuration is filled with multiple lines of narratives about who "we" are and how to (re)position us in the global context. Ongoing interplays of political and socio-cultural tensions of who "we" are as a sovereign nation under what socio-political identity are at work through the mobilization of multiple cultural narratives looming through educational practices to govern and shape children's (like Mei-Mei) everyday experience.

The example of how to "name" this specific strand of coronavirus that caused the global pandemic in 2019/2020 reflects the ongoing socio-political tensions as a project of the national imaginary in Taiwan. Officially naming it the "Wuhan Virus" reflects a political construction of Us versus Them. What's at work here is a construction of "Us the Taiwanese in Taiwan are different from Them the Chinese in China." Inevitably, childhood is an entanglement of messy knots of spacetimemattering through which multiple ideas across times and spaces are enmeshed in the mapping of the landscapes for children's lifeworlds. Childhood, in such an entanglement, is not only rhizomatic but also embraces multiple threads of socio-cultural reasoning through which ways of be(com)ing can be diffracted from a paradoxical Taiwanese construction of nationalism.

The three lines of thought here function like "loose parts" in provocations of children's play, which can be taken apart and assembled together in multiple ways. These lines of thought in relation to rhizomatic childhoods are never fixed but are fluid. There is no clear cut between the micro and macro politics of childhoods, as binary logic is too simple to capture the inter- and intra-connectedness between every possible aspect of the politics of, in, and for the concept of childhoods. My intention here is to assert that multiple conceptions of what a "good" child/student should look like and different experiences of childhood/studenthood in East Asian contexts need to be unpacked and problematized for us to engage in critical rethinking on issues of diversity and inclusion, as well as issues of educational equity (see Lee & Yelland, 2017; Whitty et al., 2020).

Some Concluding Thoughts

Seeing childhoods as entanglements opens up opportunities for us to reconsider critical questions of ethics and responsibility in childhood studies from a social justice perspective. As we foreground the invisible entanglements of histories, events, and cultural discourses/artefacts in the politics of childhoods, we can shift towards (re) conceptualizing childhoods as rhizomatic, through which we are able to recognize and acknowledge the multiple ways of be(com)ing for all children. Deleuze and Guattari's (1987) philosophical and analytical concept of the rhizome has encouraged us to look for multiplicity rather than being "trapped" with a single line of narrative. It is important to recognize the implicit and invisible dangers of a single line of narrative, for it inevitably deploys a binary logic to mobilize the stereotypical constructions of good versus bad and normal versus abnormal. What's dangerous about the dominant circulation of a binary logic in studies of childhoods is that it mobilizes a deficit view of the child in which an "Othering" practice is at work to exclude and deny the rights of all children across multiple contexts.

Throughout this chapter, with a different analytical toolbox, from a critical perspective with hopes for social justice, I have worked to challenge the construction of a narrowed childhood in which the child is thought of, disciplined, regulated, and "raised" through a set of restricted and biased socio-cultural expectations/rules/norms. I have also argued that the experiences of growing up across different spaces of lifeworlds in different geopolitical regions are to be treated and respected as multiple ways of being and becoming. Social and educational justice issues relating to diversity, inclusion and equity should not be reduced or (re)configured as "personal/family choices" and "individual responsibility" through global capitalism and a neoliberal logic through which the ways of being are prescribed through the "objective" measurement of desirable outcomes as achieving and reaching success. In summary, I assert the importance for us to expand our onto-epistemological perspectives to unsettle the dominant construction of childhood as well as to trouble the politics of childhoods. It is only through such ongoing critical inquiries that we "see" the landscapes of childhoods as fluid/dynamic so that we can challenge the troubles of the politics of childhood.

Notes

1. For researchers in the social sciences, the concept of *age cohorts* can be a useful analytical tool in which several Western-centric sociological inventions about *generations* have been coined and used in research studies. For examples, some common sociological inventions of demographic terms may include the Baby Boom Generation (born 1946–1964), Generation X (born 1965–1980), Generation Y/the Millennial Generation (born 1981–1997), Generation Z (born 1997–2010), and Generation Alpha/α (born after 2010 up to the mid-2020s). The demographic categories have been mobilized and rationalized through a populational reasoning in which an individual's age/year of birth is treated as one of the common predictors of differences when investigating and measuring public standpoint of views on a variety of contemporary issues ranging from social policy to foreign affairs (Pew Research Center, 2015).
2. For example, the Programme for International Student Assessment (PISA) is an international education outcome assessment measuring the 15-year-old student's reading, mathematical and scientific literacy level. Another example is the International Early Learning Study (IELS) for measuring the 5-year-old child's learning outcomes.
3. The political handover in 1997 marked the birth of the Biliterate and Trilingual language policy, which aimed to cultivate "new" practices of being biliterate in both written Chinese and English as well as trilingual in Cantonese, Putonghua, and spoken English. This policy shifted

the "priority" of languages used in schools as the medium of instruction and the formation of sociocultural identities in Hong Kong.
4. British National (Overseas) is a unique category of British semi-citizenship introduced in 1987 in Hong Kong. Hong Kong residents who were eligible for the British National (Overseas) passport would be born during the period of 1 July 1987 to 30 June 1997 as 1 July 1997 was the official transfer of sovereignty of Hong Kong to China.

References

Barad, K. (2014). Diffracting diffraction: Cutting together-apart. *Parallax, 20*(3), 168–187. doi:10.1080/13534645.2014.927623

Childhood. (n.d.). In *Oxford Learner's Dictionary*. https://www.oxfordlearnersdictionaries.com/definition/english/childhood?q=childhood

Deleuze, G., & Guattari, F. (1987) *A thousand plateaus: Capitalism and schizophrenia* (B. Massumi, Trans.). University of Minnesota Press.

Dolot, A. (2018). The characteristics of Generation Z. *E-mentor, 74*(2), 44–50.

Juelskjær, M., & Schwennesen, N. (2012, June). Intra-active entanglements: An interview with Karen Barad. *Kvinder, Køn & Forskning,* 10–23.

Lee, I. F., & Tseng, C. L. (2013). Young children's living and learning experiences under the biliterate and trilingual education policy in Hong Kong. *Global Studies of Childhood, 3*(1), 26–39.

Lee, I. F., & Yelland, N. (2017). Crafting miniature students in the early years: Schooling for desirable childhoods in East Asia. *International Journal of Early Childhood, 49*(1), 39–56. doi:10.1007/s13158-017-0183-7

Pérez, M. S., & Saavedra, C. M. (2017). A call for onto-epistemological diversity in early childhood education and care: Centering global South conceptualizations of childhood/s. *Review of Research in Education, 41*(1), 1–29.

Pew Research Center. (2015, September 3). *The whys and hows of generations research*. https://www.pewresearch.org/politics/2015/09/03/the-whys-and-hows-of-generations-research/

Seemiller, C., & Grace, M. (2017). Generation Z: Educating and engaging the next generation of students. *About Campus, 22*(3), 21–26.

Shatto, B., & Erwin, K. (2016). Moving on from millennials: Preparing for Generation Z. *The Journal of Continuing Education in Nursing, 47*(6), 253–254.

UNICEF. (n.d.). *The convention on the rights of the child: The children's version*. https://libguides.newcastle.edu.au/ld.php?content_id=47712050

United Nations. (1989). Convention on the Rights of the Child. Treaty Series, 1577, 3.

Whitty, P., Lysack, M., Lirette, P., Lehrer, J., & Hewes, J. (2020). Passionate about early childhood education policy, practice, and pedagogy. *Global Education Review, 7*(2), 8–23.

Wong, J. M., & Rao, N. (2015). The evolution of early childhood education policy in Hong Kong. *International Journal of Child Care and Education Policy, 9*, Article 3. https://doi.org/10.1007/s40723-015-0006-y

CHAPTER 9

Sitting With the Agency Paradox to Stand for Childhood Liberation: The Case of Critical Mathematics Education

José Martínez Hinestroza

DURING A MATHEMATICS lesson, a group of third graders engaged in an animated debate about how to subtract five minus eight. While children argued for different answers, a child, Halley (all names are pseudonyms), went to a cabinet on the back of the classroom and grabbed a container with linking cubes. Manipulatives in hand, she marched to the front of the classroom while raising her voice to demand her classmates' attention. The classroom quieted down. Announcing that they needed to act out the problem, Halley picked five cubes and said she needed to give eight to me (a researcher in the classroom). Giving me one cube at a time as she counted from one to five, Halley stopped when she had handed out all five cubes. She concluded that, since she now had zero cubes, five minus eight was impossible to solve. Concerned about some children monopolizing the discussion while others remained silent, the teacher asked the class to think quietly for a minute about Halley's idea. After a short period, the teacher drew one of the popsicle sticks labeled with the children's names and she called on Gina. Shrugging, Gina said in a low voice that it (five minus eight) was impossible.

It seems reasonable to interpret Halley's actions as evidence of agency, simplistically defined for now as acting on the world according to one's own choices and intentions. Without any prompting, Halley took the initiative to use manipulatives and demonstrate her idea. An interpretation of Gina's agency is less straightforward. The well-intentioned teacher sought to support agency by distributing talking turns. This teaching move, however, subjected Gina to comply with the adult's expectations. Although Gina proved she was following the discussion and had heard Halley, deflecting attention seemed more urgent to her.

I refer to puzzling classroom situations such as this as the *children agency paradox*, in which agency involves children taking the initiative to play the pedagogical game the adult in the room defines. The child's choices become a mirage as there are limited and preordained possible lines of action. In the example, by declining to answer, ignoring the teacher, or announcing she felt bored, Gina would likely become the target of an intervention for her to eventually speak up. Under rigid, traditional configurations of adult–child roles, the teacher and the social setting are rarely the ones deemed in need of transformation. Gina is encouraged to express her agency as long as it involves following adult-approved lines of action. Naming this paradox makes it possible to observe, analyze, and resist its problematic implications. Specifically, awareness of the children agency paradox exposes how some well-intentioned adult efforts to facilitate children's initiative and choice can, paradoxically, subjugate children to the adult's expectations.

This children agency paradox is particularly relevant in critical mathematics education (CME) because of its focus on emancipation and on the disruption of hegemonic practices to create inclusive spaces for children from historically marginalized groups (Frankenstein, 1983; Gutstein, 2007; Skovsmose, 1994). Accordingly, in this chapter, I develop a conceptualization of agency that honors the commitment of critical mathematics education to liberation. I argue that in critical mathematics education, agency involves children interacting with the world in ways that go beyond and across—that is, transgress—discourses made available to them. Recognizing these transgressive discursive practices calls for a paradigm shift from viewing children as incomplete individuals in transition to adulthood, toward recognizing the multiple ways in which children can transform their own lives and conditions. In line with this focus on CME, before zeroing in on conceptualizations of agency, in the following section, I characterize CME's roots and purposes.

Narrowing the Scope: Critical Mathematics Education

To understand the need to reconceptualize agency within critical mathematics education, in this section I trace Freirean influences on CME. I, then, characterize CME.

Tracing the *Critical* in CME

Current descriptions of critical mathematics education are grounded on two distinct, yet related, theoretical framings: the Frankfurt School and Freirean formulations of critical theory and critical pedagogy. Both theoretical framings question taken-for-granted institutions and traditions that marginalize and oppress certain groups of people (Freire, 1970; Held, 1980; Kincheloe, 2004). This central interest translates in a search for pedagogical approaches that support emancipation and the development of socially just societies (Kincheloe, 2004). By developing critical consciousness—awareness of how power and social structures influence experience—students learn to see themselves as capable of effecting change (Freire, 1970). Given its emancipatory potential, critical pedagogy is particularly relevant for disenfranchised communities to disrupt historical marginalization based on race, language, national origin, gender, and socioeconomic status, among other identity markers.

Critical pedagogy requires continuous self-examination to avoid replicating the social structures and practices that it critiques. One such practice is the type of interaction that the teacher–student dichotomy frequently evokes, where the knowledge-bearing adult makes decisions to lead unknowledgeable children to liberation. To avoid this contradiction, critical pedagogy challenges this hierarchization by reconfiguring the student–teacher relationship as one of collaboration. When students and teachers come together to tap into their unique expertise, they are better equipped to make informed decisions and subvert oppression.

Critical mathematics education emerges at the intersection between critical pedagogy and mathematics education. Foundational to CME is the belief that students can "co-determine the ends and means of their own education" (Brantlinger, 2013, p. 201). Expanding the focus beyond students' development of mathematics conceptual understanding, CME seeks to question and redefine the nature of the student–teacher relationship, what students learn, and how they use what they learn (Frankenstein, 1983, 1989; Gutstein, 2006, 2007; Skovsmose, 1994, 2000). In line with tenets from critical pedagogy, in CME students and teachers work collaboratively to use mathematics to understand power and resist oppression (Gutstein, 2006).

These origins of CME have implications for conceptualizations of agency as acting on the world and making individual choices. Unlike traditional mathematics classrooms that follow mandated scope and sequence guidelines, in CME, students and teachers influence the selection of focal mathematical concepts to explore. This dialogic decision-making increases opportunities for student choice. Given this intricate collaborative process, instantiations of CME are local and situated. That is, CME development is inseparable from the particular people who engage in it and from the social influences and situations of oppression that they face (Brantlinger, 2013). This situated nature renders CME practices open-ended and unpredictable (Aslan Tutak et al., 2011). Consistently, rather than suggesting a set of pedagogical practices, CME offers principles to guide interaction, as I discuss next.

Guiding Principles of CME

The tenets of critical pedagogy guide specific CME instantiations in relation to (1) the learning goals, (2) the students' and the teachers' roles, and (3) the object of study. First, in CME learning goals are twofold: addressing both mathematical sensemaking and the development of critical consciousness. Students develop mathematical conceptual understanding while simultaneously raising their awareness about situations of marginalization and oppression (Gutiérrez, 2002; Gutstein, 2006). Students use mathematics to understand social issues and to decide on possible transformative actions.

Second, unlike traditional mathematics classrooms that treat students as receptacles of teachers' knowledge, in CME students and teachers decide together on social issues to examine (Brantlinger, 2013). During these mathematical explorations, CME disrupts a common classroom practice whereby teachers explain how to solve a problem and students memorize and replicate these procedures (Lawler, 2012). Instead, students generate their own problem-solving strategies, relying on their own understandings to assess each other's strategies and establish courses of action.

Third, in addition to specific mathematical concepts, in CME, mathematics itself is an object of study. While students learn standard mathematical skills and ways of communicating, they also examine mathematics. Students develop critical consciousness about whose mathematical ideas are typically valued and about how mathematics can be used as a mechanism for domination (Skovsmose, 2000). This critical consciousness supports students in recognizing and challenging their own marginalization in mathematics education (Gutiérrez, 2002). Students become critical of different uses of mathematics, and they resist exclusionary forces that inhibit them from participating in ambitious mathematical activity. I contend that CME research has focused on the first two guiding principles while this third principle related to critiquing mathematics has played a secondary role.

Following these guiding principles, defining agency in CME as children making choices and acting on the world becomes tautological. In CME, the adult–child hierarchy is disrupted in favor of a balanced distribution of ways to influence mathematical activity. Students decide how to solve mathematical problems, and they rely on their own understanding to assess others' ideas. Backgrounding the third guiding principle of raising critical consciousness on how mathematics can subjugate children can result in problematic cases of the agency paradox. By assuming that the child agrees to participate in dominant mathematical practices, common characterizations of agency in CME run the risk of reproducing the subjugating trap they intend to dismantle, as I discuss in the following section.

Common Characterizations of Agency in CME

By recognizing children as competent decision-makers who can act on the world, CME is strongly related to agency. I contribute to the search for theoretical clarity that can maintain and enhance agency's explanatory power. Rather than denying the contribution of these characterizations of agency, my intention is to bring attention to the risk of falling back on the subjugation of children. Otherwise, unexamined uses of this construct run the risk of unintentionally perpetuating well-meaning discourses and practices that, paradoxically, end up restricting agency. By examining these characterizations, I also intend to reveal how agency as commonly defined may become irrelevant or may contradict tenets of CME. In this section, I note contributions and persisting tensions in common characterizations of agency.

The Possession of Critical Mathematical Agency

Abundant and diverse definitions of agency in CME send cryptic messages about this construct. As discussed before, previous research on agency in CME has defined agency as children's ability to act on the world according to their own choices (Martin, 2000; Powell, 2004; Turner, 2012). This definition is frequently prefaced by an acknowledgment of the difficulty of fully defining agency in a succinct way (Norén & Andersson, 2016). As de Freitas and Sinclair (2011) put it, "given the complexity of agency, all definitions will prove to be inadequate" (p. 134). This complexity, however, does not seem to make agency un-researchable, as authors devise ways to think and write about it. Commonly, agency is used interchangeably with autonomy, choice, self-determination, initiative, and confidence (Davies, 1991). Contributing to an "I know it when I see it" approach, in other cases, agency appears as a commonplace, and it is left undefined (e.g., see Boaler & Greeno, 2000). Several attempts to further specify agency have focused on mathematical and critical agency.

Mathematical Agency

Efforts to clarify what is meant by agency have frequently specified one type of agency: intellectual or academic agency. In CME, this translates into mathematical agency, which foregrounds the view of children as capable of generating their own problem-solving strategies without depending on others for direction or confirmation (Boaler, 2002; Lawler, 2012). This conceptualization positions all children, and children from historically marginalized communities in particular, as competent (Martínez & Ramírez, 2018; Norén & Andersson, 2016; Powell, 2004; Silva, 2020). This positioning differentiates CME from traditional mathematics classrooms where deficit views on Black and Brown, bilingual, impoverished, and female children persist. By recognizing mathematical agency, CME seeks to destabilize adult–child power imbalances. The teacher is no longer the only knowledgeable one, and the child decides how to approach mathematical activities.

Although mathematical agency has the potential of facilitating access to an academic discourse frequently denied to some children, some pitfalls follow this narrower focus. A focus on mathematical agency emphasizes children's thinking, overplaying their intentionality in what Valero (2005) has described as the myth of the schizo-mathematics-learner "with a clearly divided self: that one that has to do with mathematics, and the one that has to do with other unrelated things. Of course, those other unrelated things are secondary" (p. 5). Rather than communicating to children that a mathematician identity is available for them, an overemphasis on mathematical agency may impose the uptake of such identity. Choice becomes illusory as the only lines of action permitted are those where the child focuses his creativity on developing mathematical ideas. This sort of mathematical golden cage is still a cage that contradicts the notion of agency as acting on the world and tenets from CME.

Critical Agency

In line with CME's interest in transforming social conditions, critical agency focuses on children's ability to effect change in their lives and communities (Chao & Jones, 2016; Louie, 2019). No longer seen as passively waiting for adults to decide on their circumstances, critical agency recognizes children's awareness and perceptions of their reality. The focus is on foregrounding children's use of mathematics to explore situations that matter to them (Turner, 2012). This is a departure from traditional mathematics classrooms in which mathematical activities overrepresent an unmodifiable and unquestionable White, monolingual, middle-class dominant culture. In this sense, critical agency constitutes a pleonasm that emphasizes critical consciousness within CME rather than suggesting the existence of an opposite, noncritical agency.

Despite the importance of understanding and using mathematics as relevant to children's lives, some tensions emerge around critical agency. Critical agency may communicate that CME will deliver a power intrinsic to mathematics. The underlying assumption is that mathematical understandings are a necessary tool for children to explore their world and transform their circumstances. Mathematics learning as the central enterprise remains unquestioned, thus potentially perpetuating the subjugation to dominant mathematics discourses. Wanting the emancipatory power that mathematics arguably conveys becomes compulsory, bringing children back into their mathematical golden cage.

The Possession, Manifestation, and Development of Agency

Common characterizations of agency shed light on its important dimensions, and they carry assumptions about the nature of agency in CME. One common assumption is that agency is a possession, something to be had. Some argue that all human beings have agency, recognizing all children as competent (Silva, 2020; Turner, 2012). The expression "individual agency" is not uncommon in CME, emphasizing will, self-determination, and individuality (Martin, 2000; Powell, 2004), and differentiating individual agency from social agency (Eteläpelto et al., 2013). Agency appears to be dormant until a human actor decides to activate, exhibit, or use it (Gresalfi et al., 2009). Simultaneously, agency is described as having the power to manifest itself when a person needs it, given the necessary circumstances (Powell, 2004). In my own previous work, I have described agency as something that a person—generally teachers or other influential adults—can summon or elicit on behalf of children (Martínez & Ramírez, 2018). Agency has been similarly described as something that a person—for example, a teacher—can distribute, redistribute, or restrict (Eteläpelto et al., 2013; Louie, 2019). A commonality among these characterizations is that rather than being static, agency is fluid, constantly responding to the situation. An illustrative analogy is depicting agency as a possession you carry around in your pocket, waiting for the appropriate time to take it out and turn it on. Agency is then used during a temporally bounded interaction.

Coinciding with these characterizations is a virtually ubiquitous presentation of agency as an ability. Under this characterization, agency can be developed over time, and certain social arrangements and conditions are more conducive to this development (Chao & Jones, 2016; Powell, 2004). Instead of encapsulating agency as something absolute that one either has or does not have or uses or does not use, this characterization presents agency as something that can be exercised. The notion of exercising agency evokes agency as a right—as in exercising the right to vote—specially in CME whereby children from historically marginalized groups gain access to mathematical activity.

The previous characterizations offer implicit answers to the question of what counts as evidence of agency. Agency is portrayed as observable behaviors or actions attributable to an individual. Agency, however, is also portrayed as something that an individual senses and feels. In these cases, agency is perceived in absolute terms: It either is or is not exercised, felt, used, or manifested at any given moment. Despite the analytical feasibility that these characterizations allow, the agency paradox—whereby one interaction shows evidence of agency and subjugation simultaneously—remains. To grapple with this apparent contradiction, in the following section I bring a poststructuralist conceptualization of agency to CME.

Agency in CME as Transgressing Discourses

Poststructuralist examinations of how discourses attempt to define what is considered possible are consistent with CME's focus on critical consciousness. Moreover, poststructuralism disrupts taken-for-granted dichotomies, which can shed light on the apparent paradox of simultaneous absence and presence of agency. I draw on a poststructuralist perspective on discourse to rethink three main aspects of agency in CME: (1) the role of available discourses, (2) individual initiative and intentionality, and (3) the constitution and interpretation of agency.

Centering the Role of Available Discourses

A poststructuralist perspective defines discourse as "the complexes of signs and practices that organize social existence and social reproduction. In this view, a discourse delimits the range of possible practices under its authority and organizes how these practices are realized in time and space" (Peirce, 1989, pp. 403–404). Individuals are entangled and immersed in discourses that influence what is seen as possible. We speak ourselves into existence from within discourses: As individuals interact with the world, multiple discourses influence how we interpret reality and make sense of experience (Davies, 1991; Foucault, 1971, 1972; St. Pierre, 2000).

Consider, for instance, the case of a family of recent immigrants to the United States from Latin America and how discourses may constitute a child as bilingual. The social category of bilingual takes on multiple meanings that carry different implications. A family-oriented discourse of *latinidad* that values intergenerational communication may result in this child using Spanish at home exclusively to communicate with grandparents (Chávez, 2009). A concurrent discourse of national unity and homogenization, on the contrary, may force this child into an English-only policy at school that suppresses and punishes the use of Spanish (Ruíz, 1984). When combined with a discourse that equates mathematics understanding with power, the family may embrace the English-only policy in an attempt to support the child's academic success. Influencing these multiple discourses is the dominant adult–child discourse through which the allegedly rational and knowledgeable adult makes decisions for the child. How this child is constituted as bilingual lies at the intersection of these multiple discourses.

Although it may not be possible to escape the pervasiveness of discourses, it is possible to become aware of them and how they influence decisions (Davies, 1991; Foucault, 1971). Through discourse awareness, it becomes possible to decode, reconfigure, and resist discourses (Davies, 1991; James, 2009). In the example of a bilingual child, it is common to hear children using multiple languages in school spaces and moments that are not closely monitored by adults who enforce English-only policies (Flores, 2020). These children recognize discourses around them, and they skillfully and ingeniously transgress some discourses to favor others.

In mathematics education, in general, a discourse of exclusion persists where some children are deemed good at math and others are deemed as struggling (Parks, 2010). Teachers frequently take on the role of gatekeepers, enforcing the observance of traditional mathematical practices. In doing so, these teachers may suppress many children's cultural and linguistic practices (Barwell, 2014; Louie, 2017). A central contribution of CME is disrupting discourses that exclude children from historically marginalized groups from engaging with ambitious mathematical activity (Gutiérrez, 2002; Powell, 2004; Turner, 2012). Critical mathematics education makes available an alternative discourse that acknowledges that all children are capable of mathematical sense-making. A few studies have begun to advance a notion of agency as involving children becoming aware of, taking up, transforming, and resisting available discourses (Louie, 2019; Stinson, 2013), although continuing a discourse of universal mathematical ability and of the intrinsic value of knowing mathematics.

Complicating Individual Initiative and Intentionality

Recognizing the interaction among multiple discourses in the constitution of the individual complicates, rather than negating, characterizations of agency that center the individual's autonomy and will. Accordingly, this poststructuralist perspective has informed alternative conceptualizations of agency in mathematics education. For example, the notion of a dance of agency decenters individual, human agency to consider the interaction between the mathematician's agency and the agency of the discipline (Boaler, 2002; Pickering, 1995). When the mathematician's agency takes the lead, the individual creatively develops mathematical ideas. When the discipline takes the lead, the individual mathematician observes the dominant traditions of mathematical knowledge generation and verification. Adding nuance to the dance of agency, the notion of embodied and material agency relocates agency not in the individual or the material world, but in their interaction (de Freitas & Sinclair, 2011; Martínez & Ramírez, 2018). The tools that the mathematician uses prompt and facilitate movements and gestures that, in turn, help develop and communicate ideas.

Reconsidering how the individual is constituted and how disciplines and the material world interact with human actors, a poststructuralist perspective questions the overemphasis on intentionality in common characterizations of agency (Davies, 1991; Mazzei & Jackson, 2017). When considering childhood liberation, it is important to notice how this focus on intentionality is grounded on adults' tendency to look for causality and control (James, 2009). This is not to dismiss intentionality but to cast a shadow on its centrality, favoring "analysis that decenters the intentional human subject, and distributes agency among all of the *things* in an assemblage" (Mazzei & Jackson, 2017, p. 1096, emphasis in the original). A poststructuralist perspective acknowledges that decisions may be based on the influences of the surrounding discourses, artifacts, and tools. Rather than individual aspects or actors, it is this assemblage that acts on the world (Mazzei & Jackson, 2017). This perspective also acknowledges that desire, rather than rational decision-making, may motivate action (Davies, 1991; James, 2009). This recognition problematizes characterizations of agency as rational, individual decision-making. It also offers possibilities to rethink agency in ways that are more consistent with CME by highlighting agency in children's resistance and discursive transgressions, as I explain next.

A Poststructuralist Conceptualization of Agency in CME

Drawing on a poststructuralist perspective, I offer a conceptualization of agency in CME as involving children interacting with the world in ways that go beyond and across—that is, transgress—discourses made available to the child. Consistent with CME's interest in critical consciousness, this conceptualization of agency entails children becoming aware of how they are constituted through dominant discourses. Moving awareness to action, children may take up, transform, or resist discourses, including discourses about what agency should look like.

From a poststructuralist perspective, agency involves discursive transgressions that include resisting aspects of CME and certain adults' decisions, as well as declining invitations to take up specific identities. These transgressions help rewrite master narratives that limit what is seen as possible. Accordingly, the transgressive status of these discursive practices is provisionary. Over time, these practices can become legitimized and integrated into the discourses available to children.

In this conceptualization, agency becomes hermeneutic. Agency is interpreted and comes into existence as felt, experienced, owned, distributed, or used in multiple concurrent ways. Challenging the adult–child dualism, determining the presence and absence of agency is no longer delegated to the adult. For a child, an interaction can simultaneously evoke a sense of agency when interpreted from one discourse and a sense of subjugation when interpreted from another. Both interpretations are legitimate and constitute reality for the child. An adult observer's interpretations of agency in this interaction may be different from the child's interpretations, as adults draw on discourses available to them. In both cases, the temporal dimension that establishes what constitutes the beginning and the ending of agency is also an interpretation. Iterative interpretations from within multiple discourses may create a nuanced, multifaceted story of agency.

Far from promoting agency relativism where anything goes, this conceptualization of agency draws attention to the origins and implications of multiple interpretations. Instead of suggesting that adults conform with their interpretations of agency, this conceptualization invites critical consciousness about agency. By recognizing that dominant discourses influence how we interpret agency, we can more intentionally draw on and problematize alternative discourses. This rereading of agency from multiple discourses may raise the agency paradox to awareness, supporting the transformation of well-intentioned, yet oppressing, interactions. In short, sitting with the agency paradox (i.e., allowing it and resisting the urge to get rid of it) can help us stand for childhood liberation (i.e., support disruptions of the adult–child hierarchy).

Classroom Examples: Interpreting Agency as Transgressive Discursive Practice

To illustrate how a poststructuralist perspective can enhance interpretations of agency in ways that are consistent with CME, I draw on two examples from a third-grade classroom. There were 21 children in this third-grade Spanish-immersion classroom in the Midwest. All students were comfortable speaking both Spanish and English, although most children spoke English at home primarily. Spanish was the official language of instruction for mathematics lessons. Three students were on individualized educational plans and were pulled out of mathematics lessons three days a week to work with a teacher aide. The teacher was Valery Abad, a Spanish–English bilingual, U.S. –born Latina. I, a Spanish–English bilingual Colombian immigrant, visited this classroom regularly as part of a participatory research project on children's participation in mathematics class. I present quotes in their original language, followed by my italicized translation to English, when needed.

"I Wasn't Doing Nothing:" Multiple Agency Interpretations Around Daniel's Paper Folding

To illustrate how multiple interpretations of agency can coincide, I draw on an example from a unit where the class explored multiplication and how emotions affect our bodies (e.g., increased heart rate related to nervousness). During a whole-class discussion, one of the students, Daniel, folded a piece of paper under his table. Noticing what Daniel was doing, Valery and I decided to follow up with him. We conjectured that other children would be interested in paper folding, which we could connect with a future multiplication or fractions lesson. The following lesson, when children started working in small groups solving problems from a textbook page, Daniel proceeded to fold paper again. I approached him and asked, in what I intended as a casual, conversational tone, if I could see what he was doing. Daniel quickly clutched the paper while putting his hands under the desk, as he said, "I wasn't doing nothing. ¿Qué página?" (*What page?*), as he looked down at his textbook.

Suspecting that Daniel's apprehension came from his assumption that he could get in trouble if I caught him off-task, I attempted to reestablish trust. I said I noticed he was folding paper and I explained that Mrs. Abad and I were curious about whether what he was doing could help us with a future lesson. Still reticent, Daniel showed me the folded paper as he assured it had fallen when he opened his textbook, so he was folding it to throw it away. As I insisted that it would be helpful to learn how he folded his paper, he finally let his guard down and modeled two ways in which he could fold paper. Eventually, a few days later Daniel helped introduce a lesson in which all children folded paper, coming up with predictions on the number of equal parts there would be after a series of folds.

Episodes of what teachers and researchers frequently label as off-task behavior rarely make it to data analysis in mathematics education research (as argued by Langer-Osuna, 2018). Considering children as social actors as much as they are cognitive beings (Valero, 2005), a poststructuralist perspective does not limit interpretations of agency to children's display of normative mathematical practices. In Daniel's case, one way of interpreting agency is by focusing on transgressive discursive practices that suggest he recognized, resisted, and resignified discourses in which he was enmeshed. Folding paper instead of working diligently on his textbook was a transgression. This might not have been Daniel's intentional initiative, disqualifying it from being counted as a use of agency under common characterizations of the construct. A poststructuralist perspective, on the contrary, recognizes the roles that desire and multiple discourses play in the constitution of agency. Thus, it is reasonable to interpret Daniel's possibly unconscious desire to fold paper as related to agency.

It is unknown if and how a discourse about his ability, or lack thereof, to engage in mathematical activity as an African American child influenced Daniel's actions. If that was the case, then Daniel might have accepted this discourse and taken his position at the margin of mathematical activity. Rather than speculative and unnecessary, this hermeneutic consideration of multiple readings of the situation can prevent analyses that pathologize Daniel as an agentless, disengaged individual. Daniel may be simultaneously agentic and resisting a dominant discourse that pulls him in toward mathematical activity and subjected by another dominant discourse that pulls him toward the margin.

Daniel kept his clandestine undertaken under the table and he attempted to maintain this secrecy when I approached him. I approached Daniel authentically curious and in search of mathematical meaning in his paper folding. It is reasonable to interpret this interaction as inviting Daniel into a discourse where his mathematical ideas matter. However, as an adult in the classroom who had admittedly taken up my role as decision-maker more than once, whether this was an invitation that Daniel could decline is uncertain. By insisting on this collaboration to plan a mathematical task, Daniel, Valery, and I came together to challenge a dominant discourse whereby adults make most classroom decisions. Simultaneously, Valery and I took over an action for which we were not the intended audience. Doing so, we may have reinforced a discourse of surveillance, where children cannot escape the monitoring eye of the adults in the classroom.

"It was like tap, tap, tap, tap, tap, tap:" How Coretta Transgressed Discourses

To illustrate agency as transgressing discourses, I draw on an example from a unit with three overlapping foci: (1) representing and comparing proper fractions, (2) measuring the area of quadrilaterals, and (3) analyzing data from the state and the country to consider issues of diversity. During an activity in which children worked in pairs, they received a slip with the name of a U.S. state and its area represented as a fraction of the area of the classroom home state. For example, the pair of children who represented the

SITTING WITH THE AGENCY PARADOX

area of the classroom home state represented one square meter. If the area of the state a pair received was approximately half the area of the classroom home state, their fraction was half a square meter. Each pair received a measuring tape and masking tape to represent the area on the floor. For the second part of the task, children switched partners, observed the area they had represented, and asked questions to figure out what their fraction was. Then, children reported back to their original partner. Children compared the other pair's fraction and their original one.

Coretta and Rose worked together, and they represented an area of half a square meter. As most pairs did, they realized that the squares that the carpet pattern formed had an area of approximately half a square meter. They used masking tape to trace over one carpet square. Then, Coretta observed Jimmy's rectangle that represented three square meters. The following interaction (Table 9.1) took place:

Table 9.1. Coretta's hopscotching to measure area

Child	Utterances	Actions
Coretta:	Yours is like . . .	Observing the fraction the other group represented.
Jimmy:	Coretta, estamos en español (*Coretta, we are speaking Spanish*).	
Coretta:	Wait. I see something.	Hops on one foot in each of the six squares making up the rectangle.
Jimmy:	¿Estás hopscotchando? (*Are you hopscotching?*)	Giggles.
Coretta:	Wait. What was it?	Repeats hopping on one foot in the six squares.

Coretta went back to Rose and reported back (Table 9.2):

Table 9.2. Coretta's sonic-kinesthetic fraction representation

Child	Utterances	Actions
Rose:	What's theirs?	
Coretta:	It was like tap, tap, tap, tap, tap, tap.	Each time she says "tap," she taps the table with her finger.
Rose:	¿Qué? (*What?*)	Facial expression of confusion.
Coretta:	Nuestro es como así (*Ours is like this*) It's like 'tap' and that's it. Theirs is like tap, tap, tap, tap, tap, tap.	Hops once in the square they represented. Tapping at the table with her finger. Leans on the table with one hand, taps with the other hand, and hops.
Rose:		Both children giggle.
	¡Oh! ¡Como un hop-o-meter! El nuestro es como esto. ¿El de ellos? (*Oh! It's like a hop-o-meter! Ours is like this. And theirs?*)	Draws a short vertical line on paper.
Coretta:		Taps six times on the table.
Rose:	[No utterances] [No utterances]	Draws a line with each tap, beginning beneath the line she drew before.

Attention to multiple discursive transgressions across these interactions can support multifaceted interpretations of agency. Children transgressed discourses of dichotomies such as human–nonhuman, talk–embodiment, and language separation–translanguaging. First, children, material conditions, and mathematical notations joined in a dance of agencies as the squares on the carpet influenced how children represented their fractions. This was coincidental, as Valery and I were not aware of the area of the squares on the carpet when we planned this lesson. In this case, "agency is constituted as an enactment, not something that an individual possesses, nor something that relies on a demarcation between human/non-human" (Mazzei & Jackson, 2017, p. 1094). This interpretation of multiple agencies interacting challenges dominant discourses that assign agency to human actors only based on an assumption of intentionality.

Children challenged logocentric discourses that portray language as the ultimate expression of thought. In mathematics education, logocentric discourses have overemphasized the role of student talk in sensemaking, downplaying alternative ways of developing mathematical ideas that include silence (Martínez Hinestroza, 2020). Rather than counting aloud the number of squares that Jimmy's group had enclosed, Coretta hopped in each of these squares. Then, she silently hopped and tapped as if reproducing the cadence of the movement and sounds she perceived when hopping on the squares. With little explanation, Rose joined in this sonic-kinesthetic representation of the equal number of parts that made up their fractions, and she quietly added a visual representation using lines. These children's playfulness adds to this interpretation of agency as involving transgressing dominant discourses that mandate formal talk as the legitimate way of engaging with mathematics.

There are multiple readings of how children reacted to a discourse of monolingualism that mandates the use of one register of one language at a time, in this case, academic Spanish. When Coretta spoke in English, Jimmy reminded her they were supposed to speak in Spanish exclusively during this time of the day. It is reasonable to interpret this response as Jimmy being subjugated by a discourse of monolingualism that prevented him from seeing other language practices as acceptable. Jimmy, however, also transgressed this discourse by formulating a lexical invention—the coinage of a word that resembles the morphology and pronunciation of a language but that is not formally defined and commonly used (Dewaele, 1998). By playfully creating the word "hopscotchando," Jimmy combined discursive practices from English and Spanish. He took the English word *hopscotch*, and he followed Spanish grammar conjugation rules (i.e., adding *-ando* instead of *-ing*). Jimmy, then, simultaneously reinforced and transformed a dominant discourse on language use in the classroom.

Coretta and Rose engaged in multiple transgressive discursive practices related to language use. They flexibly used both Spanish and English, ignored Jimmy's reprimand, and skillfully included embodied and silent ways of developing mathematical ideas. Regardless of whether these were intentional choices or simply discursive practices that came naturally to them, Coretta and Rose brought these practices to their mathematical activity. They developed a line of action that evokes translanguaging's attention to how children naturally draw on their complete linguistic repertoire (García & Wei, 2014). They disrupted dominant discourses of monolingualism and logocentrism.

Conclusion: Possibilities to Further Align Agency and CME

Common characterizations of agency assume individual rational choice and the observation of normative mathematical conventions. The expression of agency occurs within the confines of formal mathematical discourses. Children whose practices fall outside these discourses are pathologized and labeled as struggling with mathematics, insecure, shy, disengaged, disruptive, or resistant. That is, fostering individual choice to act on the world entails ensuring that children choose to play their role in the didactic play set in place for them (Valero, 2005). Individual choices turn into forced choices: The illusion of introducing options while simultaneously presenting only one acceptable line of action (Davies, 1991). Supporting agency on the condition that it be used only on a predetermined endeavor renders agency irrelevant, at best, and illusive, at worst. This agency paradox is particularly significant in CME because of its focus on liberation, and the disruption of hegemonic discursive practice to make room for historically marginalized children.

To better align characterizations of agency and tenets from CME, I contributed a conceptualization of agency that avoids presenting children as agentless and extends criticality to the examination of mathematics. I proposed a poststructuralist reconceptualization of agency in CME as children interacting with the world in ways that go beyond and across—that is, transgress—discourses made available to them. Rather than adults suppressing discursive practices such as silence, off-task behavior, and informal use of more than one language, children, adults, and the material world come together to enable, support, and legitimize these transgressions. Recognizing these transgressive discursive practices calls for a paradigm shift from viewing children as incomplete individuals transitioning to adulthood to recognizing multiple ways in which children skillfully transform their own lives and circumstances.

Consistent with CME's interest in critical consciousness, this conceptualization of agency pays attention to how children are constituted through dominant discourses. Children may take up, transform, or resist discourses, including discourses about what agency should look like. This recognition of previously unavailable possibilities implies that transgressive, child-generated discursive practices are unpredictable by nature. That was the case in the classroom examples I discussed in which children, the teacher, the researcher, and the material world connected practices from multiple discourses.

I illustrated the analytical possibilities that a CME-aligned, poststructuralist conceptualization of agency can support. Recognizing agency as hermeneutic, I provided examples of how it comes into existence in multiple concurrent ways that lie at the convergence of different influencing discourses. Agency, then, appears as multifaceted and taking on multiple meanings when considered from the perspectives that specific discourses reveal. There were multiple interpretations of agency around a child's reaction of shame and denial when inquired about what an adult interpreted as a mathematical idea in his seemingly off-task behavior. Similarly, the uptake of a discourse of monolingualism coincided with transgressive discursive practices closer to translanguaging, such as the creation of lexical inventions, and embodied and silent engagement with mathematical ideas. Being comfortable with this agency paradox—that is, sitting with it and recognizing multiple interpretations—facilitated supporting children's discursive transgressions—that is, standing for childhood liberation.

Fluidifying agency in the ways presented here challenges analytic determinism that delegates the attribution of presence or absence of agency to adults. Considering both adult and child perspectives from different discourses available to them, multiple interpretations of agency become inevitable. Awareness of problematic implications of some interpretations may support those engaging with CME in opting for productive, transgressive lines of action. Ultimately, this way of rethinking agency extends and contributes to CME efforts to rehumanize mathematics education by challenging the positioning of children on the negative side of the child–adult, object–agent, emergent bilingual–English proficient dichotomies. If children are to bring their whole selves to the mathematics classroom to transform their lives, they need freedom to move across and beyond discourses, both hegemonic and transgressive.

References

Aslan Tutak, F., Bondy, E., & Adams, T. L. (2011). Critical pedagogy for critical mathematics education. *International Journal of Mathematical Education in Science and Technology, 42*(1), 65–74.
Barwell, R. (2014). Centripetal and centrifugal language forces in one elementary school second language mathematics classroom. *ZDM Mathematics Education, 46*(6), 911–922.
Boaler, J. (2002). The development of disciplinary relationships: Knowledge, practice and identity in mathematics classrooms. *For the Learning of Mathematics, 22*(1), 42–47.
Boaler, J., & Greeno, J. G. (2000). Identity, agency, and knowing in mathematics worlds. In J. Boaler (Ed.), *Multiple perspectives on mathematics teaching and learning* (pp. 171–200). Ablex Publishing.
Brantlinger, A. (2013). Critical mathematics discourse in a high school classroom: Examining patterns of student engagement and resistance. *Educational Studies in Mathematics, 85*(2), 201–220.
Chao, T., & Jones, D. (2016). That's not fair and why: Developing social justice mathematics activists in pre-K. *Teaching for Excellence and Equity in Mathematics, 7*(1), 15–21.
Chávez, K. R. (2009). Remapping latinidad: A performance cartography of Latina/o identity in rural Nebraska. *Text and Performance Quarterly, 29*(2), 165–182.
Davies, B. (1991). The concept of agency: A feminist poststructuralist analysis. *Social Analysis: The International Journal of Anthropology, 30*(1), 42–53.

de Freitas, E., & Sinclair, N. (2011). Diagram, gesture, agency: Theorizing embodiment in the mathematics classroom. *Educational Studies in Mathematics, 80*(1–2), 133–152.

Dewaele, J.-M. (1998). Lexical inventions: French interlanguage as L2 versus L3. *Applied Linguistics, 19*(4), 471–490.

Eteläpelto, A., Vähäsantanen, K., Hökkä, P., & Paloniemi, S. (2013). What is agency? Conceptualizing professional agency at work. *Educational Research Review, 10*(1), 45–65.

Flores, N. (2020). From academic language to language architecture: Challenging raciolinguistic ideologies in research and practice. *Theory Into Practice, 59*(1), 22–31.

Foucault, M. (1971). Orders of discourse. *Social Science Information, 10*(2), 7–30.

Foucault, M. (1972). *The archaeology of knowledge and the discourse on language*. Pantheon Books.

Frankenstein, M. (1983). Critical mathematics education: An application of Paulo Freire's epistemology. *The Journal of Education, 165*(4), 315–339.

Frankenstein, M. (1989). *Relearning mathematics: A different third R—radical math(s)*. Free Association Books.

Freire, P. (1970). *Pedagogy of the oppressed*. Siglo XXI.

García, O., & Wei, L. (2014). *Translanguaging: Language, bilingualism and education*. Palgrave Macmillan.

Gresalfi, M., Martin, T., Hand, V., & Greeno, J. (2009). Constructing competence: An analysis of student participation in the activity systems of mathematics classrooms. *Educational Studies in Mathematics, 70*(1), 49–70.

Gutiérrez, R. (2002). Enabling the practice of mathematics teachers in context: Toward a new equity research agenda. *Mathematical Thinking and Learning, 4*(2–3), 145–187.

Gutstein, E. (2006). *Reading and writing the world with mathematics: Toward a pedagogy for social justice*. Taylor & Francis.

Gutstein, E. (2007). Connecting community, critical, and classical knowledge in teaching mathematics for social justice. In S. Mukhopadhyay & W. M. Roth (Eds.), *Alternative forms of knowing (in) mathematics: Celebrations of diversity of mathematical practices* (pp. 300–311). Sense Publishers.

Held, D. (1980). *Introduction to critical theory: Horkheimer to Habermas*. University of California Press.

James, A. (2009). Agency. In J. Qvortrup, W. Corsaro, & M. Honig (Eds.), *The Palgrave handbook of childhood studies* (pp. 34–45). Macmillan.

Kincheloe, J. L. (2004). *Critical pedagogy primer*. Peter Lang.

Langer-Osuna, J. (2018). Productive disruptions: Rethinking the role of off-task interactions in collaborative mathematics learning. *Education Sciences, 8*(2), 87–97.

Lawler, B. R. (2012). Fabrication of knowledge: A framework for mathematical education for social justice. In T. Cotton (Ed.), *Towards an education for social justice: Ethics applied to education* (pp. 163–189). Peter Lang.

Louie, N. (2019). Agency discourse and the reproduction of hierarchy in mathematics instruction. *Cognition and Instruction, 38*(1), 1–26.

Louie, N. L. (2017). The culture of exclusion in mathematics education and its persistence in equity-oriented teaching. *Journal for Research in Mathematics Education, 48*(5), 488–519.

Martin, D. B. (2000). *Mathematics success and failure among African-American youth: The roles of sociohistorical context, community forces, school influence, and individual agency*. Routledge.

Martínez Hinestroza, J. (2020). "Hush it up!": Silence as a pedagogical resource in a language immersion mathematics classroom. *Teaching for Excellence and Equity in Mathematics, 8*(3), 8–15.

Martínez, J. M., & Ramírez, L. (2018). Angling for students' mathematical agency. *Teaching Children Mathematics, 24*(7), 424–431.

Mazzei, L. A. & Jackson, A. Y. (2017). Voice in the agentic assemblage. *Educational Philosophy and Theory, 49*(11), 1090–1098.

Norén, E., & Andersson, A. (2016). Multilingual students' agency in mathematics classrooms. In A. Halai & P. Clarkson (Eds.), *Teaching and learning mathematics in multilingual classrooms: Issues for policy, practice and teacher education* (pp. 109–124). Sense Publishers.

Parks, A. N. (2010). Metaphors of hierarchy in mathematics education discourse: The narrow path. *Journal of Curriculum Studies, 42*(1), 79–97.

Peirce, B. N. (1989). Toward a pedagogy of possibility in the teaching of English internationally: People's English in South Africa. *TESOL Quarterly, 23*(3), 401–420.

Pickering, A. (1995). *The mangle of practice: Time, agency, and science.* University of Chicago Press.

Powell, A. B. (2004). The diversity backlash and the mathematical agency of students of color. In M. Høines & A. B. Fuglestad (Eds.), *Proceedings of the 28th Conference of the International Group for the Psychology of Mathematics Education* (pp. 37–54). National Council of Teachers of Mathematics.

Ruíz, R. (1984). Orientations in language planning. *NABE Journal, 8*(2), 15–34.

Silva, J. (2020). Exploring the mathematical agency of a multilingual child with an identified learning disability. *Teaching for Excellence and Equity in Mathematics, 11*(3), 25–31.

Skovsmose, O. (1994). Towards a critical mathematics education. *Educational Studies in Mathematics, 27*(1), 35–57.

Skovsmose, O. (2000). Aporism and critical mathematics education. *For the Learning of Mathematics, 20*(1), 2–8.

St. Pierre, E. A. (2000). Poststructural feminism in education: An overview. *International Journal of Qualitative Studies in Education, 13*(5), 477–515.

Stinson, D. W. (2013). Negotiating the "White male math myth": African American male students and success in school mathematics. *Journal for Research in Mathematics Education, 44*(1), 69–99.

Turner, E. E. (2012). Critical mathematical agency in the overcrowding at Francis Middle School project. In E. Tan, A. Calabrese Barton, E. E. Turner, & M. Varley Gutiérrez (Eds.), *Empowering science and mathematics education in urban schools* (pp. 51–75). University of Chicago.

Valero, P. (2005). The myth of the active learner: From cognitive to socio-political interpretations of students in mathematics classrooms. In P. Valero & O. Skovsmose (Eds.), *Proceedings of the Third International Mathematics Education and Society Conference* (pp. 489–500). Danmarks Pædagogiske Universitet.

CHAPTER 10

"Your Children Are Having Too Much Fun": Teaching Literacy With Radical Hope

Luz A. Murillo

> We cannot reduce children to a pair of eyes that see, a pair of ears that listen, a vocal mechanism that emits sounds, and a hand that clumsily squeezes a pencil and moves it across a sheet of paper. Behind (or beyond) the eyes, ears, vocal cords and hand lies a person who thinks and attempts to incorporate into his or her own knowledge this marvelous medium of representing and recreating language, which is writing, *all* writing. (Ferreiro, 2003, p. 34)

IN THIS CHAPTER, I describe attempts to teach against the literacy miseducation of emergent bilingual children, a challenge that, together with fellow scholars, colleagues, and students, I have been wrestling with for many years. As a biliteracy scholar, I am specifically concerned here with classroom instruction as a site of historical and contemporary subjugation of children whose home languages and literacy and cultural practices are viewed as deviant from English monolingual norms. For reasons that will be apparent to many readers, teaching literacy against racial and linguistic discrimination and in support of young bilingual children is no easy task. And yet, as I hope to show, there are reasons to be hopeful, despite the many barriers facing bilingual children and their teachers, that education through literacy—this "marvelous medium of expression, of representing and recreating language" (Ferreiro, 2003, p. 34)—can contribute to educational justice long overdue.

To tell this story, I share the example of Nina, a second-year teacher in Central Texas, beginning with a vignette from her kindergarten classroom. I ground the work of bilingual children, literacy teachers, and teacher preparation programs in a review of selected literature in three areas: children's responses to literate environments, the emerging field of raciolinguistic ideologies and racioliteracies, and how dominant forms of literacy instruction have been shaped by "reading science" and capitalism. I describe an ethnographic case study of literacy instruction and learning in Nina's classroom in which we extended the concept of "kidwatching" to "teacherwatching." Through this example, I explore literacy instruction as a form of "radical hope" (Lear, 2006) with potential to transform teacher practice and preparation in favor of bilingual children. The chapter concludes with thoughts for literacy educators, teacher preparation programs, and researchers interested in challenging raciolinguistic ideologies through sustained collaboration with new literacy and bilingual education teachers beyond the time limits of their formal teacher preparation.

Literacy before Schooling

Emilia Ferreiro and Ana Teberosky (1982) emphasized the central role of language and cognition in children's early development of reading and writing. In the United States, where schools have historically envisioned and promoted literacy as a practice that occurs only in English, the great majority of children from Latinx/immigrant backgrounds and Spanish-speaking households are confronted with the task of learning without the benefit of their home language (García & Kleifgen, 2018). Foley (1997) urged researchers to challenge and deconstruct the deficit thinking and culture-of-poverty orientations that continue to inform the education of bilingual and working-class racialized children. Similarly, Flores, Tefft, and Diaz (1991) invited scholars to transform deficit myths about learning, language, and culture. Despite more than a quarter century of scholarship exposing harmful racist and English monolingual ideologies underlying literacy instruction in the United States (Dyson, 2015), Latinx students and their teachers remain subject to forms of linguistic discrimination that narrow opportunities for learning and teaching and limit the literacy development of bilingual learners.

In this chapter, I draw on theories of raciolinguistic ideologies (Chaparro, 2019; N. Flores & Rosa, 2015; García & Otheguy, 2017; Rosa, 2019) and racioliteracy ideologies (Saldivar, 2019) to understand the risks that novice teachers must take to comply with state mandates to help Spanish-speaking children develop literacy while simultaneously navigating the contradictory mandates that frame bilingualism and biliteracy as tools to transition children into English-only instruction. This ethnographic case study (Dyson & Genishi, 2005) is based on the words and actions of Nina and her kindergarten students, as well as their interactions with school administrators, fellow teachers, and bilingual families. The study demonstrates how literacy teachers of Latinx children can practice epistemic disobedience (Mignolo, 2009) in order to help linguistically racialized students thrive despite the colonizing forms of literacy education that persist in many school settings (N. Flores, 2017; Lear, 2006).

"Yo Soy un Lector y un Escritor": Fostering Radical Hope in a Bilingual Kindergarten

In the fall of 2019, I was invited, along with another of Nina's former professors, to read bilingual books with her kindergarten students. Because the date of the invitation coincided with our university's graduation ceremonies, we decided to visit while still dressed in our regalia. Our university prides itself on serving first-generation college students, and it has been designated by the U.S. federal government as a Hispanic-Serving Institution. In electing to share a bit of the university's symbolic capital with the children we were reminded of the ideological contradictions that aspirations of higher education can pose for Latinx and linguistically diverse children. On previous visits, we noticed that the hallways were decorated with pennants of famous universities and that the name and logo of the teacher's alma mater were displayed at the entrance of each classroom. In this early-exit transitional bilingual education program, the most common type of bilingual education in Texas and in the United States, children are expected to master English literacy before the end of third grade. The end of reading and writing instruction in Spanish is a linguistic and cultural sacrifice Latinx children are expected to make in the name of academic achievement. Given research indicating that young bilingual children are quite aware that school success will require them to study only in English (Moll, 2008), we were conscious of the ideological weight of our regalia.

As the children took turns trying on our caps and the colorful "Educación Bilingüe" sashes worn by our Bilingual/Biliteracy Education graduates and faculty, they asked many questions about the university. They eagerly showed us their notebooks and the portfolios Nina uses to document their growth, as well as their writing about tamales, pozole, and other foods made with *maíz* (corn) posted on the classroom walls. We were struck by the enthusiasm and literate confidence of these 5- and 6-year-old children. Clearly, they saw themselves as capable readers and writers. While telling us about their writing and drawings, the children made detailed connections to their families, homes, and pets in Texas, Mexico, and Guatemala. We were also impressed with the way Nina spoke with the children to instill in them the idea of being literate. We noticed that on the few occasions a student said, "Yo no puedo escribir/leer esto" (I can't write or read this), Nina pointed to a large poster she had created with the phrase "Soy un lector y un escritor" (I'm a reader and a writer) and invited the student to read it with her. By allowing students to read and write about ideas that interest them and by encouraging the children to identify as readers and writers, Nina was guiding them to develop a love of written language and confidence in their own biliterate abilities. This is a practice that Emilia Ferreiro, Frank Smith, and other literacy researchers have been telling us about for many years.

Synthesis of Selected Literature

Historical Background: The Vancouver Conference

In 1982, at the invitation of Frank Smith, 14 scholars from around the world and representing different disciplines met at the University of Victoria, Canada to participate in the symposium *Children's Response to Literate Environments: Literacy Before Schooling*. The aim of the symposium was to discuss the intellectual work of preschool children from perspectives in psychology, sociology, anthropology, and education (Goelman, Oberg & Smith, 1982). To organize their discussion, researchers grouped the topics and subsequent publication of their papers into three themes: literacy and culture, learning to be literate, and literacy and cognition. The interdisciplinary nature of this scholarly dialog highlighted multiple roads to literacy among bilingual children.

Notably, the research presented at the symposium had been conducted in different countries and in different languages and these multilingual and international perspectives made the conclusions relevant for literacy education around the world. Key ideas from the symposium included play and children's creative and imitative involvement with literacy activities as a key developmental stage in becoming literate; "children's contacts with literacy, literate adults, and literacy activities occur between a wide range of social domains within the family" (Goelman, 1982, p. 202); and the principle that children's encounters with literacy in different environments without formal instruction demonstrate that literacy is firmly embedded in the home and other social contexts. One important discussion centered on new research challenging the ideology that literacy develops only in the context of formal schooling, as presented by Glenda Bissex (1982):

> Children encounter literacy within meaningful social contexts and learn (as distinct from being taught) to view literacy as a way of making sense of the world. Formal instruction in literacy tends to be linear and devoid of much of the real-life social and meaningful contexts in which literacy has been observed to develop. From a child's viewpoint, real-life contexts are more powerful and meaningful than those which formal instruction tends to offer. (p. 204)

Another set of papers focused on cognitive processes and emphasized the central role the brain plays in literacy acquisition and development. Frank Smith introduced the foundational ideas that reading is primarily a matter of making sense of print, that prediction is a "natural" strategy available to all children, and that children use these behaviors while developing literacy. Although novel at the time, Smith's conclusions about reading development continue to inspire teachers and researchers who strive to understand how children learn, as brain research and language studies continue to support the original insights (Compton-Lilly et al., 2020; Smith, 2011). Jerome Bruner described the cognitive processes involved in reading and argued that literacy development is connected to the social contexts and lived experiences of children, emphasizing the relationship between cognition and culture described by Scribner and Cole (1981) as the psychology of literacy.

Among the invited scholars was Emilia Ferreiro, whose classic work with Ana Teberosky (1979/2012) *Los sistemas de escritura en el desarrollo del niño*, had just been published in English under the title of *Literacy Before Schooling*. Psychogenesis, the history of an idea or concept as influenced by the learner's personal intellectual activity (Ferreiro, 1990, pp. 12–25), was a central concept in Ferreiro's research, following the work of her former professor, Jean Piaget. Adapting Piagetian principles of psychogenesis to children's literacy development, Ferreiro and Teberosky (1982) analyzed the development of writing among Spanish-speaking children in Argentina and Mexico. They proposed that children develop literacy by building on their own knowledge and argued that it is not through school tasks such as repetition and memorization but, rather, by taking risks and understanding errors that children become literate. Ferreiro's (2003) position is that research and literacy instruction must consider the child "a person who thinks" (p. 34) and is engaged in a rich process of cognitive, social, and linguistic development while simultaneously learning to represent ideas in print.

Another important contribution at the symposium was Shirley Brice Heath's research on how White and Black middle-class and working-class families socialized their children into distinct literacy practices. Heath (1982) described the language practices in three communities in rural Piedmont Carolinas. One was a middle-class community with a history of formal schooling; one was working class, predominantly Black; and one was working-class, predominantly White. In following the children into school, Heath found that their different language practices had implications for academic success. She argued that the difficulties linguistically diverse children, including those who speak different varieties of English, encounter in schools were not due to a lack of exposure to literacy practices in their homes and communities, as was commonly assumed, but, rather, due to the schools' construction of standardized English as the norm for literacy instruction. Heath was among the first ethnographers of literacy to articulate the connections between socioeconomic class, race, language, and literacy. Although the sociolinguist William Labov wrote as early as 1969 about the educational injustices faced by African American students resulting from educators' ignorance about African American Language, it was only in 2003 that he made a direct connection between the failure of schools to acknowledge the role of language variation in literacy development and the failures of "ordinary children" (as he called African American and Latinx children in his study) to learn to read and write in schools.

Of course, a great deal of important research on early literacy has been conducted before and since 1982. I have chosen to begin with the University of Victoria symposium, designed by Frank Smith to foster interdisciplinary discussion of the interrelationship among language, cognition, and culture in the early literacy development of multilingual children. I have highlighted the seminal work of Emilia Ferreiro and Ana Teberosky on children's writing development and research by Shirley Brice Heath on the relationships among social class, language, and literacy. Collectively, these understandings form the pillars of subsequent work with Latinx children's literacy and biliteracy development, such as the Funds of Knowledge for teaching research projects conducted by Luis Moll and Norma González (González, Moll & Amanti, 2005), as well as emerging scholarship on racioliteracy ideologies.

Racist Linguistic Practices as Barriers to Literacy Learning and Teaching with Emergent Bilingual Children

Alim (2016) challenges majority discourses that describe the United States as a post-racial society. He examines how the hyper-racialization of U.S. society has shaped language and education research perspectives over many decades and, relatedly, investigations into the intersections between race and language examine how language is used to construct race and how racist ideologies influence language (see Alim et al., 2016 for research examples). This work further adds to problematizations of the abilities of multilingual and multidialectal children, the latter group being especially tied to socioeconomic and regional diversities and other issues connected to constructions of race and racial identity. For many years, deficit assumptions have, largely from a biological point of view, assumed that children from low-socioeconomic groups, African Americans, Latinxs, and some immigrant groups were intellectually inferior to their White, middle-class, English-monolingual peers. From an anthropological point of view, Douglas Foley helped us understand how the rejection of biology-based models of deficit thinking unfortunately led to deficit models based on culture. Foley (1997) explained how effectively deficit thinkers, based on the work of U.S. anthropologist Oscar Lewis on what he termed the "culture of poverty," moved from the idea of genetic inferiority to the idea of cultural and linguistic deficiencies. Specifically, these assumed deficiencies were found in African American and Latinx families and communities who lived in poverty. Although the work of Lewis was extensively disputed by scholars of different backgrounds, a pervasive idea that still informs language and literacy policies in school settings is that the "poor had a restricted, less abstract, simpler language code and cognitive reasoning style" (Foley, 1997, p. 119). This is particularly important to emphasize because language has been used to create educational programs, in general, and literacy programs, in particular, to correct the language children use in their homes and communities. These programs aimed to remediate the supposed deficiencies linguistically racialized children bring to school. An example is the work of Carl Bereiter and Siegfried

Engelmann, who initiated a direct instruction school curriculum focused on "perceived deficits in poor children's oral and written language" (Dyson, 2015, p. 200). (For a sample lesson, see a 1965 video produced by the Anti-Defamation League and archived by the Institute for Advanced Instruction at https://www.youtube.com/watch?v=Y9dg1kKdR1Q&t=82s.) It is important to note that, although many early childhood researchers have disagreed strongly with these findings, instruction based on deficit ideologies continues to dominate the public education of racialized children.

In the case of Latinx children, Spanish-dominant emergent bilinguals were featured in the work of Flores et al., (1991), who offered a rigorous analysis to debunk the assumed deficiencies of linguistically racialized children and to challenge school practices defining them as targets of remediation. These researchers explained that habitudes, "habitually unexamined attitudes, which form the basis of this deficit view of students who are not from an Anglo-middle class world," (p. 369) are harmful and have contributed to the "literacy problems" of many Latinx children. Later, Flores (2005) traced the presence of the deficit view of Spanish-speaking children in the educational literature throughout the 20th century, as summarized in the following:

> **100 years of deficit views of Spanish-speaking children**
> 1920s: The problem is "Mental retardation"
> 1930s: The problem is "Bilingualism"
> 1940s: The problem is to change Mexicans through education
> 1950s: The problem is a dual handicap and language barrier
> 1960s: The problem is cultural and linguistic deprivation
> 1970s: The problem is culturally and linguistically different child and family
> 1980s: The problems are semi-lingualism and Limited English
> 1990s: The problem is that these children are "at risk"
> 2000s: The problem is lack of English
> *2010s: The problem is "bad teachers"*
> *2020s: Who do we blame next?*

I have modified Flores' model by adding the decade 2010 to include "new" deficit discourses in which teachers are blamed for their students' low performance on standardized tests (de Saxe & Favela, 2018). I want to point out the perpetual cycle and historic hypocrisy of blaming Spanish-speaking children and families and their teachers for educational failure while ignoring structural inequalities and the lack of accountability among leaders of education agencies at the state and federal levels. As Edelsky (2006) points out, for many years, influential corporations and publishers have been shaping literacy instruction in the United States through the marketing of reading programs that fail to take into account the systematic disparities in the education of racialized children, but which inevitably portray bilingual children from a deficit perspective. As we begin the 2020s, it remains unclear who will be blamed next.

The factors behind the educational underachievement of racialized children have been well documented for many years (Kozol, 2006; Ladson-Billings, 2009; Paris & Alim, 2017). Insidiously, the normalization of this underachievement has been used to justify the creation of intervention programs intended to "help" these children do better in schools (Avineri et al., 2015; Blum, 2016). Building on years of scholarship showing that the practice of racialized linguistic discrimination is toxic for young children and harmful for their educational futures (Murillo & Smith, 2011), critical analyses of the relations between race and language make clear that the racialization of minority language speakers contributes to forms of schooling that fail minoritized students. In addition to studies of contemporary conditions of schooling, they allow us to look back upon and interrogate past practices and to see how, historically, U.S. federal, state, and local education policies and curriculum have used language as a proxy for race preventing Latinx and other non-White children from receiving a strong education (Monzó & Rueda, 2009).

The field of literacy education has recently begun to reframe understandings of the intersecting challenges linguistically diverse and racialized children encounter in schools. Within educational research more broadly, linguistic anthropologists Nelson Flores and Jonathan Rosa (2015) have led an emerging field of study of raciolinguistic ideologies to explore how language use and speakers are racialized in and out of school. A key theoretical innovation and what distinguishes raciolinguistic ideologies approaches from earlier efforts to create more equitable conditions of schooling is the emphasis on "the White listener," who continues to hear and frame speakers of minoritized languages as perennially deficient, as a subject (Rosa, 2019; Sosnowski, 2020). Thus, raciolinguistic ideologies approaches to the study of language and literacy focus not on racialized learners, but rather on the ideologies and practices of White, English monolinguals whose views and interests dominate literacy education.

Recently, scholars have begun to focus on the connections between the study of raciolinguistic ideologies and literacy. Saldivar (2019) explored how particular literacy practices produce race and how race produces particular literacy ideologies in a Spanish heritage language education program for middle school students. She found that the program, and world language teaching and learning more broadly, have been "conceptualized in ways that maintain systems of domination . . . racial and linguistic oppression" (p. 182) and argued that failure to consider broader systems of power, like racism, results in the re/production of deficit discourses. These discourses frame bilingual Latinx students as lacking language and literacy proficiency. The study documents how the rich language abilities Latinx students bring to school are evaluated almost exclusively in terms of exclusionary indicators of proficiency such as measures of grammar, functional language use, and reading proficiency.

Similarly, Chaparro (2019) describes the intersectionality of language, race, and social class in a dual language kindergarten. Using raciolinguistic ideologies theory, the study documented classroom practices as forms of language and literacy socialization aimed at young emergent bilinguals. Chaparro (2019) states:

> The term raciolinguistic socialization captures how race and class impact the way language and literacy abilities are evaluated, both formally in educational settings, and informally, in adult reflections of children's growth.... Indeed, evaluations of linguistic abilities in schools become intertwined with school literacy skills in ways that place students from socioeconomically privileged backgrounds at an advantage. (p. 2)

Chaparro expands on the works of Nelson Flores and Jonathan Rosa to demonstrate how students, teachers, and families contribute to reinforcing raciolinguistic ideologies and, as a consequence, racioliteracies. Describing the linguistic backgrounds and practices of three children, one biracial and one White (both emergent bilinguals dominant in English), and one Latinx emergent bilingual dominant in Spanish, Chaparro observed a common practice in the bilingual program, of praising the White middle-class children who are doing well in Spanish while dismissing what Latinx children can do in both Spanish and English. Furthermore, in her analysis, the White child is given the power to "help" the Latinx child to read in both Spanish and English. In contrast, "for working class immigrant children, both their Spanish and their English come into question" (Chaparro, 2019, p. 8).

This chapter draws on scholarship on raciolinguistic and racioliteracy ideologies to examine ways linguistically racialized children are taught reading skills in isolation. I argue that long-standing beliefs about such children result in literacy curriculum and instruction that severely undervalue the impressive language abilities all children bring to school, despite the extensive body of research showing that phonocentric approaches to literacy development are detrimental for emergent bilingual children (Edelsky, 2006; Garan, 2007; Noguerón-Liu, 2020). Teaching the so-called basics (i.e., phonemic awareness, phonics, fluency, vocabulary, and text comprehension) in the absence of rich linguistic context results in confusion and school failure for many children. These deficit-based practices, typically justified in the name of "scientifically based research" and, more recently, "the science of teaching reading" (Compton-Lilly et al., 2020) contribute to the fourth-grade slump, reinforce the literacy injustices linguistically racialized children face in school-based literacies (Gee, 2007; Meyer, 2002; Smith, 2006), and ignore the linguistic flexibility that multilingual children develop in their families and communities and which is necessary to read and write successfully in school (Genishi & Dyson, 2009).

Dominant Forms of Literacy Instruction Shaped by "Science of Reading" and Capitalism

Literacy "has been used, in age after age, to solidify the social hierarchy, empower elites" (Gramsci, 1971, as quoted in Gee, 2015, p. 42), and literacy instruction is the primary mechanism through which schools produce workers for contemporary forms of capitalism. Reich (2001) describes three types of workers required by "fast" or "global" capitalism: poorly paid service workers; "knowledge workers" who must bring technical, collaborative, and communication skills to the workplace and commit themselves body and soul to the company and its "core values" under conditions of little stability; and leaders who create innovation and core values and who will benefit most from the new capitalism (pp. 280–281). Gee (2015) estimates that three fifths or more of workers will fall into the first category. Given the historical positioning of immigrants and minoritized populations generally, we shouldn't be surprised that linguistically racialized children will fit in the category of "poorly paid service workers" (Gee 2015, p. 61). Elaborating on the connections between racioliteracies and poorly paid workers, Edelsky (2006) states that "one area that must be controlled is the literacy of students, more precisely of future workers (p. 5) and adds that

> corporate America (in an intensified neo-liberal world) has a new literacy requirement: It needs a labor force with the ability to read, without questioning, for technical information. Inducting youth students into school literacy through intensive phonics instruction fits the narrow type of reading ... that emphasizes the encoding and decoding of the language of software and hardware and various wares in between. Reading done freely and volitionally ... for one's own interests ... is to remain the private school curricular privilege of the already privileged. (Edelsky, 2006, p. 5)

In this sense, the narrow literacy curriculum and instruction imposed on working-class children, approximately the great majority of emergent bilingual children, can be seen as an intentional practice to concentrate human capital within privileged groups and maintain class divisions that keep poor children in low-end employment (Watkins, 2015).

A further example of the reductionist literacy curriculum and instruction practiced in the schooling of bilingual children can be found in the popular program Accelerated Reader (AR), used in thousands of U.S. elementary school classrooms to document and ostensibly promote children's progress in reading. AR is a computer-based program purchased by school districts, including Nina's, to quantify the number of words children read and to rank children based on "comprehension" tests of selected children's books. Each title is assigned a predetermined number of AR points, and schools commonly give individual prizes such as candy or rewards such as pizza parties to classrooms that have met established goals for the number of books children read. Although it is not specifically designed for emergent bilinguals the AR program is commonly used in bilingual education programs and classrooms in which most children are designated as English learners. In the following email sent by the school principal to Nina and the other bilingual kindergarten teachers, we see how the use of AR shapes literacy instruction:

> After thinking about the meeting yesterday, I would like for ya'll to get together weekly to review the writing samples from each week & AR totals. The expectations for writing and AR are:
>
>   * Working on handwriting correctly (proper size and letter formation)
>   * Kinder (independently) will write 3 sentences (capital letter w/end punctuation)
>   * AR: each student should try to get 500 words per week
>
> Please let me know what day/time ya'll will be meeting weekly. (Nina, personal communication, February 17, 2020)

It is disheartening, to say the least, to see the ignorance informing administrators' decisions about how literacy is taught, as well as the surveillance of children and teachers ("Please let me know what day/time ya'll will be meeting weekly") promoted through the use of AR. Like other repackaged reading programs, AR has been shown to be an ineffective means of creating "life-long readers" (Garan, 2007, p. 59). The emphasis on form ("correct" handwriting, including letter size and shape, capitalization, and punctuation) and quantity of reading ("500 words per week") and the disregard for children's ability to make meaning of what they read is inappropriate for emerging readers, especially for emergent bilinguals. Such practices are part and parcel of the "nonsense" (Smith, 2006) that continues to inform literacy curriculum and instruction in many schools.

Broadening the narrow view of reading and disrupting harmful forms of literacy instruction we observe in schools are urgent challenges for teacher preparation programs. How do we prepare bilingual teachers to resist and avoid reinforcing harmful raciolinguistic and racioliteracy ideologies and practices in their classrooms? "In these very hard times, there are glimmers of what might be hope" (Edelsky, 2006, p. 15) in preparing better equipped literacy and biliteracy teachers (Hoffman et al., 2020). As a biliteracy researcher and teacher educator, I want to call attention to the dangers associated with acritical literacy courses and superficial field experiences (Hoffman et al., 2019) typically required of preservice teachers in Texas and across much of the United States.

My critique and subsequent recommendations for healthier, more productive forms of literacy instruction are grounded in two decades of research and teaching experience in bilingual teacher preparation programs. In my experience, teacher education programs often reflect and promote deficit ideologies similar to those practiced in schools.

For example, faculty conversations about students' reading and writing typically revolve around the performance of pre-service teachers and program graduates on state certification tests. Program evaluation by state education agencies center on low passing rates, call on institutions to raise test scores, and remind program faculty of the state's ultimate authority to suspend teacher preparation. Each of these actions parallels the pressures that preservice teachers face to teach literacy skills in isolation.

In the same fashion, ideologies of reading and writing as practices that take place only in English and that are disconnected from children's language development are central to teacher preparation programs. The normalized literacy "problems" of linguistically racialized children are largely unquestioned within teacher preparation programs and in the state-mandated reading programs that continue to fail the emergent bilingual children they purport to educate (Burns, 2014; Cochran-Smith et al., 2018). In his analysis of *Preventing Reading Difficulties in Young Children*, (Snow et al., 1998), commonly used in literacy teacher education programs, James Gee (2007) describes how issues of racism and power are intentionally excluded from literacy education:

> It is widely believed that such issues are "merely political," not directly relevant to reading and reading research. PRD is certainly written in such spirit. But the fact of the matter is that racism and power are just as much cognitive issues as they are political ones. Children won't identify with—they will even disidentify with—teachers and schools that they perceive as hostile, alien, or oppressive to their home-based identities. (p. 12)

While critical literacy scholars are not opposed to the idea that standards can guide meaningful literacy instruction, it is important to recognize that standards tell us *what* to teach but should not be interpreted to dictate *how* teachers must teach (Moustafa, 2008).

Further complicating the relationship between standards and reading programs is that linguistically diverse and racialized students are largely absent in the standards discourse except as perceived targets of remediation. This omission is arguably by design. Certainly, many early childhood researchers and educators have long understood the importance of supporting children's home language and literacy practices (Dyson, 2015), and in too many cases, these views have been silenced or rendered ineffective by the dominance of for-profit interests (capitalism) within the public education system, in combination with racial and anti-immigrant discrimination. Furthermore, dominant views of literacy hold that reading and writing are best taught in bits and pieces and through ideologies of "grammatical correctness and mandates that are linguistically unsound" (Genishi & Dyson, 2009, p. 144) with pernicious effects, especially for linguistically diverse children. Similarly, dominant views treat reading and writing as skills that can be taught from a script and disconnected from children's language development or contexts of use, making room for competitive and dubious practices in the marketing and delivery of teacher education programs which signal that practically anybody can teach children to read and write. Given this backdrop, it is not surprising that even well-intentioned early childhood and emergent literacy practitioners may approach their work with bilingual children and families as a form of remediation that will eventually result in English monolingualism. How can we help support and sustain literacy teachers who wish to teach against such a view? In the following section, I describe kidwatching and teacherwatching as sensible and caring approaches to preparing teachers to promote biliteracy and serve bilingual children.

From "Kidwatching" to "Teacherwatching": Strategies for Promoting Healing Forms of Literacy and Literacy Teacher Preparation

Kidwatching (Owocki & Goodman, 2002) and ethnographic case studies (Dyson & Genishi, 2005) are critical pedagogical practices for preparing teachers to recognize and contest racial ideologies. Kidwatching, or "spending time observing, gathering data, interacting with children to understand how language and literacy develop" (Owocki & Goodman, 2002, p. 3), is at the core of conducting ethnographic case studies with novice literacy and bilingual educators. In my university courses, I combine these approaches by requiring preservice teachers to observe an emergent biliterate child over the course of a semester. It is important to note that many preservice bilingual teachers begin, often unconsciously, to reproduce the same colonizing racioliteracy practices they themselves experienced as children. By providing concrete tools for observing and listening carefully to children as they read and write, kidwatching can greatly impact how future teachers will work with linguistically racialized children.

With this background in mind, I want to extend the idea of kidwatching into teacherwatching as a critical component of using epistemic disobedience and engagement with decolonial epistemologies (Mignolo, 2009; Mignolo & Walsh, 2018) in teacher preparation. This teacherwatching would acknowledge and seek to contest deficit ideologies regarding the intersections among language, race, and literacy. Epistemic disobedience, in this case, means rethinking ways of teaching literacy and reconceptualizing linguistic differences to include students' worldviews and build on the linguistic strengths derived from their home and community literacy practices. To practice epistemic disobedience in literacy instruction and research we must ground our work in the understanding that legitimate forms of language and literacy exist in languages other than standardized American English. To work toward this goal, it is necessary to continue supporting teachers after they enter the profession and to accompany them in the creation of meaningful reading and writing practices for engaging racialized children. Unlearning and undoing colonizing forms of literacy instruction, where commercial reading programs maintain dominance over the particular needs of emergent bilingual children biliteracy education, requires time and teacher courage, but it is an urgently needed decolonial tool

(Mignolo & Walsh, 2018; Pennycook & Makoni, 2020) or anticolonial practice (Rivera Cusicanqui & Greidel, 2020).

Accompanying a New Teacher in Her First Years of Teaching

To illustrate the power of teacherwatching, I return to the story of Nina, the kindergarten teacher and former student who invited me to study her bilingual classroom. I chose to write about Nina's classroom for multiple reasons. She was the most engaged and dedicated student during the semester she took my university literacy classes for prospective bilingual teachers and conducted a thoughtful case study of the reading and writing development of a kindergarten student from Mexico. As an immigrant from Central America, Nina could see the talents and promises inherent in children who are developing literacy in two languages. By kidwatching and reflecting on her own history of language and literacy schooling, she became conscious of the educational and ideological limitations she experienced in high school English as a Second Language (ESL) classes upon her arrival in the United States. Furthermore, unlike many of her U.S.-born classmates in the teacher education program in Texas, Nina had not been linguistically colonized through English-only schooling at an early age. Thus, she was able to draw on her experiences as a student in Central American schools to recognize the linguistic strengths of Spanish-speaking and immigrant families. In addition, once she had her own classroom, Nina reached out for guidance in designing the best possible literacy program for her bilingual kindergarten students. In the following section, I describe how together we practiced teacherwatching to inform her practice.

Nina teaches at an elementary school in a small city in Texas with a rapidly growing population of emergent bilinguals of Mexican and Guatemalan origin. Because the school uses an "early exit" model of transitional bilingual education, Nina's first-year assignment—third grade—required her to teach primarily in English. In her second year of teaching, Nina was excited to be reassigned to a kindergarten classroom where she was permitted to teach bilingually. Knowing the importance of a bilingual classroom library, Nina borrowed 30 bilingual children's books from me, and we met often to discuss her plans for her second year of teaching. In a letter written in the first weeks of the year, Nina described her students' reaction to reading these books and her impressions of the impact on the children's engagement with reading. Her letter was written in Spanish, and I provide an English translation here:

> Buenas tardes, Dra. Murillo. Ayer empezamos a usar los libros que usted nos prestó. Hoy quedé sorprendida en ver la diferencia que existe al darles la oportunidad a los niños de escoger el libro que les gustaría leer primero. Hoy escogieron *La Llorona*. Estaban tan interesados, espantados, asustados, había de todo. Tenía ganas de llorar al verles sus caritas mientras escuchaban la historia.

> Lo mejor de todo, es que en el transcurso del día los niños continúan leyendo los mismos libros y siempre con muchas ganas y entusiasmo. Hoy se dieron cuenta que los libros tienen su nombre. Me decían, "maestra, aquí dice 'Luz' y aquí también." Y les conté que usted se los había prestado para que los leyeran y los amaran. Gracias por enseñarme cada vez que se puede un poco del montón de cosas que todavía me falta por aprender.
>
> Good afternoon Dr. Murillo. Yesterday we started using the books you loaned us. I was surprised today to see the difference that takes place when children have the opportunity to choose the book they want to read. Today they chose La Llorona. They were so interested, surprised, scared, all sorts of emotions. I almost cried seeing their faces as they listened to the story. Best of all, throughout the day the children kept reading the books with interest and enthusiasm. Today the children realized that your name is written in the books. They said, "Teacher, it says "Luz" here and here too. And I told them that you'd loaned us the books for them to read and love. Thank you for showing me that it is always possible to do a little of the many things I am still learning.

To learn about Nina's classroom, I spent each Friday during the fall of 2019 reading with students and observing her literacy instruction. I also sent some of my preservice teachers to do participant observation and help in the classroom. We met periodically with Nina to debrief about her instruction, my observations, and the university students' participation. Together we reviewed state-mandated standards, the materials the district required kindergarten teachers to use, and examples of her students' writing. Following the ideas of Ferreiro and Teberosky (1982) and Genishi and Dyson (2009), we provided notebooks for each child in order to record their daily writing and binders to collect their drawing and writing. We were engaged in a decolonial literacy project, in which we took risks to support the literacy development of the children in this kindergarten classroom, for example, minimizing the use of "Estrellita," the district-mandated prescriptive literacy program used to develop phonemic awareness in Spanish, and supplementing it as much as possible with bilingual books and teacher-designed activities based on principles from research informing the teaching of literacy for emerging readers and writers (Compton-Lilly et al., 2020; Dombey & Moustafa, 1988; Edelsky, 2006).

Based on the culturally sustainable pedagogies (Paris & Alim, 2017), she had developed in her teacher preparation program, Nina wrote a successful grant to buy books for her classroom library. These Spanish/English bilingual books, written mostly by Latinx authors and prominently displayed in her classroom, portray topics related to Latinx cultural and linguistic practices. The collection, along with a large poster Nina created with the words "Soy un lector y un escritor" (I'm a reader and a writer) was one of several features that caught the attention of all who visited her classroom. Another was the creation of a *tiendita* (neighborhood store) supplied with empty food packages children brought from home. In this favorite center, children experienced reading and writing as fun and commonsense practices needed to create a shopping list, calculate a food budget, and transact sales as shopkeepers and customers. Each time the university students and visiting professors entered the classroom the children ran toward us with a book to read or to share their notebooks and portfolios in great excitement. Furthermore, on several occasions, children have written letters inviting us to read with them and to attend a holiday potluck lunch with food prepared by their families.

In all these literacy encounters, Nina's students seemed to be making great progress in reading and writing and they were obviously developing a passion for reading bilingual books, including the big books which Nina created based on these stories. Unfortunately, the school's administration soon expressed concern that the students were not using the assigned phonics program or the worksheets adopted by the other kindergarten teachers. In November, only 3 months into the school year, Nina's teaching was observed by the assistant principal, who told her, "Your children are having too much fun and we want them to learn." Her observation and formal review did not mention the dynamic biliteracy classroom environment Nina had created or her students' enthusiasm for reading bilingual books and writing about them. A few days later, the principal sent her the email message quoted earlier, emphasizing the expectation that reading and writing instruction should focus on word counts, letter formation, capitalization, and punctuation.

Practicing Literacy Teaching and Teacher Preparation as "Radical Hope"

Through the accounts in this chapter, my intent is to encourage teachers to expect the best from Latinx children by providing opportunities to read and write on their own terms and become long-life readers and writers, even if it appears to some that their students are "having too much fun." I began the project with the hope of supporting a new teacher with limited classroom experience and much promise and to see what I could learn by extending my university teaching of preservice teachers beyond certification and into the early years of teaching. Now in her third year of teaching, Nina has been reassigned to a first-grade classroom, where she works with many of her former kindergarten students and is adding to her growing collection of bilingual books and materials she has created. In this strange and unsettling year of remote-teaching learning due to the COVID-19 pandemic, Nina and I continue to collaborate virtually to document and reflect on her growth as a literacy teacher of racialized bilingual children. She continues to receive preservice teachers from the university and has begun to mentor them as they conduct their own ethnographic case studies by reading and writing with her first-grade students. We should be grateful for the persistence of teachers like Nina, given the pressures they face to teach literacy only in the limited, reductionist ways we know are not helpful for emergent bilingual children (Garan, 2007) and the lack of recognition of their dedication and creativity, factors that cause many to leave the classroom (Petrón et al., 2019).

My hope for teacher education and early childhood literacy programs is that we develop the wisdom and courage to undertake the task of preparing literacy teachers who will challenge the racialized and language-based deficit ideologies that persist in many school and university classrooms, educators who will recognize the power orientations, marginalizations, and oppressions that are revealed through the study of raciolinguistic ideologies. A radical hope is at the center of this important work. Jonathan Lear (2006) writes that what makes hope

> radical is that it is directed toward a future goodness that transcends the current ability to understand what it is. Radical hope anticipates a good for which those who have the hope as yet lack the appropriate concepts with which to understand it. What would it be for such hope to be justified. (p. 104)

The long history and widespread practice of deficit thinking in schools about emergent bilinguals and other linguistically racialized children mean that few educators have experienced or taught in schools where the vision of literacy equity is fully realized. Thus, we can say that we are preparing teachers in the hope of moving toward this "future goodness" rather than in expectation of its immediate realization. Lear (2006) goes on to say that "the question of hope ... [is] intimately bound to the question of how to live" (p. 105), which can be extended to the practice of literacy for better futures. I am proposing that those of us who prepare literacy teachers approach our work with radical hope.

In conclusion, I invite scholars and practitioners to question, challenge, and decolonize literacy pedagogies that claim to be based on exclusive and limited views of "science" that ignore or discriminate against bilingual children. Efforts to prepare literacy and biliteracy teachers using an anticolonial framework may be met with reluctance but they are critically important (Lyiscott et al., 2018) for the dignity and school success of racialized children. As I have tried to show here, a hopeful first step is engaging with beginning teachers as researchers (Curry & Bloome, 1998), potential mentors (Hoffman et al., 2019), and, most of all, people who think (Ferreiro, 2003) rather than simply as conduits for the delivery of "new" reading programs that do not work for emergent bilingual learners.

References

Alim, S., Rickford, J., & Ball, A. (2016). *Raciolinguistics: How language shapes our ideas about race.* Oxford University Press.

Avineri, N., Blum, S., Johnson, E., Brice-Heath, S., & Kremer-Sadlik, T. (2015). Invited forum: Bridging the "language gap." *Journal of Linguistic Anthropology, 25*(1), 66–86. doi:10.1111/jola.12071.66

Bissex, G. (1982). The child as teacher. In H. Goelman, A. A. Orberg, & F. Smith (Eds.), *Awakening to literacy. The University of Victoria symposium on children's response to a literate environment: Literacy before schooling* (pp. 87–101). Heinemann Educational Books.

Blum, S. (2016). Unseen WEIRD assumptions: The so-called language gap discourse and ideologies of language, childhood, and learning. *International Multilingual Research Journal, 11*(1), 23–38. doi:10.1080/19313152.2016.1258187

Burns, J. (2014). Our impoverished view of teacher education. *Teachers College Record 108*(6), 949–995. http://www.tcrecord.org

Chaparro, S. (2019). "But Mom! I'm not a Spanish boy": Raciolinguistic socialization in a two-way immersion bilingual program. *Linguistics and Education, 50*(1), 1–12 https://doi.org/10.1016/j.linged.2019.01.003

Cochran-Smith, M., Cummings Carney, M., Stringer, E., Burton, S., Chang, W., Fernández, M. B., Miller, A., Sánchez, J., & Baker, M. (2018). *Reclaiming accountability in teacher education.* Teachers College Press.

Compton-Lilly, C., Mitra, A., Guay, M., & Spence, L.K. (2020). A confluence of complexity: Intersections among reading theory, neuroscience, and observations of young readers. *Reading Research Quarterly, 55*(1), 185–195. https://doi.org/10.1002/rrq.348

Curry, T., & Bloome, D. (1998). Learning to write by writing ethnography. In A. Egan-Robertson & D. Bloome (Eds.), *Students as researchers of culture and language in their own communities* (pp. 37–58). Hampton Press.

de Saxe, J., & Favela, A. (2018). Good teacher, bad teacher: Helping undergrads uncover neoliberal narratives that dichotomize and disguise structural inequalities. *Journal of Thought, 52*(1–2), 29–47.

Dombey, H., & Moustafa, M. (1998). *Whole to part phonics: How children learn to read and spell.* Heinemann.

Dyson, A. H. (2015). The search for inclusion: Deficit discourse and the erasure of childhoods. *Language Arts, 92*(3), 199–207.

Dyson, A. H., & Genishi, C. (2005). *On the case* (Vol. 76). Teachers College Press.

Edelsky, C. (1986). *Writing in a bilingual classroom: Había una vez.* Ablex.

Edelsky, C. (2006). *With literacy and justice for all. Rethinking the social in language and education.* Erlbaum.

Ferreiro, E. (1990). Literacy development: Psychogenesis. In Y. M. Goodman (Ed.), *How children construct literacy. Piagetian perspectives* (pp. 12–25). International Reading Association.

Ferreiro, E. (2003). *Past and present of the verbs to read and write* (A Groundwood Book). Douglas & McIntyre.

Ferreiro, E., & Teberosky, A. (1982). *Literacy before schooling.* Heinemann

Ferreiro, E., & Teberosky, A. (2012). *Los sistemas de escritura en el desarrollo del niño.* Siglo Veintiuno Editores. (Original work published 1979)

Flores, B. (2005). The intellectual presence of the deficit view of Spanish speaking children in the educational literature during the 20th century. In P. Pedraza & M. Rivera (Eds.), *Latino education: An agenda for community action research* (pp. 75–99). Erlbaum.

Flores, B., Tefft, P., & Díaz, E. (1991). Transforming deficit myths about learning, language, and culture. *Language Arts, 68*(5), 369–379.

Flores, N. (2017). Bilingual education. In O. García, N. Flores, & M. Spotti (Eds.), *The Oxford handbook of language and society* (pp. 525–543). Oxford University Press.

Flores, N., & Rosa. J. (2015). Undoing appropriateness: Raciolinguistic ideologies and language diversity in education. *Harvard Review, 85*(2), 7–29.

Foley, D. (1997). Deficit thinking models based on culture: The anthropological protest. In R. R. Valencia (Ed.), *The evolution of deficit thinking: Educational thought and practice* (pp. 113–131). Falmer Press.

Garan, E. (2007). *Smart answers to tough questions: What to say when you are asked about fluency, phonics, grammar, vocabulary, SSR, tests, support for ELLs, and more.* Scholastic.

García. O., & Kleifgen, J.A. (2018). *Educating emergent bilinguals: Policies, programs, and practices for English language learners.* Teachers College Press.

García, O., & Otheguy, R. (2017). Interrogating the language gap of young bilingual and bidialectal students. *International Multilingual Research Journal, 11*(1), 52–65.

Gee, J. (2015). *Social linguistics and literacies: Ideology in discourses.* Routledge.

Gee, J. P. (2007). Reading and language development. Beyond limited perspectives. In J. Larson (Ed.), *Literacy as snake oil. Beyond the quick fix* (pp. 10–25). Peter Lang.

Genishi, C., & Dyson, A. (2009). *Children language and literacy. Diverse learners in diverse times.* Teachers College Press.

Goelman, H. (1982). The discussion: What was said. In H. Goelman, A. A. Orberg, & F. Smith (Eds.), *Awakening to literacy. The University of Victoria symposium on children's response to a literate environment: Literacy before schooling* (pp. 214–221). Exeter Heinemann Educational Books.

Goelman, H., Oberg, A. A., & Smith, F. (1982). (Eds.). *Awakening to literacy. The University of Victoria symposium on children's response to a literate environment: Literacy before schooling.* Exeter Heinemann Educational Books.

González, N., Moll, L. C., & Amanti, C. (2005). *Funds of knowledge: Theorizing practices in households, communities, and classrooms.* Erlbaum.

Heath, S. B. (1982). The achievement of preschool literacy for mother and child. In H. Goelman, A. A. Orberg, & F. Smith (Eds.), *Awakening to literacy. The University of Victoria symposium on children's response to a literate environment: Literacy before schooling* (pp. 51–72). Exeter Heinemann Educational Books.

Hoffman, J. V., Svcerc, N., Lammert, C., Daly-Lesch, A., Steinitz, E., Greeter, E., & DeJulio, S. (2019). A research review of literacy tutoring and mentoring in initial teacher preparation: Toward practices that can transform teaching. *Journal of Literacy Research, 51*(2), 233–251.

Hoffman, J. V., Hikida, M., & Sailors, M. (2020). Contesting science that silences: Amplifying equity, agency, and design research in literacy teacher preparation. *Reading Research Quarterly, 55*(1), 255–266. https://doi.org/10.1002/rrq.348

Kozol, J. (2006). *The shame of the nation: The restoration of apartheid schooling in America.* Crown.

Ladson-Billings, G. (2009). *The dreamkeepers: Successful teachers of African American children.* Jossey-Bass.

Labov, W. (1969). *The logic of nonstandard English* (Monographs on Language and Linguistics). Georgetown University School of Languages and Linguistics.

Labov, W. (2003). When ordinary children fail to read. *Reading Research Quarterly, 38*(1), 128–131.

Lear, J. (2006). *Radical hope.* Harvard University Press.

Lyiscott, J. J., Caraballo, L., & Morrell, E. (2018). An anticolonial framework for urban teacher preparation. *The New Educator, 14*(3), 231–251. https://doi.org/10.1080/1547688X.2017.1412000

Meyer, R. (2002). *Phonics exposed. Understanding and resisting systematic direct intense phonics instruction*. Erlbaum.

Mignolo, W. (2009). Epistemic disobedience, independent thought, and decolonial freedom. *Theory, Culture & Society, 27*(7–8), 159–181. doi:10.1177/0263276409349275

Mignolo, W., & Walsh, C. (2018). *On decoloniality. Concepts, analytics, praxis*. Duke University Press.

Moll, L. C. (2008, October 16). *The subject of biliteracy* [Paper presentation]. Annual Meeting of the National Academy of Education, University of Washington, Seattle, WA, United States.

Monzó, L. M., & Rueda, R. (2009). Passing for English fluent: Latino immigrant children masking language proficiency. *Anthropology & Education Quarterly, 40*(1), 20–40.

Moustafa, M. (2008). *Exceeding the standards: A strategic approach for linking state standards and best practices in reading and writing instruction*. Scholastic.

Murillo, L. A., & Smith, P. H. (2011). "I will never forget that": Lasting effects of language discrimination on language-minority children and families in Colombia and on the U.S.-Mexico border. *Childhood Education, 87*(3), 147–153.

Noguerón-Liu, S. (2020). Expanding the knowledge base in literacy instruction and assessment: Biliteracy and translanguaging perspectives from families, communities, and classrooms. *Reading Research Quarterly, 55*(1), 307–318. https://doi.org/10.1002/rrq.348

Owocki, G., & Goodman, Y. (2002). *Documenting children's literacy development*. Heinemann

Paris, D., & Alim, S. (Eds.). (2017). *Culturally sustaining pedagogies. Teaching and learning for justice in a changing world*. Teachers College Press.

Pennycook, A., & Makoni, S. (2020). *Innovations and challenges in applied linguistics from the global South*. Routledge.

Petrón, M. A., Ates, B., & Berg, H. (2019, June 4). "You just sit there and be quiet": Latina/o bilingual educators in Texas. *Journal of Latinos and Education*. Advanced online publication. doi:10.1080/15348431.2019.1622115

Reich, R. B. (2001). *The future of success: Working and economy*. Knopf.

Rosa, J. (2019). *Looking like a language, sounding like a race: Raciolinguistic ideologies and the learning of latinidad*. Oxford University Press.

Rivera Cusicanqui, S., & Geidel, M. (2020). *Ch'ixinakax utxiwa: On decolonizing practices and discourses*. Polity.

Saldivar, E. (2019). *Racioliteracies: Race and subjectivity in the teaching of Spanish to bilingual Latinx students* [Unpublished doctoral dissertation, University of Pennsylvania]. ProQuest.

Scribner, S., & Cole, M. (1981). *The psychology of literacy*. Harvard University Press.

Smith, F. (2006). *Reading without nonsense*. Teachers College Press.

Smith, F. (2011). *Understanding reading. A psycholinguistic analysis of reading and learning to read*. Routledge.

Snow, C. E., Burns, M. S., & Griffin, P. (Eds.). (1998). *Preventing reading difficulties in young children*. National Academy Press.

Sosnowski, J. (2020). *Reinscribing and reimagining linguistic and social hierarchies in a prison-based language and literacy program* [Unpublished doctoral dissertation, University of Illinois at Urbana-Champaign]. ProQuest.

Watkins, E. (2015). *Literacy work in the reign of human capital*. Fordham University Press.

CHAPTER 11

Justice Mapping: Making Theoretical Kin With/in Childhood Studies

Tim Kinard

THE FOLLOWING IS an attempt to "make kin with" (Haraway, 2016) a version of critical race theory (CRT) and posthumanist theories by reencountering a curriculum I code-signed through narration. "Making kin seems to me the thing that we most need to be doing in a world that rips us apart from each other" (Paulson, 2019, para. 19). To make kin with CRT and new materialism(s), I grapple with CRT scholars' call to "re-centre the issue of 'race'" (Bradbury, 2020, p. 242) and posthumanist scholars' attempts to "transcend the boundaries of the human and animal, animal/human and machine, and the physical and non-physical" (Howlett, 2018, p. 108):

> "It matters what ideas we use to think other ideas (with)." (Strathern quoted in Haraway, 2016, p. 12)
>
> It matters what stories we tell to tell other stories with. (Haraway, 2016, p. 12)

I have recently had conversations with educators who employ CRT and educators who employ theories of the more-than-human. In speaking with these friends, peers, and mentors, frustrations emerge, esoteric language reinforces walls, and exoteric articulations fail to cross boundaries. At the core of these conversations are the seemingly conflicting desires to (a) focus on race-based identity and (b) blur identities' boundaries (re)enforced by recognition (Pacini-Ketchabaw & Nxumalo, 2010). Yet, I hear hope in these educators' articulations for practitioners and scholars utilizing disparate frameworks to "become enfolded in each other's projects, in each other's lives; [to] come to need each other in diverse, passionate, corporeal, meaningful ways" (Haraway, 2016, pp. 71–72).

I reencounter, through narrative wonderings, our curriculum, which was designed partly to "extend dialogue, at times beyond human interaction, to encompass materials and the environment itself" (Lawrence, 2019, p. 319), as well as to attend to calls for educators to fully humanize participation to/with students of color in an era of "anti-Black misandric violence" (Bryan, 2021, p. 747)—to meet demands for humanization and demands for posthumanization—that "*matter* matters" (Lenz Taguchi, 2010) and "Black Lives Matter." I purport neither to delineate/define/explicate the multiplicity that is CRT nor posthumanism(s) but to read/think/see (Jackson & Mazzei, 2012) our curriculum and its implementation, to become-with important scholarship.

A Pirouette

A student in a Texas public school leans over a precarious, student-designed-and-made assemblage of recycled materials. Recyclables are a mainstay of this curriculum, and this construction is a balancing act of previously used wood, plastic, and cardboard held together without glues, screws, or tape. It's a wobbly series of ramps designed to transport ping-pong balls into a cup meters away. The student waits their turn to drop a ball on the path, while another student rolls theirs. The ball misses the cup. The waiting boy exclaims, "OOoohhh!" while gracefully pirouetting. One of the construction's creators cries, "You're gonna knock it down!" Then, swiveling to locate an adult, shouts, "Ms. Peña, he's gonna knock it down!"

A Short Story of Place

Millennia before this pirouette, there was an ancient spring emanating from the land beneath this school. This spring remains vital with plants and animal/humans—a sacred site (Rocha, 2019). Countless languages have been uttered along its banks, like Caddo, from whence the word *Texas* emerged. Europeans seized the spring 500 years ago, speaking Spanish (Balestra, 2008). Centuries later, it was stolen from their descendants, the Tejanos, by English-speaking settler colonizers from the United States (Teja & Ramos, 2010). Those intruders brought another violence to Texas: cleaving economies from the land by the forced labor of enslaved Black people (Kendi, 2016). Land, people, matter, water, languages—stolen. The spring continued to bubble forth. Clear and cool, the resulting river cuts a new city in two. It divides the resulting, ever-changing city into two codependent cities: one on high ground, where English is heard. My university tops the highest hill. The river is recreational there: canoes, swimming, fishing. The other city is on low ground, a floodplain. Spanish is spoken by many there. The river is an imminent danger, always a threat. It destroys and sometimes kills (Ashford-Hanserd et al., 2020). Black people created a community here after the end of enslavement, becoming Texans. This becoming remains in progress, and a small Black community resists and resides in this multiple city (Ashford-Hanserd, et al., 2020).

The story of water, land, peoples, languages, dominance, and resistance entangles the characters of the narrative of this chapter—one in which recycled materials, teachers, students, discourse, matter, all work as agents in creating reality—realities—within a city, within its communities, and within a curriculum. This short story of a sacred spring and a city's communities is not "context" for the narrative in a school. It is not the past that I take into consideration. It is now—the "past-present" of settler colonialism (Nxumalo & Cedillo, 2017). The springs, the languages, conquest, the city (cities) are the 'now' of the curriculum as much as 4-year-olds and recyclables.

This city is a "becoming," "heterogeneity, infinitesimal, passage to the limit, continuous variation" (Deleuze & Guattari, 1987, p. 363). The school is "becoming" as the land, the water, the conquest, the economies, the peoples relate/encounter.

Entering a Curriculum without Beginnings

Back at school, just before the pirouette, the hallway bustles.

There are multiple, interactive, student-created constructions, conceptualized by 3- to 7-year-olds in this public summer program. The repurposed materials line the walls while students browse their peers' offerings, exiting and entering classrooms in a spontaneous, syncopated rhythm. The hallway is also filled with the accompanying sounds of this sort of bustle: Spanish phonemes, words, and ideas intertwine with English phonemes, words, and ideas. One can clearly hear both languages but also an intermingled symphony of similarities and differences. The hallway echoes the velar fricatives of Texas' Spanish and the monophthongs of Texas' English: The borders between blur.

Four girls have created a "store" within an appliance box. Jewelry sways in the window, crafted by students/materials in a space called the "Constructive Play Lab" (Kinard et al., 2018). I enter this narrative here, at "The Store," but in the middle—plugging into memories, notes, photos, and videos; mashing them, viewing various angles, contemplating what's beyond the borders of the video; the backstories and supporting cast of lives lived outside my view, beyond this context, which "refers to what is neither seen nor understood, but is nevertheless perfectly present" (Deleuze, 1986, p. 16): the city, its waters, its ways. Our curriculum was designed to be entered in the middle, resistant to the notion of having a "beginning" (Sellers, 2010), characterized by "heterogeneous connectivity" (Sellers, 2010, p. 559), interrupting adult control of 'knowledge,' movement, bodies, and future realities.

Collaboration and "Recognition"

My colleagues and I recognized the disparity in lived experiences on the two sides of the river. Aware that recognition can act as "foregrounding the liberal rhetoric of freedom and equality" (Nxumalo et al., 2011, p. 216), but troubled by the inequity, we recognized that those speaking Spanish at home and those speaking English at home were encountering disparate curricula at school. We took action. We sought collaboration with the school district to create a new summer program. Texas has long mandated interventionist summer school be available "for" students who speak English as a Second Language, labeled "at risk," harboring deficits (Swadener, 2000), governed by standards—policed through instructivism/didacticism. Our university also ran tuition-based "enrichment" summer programs. Troubled by both notions of "enrichment" and "intervention" based on language, we collaborated with district partners to create a blended environment, where students could test and retest the physical rules of life on a planet with gravity, chemicals, usable waste, thermodynamics, and test and retest the sociocultural rules of what it means to be in school, a family, a city, with a language, regardless of which language they spoke at home. On the day student-built contraptions line the halls, years into this careful and difficult district/university collaboration, the blended populations explore others' designs.

I have taught here since 2014, alongside colleagues, preservice teachers, and certified, bilingual teachers. Each summer more than 200 children attend. Half speak Spanish at home, half English—some both. Half attend for free, qualifying linguistically. The rest pay US$90.

Whether their families pay or the state does, the students enter the curriculum to work as theory-builders, sharing home-hewn knowledges, creating, and storytelling, encountering diverse others and a diversity of materials. Given our recognition of the deficit views of language, we committed to countering the hegemony of English, emphasizing Spanish as a language of beauty, purpose, and brilliance. We worked with predominantly monolingual preservice teachers to investigate ways English-dominant spaces damage all students' abilities to fashion new understandings and connect to multilingualism. We foregrounded Spanish, shared bilingual and Spanish mentor texts, celebrated translanguaging and the virtuosity of those brokering between two languages (García & Wei, 2014). We acted out stories told by students in home languages, made books of these stories from recyclables, built structures, played, and became "otherwise" (Shields, 2015). We encouraged the preservice teachers to embrace the moniker "emergent bilingual" (García & Wei, 2014) and transgress the borders that separate Texans.

The point of these efforts was never to "teach" language skills. It was—is—to share spaces normally defined by "bright boundaries" (Alba, 2005), borders held in fixity defining "other" (Davies et al., 2013). We resisted notions of "beginning" "instruction" with a single packet of linguistic knowledge. Languages have no beginnings; one enters in the middle of a language, which enfolds and unfolds (Ramanathan, 2006). This movement was not just about language but also our enacted curriculum. Just as I enter this narrative in the middle, at the "Store", the students employ the connectivity of their experiences and enter the curriculum, picking a spot and plugging in. I pick The Store.

Jewelry Emerges from the Lab

About an hour before the busy scene in the hallway, the halls were mostly empty, just handfuls of students coming and going. Generally, the halls are merely pathways from place to place. This is the shifting, always-in-motion, reality of the curriculum. Movement. Change. Previously, there were a few adults, some constructions—paint drying—and a group of girls walking together down the relatively quiet corridor, looking for a new venue. They chose the "Constructive Play Lab." They leave the hall and enter.

The Lab. There are no assigned times or designated groups who visit the Lab. Those who choose to enter come and go alone or in groups. The girls enter and scan the room, scrutinizing the shelves: cartons, crates, buttons, twine, fabric, toilet paper rolls, and every size of box that Amazon ships. There are also teachers, with the accoutrements of their Lab work: box cutters, glue guns, tape, Sharpies.

Three boys enter. One points to his companion's construction, "¡Queremos hacer un avión!" A teacher confirms, "¿Desea hacer un avión? Okay." She nods, looking around to model scanning the shelves for materials needed to make an airplane. The boys pick up the teacher's cue and rummage through the shelves for possibilities. One of the boys picks up a tube. "¡Uuuu, mira!"

Across the room, the girls experiment with both ideas and materials. A shared topic emerges. They begin making jewelry. The individual pieces become a collection, an assembly of ideas, materials, histories, and desires: necklaces of yarn and buttons, bracelets woven from fabric. One exclaims, "Ooh! We can make a store! We can sell them!" Her peers respond exuberantly. They find a cardboard tray, carefully arrange their creations in it, and leave the Lab.

Hopes for Becoming

Through narrative, I unfold a crinkle of memories, smoothing out recollections from the first days I recognized our city's segregated summer programs. I recognized, categorized, held identities in place by the fixity of "recognition" (Pacini-Ketchabaw & Nxumalo, 2010)—a link in a chain of citations, affirmations, admonishments defining who one "is":

> It is through citational chains, or repeated acts of recognition, that we are subjected and subject ourselves to discourses that are...in some sense prior to us, and external to us. The citational chains enable the accomplishment of

ourselves as recognizably human, autonomous beings with a viable sense of individual identity. (Davies et al., 2013, p. 682)

This repeated act creates an identity, illustrated in the static conveyance of the word *being*: *being* a girl, Latina, English-speaking, bound by recognition. But if the border of individual identity is challenged, newness becomes possible. If we reconsider the "edge" of an individual at the skin and unravel individuality into "a body-world that is always tending, attending to the world" (Manning, 2013, p. 2), then body-beyond-skin (and world-within-*through*-body) reenvisions a girl making jewelry—as not only more-than-girl *using* yarn, but also yarn-altering-girl; yarn-girl becoming-with, "doing something to each other simultaneously" (Hultman & Lenz Tguchi, 2010, p. 530). Grosz (2011) describes "the nonliving tentacles that extend themselves into the living, the provisional linkages the nonliving and the living form to enable the living to draw out the virtualities of the nonliving" (p. 36): Yarn-girl-ideas-jewelry-desires becoming-with. This connects the girl and the world through recycled materials, relational realities, possibility—but also a critical juncture where capitalist desires and colonial ideals about "precious" "jewels" intersect traditions of adornment: a dialogue.

"Life is as much about becoming as being" (Grosz, 2011, p. 65). A city's (cities') realities of conquest, water, school, languages, families, recyclables, "foldings bring into appearance not a fully constituted human, already-contained, but a co-constitutive strat[um] of matter, content, form, substance, and expression. The self is not contained. It is a fold of immanent expressibility" (p. 3). Expressibility explodes recognition—a single girl and who she "is" or "contains": Latina, English, Texan, human—becomes-with new expressions. The role of a curriculum is worth investigating in terms of these relations. In a reconsidered curriculum-*becoming*, matter, minds, what 'matters' becomes-with. Manning (2013) presents a reality in which becomings-with are "always on the way toward new foldings" (p. 26).

Through this connection making to the middle of a curriculum-becoming-with-no-beginning and lives that are in the middle of a city's story, the recognition of one student's learning unravels as "leaps of development occur[ing] in a fractal mode of relation where events build on events, each of them affecting at once the [student] and the environment" (Manning, 2013, p. 3). Because of the enfolded, lived experiences across the city, students plug into multiplicities, and "curriculum" becomes "*curricula*"—plural. I engage with the story not in terms of the learning of the individuals therein, or the "freedom" one "child" might have to "choose" an activity or a project. Instead, I encounter the movement of the city, the building, all those boxes and materials, bodies and utterances through Manning's (2013) notion that it is "incumbent on the event as it unfolds that all preconstituted constituents be transformed into propositions" (p. 114), which rewrite the future/present. Girls performing multiple futures in an enfolded "now."

Given this expressibility, or the ability to express the matter and *what* matters, to relate, to create futures in the now, I return to my entry point, in the middle.

Curricula-Becoming-Store

The group of girls takes the jewelry tray to a room called "Boxville," a classroom emptied of everything except appliance boxes. The teachers, here, also have box cutters, Sharpies, and tape. The group circumvents a sprawling assemblage of recycled boxes, combined, cut, and constructed into a "castle" by a group of students.

They choose a big box as the site. The box's construction contributes to this conversion, suggesting the architecture of the store, dialoguing with their ideas of "stores." One girl draws the "window," and the teacher slices the cardboard. Because of the manufacturing of the box, this leads to the discovery of layers of reinforcing within the box. The girls tug; the box resists. Protrusions materialize along the "window," suggesting an idea, and the girls hang trinkets on them. "Let's move it out [in the hall], so we can get customers."

New connections, relations, and encounters irrupt in the hallway. The Store creates ripples. Groups respond by designing complementary attractions. There are other stores. One with wares on a table crafted together by repurposed lumber, hammers, nails, saws, and two girls in the outdoor woodworking area. On the table are "potholders" and strips of paper—money the buyers can literally print themselves. New economies.

These consumerist connections are not the only relations fashioned from peers' and materials' encounters. "Games" emerge. Some students have fastened deconstructed egg cartons to the insides of a box, challenging peers to toss a tape-ball into the openings. One student shouts encouragement, "¡Órale!" A line forms. Cues to queue up come from lived experience, not teacher direction. The hallway soon buzzes with games, shops, and oddities. Next to one attraction is a girl holding a green sheet of paper with orange paint: "Abierto."

Contextualizing Pirouettes

Ideas burst forth as if from a hidden root system. The creativity, competitiveness, consumerism, and quirkiness become "propositions" (Manning, 2013) that "propel: they promise nothing. They create openings, intervals, fluxes of potential relations. They propose. They risk. And they move" (p. 52). This curricula-becoming, extends material into the lives of our students, which extend into curricula. The materials and bodies create provisional linkages, connecting school and beyond. The hallways become a new territory, propelled by desires, an ethic of resistance, the taken-for-granted, and the chimeric connectivity of "playwork" (Kinard et al., 2018, p. 225).

The creators of the contraption from the beginning of this narrative—with its tubes, ramps, twists, and pitfalls—bark to passersby, inviting them to roll a ball, to see if it will land in a red plastic cup. A box containing ping-pong balls sits waiting. A line forms, and students take a turn or two, trying their luck. Shrieks of laughter and defeat emanate when balls inevitably fall off the whimsically engineered track. A boy approaches. "Oh, I'll try!" He plunges his hand into the box and withdraws with a ball. "You'll have to wait!" exclaims one of the designers, pointing. "There's a line!"

"Uh-huh!" The customer nods vigorously, leaning over the device to wait his turn. A failed attempt rolls off the track. "OOHHhh!" he exclaims in solidarity and pirouettes.

"You're gonna knock it down!" says the boy who sent him to the line. He reels toward an adult. "Ms. Peña, he's gonna knock it down!"

"Calm your body, Ezekias," a teaching veteran, says from several feet away.

Policing

This narration repeats recognitions. The borders of girl, English, student, mind: recognitions. St. Pierre (2004) suggests "we might live differently if we conceived the world differently" (p. 290). She also insists that "language and reality exist together on the surface" (St. Pierre, 2013, p. 650). Limited language limits possibility. My inability to narrate without recognition limits. Justice seems reliant upon dialogue with/in group [esoteric] and across groups [exoteric] (Wray & Grace, 2007). As I attempt "plugging one text into another" (Jackson & Mazzei, 2012, p. 130) and "insert [my]selves into the material production of the texts" (p. 131) to think with theory, I search for articulations of justice.

I narrate Ezekias in the previous paragraphs using variations of *boy, waiting, plunging, withdrawing, pirouetting, nodding*. But these narrations deny "foreground[ing] one measure of how the body expresses" (Manning, 2013, p. 17). Ezekias is Black. I recognize this. So do his peers, teachers, and city.

Ezekias moves/acts/utters/behaves during this event just like his peers. There are "lines" at attractions, but many don't line up. Ezekias queues up at one point. Later, he doesn't. His peers exclaim, gesticulate, twirl, too. In reengagement with the events, I read/think/see him spin on the balls of his feet in relation to both physics and ideas. His movements are also read/thought/seen by peers and teachers.

Ezekias' movement is read as a danger. His body is read as dangerous. The students, both White and Latinx, train their eyes on Ezekias and declare his actions threatening (Bryan, 2021). The teacher acknowledges it. The students who admonish him point to no other body in the hall. Only the Black one. There are just four Black students of the more than 200 students. This number echoes the lived experiences of the Black families who have resided and resisted as a tiny percentage of this town. Ezekias is surrounded by non-Black bodies. And Ezekias is instructed to change his body.

"Calm your body, Ezekias."

Black PlayCrit and Death in a Rhizome

Bryan (2021) evokes Tamir Rice, killed by police while playing, perceived as a threat, denied "childhood" "innocence" assumptions, "subject to an adultification" (Dumas &

Nelson, 2016, p. 30). Bryan calls for a "Black PlayCrit," built on CRT to analyze reactions to Black students' playing. Black PlayCrit demands safe, supported, school-based Black play. "Children of color—suffer by being outside the public imagination of what childhood means—that is, children are worthy of protection and are entitled to play and discover" (Dumas & Nelson, 2016, p. 30). "Innocence" was not assumed of Ezekias. He was, like other Black boys, denied the "ability to enjoy the privileges and pleasures of play similar to their White children counterparts" (Bryan, 2021, p. 759).

Through Black PlayCrit, Black students become rightful players, enacting power, not held to a "script . . . handed down over generations . . . that some children are more innocent than others and Black children are not innocent at all" (Thomas, 2019, p. 66).

> Black liberatory fantasy enables Black people to create a world not yet for themselves, or invoke a radical imagination in which the colonized becomes the colonizer and the colonizer becomes the colonized. (Bryan, 2021, p. 757)

Yet, "deeply ingrained within schools' structures, processes, discourses, customs, policies, and laws" (Johnson, Bryan & Boutte, 2019 p. 6) is the denial of Black play, "undeserving of emotional and moral *recognition*" (Dumas & Nelson, 2016, p. 29). Bryan (2021) names this denial—"Play-Not": "given that Black bodies are devoid of intrinsic value under the White gaze, Play-Not acknowledges the denial of Black boys' play rights" (p. 759).

"The brilliance of children of color is rarely positioned as a starting point for discussion in early childhood studies" (Pérez & Saavedra, 2017, p. 1). Through a Black PlayCrit "recognition" of Blackness becomes necessary for Black brilliance to become assumed and Black students' right to playfully, creatively imagine become honored.

This disconnect between demands for recognition and calls to deconstruct recognition as a binding citational chain creates a dialogic impasse. As I seek to deconstruct my binding recognition of groups and individuals through the potential of becoming-with, I also seek to recognize racist acts within, *through*, a curriculum I designed. The curriculum I narrate, is connection-making, beginningless, "rhizomatic" (Sellers, 2010):

> Rhizomatics has been considered the most useful form of relative and potentially absolute deterritorialization by many scholars who are concerned with equity and social justice. However . . . the rhizome is a dangerous construct and is not necessarily liberatory, but it can initiate, "yes" newness, but also *death* or *failure*. (Cannella & Wolff, 2014, p. 8)

In order for this rhizomatic curricula-becoming to be additive, a reckoning with rhizomatic dangers must occur.

Our school is in Texas. Ezekias lives here. Texas is where Sandra Bland, a Black woman, died in jail (Heilbroner & Davis, 2018), where Breaion King, a Black teacher in *this* program was tackled by a police officer after school—*this* school (see *Traffic Stop* by Davis & Heilbroner, 2017). Texas is where Justin Howell, a Black undergraduate at my university, was shot by police while protesting the killing of George Floyd (Maxouris & Razek, 2020). Texas is where the city with the sacred spring connects to the matter of its land and matters called "history." Anti-Black violence is physical, bloody. It is also enacted daily in schools as "spirit murder" (Love, 2016). If matter is agential in new realities, and matter is named as mattering, then people who matter deserve naming, recognition. Ezekias matters. His Blackness matters.

Curriculum Deficits

Using Manning's (2013) words, White "desiring" "propels" (p. 52) anti-Blackness. It is not happenstance that Ezekias' peers and teacher police him, demand he change, become different—*be* different. This violent desire could be seen/thought/read as a twofold attempt to "fix" his identity—to *repair* his Blackness and/or to maintain the fixity of his identity. Fix him. Bind him.

In order to interrupt this fixing, many critical scholars argue for implementing top-down, content-based curricula, counterhegemonic instruction of alternate narratives of Blackness settler colonization (Asante, 2017). Just as books and stories in Spanish, and a celebration of Latinx community might create possibilities, utilization of BlackCrit lenses, along with careful self-analysis and care-full invitations for teachers to self-analyze might open borders to new territories in coming semesters. This episode could have unfolded differently in a curriculum specifically designed for anti-Black bias to be made visible, discussed, and countered, and Black genius, integrity, and accomplishment to be daily centered, "re-membered" (Johnson et al., 2019)—especially in a city where Black residents are scarce, where Brown residents are the majority and Whiteness dominates. Our program will utilize "a multiplicity of Black texts that highlight and celebrate the beauty, diversity, and positive contributions" (Bryan, 2021, p. 763) of Black people, Black brilliance, resistance, and contributions.

This is imperative and a directive in hindsight. But these changes will be enforced by teachers, reenforcing an adult/child binary. Critique of educator-led solutions to educator-created problems is important. Certainly, if adults control the knowledge in school, better that it be an interruption of anti-Black violence than an enforcement of neoliberal reform(ations) of these violences. Additionally, transformation should be participatory, not saviorism. Cole (2012) has named the "White Savior Industrial Complex" as "not about justice. It is about having a big emotional experience that validates privilege" (Cole, quoted in Aronson, 2017, p. 36). To read/think/see with the work of scholars who interrupt the construction of childhood, leads me to seek student/educator collaborated solutions to adult-created problems.

I continuously (re)learn to become-with students, peers, scholars, and notions. Our interns "recognized" Latinidad by recognizing anti-Latinx policies in top-down university classrooms. They learned to seek out Latinx resilience, resistance, creativity, brilliance, educación—it came to matter. We have far, far to go. Coming-into-encounter with Latinx brilliance, *prior to teaching*, remains important. Latinx brilliance acted with our university interns. Black brilliance seems even more pressing to highlight in a city with such a paucity of Black residents. Books are merely things in a classroom, and a curriculum is merely a map. These things that highlight pro-Blackness are not enough.

Onto-Epistemic Mattering and Anti-Blackness

Latour (2005) deconstructs intangible "social" realities. "It is always things—and I now mean this last word literally—which, in practice, lend their 'steely' quality to the hapless 'society'" (p. 68). Latour's acknowledgment of "things" relates to the design of a curricula-becoming in which recyclables co-create becomings-with. I read/think/see Latour's (2005) description of "things," so I can read/think/see *other* things:

> After all, there is hardly any doubt that kettles 'boil' water, knifes 'cut' meat, baskets 'hold' provisions, hammers 'hit' nails on the head.... Are those verbs not designating actions? (p.71)

Humans effect change in concert with "things." A curricula-becoming recognizes the agency of matter, minds, and becoming-with future/present worlds—a justice late in (be)coming. But humans create things that boil, cut, hit, through economies cleaved into and from place. Texas's economy was cleaved with racism.

Plugging into Latour's text, 'things'—race, racism, Whiteness, settler colonialism, anti-Blackness, and adultification—are agents that act across-and-with teachers and students, "doing something to each other simultaneously" (Hultman & Lenz Tguchi, 2010, p. 530). This is the "learner and the world as entangled becoming" (Lenz Taguchi, 2010, p. 47). I wonder, through the text, whether scholars utilizing the tenets of CRT ("recognizing" that racism is a reality agential in much of schooling's inequities) and scholars of the tenets of posthumanism (acknowledging limits to "recognition" as human-centric) might encounter each other's entangled becoming:

> The encounter between these two theoretical traditions leads to a provocative supposition—that it may make methodological sense to frame racism not as a passive byproduct of dysfunctional psychological or sociological processes, but instead as a protean ontological phenomenon with an agency of its own. Although regarding a social formation as agential may seem surprising, it fits

within what we have long known about institutionalized racism—that it is flexible and evolves in response to our collective efforts to resist it. (Rosiek, 2018, p. 2)

Hultman and Lenz Taguchi (2010) describe the unbound, unrecognizable agency when matter, minds, and that-which-matters intra-act:

> The girl and the sand have no agency of their own. Rather, what is understood as "agency" in a relational materialist approach is a quality that emerges in-between different bodies involved in mutual engagements and relations: muscles lifting the arm and hand. (p. 530)

If I extract the raceless and placeless girl and sand and plug in memories of Ezekias and realities of Texas, then I am presented with a map I can enter:

> [*Ezekias and racism*] have no agency of their own. Rather, what is understood as "agency" in a relational materialist approach is a quality that emerges in-between different bodies involved in mutual engagements and relations: [*anti-Blackness and Ezekias*].

In this reencounter of a passage about action across-and-with material agency, race, racism, and the other bodies in the hallway, Whiteness policed by a teachers' assumption, each "had their own specific agential qualities and potentialities and thus agency as performative agents in the entangled intra-action" (Lenz Taguchi, 2010, p. 49). Racism's "agentic qualities *makes itself intelligible* . . . with its specific qualities and potentialities" (p. 59). Ezekias and racism intra-act; Ms. Peña and anti-Blackness intra-act—becoming an assemblage in the "midst of an open-ended swirl of extensions and supplementations, changing their powers and characteristics as they pass through different assemblages" (Lee quoted in Hultman & Lenz Taguchi, 2010, p. 531).

Describing violence as encountering Ezekias while he encounters it does not shield him from it. It simply describes material reality—anti-Blackness as agent. I can recognize that the cardboard is making itself intelligible to students as they become-with, creating. I can recognize that racism, anti-Blackness, and Whiteness are making themselves intelligible as they act agentially:

> Engagement with the complexities, contradictions and capriciousness through which racialization is effected on and implicated through bodies and the ways in which bodies escape these limits, needs attunement to how systemic forces might be held in place in the intensities in everyday encounters, especially in ways that might otherwise remain obscured. (Nxumalo, 2012, p. 296)

Attunement creates a space for educators to have a conversation *prior* to enacting a curricula-becoming, so educators might become-with notions of CRT's racial realism(s) and posthumanism's material realism. Thinking with both theories might be similar to the type of dialogue-in-preparation-for-action that students engage in as part of a university course designed to open new spaces for new environmentalism, as students encounter texts about material agency prior to leading/experiencing material encounters in field-based contexts.

To extend agential realism to "things" that plug into rhizomes, like racism, and to recognize the constructions and fabrications of race as a cite of enaction, creates attunement for teachers to see/think/read their encounters—and their students' encounters—with racism, while remaining realistic about bodies and bodies undone:

> Unlike identity politics, which affirms what we are and what we know, the concept, theory, is never about us, about who we are. It affirms only what we can become, extracted as it is from the events which move us beyond ourselves. (Grosz, 2011, p. 81)

This recasting of racism as agentive, more-than discursive, is becoming-with CRT's realism, employing the additive "'and' ... an atypical expression of all possible conjunctions which it puts into continuous variation" (Deleuze & Guattari, 1987, p. 110). "The fabric of the rhizome is the conjunction, 'and ... and ... and'" (p. 27). In thinking with Haraway's notion of making kin with those things that make themselves intelligible, I can employ CRT to think/read/see my actions with/in those material realities *"and"* employ posthumanist's undoings to think-with curricula's matters, with matter mattering *"and"* Blackness mattering. Always *"and."*

Conjunctive Dialogue

This responsibility ("possibility of justice-to-come ... not intertwinings of separate entities, but rather irreducible relations"; Barad quoted in St. Pierre, 2013, p. 655) opens space in between, like the hybridity of linguistic spaces, "a special in-between zone where such metamorphoses can take place" (Beighton, 2015, p. 50).

In-between becomes dialogues of inclusion, spaces in which race-based scholarship is not separated (bound, fixed, fenced) from posthumanist scholarship, both becoming-with, making kin, neither positioning the other as "lacking" nor having a "deficit" but mutually intelligible to the other, recognizing one another—fully—"toward new foldings" (Manning, 2013, p. 26), becoming "transformed into propositions" (Manning, 2013, p. 114) taking flight into new territories for early education.

References

Alba, R. (2005). Bright vs. blurred boundaries: Second generation assimilation and exclusion in France, Germany and the United States. *Ethnic and Racial Studies, 28*(1), 20–49.

Aronson, B. A. (2017). The White savior industrial complex: A cultural studies analysis of a teacher educator, savior film, and future teachers. *Journal of Critical Thought and Praxis, 6*(3), 36–54.

Asante, M. K. (2017). *Revolutionary pedagogy: Primer for teachers of Black children*. Universal Write Publications.

Ashford-Hanserd, S., Sarmiento, E., Myles, C., Rayburn, S., Roundtree, A, Hayton, M.-P., Ybarra, E., Benitez, S., Clifford, T., Pierce, C., Williams, C., & Maleki, S. (2020). African American experiences in the Historic Dunbar Neighborhood in San Marcos, Texas. *Social Sciences, 9*(10), 177–203.

Balestra, A. (2008). *Recovering the US Hispanic linguistic heritage: Sociohistorical approaches to Spanish in the United States*. Arte Público.

Beighton, C. (2015). *Deleuze and lifelong learning: Creativity, events and ethics*. Palgrave Macmillan.

Bradbury. A. (2020) A critical race theory framework for education policy analysis: the case of bilingual learners and assessment policy in England. *Race Ethnicity and Education, 23*(2), 241–260.

Bryan, N. (2021). Remembering Tamir Rice and other Black boy victims: Imagining Black PlayCrit Literacies inside and outside urban literacy education. *Urban Education, 56*(5), 774–771.

Cannella, G. S., & Wolff, K. (2014). Conceptualizing critical qualitative research in/against global neoliberalisms: Childhood public policy assemblage(s) as example entanglement(s). *International Review of Qualitative Research, 7*(1), 1–14.

Cole, T. (2012, March 12). The White savior industrial complex. *The Atlantic*. http://www.theatlantic.com/international/archive/2012/03/the-white-saviorindustrialcomplex/254843/2/

Davies, D., De Schauwer, E., Claes, L., De Munck, K., Van De Putte, I., & Verstichele, M. (2013). Recognition and difference: a collective biography, *International Journal of Qualitative Studies in Education, 26*(6), 680–691.

Davis, K., & Heilbroner, D. (Directors). (2017). *Traffic Stop*. [Film]. Home Box Office.

Deleuze, G. (1986). *Cinema I: The movement-image*. The Athlone Press.

Deleuze, G., & Guattari, F. (1987). *A thousand plateaus: Capitalism and schizophrenia*. University of Minnesota Press.

Dumas, M. J., & Nelson, J. D. (2016). (Re)imagining Black boyhood: Toward a critical framework for educational research. *Harvard Educational Review, 86*(1), 27–47.

García, O., & Wei, L. (2014). *Translanguaging: Language, bilingualism and education*. Palgrave Macmillan.

Grosz, E. (2011). *Becoming undone: Darwinian reflections on life, politics, and art*. Duke University Press.

Haraway, D. J. (2016). *Staying with the trouble: Making kin in the Chthulucene*. Duke University Press.

Heilbroner, D., &, Davis, K. (Directors). (2018). *Say her name: The life and death of Sandra Bland* [Film]. Home Box Office.

Howlett, C. (2018). Teacher education and posthumanism. *Issues in Teacher Education, 27*(1), 106–118.

Hultman, K., & Lenz Taguchi, H. (2010). Challenging anthropocentric analysis of visual data: A relational materialist methodological approach to educational research. *International Journal of Qualitative Studies in Education, 23*(5), 525–542.

Jackson, A. Y., & Mazzei, L. A. (2012). *Thinking with theory in qualitative research: Viewing data across multiple perspectives*. Routledge.

Johnson, L. L., Bryan, N., & Boutte, G. (2019). Show us the love: Revolutionary teaching in (un)critical times. *Urban Review, 51*(1), 46–64.

Kendi, I. X. (2016). Chapter 14: Imbruted or civilized. In *Stamped from the beginning: The definitive history of racist ideas in America* (pp. 177–190). Nation Books.

Kinard, T., Gainer, J., & Huerta, M. E. (2018). *Power play: Explorando y empujando fronteras en una escuela en Tejas through a multilingual play-based early learning curriculum*. Peter Lang.

Latour, B. (2005). *Reassembling the social: An introduction to actor-network-theory*. Oxford University Press.

Lawrence, P. (2019). Dialogical agency: children's interactions with human and more-than-human. *European Early Childhood Education Research Journal, 27*(3), 318–333.

Lee, N. (2001). *Childhood and society: Growing up in an age of uncertainty*. Open University Press.

Lenz Taguchi, H. (2010). *Going beyond the theory/practice divide in early childhood education: Introducing an intra-active pedagogy*. Routledge.

Love, B. L. (2016). Anti-Black state violence, classroom edition: The spirit murdering of Black children, *Journal of Curriculum and Pedagogy, 13*(1), 22–25.

Manning, E. (2013). *Always more than one: Individuation's dance*. Duke University Press.

Maxouris, C., & Razek, R. (2020). Austin police fired at a crowd transporting a protester injured by an officer. *CNN Wire*. https://www.cnn.com/2020/06/07/us/austin-texas-police-bean-bag-20-year-old-injured/index.html

Nxumalo, F. (2012). Unsettling representational practices: Inhabiting relational becomings in early childhood education. *Child & Youth Services, 33*(3–4), 281–302.

Nxumalo, F., & Cedillo, S. (2017). Decolonizing place in early childhood studies: Thinking with Indigenous onto-Epistemologies and Black feminist geographies. *Global Studies of Childhood, 7*(2), 99–112.

Nxumalo, F., Pacini-Ketchabaw, V., & Rowan, M. C. (2011). Lunch time at the child care centre: Neoliberal assemblages in early childhood education. *Journal of Pedagogy, 2*(2), 195–223.

Pacini-Ketchabaw, V., & Nxumalo, F. (2010). A curriculum for social change: Experimenting with politics of action or imperceptibility. In V. Pacini-Ketchabaw (Ed.), *Flows, rhythms, and intensities of early childhood education curriculum* (pp. 155–176). Peter Lang.

Paulson, S. (2019, December 6). *Making Kin: An Interview with Donna Haraway*. Los Angeles Review of Books. https://lareviewofbooks.org/article/making-kin-an-interview-with-donna-haraway/

Pérez, M., & Saavedra, C. (2017). A call for onto-epistemological diversity in early childhood education and care: Centering global South conceptualizations of childhood/s. *Review of Research in Education, 41*(1), 1–29.

Ramanathan, V. (2006). Of texts AND translations AND rhizomes: postcolonial anxieties AND deracinations AND knowledge constructions. *Critical Inquiry in Language Studies: An International Journal, 3*(4), 223–244.

Rocha, M. (2019, October 9). *Indigenous People's Day celebration Oct. 13*. Hays Free Press. https://haysfreepress.com/2019/10/09/indigenous-peoples-day-celebration-oct-13/

Rosiek, J. (2018). Critical race theory meets posthumanism: Lessons from a study of racial resegregation in public schools. *Race, Ethnicity and Education, 22*(1), 73–92.

Sellers, M. (2010). Re(con)ceiving young children's curricular performativity. *International Journal of Qualitative Studies in Education, 13*(5), 557–577.

Shields, R. (2015). Ludic ontology: Play's relationship to language, cultural forms, and transformative politics. *American Journal of Play, 7*(3), 298–321.

St. Pierre, E. A. (2004). Deleuzian concepts for education: The subject undone. *Educational Philosophy and Theory, 36*(3), 283–296.

St. Pierre, E. A. (2013). The posts continue: Becoming. *International Journal of Qualitative Studies in Education, 26*(6), 646–657.

Strathern, M. (1990). *The gender of the gift: Problems with women and problems with society in Melanesia.* University of California Press.

Swadener, B. B. (2000). "At risk" or "at promise"? From deficit constructions of the "other childhood" to possibilities for authentic alliances with children and families. In L. Diaz-Soto (Ed.), *The politics of early childhood education* (pp. 117–134). Peter Lang.

Teja, J. L., & Ramos, R. A. (2010). *Tejano leadership in Mexican and revolutionary Texas.* Texas A&M University Press.

Thomas, E. E. (2019). *The dark fantastic: Race and the imagination from Harry Potter to the Hunger Games.* NYU Press.

Wray, A., & Grace, G. W. (2007). The consequences of talking to strangers: Evolutionary corollaries of socio-cultural influences on linguistic form. *Lingua, 117*(3), 543–578.

CHAPTER 12

Becoming-with Water: Collaboration, Ethico-onto-epistemologies, Experimentations, and Creativity

Mindy Blaise and Claire O'Callaghan

MANY PEOPLE AGREE that the volume of waste today is unsustainable and signals an environmental crisis. This growth in waste poses global threats to land, air, water, and public health and contributes to climate change. This is a social justice issue that affects future generations around the globe and with differing effects (Hird, 2013). At the same time, the early childhood industry is both a large producer of waste (food, paper, diapers) and a popular site for addressing waste issues (gardening, recycling, composting). One of the most common ways in which waste is addressed in early childhood education is through managerial or surveillance approaches, such as the well-known 'three Rs' (reduce, reuse, recycle). These approaches to waste are based on a stewardship model of environmental education that assumes there are specific strategies that must be taught to children to care for the environment (Taylor, 2017) and place responsibility on individuals to solve these problems. These approaches also aim to distance humans from waste by putting it 'out of sight and out of mind'. However, environmental waste research shows that such strategies are insufficient and are doing more harm than good (Hird, 2014). This is something that few early childhood programs have considered, as they eagerly (and with good intentions) sign up to quick-fix, feel-good, and easy-to-implement practices.

This chapter argues that the field of early childhood education is well placed to consider waste differently and how how 21st-century children might become active agents in critically and creatively confronting the complex waste problems that threaten their future. But to do so requires a radical shift in how waste materials and waste relations are understood in early childhood settings. It is important to note that these issues are not just about waste, but rather they are related to a broader set of multiple existential threats that we have brought on ourselves and that are triggering a cascade of ecological crises. This necessary shift is about how humans broadly relate to environments. In response, there are calls for education to be reimagined around the future survival of the planet by "learning to become with the world around us" (Common Worlds Research Collective, 2020, p. 2). To do so requires that we give up delusions of mastery and control (Plumwood, 1993) and instead see the world as uncertain and yet unfolding (Gibson et al., 2015). Therefore, our thinking and practices must change and need to be collaborative; ethical, relational, and responsive; experimental; and creative.

This chapter begins by providing an overview of how human–waste relations are being rethought in the social sciences and humanities. It then continues with a discussion of becoming-with water as an example of how early childhood educators are pedagogically engaging with a site-specific material, such as water, in ways that produce ethical water–child relations that are not solely based on human exceptionalism (Haraway, 2008). These perspectives are aligned with how material feminists, such as Karen Barad (2007) and Hillevi Lenz Taguchi (2009), suggest that it is not only humans that have agency and act upon the world. Rather, all matter is agentic and can be understood as having agency in relations. Additionally, there are many non-Western thought traditions that presuppose that there are infinite human and more-than-human worlds within worlds, all of which are animate and radically interdependent (Escobar, 2018). This interdependency has always grounded Indigenous ways of knowing and being in reciprocal relationships with Country and all its creatures (Kwaymullina, 2020; Nannup, 2020; Rose, 1992).

To set the scene for how early childhood practice might respond differently to the waste crisis, the Canadian collaborative and experimental project "Material Encounters" will be introduced, in which researchers worked with early childhood educators to become-with common materials, such as paper, paint, charcoal, clay, and blocks found in early childhood spaces (Pacini-Ketchabaw et al., 2016). This project laid the theoretical and methodological groundwork for rethinking waste materials, waste practices, and waste relations in early childhood education. Building on this project, a large international study is currently underway that involves transforming children's relations with waste (Pacini-Ketchabaw, 2017) across sites located in Canada, Australia, and Ecuador. Although these inquiries are exploring site-specific materials, such as water, toxic water, plastics, microplastics, and food, this chapter highlights those projects that are related to water. These water projects are inspired by Donna Haraway's (2008) scholarship of human response-ability in more-than-human relationships, grounded in kinship and encounters rather than in disparity. Because these inquiries are still in progress, rather than reviewing major findings, this chapter shows how these studies are grounded in *collaboration, ethico-onto-epistemologies, experimentations,* and *creativity* to support the radical rethinking and remaking of human–environment relations that are required to shift from controlling and managing water, toward becoming-with this important and vital natural resource.

Rethinking Human–Waste Relations: Purity and Materiality

Cultural studies scholar and sociologist Gay Hawkins (2006) makes sense of waste beyond moralistic environmental stewardship approaches by considering the ethics, habits, and practices that shape what humans do with waste. For Hawkins, psychoanalytic explanations of human–waste relations, which tend to focus on the abject, are limiting because waste is reduced to a phobia and positioned as a threat to one's self. In the home, failing to keep one's space neat and tidy, implies that the person is unable to manage their life in an orderly way, and is an unclean person. These ideas about the improper or impure are connected to pure and innocent childhoods (Taylor, 2017), which society, including education, tries to maintain. Critiques of childhood innocence show how concerns about purity are cherished throughout early childhood and are evident in traditional theories of development (Cannella, 1997; Robinson, 2008) and work to distance young children from the "inappropriate" such as sex/uality, death, and AIDS (Silin,1995) or pleasure (Tobin, 1997). Waste is simply another element that works with these discourses of innocence and purity in early childhood.

Alexis Shotwell (2016), building and expanding on Mary Douglas's (1966) analysis of purity practices, argues against purism because it is "one bad but common approach to devastation in all its forms" (p. 8). Purism shuts down thinking in complex ways about waste, our relations with it, and how we are co-constituted with the world. It fails to recognise that "we" are never pure or that humans are living in a permanently polluted world. Most significantly for Shotwell (2016), purism closes down possibilities of taking collective action about waste and instead places responsibility on the individual to become a better citizen and make a change.

Hawkins's (2006) critical approach to thinking about humans' relations with waste attends to the materiality of waste and the "recognition of the self's creation in and through relations with waste matter" (p. 12). Paying constant and close attention to the materiality of waste opens up opportunities to see waste as "both a provocation to action and itself a result of that action" (p. 13). This approach to understanding waste creates opportunities to consider human-waste relations within an ethico-onto-epistemological—a term coined by feminist physicist-philosopher Barad (2007), to describe the entanglement among ethics, ontology, and epistemology when engaging in knowledge production with the world and its human and nonhuman inhabitants—frame and might be a productive approach for transforming human–waste relations without turning to guilt, moralism, or despair.

Challenging Human Exceptionalism, Agency, and Hierarchical Thinking

In their arts-based collaborative inquiry "Material Encounters", Veronica Pacini-Ketchabaw et al. (2016) pay attention to common materials 'in action' found in early childhood settings (i.e., paper, charcoal, paint, clay, blocks). By focusing on materiality and the lively and agentic interactions between all kinds of matter (Alaimo & Hekman, 2008; Barad, 2007; Bennett, 2010), their work challenges ideas about human exceptionalism, agency, and hierarchical thinking. Instead of assuming that it is only humans that have agency, they work with early childhood teachers to consider agency as collective, more-than-human, and relational. They do this by shifting the perspective from how children act on materials to how materials are shaping children. This focus on how materials are shaping children requires educators to rethink deeply rooted cultural dichotomies (animate vs. inanimate, active vs. passive) that lead us to think of ourselves as animate agents who act on passive, inanimate waste materials.

The work initiated in the "Material Encounters" inquiry (Pacini-Ketchabaw et al., 2016) is part of a growing body of educational research arguing that more complex ways of understanding human–environmental relations are needed that address the complexity of our times (Lloro-Bidart, 2017; Taylor, 2017), including waste, or in the case of this chapter water. A recent working paper for the United Nations Educational, Scientific and Cultural Organization Futures of Education initiative, written by the Common Worlds Research Collective (2020) shows how education is directly implicated in the crisis of climate change and our future survival depends on reconceptualising education in ways that make a radical "paradigm shift from learning about the world in order to act upon it, to learning to become with the world around us" (p. 2).

Building on the concepts initially explored around materiality, a large, international, and interdisciplinary inquiry is exploring children's relations with waste (Pacini-Ketchabaw, 2017). This project aims to rethink the Rs (reduce, reuse, recycle) by intentionally keeping a site-specific waste material 'in sight and in mind'. The theoretical approach is informed by new materialist conceptualisations of waste emerging from the environmental social sciences and humanities. Four premises ground the project: (1) Waste materials are not static, (2) it is not just humans that make things happen, (3) humans and waste materials exist in entangled relationships and affect one another, and (4) entangled human/waste relations have ethical implications (Pacini-Ketchabaw, 2017).

Becoming-with Water

In early childhood settings, water is usually viewed as a resource to learn about, rather than with. This is done either at the water table or through carefully planned experiences. For example, water is factually engaged with where information is either presented or represented to children through the water cycle, learning about the properties of water, and the Rs (reduce, reuse, recycle). This approach, however, is problematic in the current climate crisis as it does not address the concern for, engagement with, or relationality with water. Instead, it positions water as something separate from humans (Neimanis, 2016).

To decenter the human and establish new relations with water is to bring colonial binaries such as nature/culture closer together (Berry et al., 2020). A common worlds pedagogy fosters the entanglement of more-than-human others, such as water, and disrupts settler-colonial 'romantic' relations with place. Fikile Nxumalo's (2016) concept of refiguring presences is a form of "anti-colonial interruption" (p. 643), a method to disrupt the everyday settler-colonial formations in early childhood education settings. It draws attention to everyday encounters with more-than-human presences. In doing this, Nxumalo (2016) "take[s] inspiration from Indigenous knowledges, which are rooted in more-than-human reciprocal relationalities that are situated in place" (p. 645). Including but not limited to North American, Australian, and African Indigenous knowledges, the more-than-human is not an unfamiliar concept with many everyday encounters being based on shared non-hierarchical relations. In other words, more-than-human others are brought to the foreground through Indigenous knowledges (Nxumalo, 2016).

In Whadjuk Noongar boodjar, the place where we (Mindy and Claire) live and work, water is sacred in Noongar culture and is the giver of all life. Because Noongar knowledge is lived every day, water is known not by learning the facts about this resource, but by breathing, feeling, seeing, and tasting it. Water is connected to so much that humans simply cannot see (Nannup, 2020). First Nations People around the world have deep connections with water and consider water as a "relative with whom we engage in social (and political) relations premised on interdependency and respect" (Yazzie & Baldy, 2018, pp. 2–3). Considering water as kin means that water demands respect and care (Rose, 2016). These demands are considered when Fikile Nxumalo and Marleen Tepeyolotl Villanueva (2020) bring attention to decolonial more-than-human relationalities between humans and water in their project with a creek in Austin, Texas. For example, they unsettle the settler-colonial, human-centric approaches to nature (water) in early childhood through their frequent visits to a waste-filled creek. But it is not just the frequency that is of importance. It is the intentional anti-colonial practices that disrupt linear and predictable approaches to knowledge that they aim to unsettle that is of significance. One of the ways that they do this is when Marleen, who is Pame, an enrolled member of Mexica Kalpulli Tlatlpapaloti and a member of the Miakan/Garza

Coahuiltecan Band of Texas, taught the children a Coahuiltecan song *for* the water. As part of this encounter, the creek was first asked permission to share the song as a sign of respect, love, remembrance, and responsibility for the water. Singing for the water and asking permission might seem unimportant, but they are necessary for changing child–river relations from a relation based on children extracting information about water, towards children who are reverent towards water. It is a radically different kind of relationship that is not focused on the child and what they are learning, but it is creek and all the relations that creek activates. Throughout creek encounters, Marleen helps children become oriented towards the relational ontologies that connect children with water. These include becoming aware of the emotional capacity and physical healing of water, human–water body inseparability and noticing the veins of multiple water bodies. These orientations towards water are also situated pedagogical practices. Situating water requires that we become more aware of the daily practices and repeated encounters through which we locate ourselves in relation to water. In turn, we need to acknowledge the wealth and complexity of these watery relations, including how we share these relations with many animal and plant others (Chen et al., 2013).

Becoming-with Water Through Collaboration, Ethico-Onto-Epistemology, Experimenting, and Creativity

The next section defines four interconnected practices that are valued across several water projects. Collaboration, ethico-onto-epistemologies, experimentations, and creativity play out in projects that are attempting to reshape water and water–child relations in early childhood education. These practices support and make possible the paradigm shift from simply reducing, reusing, and recycling water to becoming-with water.

Collaboration

The projects that are becoming-with water acknowledge the collective agency and interdependence of all earthly beings. These projects insist that humans are not living somehow separate from nature, but instead, they are intimately entangled with natures. There is also the belief that these waste problems cannot be solved alone. Therefore, these inquiries are carried out collaboratively between researchers, teachers, children, and water. Watery relations between creeks and children, colonial pasts and presents, inside and outside water tables and containers, and water movements that help make connections are the main focus of these projects.

Because making a paradigm shift is hard work, project participants (including water) are always working together. Not only does this happen through monthly meetings involving researchers and educators, but it also occurs through the ways in which the research teams engage with and include water in their thinking. In 2009, an international and interdisciplinary network of early childhood researchers and teachers interested in rethinking early childhood environmental education was established through the Common Worlds Research Collective (Kummen et al., 2020). This has now expanded across the projects' sites through social media and online platforms that support blogging, microblogs, and resource sharing. Meetings occur in person and online and are where emerging and imperfect ideas and practices are shared, examined, produced, and troubled. It is where dialogue, generative critique, and speculation occur. But collaboration is not just for humans. Paying close and constant attention to the liveliness of water makes room for collaborations with the more-than-human. Narda Nelson and Nicole Land (2017) blog about Worm River, located in Haro Woods, situated on the traditional lands of the Lekwungen people, in what is now known as Victoria, British Columbia, Canada. Their blog posts show how water, plants, children, *E. coli*, and rubber boots are becoming together. Not only do these blog posts record more-than-human collaborations, but they also provide a way for research team members across the world to stay informed and connected.

Another example of how water collaborations are happening and how these are made possible by working together is discussed by educators as they share how they initially began thinking with water at a childcare centre in Victoria, British Columbia, Canada (Clark & Nelson, 2014). Interviews with educators about a water inquiry they took part in show how important working together is to make the necessary paradigm shift from thinking about to becoming-with water. Over several months, educators engaged with water closely by allowing water to move and travel throughout the centre. This involved removing the water table and making water abundant in different ways. Initially they were hesitant to do this because of safety concerns. However, by working through these uncertainties together, and through collaborative dialoguing and questioning, they realised how removing the water tables enabled them to see water differently. It gave the educators the confidence to experiment with water outside of the constraints of the water table. As a result, they saw how children's relations with water changed. The discussions about how these educators began thinking and practicing differently with water collectively are significant because publications rarely show how projects are initiated. Over time, water became more of a partner, rather than a resource to manage, and the educators became more confident about what it might mean to think-with water.

Similar themes about keeping water in sight and in mind, are found in water thinking done by Ashley Do Nascimento (2019). Inspired by the popular children's song "Rain, Rain, Go Away", Do Nascimento speculates what is made possible by inviting rain to "come again another day" rather than to "go away" in early childhood education. By considering rain through water subjectivities, the gendered politics of water, and the intersections of Indigeneity, race, and water, Do Nascimento invites us to think alongside and with water in critically attuned ways. For instance, acknowledging that we are all water bodies and have multiple watery relations helps us notice where and how we are situated in relation to water (Neimanis, 2013). This noticing is necessary for making us accountable to water that we all too often are only interested in considering as a resource to manage, control, and use, rather than something we are constantly in collaborative relations with.

Ethico-onto-epistemology

Ethico-onto-epistemology is a term coined by feminist physicist-philosopher Karen Barad (2007) to describe the entanglements among ethics, ontology, and epistemology when engaging in knowledge production *with* the world and its human, non-human, and more-than-human inhabitants, including water. This is a non-dualist understanding of the world, where nothing can be (or ever was) a neat, tidy, and separate 'nature' or 'culture', instead the world is naturecultures (Latour, 2004; Haraway, 2004). Thinking in naturecultures has consequences for all the dualisms (man/woman, human/nonhuman, fact/story) because they are mutually constituting each other. Nothing is falsely separated from each other. Humans encounter nature (water) not somehow above it but materially, discursively, figuratively, and relationally (Barad, 2007; Lenz Taguchi, 2009). This is a process of mutual and interdependent becoming and is closely aligned with collaborative practices. Hillevi Lenz Taguchi's (2009) scholarship is significant because it shows how ethico-onto-epistemology is critical for moving beyond the theory–practice divide in early childhood education and, in doing so, is part of a feminist ethic that is always challenging Cartesian dualisms and hierarchies.

Working ethico-onto-epistemologically is productive and generative, not reductive. As an ethical project, it also means that the materials, such as water, used in early childhood settings are non-innocent. Because early childhood education is situated within discourses of childhood innocence (Cannella, 1997; Robinson, 2008), any attempt to bring in non-innocence, even if it is based on political and cultural histories, will be tricky. For instance, the clay that is used at the art table came from someplace. This place, possibly a creek bed or maybe a claypan, might have been polluted, or long ago, it could have been a place of ceremony for Indigenous people. The clay that children squeeze and mold into shapes or figurines holds memories and histories, which are never innocent. These histories are useful for considering the complexities of child–waste relations, which are missing from the ways in which waste is usually considered in early childhood settings. However, there will be many adults who will consider these non-innocent histories inappropriate for young children because it challenges purity and innocent myths that ground early childhood.

One of the water projects that engage directly with non-innocence is found in a water inquiry conducted in Nogales, Cuenca, Ecuador (Berry et al., 2020). Like Nxumalo and Villanueva (2020), this project resists pure and innocent notions of childhoods and worlds. By using a common worlds conceptual framing in this project, a commitment is made to decentering the human as the sole focus of inquiry and to situating lives within shared, yet unequal, common worlds (Latour, 2004). Situating is an ethico-onto-epistemological practice and allows these researchers to trace the taken-for-granted ways that purity functions throughout educators' documentation of their river walks with children. Dismantling and then resituating these familiar purity discourses required an understanding of the here-and-now interdependencies of complicated waste–river–child lives. Dismantling purity discourses occurred in two ways. First, educators were invited to share their childhood river memories, and second, plastics were intentionality kept 'in sight and in mind' during river walks. These dismantling practices made it possible for ethical river walks to happen. In other words, it opened up space to notice and to encounter the non-innocence of the town's rivers. Instead of wishing the impurities of the river away, new contaminated river stories were told, where children, adults, river, animals, plants, and waste are bound together, rather than kept falsely apart.

Experimentation

Experimentation is situated within experimental empiricism (Deleuze & Guattari, 1994). It is a matter of working collectively to produce something new. Taking a more experimental approach to climate change, the environment, waste, or water is not about conducting a carefully controlled experiment with variables to try to determine the cause and effects of these issues or how children will fix them. Instead, this kind of experimentation is a more open and curious attitude for trying out different ways of living-with worlds, environments, waste, and water. An experimental approach is open to uncertainty and does not establish an end point. Because it is responsive to what is in front of us right now and requires us to respond, there are never any guarantees or final solutions. This is what makes these teaching and research pedagogies ethical.

Another water project that is grounded in experimentation is happening in Whadjuk Noongar boodjar, also known as Perth, Western Australia. Here, Claire O'Callaghan's (2021) master's research involves exploring water in an early learning centre with educators and children, through methods of curious practice (Buchanan et al., 2015; Despret, 2016; Haraway, 2015). As an experimental approach, curious practice embodies unique methods of paying attention, such as politeness (polite inquiry), visiting, and questioning. This water project invites Claire, educators, and children to "go visiting, to venture off the beaten path to meet unexpected, non-natal kin, and to strike up conversations, to pose and respond to interesting questions" (Haraway, 2015, p. 8). An example of this is when Claire deliberately takes a slow approach or orientation towards water by taking time to walk, to sit and to listen. This is not always easy to do, because there is the expectation that adults should know immediately and with certainty. Claire reflects in her field notes,

> I perch on the edge of the rockery, situate myself with water, noticing movement in puddles. A child approaches and asks, 'What are you doing Claire?' to which I respond, 'I am learning with water, do you want to learn with us?' Our

conversation continues with the child questioning me with intrigue but also confusion 'but you don't need to, you already know everything Claire, because you're a grown up.' I often wonder if my practice of visiting and questioning with slow intention is observed with outside eyes as 'passive' and uninteresting, uncharacteristic of typical early childhood practice. There were days that I would merely sit, watch and wait—whether it be in the rain, on the rockery, on the grass or near a tap. It was common for educators to approach me similarly with the question 'What are you looking for today?' my response being, 'I don't know'. A difficult experimental practice to explain to those who might not fully understand.

Experimenting with a curious practice entails Claire beginning each site visit by spending time with place, to walk and notice where water is sitting and to imagine where water was and is no longer. This practice brings something new for Claire, educators, and children to notice, to question, and to pay attention to. Vinciane Despret's (2016) politeness invites the unknown to emerge as field notes show:

> After an evening of heavy rain, the early learning centre was filled with water. Water was everywhere. Droplets were on plant leaves, puddles in chair seats, scraps of soaking paper, and damp concrete paths. The smell of rain mixed with dirt was lingering in the air. In the distance, I notice one boy crouching down towards a muddy puddle and then ever so slightly dipping his foot onto the surface. He notices the slight movement of water as his foot creates small ripples. He then pauses in silence. After some time, the boy introduces water to stick, announcing "stick in the water." The boy continues this pattern of pausing as he notices water further, by dipping his fingers in and out of the muddy puddle. (O'Callaghan, 2021, field notes)

Paying attention to water invites curious practices of noticing, stillness, and silence as human and more-than-human entities respond *with* each other. The water and the boy come together, not as separate entities but also as one body forging reciprocal relations. It is a responsibility towards more-than-human and human others and an ability to meaningfully respond, not just to them, but with them (Zurn & Shankar, 2020). Claire's role as the researcher is about being situated, listening attentively, paying attention, and becoming attuned to the boy and water presences (Duhn & Galvez, 2020). This project invites children to encounter water and water to encounter children. These water–child encounters based on curious practices evoke reciprocal and meaningful relationships to occur.

An example of how one project engaged in experimentation involved educators and researchers becoming-with water logics and Indigenous Canadian artworks

(Pacini-Ketchabaw & Clark, 2016). Working collaboratively with a childcare centre located in the unceded First Nation territories of what is now called British Columbia, Canada, this project was initiated by drawing from Astrida Neimanis's (2009) scholarship on hydro-logics. Neimanis (2013) refers to logics as the "specific capacities of certain bodies to affect other bodies" (p. 30). These hydro-logics include a myriad of water sensibilities such as gestation, dissolution, communication, differentiation, archive, and unknowability. For example, an encounter with water as ice invites children to experience this substance as something solid, not fluid as Claire observes in the water research she is conducting:

> As children continue their water play, relationships with the ice develop and change, as does the shape and composition of the ice; it drops, it shatters, it is devastating. A boy takes a piece of the shattered ice and disappears. Later he returns with a carefully wrapped shard of ice and states, 'I didn't want the ice to be hurt.' He proceeds to carry this ice for the rest of the morning, eventually packing it in his bag 'to show Daddy.' (O'Callaghan, 2021, field notes)

This example illuminates that water is more than just fluid. Neimanis's (2009) hydro-logics of communication assists in explaining the complex relationship formed between child and ice, one of more than mere materiality but as a medium for communication of empathy, compassion, and care. Likewise, the hydro-logics of differentiation explain the block of ice turning to shattered, shards of ice to then waterdrops and finally to pools of water. This is what Neimanis (2013) might say is the "continual reorganisation and redistribution" (p. 31) of water.

These hydro-logics foreground water's liveliness and multiple qualities that push educators to move beyond considering it as just fluid (Neimanis, 2013). Hydro-logics helped researchers and educators in this water study (Pacini-Ketchabaw & Clark, 2016) think and see water beyond water play in early childhood. As a result of these new ways of considering water, four intentional water experimentations were conducted, and the authors show how they opened up new ideas and ways of understanding water.

Each experimentation involved bringing hydro-logics together with an Indigenous Canadian artwork. For example, to address the histories and presences of settler colonialism, this group explored sinking, floating, and splashing waters as evident in Anishinaabe artist Rebecca Belmore's art piece *Fountain*. The artworks challenged their thinking about water and pedagogy beyond the water table. Interestingly, by responding to these artworks, the educators and researchers were also responding to water. This, in turn, put into motion new relations with water that fell outside of managing and knowing about water. The article does not provide a set of instructions on how to do this kind of water thinking and relating, but it does gesture towards the power and importance of art by "adopting an attitude of humility and curiosity towards water" (Neimanis, 2013, p. 37).

Creativity

Arts-based practices are methodological tools often used by educational researchers as a way to craft more expansive understandings of social and physical worlds (McNiff, 2017). Arts-based practices are varied, including literary forms, performative forms, visual arts, audiovisual forms, multimedia forms, and multimethod forms (Leavy, 2017). All the water inquiries employ some kind of arts-based practice that stimulates new ways to see, think, and relate with water.

At the Art Gallery of Western Australia (AGWA), young children participated in a workshop designed and led by artist-researcher-educator Lilly Blue called *Conversations With Rain*. The workshop encouraged children to focus on the ontologies of water by paying close attention to how rain moves, smells, sounds, and tastes. Poetic practices of sensing, noticing, moving, and experimenting were used to create a holistic experience for children to think and become-with water, as well as privileging Western Australian Aboriginal water knowledges. For example, the workshop began by inviting children to notice and respond to Australian Aboriginal artist Ngarralja Tommy May's (2016) artwork *Raining on Kurtal*. This was done by first having children focus specifically on the rain movements in the artwork and then following those movements with their bodies. With fingers in the air and using their whole bodies, children traced the downward forces of the white etched drops. This progressed to invitations of sound creation by shredding, ripping, and crumpling paper and tapping pencils. These child-made rain sounds were recorded and combined to create the soundscape *Sound of Rain* (Art Gallery of Western Australia, 2019), which was exhibited as part of "The Botanical: Beauty and Peril". This relationship with rain continued in the teacher resource, *Unlocking Imagination, Conversations With Rain: Response Journal* (Blue & Pollitt, 2019), in which water noticings and responses are encouraged. For example, one of the invitations in the response journal asks readers to "tear off a small part of this page and scrunch it next to your ear to make it sound like a tiny rainstorm and then use it to make a miniature paper sculpture". These creative experiences recognise that children and rain are entangled and always in relation, highlighting poetic and artistic responses as a radical way of relating to and with water.

Using creative writing and photography Mindy Blaise and Vanessa Wintoneak (in press) show how a river, young children, plants, and animals are constantly (re)forming relations. During a year-long water walking project, researchers, educators, and a small group of preschool-aged children experimented walking-with, rather than walking-to, Derbarl Yerrigan. Derbarl Yerrigan is a significant river in Whadjuk Noongar boodjar. Photography was used as a technique for noticing, caring for, and speculative imaginings with Derbarl Yerrigan (Haraway, 2015; Puig de la Bellacasa, 2017). For example, the animal and plant species that children encountered on their walks were photographed. Then, these images were edited in ways that presented these animal–river relations as entwined, entangled, and relational. Black-and-white photographs were created and highlighted the specificities of decomposing fish bodies, in relation to sand, seagrass, shells, and water. Next, children responded to the photographs by painting and storying. Walks were repeated, often with these photographs. Photography also allowed the researchers to document moments when Derbarl Yerrigan was caring for and in relation to dead blowfish. Finally, photography activated speculative imaginings of ways in which river relations were (re)forming between children, fish, seagrass, wind, and much more. The cultivation of this kind care; care that is situated, a doing, and affective is inspired by María Puig de la Bellacasa's (2017) more-than-human speculative ethics. In addition to photography's ability to play a part towards (re)forming relations, creative writing was also used by the authors to work with questions of how early childhood education might imagine, get to know, and otherwise tell lively stories that present new imaginations with this river. Arts-infused writing, with attention to sensation, affect, absences and presences, was used to articulate perceptions emerging within child–blowie–river relations. The lively stories of these water encounters seep beyond what readers expect and make room for new water relations to form.

Conclusion

This chapter has reviewed several projects that are keeping water 'in sight and in mind' and provides a glimpse into how researchers, early childhood educators, and young children are attempting to shift from thinking of or about water as a resource needing to be managed to becoming-with water in their everyday lives. This shift is important because it is argued that becoming-with is related to learning how to become with the world around us, and this is needed because our future survival depends on our capacity to think and relate with the world differently (Common Worlds Research Collective, 2020). Broadly, becoming-with water encourages relational thinking and connection making, and water is a matter of relation and connection. By drawing from the environmental humanities and feminist new materialisms, these projects understand that water is not static, that it is not just humans who have agency, that humans and water exist in an entangled relationship and affect one another, and that entangled human/water relations have ethical implications (Pacini-Ketchabaw, 2017). These perspectives about materiality, agency, and hierarchies challenge many taken-for-granted understandings of waste and our relations to environments.

Doing this kind of research is not easy because it demands a radically different way of understanding water, its materiality, agency, and our relationships to it. Radical thinking is not always welcomed in neoliberal schooling spaces. These projects are based on the premise that our relations to any specific water body (puddle, raindrop, creek, river) affects our way of knowing it. Put simply, how we become-with water matters. If we are to be responsible to water, then we can no longer afford to only know about it. Instead, we are obliged to become-with water, in all its watery forms and ways. Although there are no procedures or steps to follow in doing this kind of work, this chapter provides insight into how researchers, educators, and children are collaborating with each other and the world, drawing from ethico-onto-epistemological perspectives, taking an experimental attitude, and creatively addressing water in their specific sites. This work is inspiring, generative, ethical, and necessary for making a difference in how we relate to waste.

References

Alaimo, S., & Hekman, S. (Eds.). (2008). *Material feminisms*. Indiana University Press.

Art Gallery of Western Australia. (2019). Sound of rain [song]. On *The botanical: Beauty and peril*. Soundcloud.

Barad, K. (2007). *Meeting the universe halfway: Quantum physics and the entanglement of matter and meaning*. Duke University Press.

Bennett, J. (2010). *Vibrant matter: A political ecology of things*. Duke University Press.

Berry, A., Vintimilla, C. D., & Pacini-Ketchabaw, V. (2020). Interrupting purity in Andean early childhood education: Documenting the impurities of a river. *Equity & Excellence in Education*, 53(3), 276–287. https://doi.org/10.1080/10665684.2020.1785974

Blaise, M., & Wintoneak, V. (In press). (Re)forming river-child-blowie relations: Questions of noticing, caring, and imagined futures with the unloved and disregarded. *Feral Feminisms*.

Blue, L., & Pollitt, J. (2019). *Unlocking imagination: Conversations with rain response journal*. Art Gallery of Western Australia.

Buchanan, B., Chrulew, M., & Bussolini, J. (2015). On asking the right questions: An interview with Vinciane Despret. *Journal of the Theoretical Humanities*, 20(2), 165–178. https://doi-org.ezproxy.ecu.edu.au/10.1080/0969725X.2015.1039821

Cannella, G. S. (1997). *Deconstructing early childhood education: Social justice and revolution*. Peter Lang.

Chen, C., MacLeod, J., & Neimanis, A. (Eds.). (2013). *Thinking with water*. McGill-Queen's University Press.

Clark, V., & Nelson, N. (2014). Thinking with paint and water: An interview with Terry Wilson, Deanna Elliott, Diana Foreland, and Teresa Dixon. *International Journal of Child, Youth and Family Studies*, 5(4.2), 854–864. https://doi.org/10.18357/ijcyfs.clarkv2.5422014

Common Worlds Research Collective. (2020). *Learning to become with the world: Education for future survival* (Education Research and Foresight Working Paper 28). UNESCO.

Deleuze, G., & Guattari, F. (1994). *What is philosophy?* Columbia University Press.

Despret, V. (2016). *What would animals say if we asked the right questions?* University of Minnesota Press.

Do Nascimento, A. (2019). "Rain, rain, go away!" engaging rain pedagogies in practices with children: From water politics to environmental education. *Journal of Childhood Studies*, 44(3), 42–55. https://doi.ord.10.18357/jcs00019173

Douglas, M. (1966). *Purity and danger: An analysis of concepts of pollution and taboo*. Routledge.

Duhn, I., & Galvez, S. (2020). Doing curious research to cultivate tentacular becomings. *Environmental Education Research*, 26(5), 731–741. https://doi.org/10.1080/13504622.2020.1748176

Escobar, A. (2018). *Designs for the pluriverse: Radical interdependence, autonomy, and the making of worlds*. Duke University Press.

Gibson, K., Rose, D. B., & Fincher, R. (Eds.). (2015). *Manifesto for living in the Anthropocene*. Punctum Books.

Haraway, D. (2004). *The Haraway reader*. Routledge.

Haraway, D. (2008). *When species meet*. University of Minnesota Press.

Haraway, D. (2015). A curious practice. *Journal of the Theoretical Humanities, 20*(2), 5–14. https://doi.org/10.1080/0969725X.2015.1039817

Hawkins, G. (2006). *The ethics of waste: How we relate to rubbish*. Rowman & Littlefield.

Hird, M. J. (2013). Waste, landfills, and an environmental ethics of vulnerability. *Ethics and the Environment, 18*(1), 105–124. https://doi.org/10.2979/ethicsenviro.18.1.105

Hird, M. J. (2014, September 27). Waste[Ed]: Colonial legacies in the Anthropocene. In Common Worlds Research Collective, *Learning to inherit in colonized and ecologically challenged lifeworlds* [Symposium]. University of Victoria, British Columbia, Canada. https://www.youtube.com/watch?v=hksHLkMvjpw

Kummen, K., Pacini-Ketchabaw, V., Blaise, M., & Taylor, A. (2020, September 25–26). *Common world pedagogies: Interview part 1* [Keynote panel session]. North Shore Early Childhood Conference: To Learn, To Wonder, Vancouver, BC, Canada. https://youtu.be/RFTc-IG58O0

Kwaymullina, A. (2020). *Living on stolen land*. Magabala Books.

Latour, B. (2004). *The politics of nature: How to bring the sciences into democracy*. Harvard University Press.

Leavy, P. (2017). Introduction to arts-based research. In P. Leavy (Ed.), *Handbook of arts-based research* (pp. 3–21). The Guilford Press.

Lenz Taguchi, H. (2009). *Going beyond the theory/practice divide in early childhood education: Introducing an intra-active pedagogy*. Routledge.

Lloro-Bidart, T. (2017). A feminist posthumanist political ecology of education for theorizing human–animal relations/relationships. *Environmental Education Research, 23*(1), 111–130. https://doi.org/10.1080/13504622.2015.1135419

May, N. T. (2016). *Raining on Kurtal* [scratched enamel on tin]. Art Gallery of Western Australia, Western Australia.

McNiff, S. (2017). Philosophical and practical foundations of artistic inquiry: Creating paradigms, methods, and presentations based in art. In P. Leavy (Ed.), *Handbook of arts- based research* (pp. 22–36). Guilford Press.

Nannup, N. (2020). *Walk with the Waugal* [Video]. Water Corporation. https://www.watercorporation.com.au/Education/Water-in-Aboriginal-culture/Walk-with-the-Waugal-videos

Neimanis, A. (2009). Bodies of water, human rights, and the hydrocommons. *TOPIA: Canadian Journal of Cultural Studies, 21*(1), 161–182. https://doi.org/10.3138/topia.21.161

Neimanis, A. (2013). Feminist subjectivity, watered. *Feminist Review, 103*(1), 23–41.

Neimanis, A. (2016). *Bodies of water: Posthuman feminist phenomenology*. Bloomsbury Academic.

Nelson, N., & Land, N. (2017, February 25). The water isn't running today. *Common Worlding with Children*. https://commonworldsblog.wordpress.com/2017/02/25/the-water-isnt-running-today/

Nxumalo, F. (2016). Towards 'refiguring presences' as an anti-colonial orientation to research in early childhood studies. *International Journal of Qualitative Studies in Education, 29*(5), 640–654. https://doi.org/10.1080/09518398.2016.1139212

Nxumalo, F., & Villanueva, M. T. (2020). (Re)storying water: Decolonial pedagogies of relational affect with young children. In B. Dernikos, N. Lesko, S. D. McCall, & A. Niccolini (Eds.), *Mapping the affective turn in education: Theory, research and pedagogy* (pp. 209–228). Taylor & Francis.

O'Callaghan, C. (2021). *Paying attention to water relations: Poetic inquiry and pedagogical documentation and curious practices* [Unpublished master's thesis]. Edith Cowan University.

Pacini-Ketchabaw, V. (2017). *Rethinking the three R's: Transforming waste practices in early childhood education*. Insight Grant, Social Sciences and Humanities Research Council of Canada.

Pacini-Ketchabaw, V., & Clark, V. (2016). Following watery relations in early childhood pedagogies. *Journal of Early Childhood Research, 14*(1), 99–111. https://doi.org/10.1177%2F1476718X14529281

Pacini-Ketchabaw, V., Kind, S., & Kocher, L. L. M. (2016). *Encounters with materials in early childhood education*. Routledge.

Plumwood, V. (1993). *Feminism and master of nature*. Routledge.

Puig de la Bellacasa, M. (2017). *Matters of care: Speculative ethics in more than human worlds*. University of Minnesota Press.

Robinson, K. H. (2008). In the name of 'childhood innocence': A discursive exploration of the moral panic associated with childhood and sexuality. *Cultural Studies Review, 14*(2), 113–129. https://doi.org/10.5130/csr.v14i2.2075

Rose, D. B. (1992). *Dingo makes us human: Life and land in and Australian Aboriginal culture*. Cambridge University Press.

Rose, D. B. (2016). Lively water. *Deborah Bird Rose: Love at the Edge of Extinction*. https://webarchive.nla.gov.au/awa/20190725101448/http://pandora.nla.gov.au/pan/177305/20190725-1730/deborahbirdrose.com/2016/03/14/lively-water/index.html

Shotwell, A. (2016). *Against purity: Living ethically in compromised times*. University of Minnesota Press.

Silin, J. G. (1995). *Sex, death and the education of children: Our passion for ignorance in the age of AIDS*. Teachers College Press.

Taylor, A. (2017). Beyond stewardship: Common world pedagogies for the Anthropocene. *Environmental Education Research, 23*(10), 1448–1461. https://doi.org/10.1080/13504622.2017.1325452

Tobin, J. (Ed.). (1997). *Making a place for pleasure in early childhood education*. Yale University Press.

Yazzie, M. K., & Baldy, C. R. (2018). Introduction: Indigenous peoples and the politics of water. *Decolonization: Indigeneity, Education & Society, 7*(1), 1–18.

Zurn, P., & Shankar, A. (Eds.). (2020). *Curiosity studies: A new ecology of knowledge*. University of Minnesota Press.

CHAPTER 13

Entanglements of Neoliberalism, Childhoods and Environmental Justice

Kylie Smith, Casey Myers, and Marek Tesar

THIS CHAPTER IS concerned with the effects of neoliberal education practices and the commodification and marketisation of early childhood services and the governing of educators, parents, and children in three countries (Myers et al., 2017; Perez & Cannella, 2011; Sims & Waniganayake, 2015; Smith et al., 2016). Neoliberal childhoods are framed around intervention discourses of 'giving children the best start in life' to ensure they become productive adult citizens who will contribute, rather than be a financial burden in their home, educational settings and broader society. These neoliberal childhoods are entangled with/in discourses of individualism and developmental norms; success or 'good childhoods' are measured based on universal learning outcomes, physical, and cognitive growth, and various notions of well-being. In particular, we attend to the ways in which children's well-being and the notions of environment are mutually constructed. Neoliberal childhoods become an economic unit to be built, assessed and measured. Recording and reporting on this economic unit are used to demonstrate not only the child's growth and development but also used as a discipline device in teaching and parenting (Gibson et al., 2015). Neoliberalism asks, Have teachers and families guided and instructed the child to enable them to reach their full economic potential? We ask, What are the implications of individualism and environmental justice?

With these neoliberal discourses in mind, this chapter examines childhoods in light of a global pathological obsession with 'growth'. Economic growth from a neoliberal perspective is about healthy outcomes, and from a health and environmental perspective, unstoppable growth means something that is cancerous or invasive. This chapter explores ideals around growth and development in young children and all the dividends-related discourses perpetuated by neoliberalism and edu-capitalism. When a focus is on individual growth, success and the ongoing consumption of knowledge, time, space environment and materials, what does that mean for communities and environmental sustainability? What is the interplay between '(over)abundance' and 'enough' when it comes to the spaces and places of childhood? We problematise the possibilities within the entanglements of neoliberalism and childhoods through three narratives from each of our particular time–space–place—the United States, Australia and New Zealand. From these three perspectives, we draw on particular posthuman relationalities to create knots, to disrupt or to cause stutters in growth discourses in order to envision more environmentally just childhood worlds. Each perspective grapples with its own entanglement of neoliberal childhoods—first, childhood, toys and environmental cost; second, early childhood education frameworks and the human-centric consumption of environment as learning; and, finally, the potentiality of entanglements with Indigeneity, pedagogy and place. We chose these three narratives because they are part of the everyday that often unfold without critique. In disrupting psycho-developmental and economic logics of growth, we consider multi-temporal, multi-scalar childhood(s) and the possibilities of childhood activists and geopolitical warriors (Myers, 2019).

Growth, Development, and Consumerism in the United States: Cannibalising Technologies in Contaminated Childhoods

Entangled with and through neoliberal individual competitive subjects that produce evidence of success through consumption, the ethics of a consumer culture and the intra-actions with the more-than-human are often left unaddressed. Neoliberal policy and practice operate under the guise of maximising human flourishing, but the ways in which 'human' and 'flourishing' are defined leave unanswered questions about the specificity of children's relationships with more-than-human others. For example, what is the impact of a child reaching their economic and 'potential' on the biologies and ecologies that are invisible in neoliberal metrics of success? What is the environmental cost of a 'good' childhood? Within the United States in particular, the ways in which *toys* have come to embody neoliberal child/hoods speaks to these questions. Critical exploration of the *neoliberal toy* reveals the ways in which a focus on 'growth' and 'development' has come to be enacted as *cannibalising technologies*—violent mutations that illuminate asymmetrical power relations, undoing themselves for economic gain.

For more than 20 years, critical consideration of the role of toys in childhoods has allowed scholars to "acquire an insight into how adults define childhood, how children's play is valued, and how children are regarded as modern consumers" (Korsvold, 2010, p. 31). Furthermore, toys have emerged as integral to the co-occurring phenomena of consumer culture and child/hoods. Toys exist within a complicated matrix of children's peer and familial relationships, children's and their parents' desires for normalised participation within peer culture, and market forces driving the creation and production of objects for children's consumption (Buckingham, 2011; Cook, 2009; Pugh 2009).

We can understand the ways in which idealised childhoods materialise as/in toys as a less explicit form of edu-capitalism (Blackmore, 2014; Smith, et al., 2016), wherein neoliberal economics entangle not with educational policies, *per se*, but with a kind of informal educational praxis of how to raise the ideal child. In the United States specifically, the rise of the neoliberal toy can be traced to the middle of the 20th century, as popular understandings from developmental psychology about the learning potential inherent in children's play were distilled into educational and economic policy. After the Second World War, toys were being marketed as educational and economic tools that helped children to "develop initiative, imagination, dexterity—toys that prepare for careers" (Byrne, 2016, p. 56). These toys became a way to materialise a growing and developing child, rather than simply an entertained or occupied child.

The rise of the educational toy industry aligned with advances in the mass production of plastics. Currently, the manufacturing of toys is the most plastic-intensive industry on the planet, of which the United States represents the largest market share (United Nations Environment Programme, 2014). However, because of domestic industrial and labour regulations, the vast majority of the plastic toys marketed toward and consumed by American children are produced overseas. Becker et al. (2010) state:

> Toy production and consumption occur in a global system characterized by large, complex supply chains with constant downward pressure on prices. In many cases, product design and marketing occur primarily in developed countries, with manufacturing outsourced overseas. Demand for low cost products creates pressure for companies to externalize environmental and social costs, resulting in unsafe working conditions, environmental pollution, and a drive toward using the cheapest and often toxic materials. (p.7798)

The same regulatory gaps that allow for the global toy industry to thrive economically create loopholes by which known neurotoxic, carcinogenic, and endocrine disrupting chemicals, such as heavy metals, phthalates, dioxins and brominated compounds, may be present in the toys themselves (DiGangi & Strakova, 2015; Guzzonato et al., 2017). Additionally, industrial waste known as *persistent organic pollutants* (POPs) can result from the production of plastic toys, *especially* toys using recycled plastics. POPs are defined by the World Health Organization as "chemicals of global concern due to their potential for long-range transport, persistence in the environment, ability to bio-magnify and bio-accumulate in ecosystems, as well as their significant negative effects on human health and the environment" (2020, para. 1). It's been well established that children are more vulnerable to environmental hazards than adults are due to their particular biology and physiology; children are more heavily exposed to toxins in proportion to their body weight, and these toxins have a greater long-term impact, including brain damage, cancer and developmental and learning problems (Schneider & Freeman, 2000).

So what can we make of the neoliberal toy and the ways in which it materialises the ideal child and constructs our notions of growth and development? The same cognitive constructivist perspective that afforded the rise of the educational toy allows us to relegate toys to passive tools that facilitate children's knowledge about the world around them. The same socio-cultural perspective that affords us the criticism of mass-market toys, and the popular culture these toys are thought to represent, allows us to relegate toys to objects on which the cultural ideals of corporations are inscribed. The reality is, however, that dominant cultural and educational discourses do not leave space for the unfathomably negative biological and ecological ways in which plastic toys and their industrial by-products impact children. The neoliberal project to develop and grow children to their fullest potential through educational toys is undoing itself through a toxic network of mostly *unseen* actors—neurotoxins, endocrine-disrupting compounds, and carcinogens (not to mention tons of plastic swirling in a seemingly far-away ocean gyre). Our humanist sense of toys as tools for children's learning or as passive objects belies a hierarchy by which plastics do not abide.

Growth, Development, and Consumerism in Australia: Policy and Environment(s) as a Tool for Learning

These environmental "messes" we make unfold globally on a daily basis in our "backyard" or through the media. Waterways are polluted, dammed or redirected to be used for industrial production or human consumption (hydration and recreation); land is blown up, brutalised and scarred as minerals are carved from the earth for human adornments or comfort (coal/heating, diamonds/opals/jewellry, clay/housing and structures); trees are felled from the forest floors for human lifestyles (space, building materials, paper, fuel), leaving land barren and animals, birds, insects homeless and in search of food and safety. Animals, fish and birds are killed for human 'survival' (nutrition, clothing) or leisure and recreational activities; air is polluted through the burning of fuel for human mobility (cars, trains, trams, buses, boats, planes), and comfort (heating, cooling, cooking). More-than-human environments and species are commodities and individual or national resources that are taken, priced, traded, sold, consumed and 'owned' by humans, generating income for individuals and nations. In Australia and globally, counties ride on the back of the economic global trade of food, energy, consumables, building, transport and tourism for financial prosperity which is equated to the promise of a good life for all hard-working citizens. The marketisation and privatisation of materials and resources create economies that build wealth or promise of fair pricing, quality service, and accessibility to 'all' through a competitive market. Robertson (2007) writes,

> By casting elements of the environment as "services" which provide value to human societies, they hope to stimulate environmental conservation through privatization and ownership. Following a line of logic that runs from Locke through Walras to Coase, the main thrust of these efforts has been to define new elements of the environment as property, distribute the rights to its ownership, and hope that markets and prices follow as rain follows the plow. (p. 503)

Debates on the reasons of and the (non-)realities of global warming, and the effects (bush fires, drought, floods, bleaching of coral, increased temperatures, melting snowcaps) rage among scientists, environmental activists, politicians, entrepreneurs, industrialists and climate sceptics or deniers. As governments navigate ways to deny global warming and placate industry and voters, discussion, debate and policy development around the regulation of consumption and trade of more-than-human species continues to be human-centric. Solutions are negotiated to continue building the finances of the state and to produce a thriving economy while placing regulations such as quotas that to some effect reduce 'damage' and provide the least inconvenience to human citizens. One example is the emissions-trading schemes whereby governments or industries put a cap on environmental pollution as a way to continue production and consider environmental impact, public perception of the problem and the outward-facing marketing of ethical practice. Furthermore, Felli (2015) describes as 'environmental integrity or justice' to the consumer, their relative merits on criteria such as efficiency, environmental integrity or justice (p. 3). The human/more-than-human binary continues to play out in these spaces as the consumption and comfort of the individual are the prize or reward for the hard-working neoliberal subject. The evidencing of the productive human citizen is the quantity of ownership and consumption of materials as an economic unit and the comfort these materials provide and are displayed to the world. This neoliberal endeavour of building evidence of success through achievement of materials starts in childhood where very young children learn to engage with discourses of material self-interest. More-than-human environments and species are understood as passive objects to be consumed or saved by adult/child humans (Nxumalo, 2017, 2018). This humanistic approach to 'saving' the planet is required to ensure survival and the future of the next generation of human species.

Recognising continued tracings of sustainability and environmental human saviour discourses with neoliberal and edu-capital culture provides opportunities to analyse the current Australian early childhood curriculum framework and the effects for practice. In Australia, there is a growing number of early childhood services offering bush kindergarten and river or beach kindergarten in urban and regional communities. These kindergarten settings can be located in environments close or at a distance to the physical structure of a kindergarten. As part of a funded weekly 15-hour kindergarten program, children go out into the environment for one or two sessions across the week.

The programs are inspired by European forest preschools (Elliott & Chancellor, 2014), to support children to engage with 'nature' and the environment, and are framed within humanist developmental ideologies reproducing growth capital, discussed earlier in the chapter. Within these settings, more-than-human species in natural environments are objects, tools or sites of learning and growth to be consumed by child human species without agency and to be used to explore and build skills and knowledge. The Victorian state government (Department of Education and Training, 2020) links bush kindergarten with children's health and well-being and a site to extend the educational program.

> The development of bush kinders reflects the mounting body of evidence that outdoor activities such as exploring natural environments, are beneficial to children and contribute to improving children's health and wellbeing.... Bush kinders are generally located in natural environments away from the education and care service and provide valuable opportunities for children to explore the natural environment and to extend the educational program. (Department of Education and Training, 2020, para. 1).

This natural environment becomes an annex of the early childhood classroom that is planned, structured, shaped and explored as a passive object without agency to be consumed for learning and development:

> An educational program must be planned, documented and delivered to children attending the bush kinder and should enhance children's learning and development and be based on an approved learning framework (section 168; regulations 73 to 76). (Department of Educational Training, 2020, para. 9)

Educators guided by *Belonging, Being & Becoming, The Early Years Learning Framework for Australia* (EYLF; Department of Education, Employment and Workplace Relations, 2009) develop learning outcomes, produce and evaluate a program and evaluate and report on the learning that is seen and assessed. The EYLF provides an invitation to support sustainability and environmental education under Learning Outcome 2: Children are connected with and contribute to their world. The EYLF narrative calls for children to

- become socially responsible and show respect for the environment
- demonstrate an increasing knowledge of, and respect for natural and constructed environments
- explore, infer, predict and hypothesise in order to develop an increased understanding of the interdependence between land, people, plants and animals

- show growing appreciation and care for natural and constructed environments
- explore relationships with other living and non-living things and observe, notice and respond to change
- develop an awareness of the impact of human activity on environments and the interdependence of living thing. (Department of Education, Employment and Workplace Relations, 2009, p. 32)

The potential for early childhood educators and children to interact with human and more-than-human species, consider the ethics of enough and disrupt consumer culture within not just bush kindergarten but also other early childhood settings is there. However, the reality is that if we continue to draw on human centric discourses that draw on psycho-developmental epistemologies then the same economic growth endeavours will be perpetuated. Activities that focus on climbing trees, rocks and boulders to develop gross motor skills; rolling in grasses, sand and leaves and exploring mud and water as a sensory experience; and investigating weather, tides, erosion, fauna and flora as a STEM (science, technology, engineering and mathematics) experience continues to trace consumption, learning and growth discourses. Epistemological shifts that decenter the human hierarchy and considers more-than-human possibilities is an imperative.

While early childhood curriculum and policy in many spaces continue to focus on humanist environmentalism there is a growing early childhood scholarship around more-than-human pedagogy and children's encounters with land (e.g,. Nxumalo, 2017) and insect and animal species (e.g., Pacini-Ketchabaw & Nxumalo, 2016; Taylor & Pacini-Ketchabaw, 2015). Nxumalo, (2018, 2017) in her writing calls for the need for geotheorising that recognises thousands of years of Indigenous ways of knowing and honouring place to consider the binary and hierarchical discourses resulting in the consumption and destruction of more-than-human worlds. Nxumalo (2017) calls attention to the "entangled settler colonial governance and anthropogenic extractivism" (p. 559). She explains:

> Geontology is in dialectical opposition to colonial bio-ontologies that have maintained hierarchical relationships between life and non-life and served as justification for human exploitation of those places and spaces deemed non-life, such as seen in the dominance of environmentally damaging extractive relations with land in the Anthropocene. (Nxumalo, 2017, p. 565)

Next we consider geotheorising, pedagogical encounters and environmental justice as non-linear moments. In exploring temporality and becoming in a more-than-human world, we consider the operation of colonial human power and privilege and the possibilities for childhoods when Indigenous ways of knowing with place come to the foreground.

Growth, Development, and Consumerism in Aotearoa (New Zealand): Temporality and Becoming in a More-than-Human World

The long-standing entanglement of neoliberalism, growth and childhoods with environmental justice is in this section positioned in relation to the more-than-human world in the Anthropocene (Malone et al., 2020). Childhoods, in itself a temporal encounter, begs the questions, 'Where are the children in relation to the environmental justice, and what justice shall we provide for children's future?' and, in particular, 'What expectations do we have for indigenous childhoods, for their aspirations, for example, in Aotearoa New Zealand, for Māori to grow up, teach, learn and play as Māori children? As such, the idea of time and temporality—and indigeneity—are critical to intergenerational environmental justice, and it is not possible to negotiate 'the future', 'the temporal', the 'growth' without working with the histories of the present.

The concern of growth, of 'more', has become a common refrain. Childhoods and time are associated with growth—both real, physical and the metaphor of 'more'—the economies of childhoods associated with environmental (in)justice. More has become a part of 'good', of the process of moving towards a better space. In such a space, childhood becomes an economic unit to be assessed and measured. The question that we ask in this section is how such an approach may change with and in relation to the context of Aoteaora New Zealand. How does the idea of growth translate into Indigenous thinking of the land, of the resistance that will position Māori childhood alongside environmental justice, and what agency is in place?

As the sociology of childhood reminds us, human subjects have agency. However, this concept is not necessarily in traditional scholarship extended to young children (and even more so to indigenous children) or to non-human entities (as they are not considered to be ontologically complete, or not alive). The new sociology of childhood considers children as independent social actors and capable of making decisions about their lives and their ability to demonstrate this capacity contributes to the governance of their issues (James et al., 1998). In critical posthumanism, it is considered not as much who has an agency but, rather, how agency is shared in relation to nature (Braidotti, 2013). The world reflects the idea that we may sense but not know agency, and as not only through critical posthumanism but also through Indigenous Māori lens, agency is shared among adults, children, water and land. The land and water have long had and shared deep history and agency, as Young (2017) demonstrates relations with the Whanganui River in the North Island:

> The tribes of the Whanganui take their name, their spirit and their strength from the great river which flows from the mountains of the central North Island to the sea. For centuries the people have travelled the Whanganui River by

canoe, caught eels in it, built villages on its banks, and fought over it. The people say, 'Ko au te awa. Ko te awa ko au' – I am the river. The river is me.

The Whanganui River was in 2017 granted the rights, responsibilities and liabilities of a legal subject, through the intra-relationality of river-water becoming-subject. This legal process fundamentally challenged Western notions of child/time/flow/river/shared/agency, as singular entities with clearly assigned subjectivities. At the same time, however, this act affirms the anthropocentric exceptionalism of human power, whereby granting a right, of being human, as a desirable, agentic legal state. And all the while, the earth, too, responds and reacts. As Latour (2014) says, it moves, in relation to what occurs on, in, and around it.

Childhoods—especially indigenous childhoods—are part of the concept of water assemblages. They open up possibilities for multiple conceptions, as the river offers relational and ethically concerning opportunities for diffracting physical environments through diverse cultural legends, food practices, contaminations, leisure activities, child's being and play. As Malone et al. (2020) say:

> Imagine, the ultimate non-static, temporal, river-becoming-human, the fluid boundaries between acts, orientations, knowledges, affects and responses; variously gushing, trickling, mini or major streams, running alongside each other, sometimes entwining, sometimes not, seeping into the silt, earth, clay, porous river sands and stones in, on and through which they pass. (p. 171)

The banks of a river becoming human are children's playground and part of their lifeworlds. Banks of rivers becoming Indigenous children's rhizomatic learning environments, entangled with non-static multiplicities, always shifting and changing. The growth and temporality of childhoods open us up to seeing the many different ways of understanding meaning, of viewing diverse 'organisations of power' and, in particular, of creating spaces for the multiple shifting and changing circumstances that we need to allow for as experienced by and 'powered' by children. It is the "increase in the dimensions of a multiplicity that necessarily changes in nature as it expands its connections" (Deleuze & Guattari, 2013, p. 7). This view of assemblage—of indigeneity, growth, becoming and river—underscore key challenges to Western thinking about childhoods, pursuing linear expectations for children and cementing the established hierarchies in place.

The significance of physical or affective spaces—childhood environments, such as rivers—become as felt, sensed, acted on as childhoods' social environments. In other words, the other forces or energies, metaphysical relationships to (Indigenous) land, place and water, may have to do with time, for example, which is more than a linear, forward-moving conception. Even when histories are considered, time may relate to more than the dominant focus on progress. Rather, it becomes a sense of past, present and future and of growth. Place, too, becomes more than a delineated, identifiable, ownable overt positioning. Fiore's (2018) emphasises that all matter is an ongoing historicity, a congealing of agency whereby matter and time intra-act. When the Whanganui River was granted rights, let us remind us of the argument that was presented:

> The metaphysical reality that the law recognizes is one that remains quite alien to the western mind: "I am the river, and the river is me." That's how the Iwi express their relationship to the Whanganui; the two are indivisible, an utterly organic whole. The river is not a mere "resource" to be managed. (Boiller, 2017, para. 2)

Understanding the river as 'an utterly organic whole' reinforces inseparability of humans, adults and children from time and place. It also challenges the dominant Western way of seeing children as separate from the idea of growth around us and, instead, focus on the singular temporality of growth as a 'development' (Tesar, 2016). Furthermore, Ceder (2018) explains the intra-relationality of entities entangled in each 'being', through what Barad terms *relata*. The notion of *relata* stresses the non-universality of children's development over time and disrupts many conventional developmental theories on how children grow in stages and how they should learn and play. Furthermore, they question what children should learn at different times in their lives, and what resources and support they should be given, be introduced to, or encounter in relation to their 'growth'. The basis of relata is the closely entangled evolution, and the reciprocal effect of and within, intra-relationships that children have with all that is acting with and on them at various times. This exemplifies a posthuman intra-relational view on children's growth rather than a linear idea of the growth of their bodies. The intra-relationships occurring in these posthuman "connectednesses" lead to and become as assemblages of space-time.

Indigenous thought provides us with the temporal impact on place and children's lives. In Aotearoa (New Zealand), Indigenous Māori children's lives are impacted through time by relationships with place. Ritchie and Skerrett (2014) relate how the articles of the Treaty of Waitangi, the treaty signed by Māori chiefs and the British Crown in 1840, continue to govern Māori relationships to place, and to 'things of value'. Article Two of the Treaty promises that Māori would retain "their absolute chieftainship (*tino rangatiratanga*) over their lands, villages, and everything of value" (p. 3). Land and place hold deep meaning to Māori *whānau* (families), bearing witness to the belief not only that the people are not only *of* the land but also that they *are* the land and that the land is the people. The colonial history of New Zealand, including years of unrest and dissatisfaction with marginalising practices and loss of family land, have served to diminish the promised tino rangatiratanga. They may lead to an almost complete loss of 'things of value' including tangible and intangible 'things', such as for children to lose the Māori language, and the right to live as Māori. According to Ritchie and Skerrett (2014), Māori children might perform their inter- and intra-connectedness with their physical and sensed surroundings, in their exercising of handed-down thought, orientations, attitudes, being, behaving, doing. That is, they make relationships with their surroundings on the basis of the meanings and belief systems that they are imbued with over time. This may sometimes involve metaphysical relationships and relationships evoked through mythological connections and storying over time and place. Mika (2017) elaborates on an Indigenous education when he writes about a metaphysics of presence. When children respond or react to a particular memory, of a past experience, friend, idea or thing, or to a particular occurrence in their place, they perform these 'infinite connections and co-constitutive realities', or philosophy as a method (Tesar, 2020).

Young Activists as Geopolitical Warriors

This chapter has explored the entanglement of neoliberal discourses of child/hoods, growth and development and the more-than-human world across the United States, Australia and New Zealand. What brings hope for environmental justice in the present and future is the way children and young people are becoming politically active in speaking back to policy and practice. Greta Thunberg's speech to the United Nations on climate change in September 2019 highlighted the power of global child/hood activism. Her speech called out the neoliberal consumer discourses driven by governments and industries across the world and demonstrated the growing web of young geopolitical warriors in transnational spaces and places. During 2018 and 2019, primary and secondary school student strikes for climate change action were seen across nations. Governments like Australia marked these childhood activists as ill informed and urged students to stay in the classroom and learn what they need to so that they are productive citizens and have the capacity to extract and consume natural resources. In response to student demonstrations, in 2018, the resources minister, Matt Canavan, on Sydney radio station 2 GB commented:

> Walking off school and protesting, you don't learn anything from that. . . . The best thing you learn about going to a protest is how to join the dole queue. . . . That's what your future life will look like, up in a line asking for a handout, not actually taking charge of your life and getting a real job. (ABC News, 2018, 'You Don't Learn')

Completely missing the essence of children's concerns Canavan went on to say:

> I want kids to be at school to learn about how you build a mine, how you do geology, how you drill for oil and gas, which is one of the most remarkable scientific exploits of anywhere in the world that we do. (ABC News, 2018, 'You Don't Learn')

This followed a comment by the prime minister of Australia, Scott Morrison, earlier in that week: "We don't support our schools being turned into parliaments. What we want is more learning in schools and less activism in schools" (ABC News, 2018, 'You Don't Learn').

While we continue to grapple with the negative impact of neoliberal ideals and enactments of growth and the need to imagine other presents and futures, we need to consider theories and pedagogies in early childhood that support child/adult/educator/parent to critically engage and disrupt growth, development and edu-capital assemblages. Childhoods as a space for continual material yearning and the markers of success based on the consumption of growth and material capital (toys and knowledge) governed by the state through adults makes it difficult for reimagined more-than-human child/hood activism. A starting point is respect for the thinking and knowledges of those who are younger, as well as for the agency that they continually exhibit. Second is the recognition and respect for the multiplicity of Indigenous knowledges and learnings that have been in existence for thousands of years. Third, the need to intra-act with more-than-human species and materials and call attention to the effects of neoliberal and edu-capital policies that drive learning, growth and development discourses and the effects of this consumption on the environment. Fourth, consider how activism continues to remap consumer discourses so that the 'saving' of environments is not focused on the future survival of human species but a continual ethical encounter with human and the more-than-human. There must be urgency within activism around neoliberal childhoods to work harder at comprehending what relationships both preexist and outlast us, so that we may be humbled into seeking justice with and for children that encompasses and honors multiplicity of places, spaces, times, and agents.

References

ABC News. (2018, November 29). Students strike for climate change protests, defying calls to stay in school. *ABC News*. https://www.abc.net.au/news/2018-11-30/australian-students-climate-change-protest-scott-morrison/10571168

Becker, M., Edwards, S., & Massey, R. I. (2010). Toxic chemicals in toys and children's products: Limitations of current responses and recommendations for government and industry. *Environmental Science & Technology, 44*(21), 7986–7991.

Blackmore, J. (2014). Cultural and gender politics in Australian education, the rise of edu-capitalism and the 'fragile project' of critical educational research. *Australian Educational Researcher, 41*(5), 499–520.

Bollier, D. (2017, July 3). *I am the river and the river is me*. Resilience. https://www.resilience.org/stories/2017-07-03/i-am-the-river-and-the-river-is-me/

Braidotti, R. (2013). *The posthuman*. Polity Press.

Buckingham, D. (2011). *The material child: Growing up in consumer culture*. Cambridge: Polity.

Byrne, C. (2016). *They came to play*. Toy Industry Association, Inc. New York.

Ceder, S. (2018). *Towards a posthuman theory of educational relationality*. Routledge.

Cook, D. T. (2009). Children as consumers. In J. Qvortrup, W. A. Corsaro, & M. Honig (Eds.), *The Palgrave handbook of childhood studies* (pp. 332–346). Palgrave.

Deleuze, G., & Guattari, F. (2013). *A thousand plateaus: Capitalism and schizophrenia* (B. Massumi, Trans.). Bloomsbury Academic.

Department of Education, Employment and Workplace Relations. (2009). *Belonging, being and becoming: The Early Years Learning Framework for Australia*. Australian Government Department of Education, Employment and Workplace Relations for the Council of Australian Governments, Commonwealth of Australia.

Department of Education and Training, (2020, December 20). *Bush Kinder*. Victorian State Government. https://www.education.vic.gov.au/childhood/providers/regulation/Pages/bushkinders.aspx

DiGangi, J., & Strakova, J. (2015). *Toxic toy or toxic waste: Recycling POPs into new products*. Arnika.

Elliott, S., & Chancellor, B. (2014). From forest preschool to bush kinder: An inspirational approach to preschool provision in Australia. *Australasian Journal of Early Childhood, 39*(4), 45–53.

Felli, R. (2015). Environment, not planning: the neoliberal depoliticisation of environmental policy by means of emissions trading. *Environmental Politics, 24*(5), 641–660.

Fiore, E. (2018). Posthuman performativity. In R. Braidotti & M. Hlavajova (Eds.). *Posthuman glossary* (pp. 359–360). Bloomsbury Academic.

Gibson, M., McArdle, F., & Hatcher, C. (2015). Governing child care in neoliberal times: Discursive constructions of children as economic units and early childhood educators as investment brokers. *Global Studies of Childhood, 5*(3), 322–332.

Guzzonato, A., Puype, F., & Harrad, S. J. (2017) Evidence of bad recycling practices: BFRs in children's toys and food-contact articles. *Environmental Science Process Impacts, 19*(7), 956–963.

James, A., Jenks, C., & Prout, A. (1998). *Theorizing childhood*. Polity Press.

Korsvold, T. (2010). Proper Toys for proper children: A case study of the Norwegian company A/S Riktige Leker (Proper Toys). In D. Buckingham & V. Tingstad (Eds.), *Childhood and consumer culture* (pp. 31–45). Palgrave.

Latour, B. (2014). Agency at the time of the Anthropocene. *New Literary History, 45*(1), 1–18. doi:10.1353/nlh.2014.0003

Malone, K., Tesar M., & Arndt, S. (2020). *Theorising posthuman childhood studies*. Springer.

Mika, C. (2017). *Indigenous education and the metaphysics of presence: A worlded philosophy*. Routledge.

Myers, C. Y. (2019). Environmental justice in the shadow of the hyperobject: Reflections on (not) saving the community garden. In J. Kroeger, C. Y. Myers, & K. Morgan (Eds.), *Nurturing nature and the environment with young children: Children, elders, earth*, (pp. 36–44). Routledge.

Myers, Y. C., Smith, K., & Tesar, M. (2017). Diffracting mandates for reflective practices in teacher education and development: Multiple readings from Australia, New Zealand, and the United

States. *Journal of Early Childhood Teacher Education*, 38(4), 275–288. https://doi.org/10.1080/10901027.2017.1389788

Nxumalo, F. (2017). Geotheorizing mountain–child relations within anthropogenic inheritances. *Children's Geographies*, 15(5), 558–569.

Nxumalo, F. (2018). Stories for living on a damaged planet: Environmental education in a preschool classroom. *Journal of Early Childhood Research*, 16(2), 148–159.

Pacini-Ketchabaw, V., & Nxumalo, F. (2016). Unruly raccoons and troubled educators: Nature/culture divides in a childcare centre. *Environmental Humanities*, 7(1), 151–168.

Perez, M. S., & Cannella, G. S. (2011). Disaster capitalism as neoliberal instrument for the construction of early childhood education/care policy: Charter schools in post-Katrina New Orleans. *International Critical Childhood Policy Studies Journal*, 4(1), 47–68.

Pugh, A. J. (2009). *Longing and belonging: Parents, children and consumer culture*. University of California Press.

Ritchie, J., & Skerrett, M. (2014). *Early childhood education in Aotearoa New Zealand: History, pedagogy and liberation*. Palgrave Macmillan.

Robertson, M. (2007). Discovering price in all the wrong places: The work of commodity definition and price under neoliberal environmental policy. *Antipode*, 39(3), 500–526.

Schneider, D., & Freeman, N. (2000). *Children's environmental health: Reducing risk in a dangerous world*. American Public Health Association.

Sims, M., & Waniganayake, M. (2015). The performance of compliance in early childhood: Neoliberalism and nice ladies. *Global Studies of Childhood*, 5(3), 333–345.

Smith, K., Tesar, M., & Myers, C. Y. (2016). Edu-capitalism and the governing of early childhood education and care in Australia, New Zealand and the United States. *Global Studies of Childhood*, 6(1), 123–135.

Taylor, A., & Pacini-Ketchabaw, V. (2015). Learning with children, ants, and worms in the Anthropocene: Towards a common world pedagogy of multispecies vulnerability. *Pedagogy, Culture & Society*, 23(4), 507–529.

Tesar, M. (2016). Timing childhoods: An alternative reading of children's development through philosophy of time, temporality, place and space. *Contemporary Issues in Early Childhood*, 17(4), 399–408. doi:10.1177/1463949116677924

Tesar, M. (2020). Philosophy as a method: Tracing the histories of intersections of 'philosophy', 'methodology' and 'education'. *Qualitative Inquiry*. Advanced online publication. https://doi.org/10.1177/1077800420934144

United Nations Environment Programme. (2014). *Valuing plastics: The business case for measuring, managing and disclosing plastic use in the consumer goods industry*.

World Health Organization. (2020). Persistent organic pollutants. https://www.who.int/foodsafety/areas_work/chemical-risks/pops/en/

Young, D. (2017). Whanganui tribes – Ancestors. In *Te Ara – the Encyclopedia of New Zealand*. http://www.TeAra.govt.nz/en/photograph/2176/tamateas-cave

**STIRS OF ECHOES:
20TH-CENTURY
CHILDHOODS
IN THE 21ST**

CHAPTER 14

Figurations of the Child in Swedish Early Childhood Education

Therese Lindgren

> From worrying about the turbulent present and the uncertain outcomes of the future, the step to worrying about the conditions of children's upbringing and welfare is short. Children embody the future, which is why the vitality and survivability of civilization ultimately depends on their viability—physically, psychologically and socially. (Kristjánsson, 1999, p. 30, my translation)

THE STORY OF the Swedish preschool child is unique, in the way that young children's upbringing and education have been part of state care since the early 1940s. Today, early education and care is a state-subsidized right, available for all children from 1 year of age. Since most of Sweden's 1- to 5-year-olds are enrolled in preschool programs (85%), attendance is the norm (Skolverket, 2020). The specialist knowledge, created within or in close connection to the institution, therefore has a significant influence on the general perception of children, children's development, and learning. However, what is regarded as the best available knowledge is constantly changing in step with societal development, political reforms, and trends within the research field (T. Lindgren, 2018). The history of the Swedish preschool child intertwines with the general political, economic, and social development in the country (Martin Korpi 2007; Sjöstrand Öhrfelt, 2019).

This chapter unpacks some of the different prominent figurations of the preschool child found in portions of Nordic early childhood education (ECE) history using Sweden as the exemplar, what these figurations respond to, and in what contexts they are being brought to life. However, it is not possible to make a nuanced comprehensive account of history (and all its different figurations of the child) within the limits of these pages. As a reader, you should keep in mind that the historical depictions made here are painted with a broad brush. Instead, some historical threads are traced in an effort to illustrate the ever-changing nature of the preschool child as a figure and the ideas, hopes, and fears, about society and the future, that are embedded in the different figurations.

The relevance for the international reader lies in the fact that Sweden internationally has been regarded as a "model country" in the way that early education and care are combined within the framework of one institution available for all. Furthermore, the development of ECE in Sweden can hardly be regarded as a local national phenomenon since the Swedish preschool is on par with international policy movements and ideas about transnational childhoods (Sjöstrand Öhrfelt, 2019).

The theoretical framework of this chapter is influenced by Claudia Castañeda's work and use of the concept "figuration". Figuration can be used as an analytic tool in examining how the youngest in society are being made as historically and culturally specific figures. As an example, Castañeda (2001, 2003) examines poststructuralist and feminist theories of the subject. In these theories the child figures as a raw and unfinished "not-yet subject"—that is, the ontological origin of the adult. As such, the child becomes a resource in the retheorization of the subject in opposition of the hegemonic order of the world. However, figurations are temporary stabilizations of nodes and interconnections and are therefore not definite nor definitive. Furthermore, they are not only operating in the planes of discourse but are "the simultaneously material and semiotic effects of specific practices" (Castañeda, 2003, p. 3). By describing the material and discursive practices through which a figuration occurs and the power relations associated with these practices, it can be located—not only within specific discursive domains but in time and space as well. As an analytic tool, figuration accounts for 'the means through which the child is brought into being *as* figure, as well as the bodies and worlds this figure generates through a plurality of forms' (Castañeda, 2014, pp. 3–4).

Building the Welfare State

In Sweden, childcare has been provided in various forms since the 19th century. The industrialization and urbanization processes in the latter part of the 19th century brought on vast social changes and the family dissolved as an economic unit (Persson, 1994). While their parents worked, children were often left to their own devices. The changed situation in the home raised concerns and debate amongst the high and middle classes about the crisis of the moral order and the collapse of society. The people, and the children of the people, were thought to be in desperate need of cultivation (Tallberg Broman, 1995). Based on charity, the first early forms of childcare institutions emerged in an aim to clean and feed the children of poor, single, working mothers. Anne-Li

Lindgren and Ingrid Söderlind (2019) describe that attention was drawn to children's physiological and medical needs, which was on par with the upper classes' growing interest in health, hygiene, and nutrition. If the children of the working class were offered better living conditions, maybe society could develop as a whole in accordance with bourgeoisie ideals. The charitable efforts contained equal parts of support and discipline in the way that those who stood on the receiving end were expected to embrace the values and ideals of the philanthropists.

Figure 14.1. Interior from Engelbrekt's infant crèche (barnkrubba). Photo: Wilhelm Lamm, 1909-1913. Stockholm City Museum. Picture nr. SSMF068128.

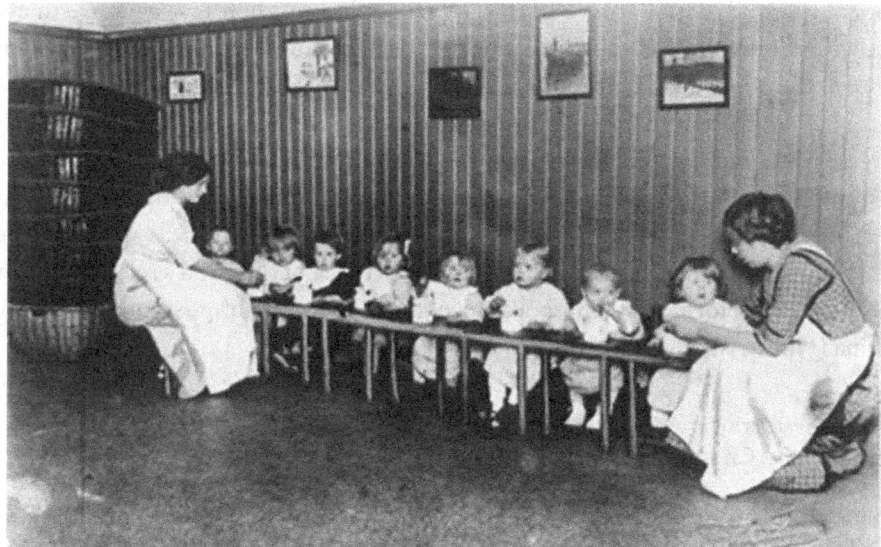

The Nature-Romantic Child

The changed conditions of the home brought a new image of the child, freed from family and production. With the separation from adulthood, the interest in children's upbringing and education grew. In 1900, Ellen Key's *The Century of the Child* was published describing the child as carrying the seed of the evolution of the human soul and hence the key to a higher civilization. In this figuration, the fate of the future rested in the hands of the child. Then, like now, the child harbored the hope for a better future and social change.

That the child is the opportunity and the education the means by which social change could be brought about is an idea that also permeated the Fröbel Kindergarten (Barnträdgård) movement. Inspired by Friedrich Fröbel's pedagogical ideas, the pioneers of kindergarten emphasized the importance of knowledge about the child's unique essence and nature, a nature that became prominent for the adult if the child was allowed to act on their own (Hultqvist, 1990). In kindergarten, this nature would be given space and nourishment in the form of nature experiences, educational household activities, and aesthetic expressions. In its design, kindergarten was similar to the home (Lindgren & Söderlind, 2019). In the kindergarten, however, the child would not be educated, but developed (Tallberg Broman, 1995). The strong notion that the educational activities offered in preschool should be distinguished from the classroom teaching of the school, which is expressed in a traditional Nordic ECE discourse, largely stems from this idea from the Fröbel movement. In an attempt to free the child from their cultural and traditional heritage, kindergarten would offer an educational and moral space beyond the contemporary social, cultural, and economic state of affairs. Here, with the right support, the child would grow and develop according to their inner nature in accordance with the divine, the true, the good, and the beautiful. The kindergarten became a symbol of the opposite of culture, that is to say nature, albeit disciplined and arranged (Hultqvist, 1997a). In the Fröbel movement, a nature-romantic figuration of the child emerges that is not entirely different from that portrayed by Jean Jacques Rousseau in his Émile (1896/2003). Fröbel himself encountered Rousseau's thoughts via Johann Heinrich Pestalozzi, which left a great impression on Pestalozzi's ideas about child-centered teaching, self-activity, and the crucial importance of the child's relationship with the mother. Therefore, the woman was also given a prominent position in the Fröbel doctrine (Hultqvist, 1990).

Figure 14.2. Interior from a kindergarten in Norrköping. Photo: Engrid Hedlund, Year Unknown. Mölndal City Museum.

However, the first kindergartens that were opened in Sweden in the late 19th century were aimed at the wealthy few. This was because the activities were subject to a fee. With the help of municipal grants, the first public kindergarten was started by sisters Ellen and Maria Moberg in 1904 (Hultqvist, 1990). The sisters were not only active in national and international networks but also started the Fröbel Institute for the training of kindergarten teachers. The training, which was called "seminars," was designed by women and for women and originated from the bourgeois women's movement and their demands for education and work (Tallberg Broman, 1995).

To sum up, it is against the background of strong urbanization processes and the separation from adult life and production that the figuration of the nature-romantic child is brought to life. Resting in the cradle of recipient democracy the nature-romantic child symbolizes innocence, originality, and formability. However, the child is constantly being threatened by the stagnating influence of tradition and culture that motivates the institution as an educational and moral space beyond culture, a space in which the child could grow and develop in accordance with the natural and divine.

Building the People's Home

In the 1930s, a critique of the Fröbel doctrine's dominance in child pedagogy grew. In the book *Stadsbarn* (City Children), Alva Myrdal advocated a merger of all different forms of childcare into so-called bigger nurseries (*storbarnkammare*). The approach was a social pedagogy with an emphasis on individuality, independence, innovation, social awareness, and the love for work (Tallberg Broman, 1995). Myrdal expressed that the moral approach to children and children's upbringing represented by the kindergarten movement needed to be replaced with rationalism and science (Myrdal, 1935). In the search for a science-based knowledge of children, child development, and learning, child psychology experienced its breakthrough. During the development of the Swedish welfare society, where rationality and scientific knowledge were held high, development psychology was able to offer the theoretical and technical language about the child and child development, which, according to Myrdal, among others, was lacking in the Fröbel kindergarten movement (Tallberg Broman, 1995; Hultqvist, 1990). Assuming that there is such a thing as context-independent universal knowledge about the child, Myrdal thought developmental psychology to be directly useful as a basis for modern educational practice (Hultqvist, 1997b). Myrdal found inspiration in, among others, Arnold Gesell's works (Hammarlund, 1998). With a focus on the stages of development, behavioral patterns, learning processes, and child observations, the knowledge of the child was to be mapped and the mystery surrounding the child's being dispelled.

During the same period, ideas about the people's home started to take shape. Through extensive government investigations and reports, based on rational considerations and the best available knowledge, various societal issues were addressed in order to find optimal solutions (Dencik, 1995). The birth rate was low, and in order to reverse the bad trend and increase the number of births, various family policy reforms were carried out which resulted in the government taking over part of expenditures of families with children (Persson, 1994). In the book *Crisis in the Population Question*, Alva and Gunnar Myrdal (1934) showed connections between poverty, housing shortages, disadvantaged social conditions, and childlessness. With the idea of "the bigger nursery" (*storbarnkammaren*), Alva Myrdal laid the foundation for social and population policy-driven public childcare, which would coordinate the collective care of children and, to the extent that the home environment was insufficient, would act as a compensation for this. In the emerging modern welfare state, the bigger nursery posed as a transitional program between the kindergarten of the Fröbel movement and a state preschool program (Hultqvist, 1990). With reason and a rational lifestyle, traditionalism, old-fashioned lifestyles, and ways of thinking would be suppressed:

> In their future lives, however, the children would be less able to rely on their parents than before. Already, such an obvious phenomenon as the greater occupational mobility and geographical mobility make[s] it necessary for us to psychologically more detach each new generation from the older one. We must not impede our children with one-sided fixations to ourselves and with all too one-sided focus on our very habits and attitudes to life. Therein lies another reason to start early in partially detaching their upbringing environment from the small and private family circle. (Myrdal, 1935, p. 301, my translation)

In Alva Myrdal's portrayal of childcare and the state's takeover of the child's education and upbringing, issues of social differences were dealt with in the background. In Hultqvist's (1990) words, upbringing was given a supposedly apolitical character. In the figuration of the child that arose in the focal point between the achievements of child psychology and the social policy project that aimed to detach the child from the home environment, the child figures as autonomous and in nature independent of their social and cultural environment. Disconnected from their parents, the child is made a subject of educational and psychological intervention. The new era required a new adaptable and flexible citizen with the ability for good independent judgment (Dahlgren & Hultqvist, 1995). However, it is worth noting that only a small part of the country's children were covered by state childcare in the 1930s. Alva Myrdal's "bigger nurseries" did not have the great impact that the vision promised but has nevertheless inspired the design of today's Swedish ECE and the ideas about the reduction of irregularities through state provision of care that motivate it.

For the Sake of the Child

The debate on the motives and purpose of ECE institutions reached its peak in the middle of the 20th century. During the Second World War, the demand for female labor increased, which also influenced the view of the role of the mother. Employment and parenthood did not necessarily have to be mutually exclusive (Hammarlund, 1998). However, there was no consensus on the matter. The child's needs for maternal care were set against the preschool's pedagogical and social motives, women's right to gainful employment, and the growing need for female labor in the labor market and the public sector. This conflict took practical form in the creation of different forms of childcare. On one hand, there were half-day forms of preschool/playschool with clear pedagogical ambitions and, on the other hand, full-day childcare in the form of day-care centers (Lindgren & Söderlind, 2019). Tallberg Broman (1995) describes how preschool/playschool in the 1940s was prioritized by teachers, officials, and politicians on the basis of perceptions of the child's needs and well-being. However, these views shifted over time and the full-day institution merged with the half-day in the way that day-care centers also began to put emphasis on pedagogical and social motives. In other words, the day-care centers simply began to take the form of preschool/playschool but with longer opening hours. Developmental psychological ideas combined with conceptions about parents' inability to prepare their children for an uncertain and changing future (Riddersporre & Persson, 2010) justified ECE institutions as being "for the sake of the child" (1946 års kommitté för den halvöppna barnavården, 1951). When Parliament decided on the first state grants for both half-day and full-day childcare in Sweden in 1944, even the youngest citizens became part of the responsibility of the state.

The Swedish Preschool Model

As described, the family has been a central subject of political reforms for social change since the interwar period. In addition to the social and labor market policy incentives for preschool described so far, the issue of gender equality was added during the 1970s. In the 1970s, a number of reforms were carried out affecting the situation of the home, such as the 40-hour working week, 6 months' shared parental insurance, and the prohibition of physical discipline in the home. The increased influence of the state on family life and the general demand for public joint childcare distinguish the Nordic countries from the rest of the world (Lindgren & Söderlind, 2019). One could conceptualize this era as the beginning of the institutionalization of childhood (Kampmann, 2004). An extensive expansion of public childcare led to more parents working; at the same time, childbearing continued to increase. The Swedish preschool model, which unites labor market, family, equality policy, and pedagogical ambitions, began to arouse international interest. This includes Swedish parents reporting the highest employment rate in the world (Persson, 1994).

Significant for the development of the preschool was the 1968 Commission on Nursery Provision (Socialdepartementet, 1972)—drawing up ideological, pedagogical, and organizational guidelines for municipal planning for childcare. In the commission, the different forms of both part-time and full-time childcare were merged within the framework of the concept of preschool. In the study, which focused on children's cognitive, social, emotional, and linguistic development, the theories of Jean Piaget's developmental psychology and Erik H. Eriksson's social psychological studies were paired with "pedagogical dialogue" as a practical tool (Persson, 1994). The model for the so-called pedagogical dialogue was framed within cognitive and psychodynamic theory—assuming that the child actively seeks knowledge and experience through interactions with the environment. The child's social, emotional, and linguistic development, as well as the development of their own self, were described as dependent on sharing these experiences in dialogue with other children and adults. The goal was formulated as children's gradual development of democratic norms and values (Socialdepartementet, 1972). The child's need for rich opportunities for interactions and dialogue motivated the right to a preschool that met this need—it was simply considered to be in the child's own interest.

The Vulnerable Child and the Child at Risk

In the late 1970s, the developmental psychological view of child development was criticized for being too uncritical and simplistic. Instead of blindly focusing on the individual child's development and psychological processes, the surrounding world, and the child's cultural and social environment, also needed to be taken into account. The criticism opened to some extent up to new ideas. The report that the Preschool Committee published in 1985, as well as in the pedagogical program with advice and instructions for preschools that were drawn up by the National Board of Health and Welfare two years later (Allmänna förlag, 1987), highlights how preschool activities also needed to be illustrated from a social and societal perspective. Child development had to be understood in relation to external circumstances:

> Child development is often seen as a completely legal course of events where different physical and psychological development steps follow each other in a certain pattern. . . . But the psychological development is more complex even though it has a statutory nature in an overall manner. . . . Children are born e.g. into special relationships through their parents. These are included in the socio-economic and cultural context of society. The parents' world and what it represents will also be the child's world with long-term consequences for the child's development. (Utbildningsdepartementet, 1985, pp. 31–32, my translation)

In the figuration of the child that occurs when the child's development is put in relation to the parents' world, the child becomes vulnerable in the way that the social and cultural world has direct consequences for the child's development and life opportunities. The former natural and, in many aspects, autonomous preschool child was given more relaxed contours when viewed in the light of their economic, cultural, and social context. In the welfare state, society carried considerable responsibility for the child and the child's development from a lifelong perspective and in relation of the figuration of the "vulnerable" child, the compensatory mission of preschool was confirmed and strengthened.

The Competent Child

In the late 1980s, the pressure on available preschool placements increased dramatically. As many municipalities could not meet the demand, municipal grants were given for the start-up of private activities, such as parent cooperatives. A few years later, the liberal-conservative government introduced the right of free establishment in childcare (Martin Korpi, 2015), which meant that state aid was also granted to private preschools.[1] This was the starting point for an increased market adaptation of the preschool, whereby families' ability to choose childcare themselves increased and with this competition between preschools (Dahlberg et al., 1991). The high demand, however, remained, and the situation did not get any easier as Sweden entered into a financial crisis in the early 1990s, which caused austerity and savings in the public sector. Childcare was one of the sectors in which the greatest rationalizations were being made. Despite the extensive expansion of capacity, the costs were not increased (Barnomsorg och skolakommittén, 1997). This, of course, had different consequences, not least for the composition and size of classes. The organizational changes required a socially functioning and capable child. That is, a child who is able to make bonds with several different adults, who expresses their needs and wishes in a larger group and who learns from and with other children of the same age.

At the same time, as preschool institutions underwent major changes related to expansions and savings, childhood sociology and the idea of the competent child (Barnomsorg och skolakommittén, 1997) made an impact internationally (see, e.g., Juul, 2001). By sociologists such as Chris Jenks (1996) and Allison James and Alan Prout (1990), childhood was explained as socially constructed and therefore also historically and socially situated. The child was highlighted as an active social actor and a cultural co-constructor. In this way, the more or less passive recipient of the influence of culture and society described earlier was challenged. The competent child soon became a nodal point in the Nordic preschool discourse. Kampmann (2004) describes how the adult gaze was moved from the child's external observable development and performance to the child's inner life to the child's feelings and individual opinions. The child's genuine insight and knowledge of their own situation and context received increased attention.

The spirit of the time is reflected in the UN Convention on the Rights of the Child, which was ratified in the early 1990s, having a major impact on both the political and the general debate in the Nordic countries. Brembeck, Johansson & Kampmann (2004) describe how the child's recognition as a citizen, equivalent to the adult, raised questions about how the child's participation in decision-making could be organized. The child's new status had effects not only on possible ways of responding to and treating the child but also on the expectations of the child as competent, self-reflective, self-evaluating, and rational. By placing the child in an institution from an early age, the child would be socialized into a community and trained to express and formulate their own needs and desires. The authors track two main figurations of the competent child. The first relates to human rights and portrays a universal child with the right to be respected regardless of age or background. The second relates to the welfare state and the expectation of the child as sensible, responsible, and adaptable.

The Swedish Preschool Becomes Its Own School Form

During the 1990s, the former state centrally controlled Swedish education system was communalized, accompanied by the breakthrough of New Public Management in the public sector (Agevall, 2005). One of the most radical reforms for Swedish preschool took place in 1996, when the responsibility of childcare and ECE was transferred from the Ministry of Health and Social Affairs to the Ministry of Education. With the National Agency for Education as the new supervisory authority, the preschool became part of the Swedish education system with its own curriculum (Barnomsorg och skolakommittén, 1997; Skolverket, 1998). Gunilla Halldén (2007) explains the transition as a clear indication that the preschool was no longer a labor market policy project but now one of educational policy. In other words, the emphasis on the motivation of state-funded childcare and education shifted from parents' opportunities for employment to younger children's right to education.

The Swedish preschool's first curriculum (Skolverket, 1998) meant a change in the view of the purpose and content of ECE (Tallberg Broman, 2010). The now publicly funded preschool would be led by professional teachers according to state-formulated national goals and guidelines. The preschool's organization and structure became more and more similar to the school (Dahlgren & Hultqvist, 1995), and as for the school, the question of evaluating the quality of the education and goal achievement came to weigh heavily. With the increasing management of goals and results, stricter requirements were made on the competent, flexible, and lifelong-learning child who, like the adult, harbored flexibility and adaptability in order to better handle contemporary challenges and changes (Halldén, 2007).

In the late 1990s, the Swedish welfare discourse started to ebb out. Visions of universalism and homogeneity were challenged by ideas of pluralism, individualism, and diversity (Hultqvist, 1997a). The breakthrough of childhood sociology was mentioned earlier, and with this, an idea of the socially constructed childhood was disseminated. Since the child's subject itself was seen as a construction, there could no longer be any natural or essential child (e.g., James & Prout, 1990). Hultqvist and Dahlgren (1995) describe the spirit of the time of change and how the development of various post-isms flourished in attempts to capture the new age and its challenges. These ideas were intercepted within the Reggio Emilia–inspired pedagogical movement, which quickly gained ground in both research and practice (Barnomsorg och skolakommittén, 1997; Dahlberg et al., 1999).[2] In the Swedish adaptation, the Reggio Emilia–inspired pedagogy was framed in by power-critical and postmodern perspectives (Dahlberg et al., 1999; Lenz Taguchi, 1997) and was often expressed as a resistance and

> a counterforce to the reform development that has been going on in the education system since the 1980s. Not only in Sweden but also internationally. A reform development that can be linked to global economic competition and that is expressed in a new governance rationality and new governance models. Governance models that today are increasingly linked to leadership philosophies such as "new public management", "total quality management" and "public choice". (Dahlberg & Elfström, 2014, p. 268)

Ever since the Reggio Emilia approach to ECE was mentioned for the first time in a state inquiry, that is, in the memorandum to the preschool curriculum (Barnomsorg och skolakommittén, 1997), teachers, as well as committees and ministers, have made a pilgrimage to the province of Reggio Emilia. Martin Korpi (2015) explains the impact of the Reggio Emilia approach in the way that "in some respects it resembled that of the Swedish preschool, but in a more audacious and sharper form" (p. 64). Once again, criticism was directed toward developmental psychological perspectives in ECE research and practice as well as the modernist organization of the world and the divisions between feeling and reason, nature and culture, body and mind, and the like (Dahlberg & Elfström, 2014). The Reggio Emilia movement strengthened the effort to protect the uniqueness of ECE (dating back to the Fröbel movement), as something separate from the school both in terms of pedagogy and content (Halldén, 2007) and claimed to move beyond curricula, evaluation, and school preparation by instead focusing on the larger questions about life and about being together with others in the world (Dahlberg et al., 1999). Framed within a postmodern social constructionist theoretical framework, the child was articulated as a decentered and pluralistic subject, embodying possibilities and change. The so-called rich competent child encountered within the Reggio Emilia philosophical approach figured as the opposite to the passive decontextualized child of developmental psychology, bringing the promise of a more democratic, equal, and fair world. Interestingly, this "counterforce to the reform development" emerged in close connection with the projection of the preschool's first curriculum (Skolverket, 1998) and its sharpened focus on goals and results.

The Child as Resource and Investment

Moving into the new millennium, the first international "Starting Strong" conference was held in Stockholm in 2001, with the Organisation for Economic Co-operation and Development (OECD) and the Ministry of Education as hosts. In an introductory speech John P. Martin (former director for Employment, Labour and Social Affairs at the OECD) presented three major policy objectives: (1) strengthening short-and long-term outcomes and lifelong learning through early investment in high-quality ECE, (2) fostering equity and social integration objectives in order to break cycles of disadvantages and child poverty (targeting immigrant and minority communities), and (3) promoting equal opportunities for women and men to participate in the labor market with the help of "family-friendly" policies. This logic and way of talking about ECE and what motivates preschool permeate the two first decades of the 21st century. The fact that Sweden was one of the 12 countries participating in the review of ECE policy resulting in the first Starting Strong report (OECD, 2001) shows the entanglement between Swedish education policy and international education policy. In an international policy context, the young child was represented as a rather unexploited resource, flexible and adaptable, vulnerable due to their potential unfortunate background but nevertheless competent enough to be educated (Lindgren & Sjöstrand Öhrfelt, 2019). The emphasises on flexibility responded to the challenges of a fast-shifting global economy, rapid digital development, and changing demographics.

In the wake of the global financial crisis of 2007–2008, the European Commission published a report titled *Europe 2020: A Strategy for Smart, Sustainable and Inclusive Growth*, stating that the said crisis wiped out years of economic and social development with long-term challenges such as globalization and an intensified pressure on resources. In this narrative of a world in crisis (financial, ecological, political, refugee, etc.), eyes were anew turned toward preschool and the education of young children (OECD, 2012). Studies were done that showed the preschool's socioeconomic benefits and socially equalizing effects (Heckman & Masterov, 2007). Here, the child's socioeconomic background, with a strong emphasis on the parents' level of education, was once again highlighted as a decisive influencing factor for the child's future academic performance. It is argued that early intervention could reduce this potential growing academic gap between socioeconomic groups while at the same time maximize the return on education (UNICEF, 2002).

The knowledge-based economic discourse implemented in both the Swedish and international ECE policy is reflected in preventive programs and financially related efforts aimed at the population in order to achieve certain goals. These efforts may be both government-imposed or initiated by international non-governmental organizations such as the OECD (Sjöstrand Öhrfelt, 2019). Because the European Union and the OECD are mainly economic organizations, the main content in their policy work is targeting success factors and economic anomalies in the form of risks and uncertainties (T. Lindgren & Sjöstrand Öhrfelt, 2019). The future is described in policy as uncertain and threatened in the way we seem to face vast political, social, economic, and ecological challenges (European Commission, 2010; OECD, 2012, 2017). The child figures as an investment and an opportunity, as capital or resource to ensure a positive outcome. The child *is* the future. However, the child is described as vulnerable in the way that the child's socioeconomic background and the academic performance of parents can put a spanner in the works. This is where the institution is needed in order to free the child from their potentially disadvantaged academic heritage and from socially and culturally poor home conditions.

Returning to the national level and the effects of international policy, the Swedish curriculum for preschool has undergone two major revisions (Skolverket, 2010; 2019) since its introduction. The first revision was made in connection with the introduction of a new Education Act (SFS 2010:800). Here, goals and guidelines concerning children's knowledge development in the subjects of language, mathematics, science, and technology were clarified, which clearly reflects the European Union's and OECD's educational strategic objectives (Halldén, 2007). It is also knowledge of these subjects that is evaluated in the context of OECD's education study PISA (Programme for International Student Assessment). In the review of the Swedish curriculum made in OECD's report *Quality Matters in Early Childhood Education and Care: Sweden 2013*, several areas of development were highlighted. Among these areas were, for example, increased harmonization with compulsory school curricula and an emphasis on subject areas that respond to societal changes such as sustainable development and children's health. That is,–areas that were later also addressed in the latest revision of the curriculum (Skolverket, 2019).

Although some attempts have been made, the voices that have expressed opposition within the Swedish ECE policy, research, and practice (not seldom with their feet in the Reggio Emilia movement)[3] to the higher management of goals and results of the preschool and the knowledge-economic discourse that is accompanied by the same, have been ebbing out during the past decade.

The Orphan

Through the brief historization of Swedish ECE made in this chapter, I aim to show how the Swedish preschool child is brought into being as a figure in "the (adult) making of worlds" (Castañeda, 2003, p. 1). Through enlightenment and emancipation, the preschool child is to be equipped, both theoretically and through educational intervention, to be able to handle both contemporary problems and imagined challenges of tomorrow (Biesta, 2015; Carneiro et al., 2015). Recurring across the history of the young institutionalized child is the idea that the child can be emancipated and released from a future predestined by background conditions (connected to class, culture, and socioeconomic environment). In this context, it is worth noting that another Swedish government report (Utbildningsdepartementet, 2020) has been published aiming to investigate (a) how participation in preschool among children aged 3 to 5 can be increased and (b) how children's language development in Swedish (i.e., in the case of newly arrived children) can be strengthened. In the report, it is stated that it is more common for children who are not enrolled in preschool to have parents with low education, no employment, or with an immigrant background. The measures proposed include that municipalities should be obliged to conduct mandatory outreaching activities, that all children should be offered a place at the age of 3 regardless of whether the parents have applied for it or not, and that preschool should be compulsory for all children from the age of five.

The strive to emancipate, or save, the child from contemporary economic, social, and cultural conditions, while at the same time expecting the child to enable vast societal and economical change, seems to run like a red thread through the history of the preschool child.

I argue that it is in this process of liberation, in the pursuit of decoupling the child from either their social and economic background and family in an effort to "save" the child from the contemporary conceptions and norms of society as well as "misguided" ideologies and worldviews, that the child becomes "orphaned." In the figuration of the child as "orphan", the child embodies the spontaneous and the not-yet-determined—a space for opportunity, intervention, and change. Based on the fact of being new in the world, the child is attributed the ability for transformation. Castañeda (2003) explains that it is in the articulation of the child as a potentiality that the child's accessibility and value as a cultural and political resource seem to be found. Whether the child has been figured as natural/mythical, essential/rational, or as competent and pluralistic throughout the Swedish history of ECE, the child is attributed to the power of reconfiguring both the subject and society, provided that the child is brought up and educated, of course, in the "right" way. Through the encouragement, experience, and insight that the institution can offer, the child is expected to want and be able to create a better society and more sustainable world. This ambition testifies to an enormous amount of confidence in what institution and education can achieve, which can be found both in the pioneers of the kindergarten such as with Alva Myrdal, as well as in the Reggio Emilia–inspired pedagogy and, not least, within the visions of the future and intervention programs that are visible in transnational policy from organizations such as the OECD.

Notes

1. Sweden is unique in the way that tax-financed schools and preschools are allowed to be run by commercial venture capital companies.
2. One of these initiatives resulted in the research network Reconceptualizing Early Childhood Education and Care (https://receinternational.org), initially established for the purpose of challenging the dominance of psychology and developmentalist theory by drawing on, for example, feminist, postcolonial, and postmodern perspectives.
3. As an example, in 2012 the Swedish National Agency of Education (Skolverket) published a support material (Skolverket, 2012) aiming at aiding teachers in their work with documenting, following up, and evaluating educational practice. The tool promoted in the support material was "pedagogical documentation" (a tool associated with the Reggio Emilia pedagogical approach) framed within a "new" postconstructionist/posthumanist theoretical framework. From the theoretical point of view offered in the support material, the traditional Western educational ideal was claimed to fall short of understanding and describing the transdisciplinary nature and relational complexity of learning as well as the interdependence between the child and the world. In the posthumanist narrative, the child was portrayed as harboring an inherent capacity for transformation and multiple potential becomings, making the child especially suitable for the posthuman condition. In any case, the support material (Skolverket, 2012) was withdrawn, and as I proceed to discuss, the development of Swedish ECE policy continued in the opposite direction. For a more detailed account of the entry of posthumanism into Swedish preschool, see Therese Lindgren (2019) and Therese Lindgren and Magdalena Sjöstrand Öhrfelt (2019).

References

1946 års kommitté för den halvöppna barnavården. (1951). *Daghem och förskolor: betänkande om barnstugor och barntillsyn* (SOU 1951:15) [Day-care centres and preschools: report on nurseries and childcare]. Victor Pettersons Bokindustriaktiebolag. http://urn.kb.se/resolve?urn=urn:nbn:se:kb:sou-764826

Agevall, L. (2005). *Välfärdens organisering och demokratin: - en analys av New Public Management* [The organization of welfare and democracy - an analysis of New Public Management]. Växjö University Press.

Barnomsorg och skolakommittén. (1997). *Att erövra omvärlden: förslag till läroplan för förskolan: slutbetänkande* (SOU 1997:157) [Conquering the outside world: a proposal for a curriculum for the preschool: final report]. Fritze. https://www.regeringen.se/49b722/contentassets/c6efb6f855df4585b7f6504e937c8c7f/sou-1997157a

Biesta, G. (2015). What is education for? On good education, teacher judgement, and educational professionalism. *European Journal of Education, 50*(1), 75–87. https://doi.org/10.1111/ejed.12109

Brembeck, H., Johansson, B., & Kampmann, J. (Eds.). (2004). *Beyond the competent child: Exploring contemporary childhoods in the Nordic welfare societies*. Roskilde University Press.

Carneiro, R., Desjardins, R., Gordon, J., & Looney, J. (2015). Editorial. *European Journal of Education, 50*(1), 1–9.

Castañeda, C. (2001). The child as a feminist figuration: Toward a politics of privilege. *Feminist Theory, 2*(1), 29–53. https://doi.org/10.1177/14647000122229361

Castañeda, C. (2003). *Figurations: child, bodies, worlds*. Duke University Press.

Dahlberg, G., & Elfström, I. (2014). Pedagogisk dokumentation i tillblivelse [The becoming of pedagogical documentation]. *Pedagogisk forskning i Sverige, 19*(4–5), 268–288.

Dahlberg, G., Lundgren, U. P., & Åsén, G. (1991). *Att utvärdera barnomsorg: om decentralisering, målstyrning och utvärdering av barnomsorgen och dess pedagogiska verksamhet* [Evaluating childcare: on decentralization, goal management and evaluation of childcare and its educational activities]. HLS.

Dahlberg, G., Moss, P., & Pence, A.R. (1999). *Beyond quality in early childhood education and care: Postmodern perspectives.* Falmer.

Dahlgren, L., & Hultqvist, K. (Eds.). (1995). *Seendet och seendets villkor: en bok om barns och ungas välfärd* [Seeing and the conditions of seeing: a book about the welfare of children and young people]. HLS.

Dencik, L. (1995). Välfärdens barn eller barns välfärd? Om till-syn, hän-syn och fel-syn [The children of welfare or child welfare?]. In L. Dahlgren & K. Hultqvist (Eds.), *Seendet och seendets villkor: En bok om barns och ungas välfärd.* (pp. 63–101). HLS.

Eilard, A. (2010). *Barndomens förändrade villkor: förutsättningar för barns lärande i en ny tid* [Changing conditions of childhood: conditions for children's learning in a new age]. Skolverket.

European Commission. (2010). *Europe 2020. A strategy for smart, sustainable and inclusive growth.* European Commission. https://ec.europa.eu/eu2020/pdf/COMPLET%20EN%20BARROSO%20%20%20007%20-%20Europe%202020%20-%20EN%20version.pdf

Halldén, G. (2007). *Den moderna barndomen och barns vardagsliv* [The modern childhood and children's everyday life]. Carlsson.

Halldén, G. (2009). Barnperspektiv: Ett ideologiskt laddat begrepp och oprecist som analytiskt verktyg [Child perspectives: An ideologically charged concept and imprecise analytical tool]. *Locus, 409*(3), 4–20.

Hammarlund, K. G. (1998). *Barnet och barnomsorgen: Bilden av barnet i ett socialpolitiskt projekt* [Child and child-Care. Images of the child in a social welfare project]. [Doctoral dissertation, Gothenburg University]. http://urn.kb.se/resolve?urn=urn:nbn:se:hh:diva-295

Heckman, J. J., & Masterov, D. V. (2007). The productivity argument for in-vesting in young children. *Applied Economic Perspectives and Policy, 3*(29), 446–493. http://nbn-resolving.de/urn:nbn:de:101:1-20080402495

Hultqvist, K. (1990). *Förskolebarnet: en konstruktion för gemenskapen och den individuella frigörelsen: En nutidshistorisk studie om makt och kunskap i bilden av barnet i statliga utredningar om förskolan* [The preschool child: a construction for the community and the individual liberation: A contemporary historical study of power and knowledge in the image of the child in state investigations of preschool]. [Doctoral dissertation, Stockholm University].

Hultqvist, K. (1995). En nutidshistoria om barns välfärd i Sverige [A contemporary historical study of child welfare in Sweden]. In L. Dahlgren & K. Hultqvist (Eds.), *Seendet och seendets villkor: En bok om barns och ungas välfärd* (pp. 141–160). HLS.

Hultqvist, K. (1997a). Förskolan och "barnets natur" [The Preschool and "the nature of the child"]. *Didactica minima, 11*(3), 6–18.

Hultqvist, K. (1997b). Changing rationales for governing the child: A historical perspective on the emergence of the psychological child in the context of pre-school-notes on a study in progress. *Childhood, 4*(4), 405–424. https://doi.org/10.1177/0907568297004004003

Hultqvist, K., & Dahlberg, G. (Eds.). (2001). *Governing the child in the new millennium.* Routledge Falmer.

James, A., & Prout, A. (1990). *Constructing and reconstructing childhood: con-temporary issues in the sociological study of childhood.* Falmer.

Jenks, C. (1996). *Childhood*. Routledge.
Juul, J. (2001). *Your competent child: Toward new basic values for the family*. Farrar, Straus & Giroux.
Kampmann, J. (2004). Societalization of childhood: New opportunities? New demands? In H. Brembeck, B. Johansson, & J. Kampmann (Eds.), *Beyond the competent child: Exploring contemporary childhoods in the Nordic welfare societies* (pp. 127–152). Roskilde Universitetsforlag.
Key, E. (1900). *Barnets århundrade: studie* [The century of the child]. Bonnier.
Kristjánsson, B. (1999) Hverdagslivet og tidens problematik. Nogle erfaringer fra en nordisk undersøgelse af børns opvækstvilkår [Everyday life and the problems of time. Some experiences from a Nordic investigation of the conditions under which children are brought up] in L. Dencik and P. S. Jørgensen (Eds.) *Børn og Familie i det Postmoderne Samfund* [Children and Family in the Postmodern Society] (pp.132-155). Hans Reitzels Publishing.
Lenz Taguchi, H. (1997). *Varför pedagogisk dokumentation? Om barnsyn, kunskapssyn och ett förändrat förhållningssätt till förskolans arbete* [Why pedagogical documentation? About perspectives on children, knowledge and a changed approach to working in preschool]. HLS.
Lenz Taguchi, H. (2010). *Going beyond the theory/practice divide in early childhood education: Introducing an intra-active pedagogy*. Routledge.
Lindgren, A., & Söderlind, I. (2019). *Förskolans historia: Förskolepolitik, barn och barndom* [The history of preschool: Preschool policy, children and childhood]. Gleerups.
Lindgren, T. (2018). *Föränderlig tillblivelse: Figurationen av det posthumana förskolebarnet* [The figuration of the posthuman child] [Doctoral dissertation, Malmö University]. https://muep.mau.se/bitstream/handle/2043/26303/Lindgren_muep.pdf?sequence=2&isAllowed=y
Lindgren, T. (2019). The figuration of the posthuman child. *Discourse. Studies in the Cultural Politics of Education*, *41*(6), 914–925. https://doi.org/10.1080/01596306.2019.1576589
Lindgren, T., & Sjöstrand Öhrfelt, M. (2019). Orphans of our common worlds. *Educational Theory*, *69*(3), 283–303. https://doi.org/10.1111/edth.12369
Martin, M. J. (2001, June 13–15). *Introductory presentation* [Paper presentation]. Starting Strong: Early Education and Care, Stockholm, Sweden. https://www.oecd.org/education/school/2535215.pdf
Martin Korpi, B. (2007). *The politics of preschool: intentions and decisions underlying the emergence and growth of the Swedish pre-school*. Ministry of Education and Research. https://www.government.se/49d31b/contentassets/4b768a5cd6c24e0cb70b4393eadf4f6a/the-politics-of-pre-school---intentions-and-decisions-underlying-the-emergence-and-growth-of-the-swedish-pre-school.pdf
Murris, K. (2016). *The posthuman child: Educational transformation through philosophy with picturebooks*. Routledge.
Myrdal, A. (1935). *Stadsbarn: En bok om deras fostran i storbarnkammare* [Urban children: a book about their upbringing in large nurseries]. Kooperativa förb.
Myrdal, A., & Myrdal, G. (1934). *Kris i befolkningsfrågan* [Crisis in the population question]. Bonnier.
Organisation for Economic Co-operation and Development. (2012). *Starting strong III: A quality toolbox for early childhood education and care*. OECD Publishing. https://read.oecd-ilibrary.org/education/starting-strong-iii_9789264123564-en#page1
Organisation for Economic Co-operation and Development. (2017). *Starting strong 2017: Key OECD indicators on early childhood education and care*. OECD Publishing. https://read.oecd-ilibrary.org/education/starting-strong-2017_9789264276116-en#page1
Pedagogiskt program för förskolan. (1987). [Pedagogical programme for the preschool]. Kundtjänst, Allmänna förlag.

Persson, S. (1994). *Föräldrars föreställningar om barn och barnomsorg* [Parents' conceptions about children and childcare]. [Doctoral dissertation, Lund University].

Persson, S. (2008). *Forskning om villkor för yngre barns lärande i förskola, förskoleklass och fritidshem* [Research on conditions for younger children's learning in preschool, preschool class and leisure centers]. Vetenskapsrådet. https://www.vr.se/download/18.2412c5311624176023d2 5ad7/1529480531339/Forskning-om-villkor-for-yngre-barns-laerande_VR_2008.pdf

Riddersporre, B., & Persson, S. (Eds.). (2010). *Utbildningsvetenskap för förskolan* [Educational science for the preschool]. Natur & kultur.

Rousseau, J. (2003). *Emile or treatise on education*. Prometheus Books. (Original work published 1896).

SFS 2010:800. *Skollag* [Education Act]. Utbildningsdepartementet. https://www.riksdagen.se/ sv/dokument-lagar/dokument/svensk-forfattningssamling/skollag-2010800_sfs-2010-800

Sjöstrand Öhrfelt, M. (2019). *Ord och inga visor: Konstruktioner av förskolebarnet i kunskapsekonomin* [Use it or lose it – constructions of the preschool child in the knowledge economy]. [Doctoral dissertation, Linnaeus University]. http://lnu.diva-portal.org/smash/get/diva2: 1329400/FULLTEXT01.pdf

Skolverket. (1998). *Curriculum for the preschool Lpfö 98*. http://www.svenskaskolan.ch/Foerskolan/ Lpfoe98_revised2010_ENG.pdf

Skolverket. (2004). *Förskola i brytningstid: Nationell utvärdering av förskolan* [Preschool in a period of transition: A national evaluation of the preschool]. Skolverket.

Skolverket. (2008). *Tio år efter förskolereformen: Nationell utvärdering av förskolan* [Ten years after the preschool reform: A national evaluation of the preschool]. Skolverket. https://www. skolverket.se/download/18.6bfaca41169863e6a6572dc/1553960523718/pdf2096.pdf

Skolverket. (2010). *Curriculum for the preschool: Lpfö 10*. Skolverket. http://www.svenskaskolan. ch/Foerskolan/Lpfoe98_revised2010_ENG.pdf

Skolverket. (2012). *Uppföljning, utvärdering och utveckling i förskolan: Pedagogisk dokumentation* [Follow-up, evaluation and development in preschool: Pedagogical documentation]. Skolverket.

Skolverket. (2019). *Curriculum for the preschool, Lpfö 18*. Skolverket. https://www.skolverket.se/ download/18.6bfaca41169863e6a65d897/1553968298535/pdf4049.pdf2019

Skolverket. (2020). *Barn och personal i förskola 2019* [Children and staff in preschool 2019]. Skolverket. https://www.skolverket.se/download/18.6b138470170af6ce914ef2/1585554485184/pdf6542.pdf

Socialdepartementet. (1972). *Förskolan. Del 1. Betänkande angivet av 1968 års barnstugeutredning* (SOU 1972:26-27) [Preschool. Part 1. Report stated by the 1968 commission on nursery provision]. Liber förlag. https://lagen.nu/sou/1972:26?attachment=index.pdf&repo=soukb &dir=downloaded

Taguma, M., Litjens, I. & Makowiecki, K. (2012). *Quality matters in early childhood education and care Sweden 2013*. Organisation for Economic Co-operation and Development (OECD).

Tallberg Broman, I. (1995). *Perspektiv på förskolans historia* [Perspectives on the history of the preschool]. Student-litteratur.

Tallberg Broman, I. (2010). Gladare och livsdugligare små medborgare [Happier and more viable little citizens]. In J. Qvarsebo & I. Tallberg Broman, (Eds.) *Från storslagna visioner till professionell bedömning: om barndom, utbildning och styrning* (pp. 29–42). Holmbergs. http://muep.mau. se/bitstream/handle/2043/10414/RoU%202010.2.pdf?sequence=1&isAllowed=y

UNICEF. (2002). *A league table of educational disadvantage in rich nations*. Innocenti Research Centre.

United Nations Convention on the Rights of the Child, 20 November 1989, https://www.ohchr. org/en/professionalinterest/pages/crc.aspx

Utbildningsdepartementet. (1985). *Förskola-skola: Betänkande av Förskola-skola-kommittén* [Preschool-school: Report from the Preschool-school committee] (SOU 1985:22). Liber/ Allmänna förlag. https://lagen.nu/sou/1985:22?attachment=index.pdf&repo=soukb&dir= downloaded

Utbildningsdepartementet. (2020). *Förskola för alla barn – för bättre språkutveckling i svenska* [Preschool for all children - for better language development in Swedish] (SOU 2020:67). Elanders Sverige AB. https://www.regeringen.se/4ad046/contentassets/73de9759ac8a41548fe7a7a7e3641b73/ forskola-for-alla-barn--for-battre-sprakutveckling-i-svenska-sou-202067

CHAPTER 15

Innocence and Parenting in Difficult Times

Emily L. Murphy and Hannah Dyer

Childhood in Crisis

IN 2020, A global pandemic caused confrontation with theories of childhood and perceptions of what a child needs to feel a sense of belonging and security. Due to COVID-19, schools and childcare centres in many nation-states, including Canada, from where we write, were closed. Children were kept at home in isolation, often with only their immediate family, and without physical access to social programs and extended communities. While the pandemic caused loss of employment and job insecurity for many, a fiery debate circulated that pitted those with children at home against those without. While many suggested that having children was a choice one must "deal with", despite circumstances, arguments were made that having children confined to the home meant that parents would be unable to produce adequate amounts of work and would struggle to properly care for themselves. Meanwhile, others suggested that caring for children should not be considered inherently more important than other forms of care and dependence. In a much-circulated *New York Times* article about parenting during the pandemic, "Parenting Was Never Meant to Be This Isolating", Jessica Grose (2020) made the point that parents who expressed ambivalence towards caring for their children after the sudden closure of schools were being condemned. Grose (2020) points out that many believe "selfish parents get too many perks and benefits yet still complain about kids who should be their sole responsibility" (para. 1), an opinion that has been expressed with force during the pandemic. In providing a social history of childhood in North America, Grose (2020) draws on the work of Robin G. Nelson to insist that "even the idea that children are an active 'choice' for most people erases the history of forced sterilization of Black, Native American, Asian and Latina women" (para. 8). The gendered impacts of the closure of schools and childcare centres are also expressed in her commentary: "analysis from the National Women's Law Center suggests that of the 1.1 million workers who dropped out of the labor force last month, 80 percent were women" (Grose, 2020, para. 10).[1] In Canada and the United States, patterns of injustice and the ways they cut across children's subject formation and parent's ability to provide protection have been amplified during the pandemic.

Driven to understand the tensions and lines of commentary surrounding parenting during the pandemic, this chapter turns to the field of critical childhood studies to offer a theoretical framework for conceptualizing childhood as a site of collective responsibility. Hidden beneath social commentary about parenting are theories of childhood. We move to a study of discourses of innocence and purity, long-held points of analysis in the study of children and childhood, hoping to gather techniques for confronting discourses of childhood that eclipse the needs of children during moments of social crises. Children are often ensnared in debates about politics (e.g., Berlant, 2004; Dyer, 2020; Edelman, 2004; Garlen, 2019) and commentary on parenting during the pandemic provides a powerful case of how children are eclipsed by adult's theories of what children need. In a consistently useful introduction to his edited collection, *The Children's Culture Reader*, Henry Jenkins (1998) turns his attention towards the formulation of childhood innocence. He writes carefully about the seductions of the innocent child and its available manipulations for the purposes of adult anxiety, ideology, and conflict—warning against the harm that discourses of innocence can produce. As James Kincaid (2004) so powerfully argued, childhood innocence "allows the admirer to read just about anything he likes into (the) vacancy of the innocent child" (p. 10). The notion of childhood innocence has been thoroughly critiqued along these lines by scholars seeking to deconstruct and reconceptualize childhood (e.g., Bernstein, 2011; Bloch, 1987, Cannella, 1997; Dyer, 2020; Egan & Hawkes, 2008; Garlen, 2019; James, Jenks & Prout 1998; Jenkins, 1998; Kincaid, 1998; Meiners, 2015; Robinson, 2008, 2013; Walkerdine, 1997, 2001). As many critical theorists of childhood assert, assumptions of innocence lay nestled within theories of normative development (Bloch, 1987; Burman, 1994/2017; Kincaid, 1998). One common example provided concerning the damage of "normal" child development is its assumption that childhood sexuality is naïve and nascent, referred to only in limited terms such as "slowly developing" (Taylor, 2010; see also Silin, 1987).

If we take methodological instruction from critical studies of childhood across a range of disciplines (and now often being labelled "critical childhood studies") in this moment of crisis and debate about collective childcare, we might reroute our thinking concerning the contradictions between notions of childhood innocence and the actual nuisance they cause when at home 24 hours a day. Rather, we might think through their complex agency. Indeed, as we suggest, underneath animosity between those who have children or are responsible for them, and those who do not, are deeper feelings about childhood itself and what it means to embrace children's nuisance, their possibilities, and our relationships with them as human beings rather than oversimplifying them and ourselves through constructs like innocence. Parental expressions of ambivalence are not necessarily harmful but, rather, attest to the complicated labour of attending to those who are younger. In order to access the deeper affective life of childhood and its social relationship to crises, we draw on critical childhood studies' theorizing of innocence and its related harms. Doing so requires the blasting apart of expectations of purity placed on both children and their caregivers and respect for the patience required to greet the child's many demands. For us, this is not about a romanticized lateralization of power between children and adults—because, when ethically wielded, the adult's experience can protect children from material harm.

It is important to note, as Garlen (2019) reminds us, that "to interrogate the construct of childhood innocence is not to suggest that children should not be lovingly cared for" (p. 55). Indeed, those who care for children—childcare workers, teachers, and parents—are often already familiar with the child's complex demands. Early childhood educators (ECEs), for example, have unrivalled expertise in handling children's complex emotional and social needs but are consistently undermined and ignored. ECEs often have an improvisational relationship with the children they work with, premised not on the belief that adults know what is best for them but that they deserve care. As with all human beings and perhaps other creatures, children can be both generous in their loving and monstrous in their hating, which means caring for them is hard work. They are warm, forceful, needy, and innovative, not incubators for the adult's desired futures or simply successors to the adult's failures, but often aspiring to usher in a world not yet recognizable to us. Leaving childcare concerns to the private space of the family or guardian runs dangerously close to the neoliberal discourse and practice of privatization. As Grose (2020) points out, the sense that parents can and should presume responsibility for their children is also deeply racialized and classed terrain. Not all families have been treated fairly under the neoliberal imperatives of privatized parenting. Relatedly, Simon Black (2020) notes, childcare workers and ECEs receive low wages and have a thick history of being treated unjustly. Ideally, a newfound respect for the profession, and for the patience needed to attend to children's complex personhood, will arise from the pandemic and insight will be gained into how important their work is. And yet, as Grose (2020) makes clear, many are still resistant to recognizing that ambivalence surrounding childhood, even in relation to one's own children, can be productive. This ambivalence often means an open embrace of the hard work of being with children and that is because they are at once demanding, smart, assertive, sensitive, and ambivalent about us adults too.

During the pandemic, and as described in Grose's (2020) writing, what seemed to spark moral outrage was parents' description of ambivalence towards their children and difficulty in caring for them. In this way, parents were articulating their children's complex needs and undermining assumptions of their innocence. Critical childhood studies have rendered the child too complicated for assumptions of its innocence. And yet, more work must be done to understand the psycho-social machinations of purity that deny justice to all children and their caregivers. In an effort to understand the contemporary impact of discourses of purity on children, we offer a rethinking of innocence that provokes childhood studies to better care for the children it writes about—all the while knowing that the adult's theories of childhood are made from our own anxieties and psychic projections. Sourced differently, childhood is not a period of purity, but a set of temporal, social, and geographic entanglements that constitute a complex subjectivity. Furthermore, as Robin Bernstein (2011) has eloquently written, "the child" is not a pure category in and of itself, but rather "retains racial meanings" and "hide[s] them under claims of holy obliviousness" (p. 8).

Critical childhood studies offer a potential rerouting of childhood away from antinomy between those with and those without children and towards not only adults' and children's enmeshment in each other's stresses and needs but also the adult's responsibility towards those who are vulnerable. Scholars such as Valerie Walkerdine (1997, 2001) and Erica Burman (1994/ 2017) suggest that adults and children are not so easily made distinct, as childhood innocence and adult desires are deeply entwined. It is this psychical entanglement that underpins much of adult's concerns about childhood, such that ascriptions of innocence and the rhetoric of protection offer more "protection" to adults than to children. Indeed, Walkerdine (2001) suggests that

> the idea of a sanitized natural childhood in which things are kept at bay, having no place in childhood, becomes not the guarantor of the safety of children from the perversities of adult desires for then but a huge defense against the acknowledgement of dangerous desires on the part of adults. In this analysis 'child protection' begins to look more like 'adult protection'. (p. 29)

Critical studies of childhood have carefully shown how childhood(s) are deeply situated in social, cultural, and historical contexts and that neither the 'childhood' that has come to be known through modern Euro-Western discourse nor innocence as its necessary condition are by any means natural (see Cannella, 1997; Kehily & Montgomery, 2004). Indeed, Euro-Western understandings of childhood as a period of innocence and ignorance are intimately entwined with Judeo-Christian narratives of purity, rooted in the Garden of Eden as an idyllic, natural, and asexual space—a space corrupted by knowledge (Cannella, 1997; Kline, 1995; Taylor, 2010). As this field of research shows, it was not until the 18th century that religious notions of a pure space of innocence were transmuted into childhood, transforming the Puritan portrait of children as inherently sinful into this Enlightenment picture of children as pure and perfect (Cannella, 1997; Garlen, 2019; James et al., 1998; Taylor, 2010).

At the centre of our theorizing is a critique of the expectation of purity in relation to children themselves and their parents. Guided by critical childhood studies, we put pressure on the entanglements that arise from our connectedness to children, as we once were categorized as such, but more so, to grasp at the realities of a childhood we never experienced. In order to do so, we first offer engagement with Alexis Shotwell's (2016) debasement of purity for its decollectivizing tendencies, and then we turn to critical childhood scholars who provide a commentary on the insidious impacts of innocence (e.g., Bruhm & Hurley, 2004; Garlen, 2019; Meiners, 2015; Nxumalo & Cedillo, 2017; Sedgwick, 2004). Finally, we turn to D. W. Winnicott's (1971/2001) writing on the good-enough mother for its capacity to describe the usefulness of ambivalence towards children, which is distinct from maltreatment or harm.

Innocence, Purity, and the Child's Complex Demands

In *Against Purity: Living Ethically in Compromised Times*, Alexis Shotwell (2016) suggests that contamination is not a reason to withdraw from responsibility but a starting point for political action and ethical relationships with others. She resists the demand for purity in the realm of politics and, rather, embraces the messy contradictions of living in a world imbued with toxicity. Shotwell (2016) reminds us that there is no space of innocence to return to and "champions the usefulness of thinking about complicity and compromise as a starting point for action" (p. 12). She makes it clear, however, that "people are not equally responsible or capable, and are not equally called to respond" to change the world and that harm and protection are unevenly distributed (p. 9). Purism, Shotwell (2016) proposes, "shuts down precisely the field of possibility that might allow us to take better collective action against the destruction of the world in all its strange, delightful, impure frolic" (p. 9). Shotwell's writing on purity is helpful in thinking about childhood and parenting. The rhetoric of childhood innocence is, of course, based on assumptions of their purity. But parents and caregivers, too, are often expected to express purity in relation to the work of caring for children. Expectations of purity remain insufficient to the child's aggression, complexity, and intellect. Shotwell (2016) further suggests that

> what's needed, instead of a pretense to purity that is impossible in the actually existing world, is something else. We need to shape better practices of responsibility and memory for our placement in relation to the past, our implication in the present, and our potential creation of different futures. (p. 14)

The propensity to install the child as the purist example of humanity and history has not worked out well for either children or adults. As we describe in the following, critical childhood studies have carefully asserted that not only lines of inquiry but also extensions of material support are withheld when the child's purity is assumed inherent.

For Shotwell (2016), "purism is a decollectivizing, de-mobilizing, paradoxical politics of despair" (p. 16). Seeking a political stance of purity is, for Shotwell, often a defensive form of individualism that shuts down collective action against devastation. Critical childhood studies have also made this point in relation to the expectation of purity imposed on children and their caregivers. Because the child's discrete personhood is always already wrapped up in connectivity with their social relations and embedded in a world broken by colonialism, genocide, and homophobia, the child cannot be pure. The intention to break open childhood innocence, and think against purity, is also a mode of self-critique. Within the field of childhood studies, for example, psychoanalytic thought has helped remind us that our own childhood experiences help shape our subjective opinions of what children need (Farley, 2018). Dreams of harmonizing children's future with our own politics, Lisa Farley (2018) has shown, has also to do with unconscious attachments to our own childhoods. Making this known means that it becomes possible to think with what would otherwise be incongruous or too deeply repressed. Rather than protecting children from harm, "innocence, when constructed as blissful ignorance of 'adult' social realities, renders children more vulnerable to the very dangers from which we seek to protect them" (Garlen 2019, p. 64).

The Innocent Child in Pure Nature

Most recently, some posthumanist early childhood educators demonstrate a further shift away from Rousseauian logics that position children as empty and "pure" beings of nature, without complex desires or agency, and towards an acknowledgement that children's lifeworlds are "imperfect and complex" and come with multiple legacies (Pacini-Ketchabaw & Kummen, 2016, p. 432). The repetitive invocation of "the child" in ways that "avoid such complexities" in modernist, Euro-Western society perniciously erases the geographically situated, gendered, racialized, sexualized, and classed experiences of children (Meiners, 2015 p. 121). Through a posthumanist lens, however, children are acknowledged as complexly entangled beings, existing in excess of innocence, and asks how we stay with their complexity rather than repress it. Nxumalo and Cedillo (2017), for example, point to Black feminist geographies to think through children's complex entanglements with place, history, and social constructs, suggesting that such perspectives shift away from "child-centered developmental environmental pedagogies toward pedagogies that bring attention to children's entanglements within multiple human and more-than-human relations" (p. 107). The notions of situatedness and complex entanglement championed by Nxumalo and Cedillo (2017) offer generative implications for rethinking the value of "innocence" as it applies to childhood. They remind us of "the paradoxical assumption that children and nature belong together, as sites of innocence and purity, not as always-already entangled and unevenly co-constituted participants in world-making" (p. 101).

Nxumalo and Cedillo (2017) provide a study of children's "forest schools," and other modes of place-based early childhood education, in order to grapple with the damaging conflation of childhood, innocence, and nature. Here, forest school refers to a method of outdoor education delivery whereby children engage in open-ended play and learning in "natural" (i.e., outdoor) spaces. Such programs, they argue, are rooted in the nature–culture binary, and colonialism and anti-Blackness are implicated in such discourses that separate the "human" from the "non-human." Historically and at present, many are routinely denied access to the category of "fully human" along lines of race, gender, geography, class, and sexuality (Nxumalo & Cedillo, 2017; Wynter, 2003). As Nxumalo and Cedillo (2017) make clear, nature pedagogies often "side-step the colonial, raced, and gendered politics impacting accessibility and affordability of outdoor recreation programs" (p. 101). Alongside immense environmental precarity, the assumption that children and nature walk hand and hand towards purity has fueled a recent proliferation of forest schools and nature pedagogies—perhaps in a future-oriented effort to meet the societal demand for purity which Shotwell (2016) thinks against. Thinking through the rationalizations of such pedagogies exposes some of the asymmetries present in conceptions of the child and its presumed innocence (Dyer, 2020). Following Judith Butler (1988), Julie Garlen (2019) positions childhood as "an identity instituted through habitual acts" rather than a simple descriptor for a period in human development, and as such "the child" is not necessarily a universal, or even "natural" figure (p. 57). Rather, she continues, "childhood is produced and maintained through the rhetoric of protection, which justifies protective practices and policies" (Garlen, 2019, p. 57). Such protective practices and policies, carried out in the name of care, often lead to harm and injustice in the material lives of children and their caregivers—particularly those minoritized along lines of race, class, sexuality, and gender.

As Pacini-Ketchabaw and Kummen (2016) have shown, an epistemological division between nature and culture/society unpins much of post-Enlightenment Euro-Western thinking about childhood. Where nature is positioned as "mute, pure, and separate," culture operates as a corrupting force (Nxumalo & Cedillo, 2017, p. 101). Through the marriage of children and nature, a "EuroWestern assumption underpins what counts as 'normal' childhood experiences of nature" (Nxumalo & Cedillo, 2017, p.101). This assumption positions childhood as an epoch of purity and ignorance, scripting what Julie Garlen (2019) terms "an expectation for what children's experiences '"should' be like" and an expectation of how parents should operate to "protect" this state of supposed "innocent ignorance" (p. 55). Indeed, nature pedagogies and assumptions of the innocent child in nature pay little attention to environmental justice issues, nor to asymmetries in children's inheritances of such issues (Nxumalo & Cedillo, 2017). Nxumalo and Cedillo (2017) encourage thinking of place as storied: "more-than-human bodies, specific stories, ontologies, histories, as well as humans are all lively and entangled participants in the shaping of place" (p. 103). They describe how Black feminist geographies think through "children's place relations in ways that trouble the nature/culture and human/

non-human binaries and that critically interrogate deficit or empty views of Black people's relations to so-called natural places" (Nxumalo & Cedillo, 2017, p. 106). The study of erasures of place, and the situatedness of children who are differently entangled along lines of race, class, sexuality, and gender, is shaded with meaning in the wake of COVID-19. Closures of schools, day cares, and social programs meant many children were confined to their homes and, for many, has exacerbated the felt presence of social and economic inequalities. This moment raises questions and concerns around topics such as who has access to nature and why this is seemingly important: Who has access to the sprawling backyard filled with lush greenery or a private space to quarantine if needed? The Rousseauian logic of the child in nature is laden with assumptions that position wealthy, White childhoods as the ideal—while poor, non-White, and/or urban families who cannot offer such a childhood are positioned as inherently deficient (e.g., Garlen, 2019; Meiners, 2015).

Childhood Innocence as an Imposition of Sociocultural Agendas

In "Trouble with the Child in the Carceral State", Erica Meiners (2015) shows how the notion of "a better future for our children" is commonly invoked to justify a range of socio-political campaigns, which include environmental protections as well as arguments in favour of new prisons and against abolition (2016). The criminal justice system, Meiners (2015) suggests, acts as a site through which the boundaries of childhood are constructed: "policing, punishment, prisons and their associated carceral systems continually redefine who qualifies as a child" (p. 121). What is protected in the expansion of prisons and other carceral apparatus is supposedly innocence. But, as Meiners (2015) carefully explains, while some individuals benefit from protections employed in the name of the child, not everyone has access to childhood or its presumed innocence, such as the "twelve-year-old boys who are charged as adults and nine-year-old girls who are held as juveniles in detention centers" (p. 124). Meiners (2015) proposes that "charting racial disproportionality at every level of the juvenile justice system clearly shows that youth of color do not have the same access to innocence and are not understood as sensate in the same way that white youth are" (p. 131), and as others have argued, Black children are not afforded the same assumption of innocence as other children (Bernstein, 2011; Garlen, 2019; Patton, 2014). For example, "although children of color ... experience sexual violence, their bodies command less white empathy, and the child's innocence (or mother's) is not assumed and must be proved" (Meiners, 2015, p. 129). The case of Cyntoia Brown offers a poignant illustration of asymmetries in assumed innocence. Cyntoia, a victim of child sex trafficking, was tried as an adult at 16 years old and sentenced to life in prison after she killed a man who bought her for sex. Cyntoia was offered no protective shield of innocence even though the fear of child sex trafficking and the image of the sexually abused little girl seem to most fervently ignite protective rhetoric, arguably because of racism. Indeed, numerous scholars and activists have spoken to the systemic racism that positions non-White children as culpable and potentially dangerous, thus denying them the shelter of childhood innocence (e.g., Bernstein, 2011; Dyer, 2020; Garlen, 2019; McKeon, 2016; Meiners, 2015; Patton, 2014). It was only after public outcry that Cyntoia was finally granted clemency in 2019, after serving 15 years in prison.

Writing against innocence as inherently protective, a body of literature in gender and sexuality studies has also contested the homophobic and often transphobic tendencies that arise in theories of children's development (e.g., Bruhm & Hurley, 2004; Dyer, 2020; Edelman, 2004; Gill-Peterson, 2018; Robinson 2008; Sedgwick, 2004, Silin 1995, Stockton, 2004). As Garlen (2019) makes clear, children who experience homoerotic desires or "who question traditional gender roles, witness violence, or suffer abuse, are afforded no opportunities to acknowledge these experiences" (p. 64). Perhaps this is because "experience ... is hard to square with innocence" (Stockton, 2004, p. 298), and so children's whose experience exceeds the bounds of normalcy are offered no shelter under the umbrella of "innocence" and, instead, are cast into the category of "traumatized" (Dyer, 2017; Stockton, 2004). Discourses of vulnerability and exploitation that accompany childhood innocence devalue the child's sexuality—particularly for those children "whose play confirms neither the comfortable stories of child (a)sexuality, nor the supposedly blissful promise of adult heteronormativity" (Bruhm & Hurley, 2004, p. ix). Indeed, as Eve Sedgwick points out in her prominent essay, "How to Bring Your Kids Up Gay," the wealth of parenting material focused on raising children towards "non-gay" outcomes has historically suggested that queerness is not a desired outcome. And, as Meiners (2015) later adds, anti-bullying policies and their punitive practices are "often drafted on the bodies of [dead] queer white children," and thus, "do little to challenge the expectation of heterosexuality nor do they excavate heteronormativity" (p. 133).

To speak of childhood sexuality, particularly queer desires, in a culture that construes children as pure and innocent, "all too quickly invoke[s] the specter of the pedophile, which all too quickly destroys one's political credibility" (Bruhm & Hurley, 2004, p. xxiii). With the boundaries of "innocence" armed by protective rhetoric, childhood sexuality is often confined to discourses of trauma and deviancy. Gill-Peterson's (2018) work in *Histories of the Transgender Child* is also generative to a study of purity in childhood. Gill-Peterson suggests that a pairing of children with theories of unfinishedness and plasticity, laden with Rousseauian logics, has acted as a key site of medicalized violence against transgender children, particularly Black, Brown, and disabled transgender children—whose bodies are viewed as sites of experimentation and whose social realities have been both denied and pathologized. Farley and Kennedy (2016) have "heed[ed] Sedgwick's call to work against the 'new pathologization' of the child with a view to illustrating how the transgender child, too, is at work on the process of embodiment" and ask "what theoretical frameworks are needed to help adults narrate the psychic life of the child's transgender embodiment, and to note both its pleasure and distress without resorting to the language of pathology?" (p. 167).

In the next section, we further elaborate on the entanglements and co-constitutive forces of the adult's socio-political agenda and the child's desires by turning to D. W. Winnicott's (1971/2001) endorsement of ambivalence towards children. The adult tasked with the responsibility of caring for a child, Winnicott proposes, should not be subservient to the child's every demand but offer the world's chaos in careful doses.

The Good-Enough Mother, Ambivalence, and Purity

D.W. Winnicott's (1971/2001) notion of the "good enough mother" disrupts the ambient ringing of purity heard and felt in relation to parenting. In *Playing and Reality*, Winnicott offered a theory of parenting that refused the romance of parent's purity and the child's innocence. Along with Diane Eyer (1992) and Madeline Grumet (1988), Winnicott complicates theories of attachment by emphasizing the relational world of child development. First publishing his work in the 1930s, Winnicott, a British paediatrician and psychoanalyst, implored parents to ignore idealized depictions of caring for children and recognize the productivity of their own ambivalence towards their children. Winnicott wrote against the backdrop of World War II and his theories of childhood were inflected with an inheritance of Freudian thought but revised to reflect the great challenges of working with children. Like Freud, Winnicott believed that our earliest relationships as children formed the basis for the adult's subjective experiences. Lisa Farley (2011) helps to situate Winnicott's thinking within a geopolitical context:

> During World War II, Winnicott oversaw the placement of approximately 285 youth who had been separated from their families in anticipation of German air raids. In this ominous context, Winnicott had become anxious about the effects of a child's premature separation from home. With two other psychiatrists, John Bowlby and Emanuel Miller, Winnicott penned a letter to the British Medical Journal on December 16, 1939. All three psychiatrists were sure that forced separation would cause an 'emotional black-out' that they believed could manifest later in a 'psychohistorical theme' (to return to Lifton's language), which, at the time was called 'juvenile delinquency.' Winnicott saw it as his task—and the task of foster parents—to provide a reliable environment in which evacuated youth could risk a relationship to the fact of separation (and accompanying feelings of absence) that would otherwise be lost to the 'emotional black-out' of repression. In this context, Winnicott increasingly turned his attention to the child's defensive projections of aggression associated with the separation. (pp. 19–22)

Winnicott, speaking primarily to mothers but also addressing others who cared for children, thought that it was harmful for caregivers to ignore the complexity of their feelings towards children, suggesting that they should not strive for ideals but rather, simply, to be 'good enough' parents. He writes,

> the good enough mother (not necessarily the infant's own mother) is one who makes active adaptation to the infant's needs, an active adaptation that gradually lessens, according to the infant's growing ability to account for failure of adaptation and to tolerate the results of frustration. (Winnicott, 1971/2001, pp. 13–14).

Here, it is not the mother's perfection that is important to the child's development but her disappointments. A good-enough mother, according to Winnicott, will allow the child to adapt to her failures and feel frustration when she does not immediately meet their demands. "If all goes well", which is Winnicott's phrase for development, the mother can be "hated as well as loved" by the child (and vice versa). It is precisely this ambivalence that is too often denied when children are presumed pure and their caregivers assumed in full control of their emotions and circumstances. We follow Winnicott into understanding the mother's ambivalent relationship to the child as both carefully crafted and a result of the overwhelming labour of being responsible for another's well-being.

Winnicott (1971/2001) writes provocatively about children's purposeful ambivalence towards their caretaker: "this is the preliminary task of weaning, and it also continues as one of the tasks of parents and educators" (p. 17). In this space of what he terms "disillusionment", the child can learn to psychically survive in a world that does not always conform to their wishes and where they must also adapt to the needs of others. Farley (2011) explains that "for the good enough mother, the capacity to 'hold' the baby's projections could create a potential space of communication" (p. 12). Winnicott's good-enough parent provides us with a way to think against imperatives of purity and embrace ambivalence in relation to children and childhood. Transposed to the context of pandemic and related debates about whose responsibility it is to offer care to the child, Winnicott's reflections on disillusionment are incisive. The parent may hope to take full responsibility for their child's well-being, but anxiety arises from the recognition that it is an enormous task to support "the child's capacity to survive a world that exceeds and can oppose one's expectations of it" (Farley, 2009, p. 542). If we take Winnicott's theory of development seriously, then the affective traces of disillusionment left on the child's future subjectivity are central to their ability to withstand or make meaning from future crises.

In thinking about the rhetoric of protection and the "nurturing" parent, Garlen (2019) has further complicated the notion of a protective parent, showing how structures of child protection are deeply racialized and gendered terrains. "The rhetoric of protection", she explains, justified the forced removal of Indigenous "children from their homes in order to provide the 'appropriate' conditions of childhood, and perpetuated stereotypes about Black and poor White mothers as morally deficient" (Garlen, 2019, p. 63). Reading Winnicott alongside Garlen and other critical theorists of childhood raises questions about how narratives of protection can seek to erase complex entanglements between parenting advice, childhood, socio-economic perspectives, sexism, and racism. We find use in Winnicott's proposal that adults might find value in their ambivalence towards children and highlight scholarship that has shown how the state is also ambivalent in its treatment of childhood, offering asymmetries of both protection and harm. Critical work related to childhood offers sharp critiques of the rhetoric of innocence and its attendant policies and procedures, showing that the act of caring for children is wrought with the toxicity of genocide, racism, sexism, carcerality, homophobia, and even anti-Blackness and misogyny as specific examples and that the protections offered by innocence are not evenly circulated.

Conclusion

This chapter has offered critique of imperatives of purity in relation to parenting and childhood. As the field has demonstrated, assertions of children's purity and innocence without attention to their complex entanglements in material histories of harm and social conflict, damage the adult's ability to be with the child respectfully and carefully. We have retraced the conceptualization of innocence in childhood studies in order to understand why children and their caregivers are often hurt by discourses of purity. We have sought to engage the subjective dimensions of purity as it appears in discourses of childhood so that assertions of children's difficult complexities are not disjunctive proclamations but acceptable perspectives, even while we love them. The notion of childhood innocence produces a particular "childhood", and as critical childhood scholars have argued, this vision of "childhood" perpetuates material harm and social injustices along racial, sexual, gendered and classed lines.

Drawing on the work of critical childhood scholars and beyond (e.g., Burman, 1994/2017; Cannella 1997; Dyer, 2020; Garlen, 2019; Meiners, 2015; Nxumalo & Cedillo, 2017; Pacini-Ketchabaw & Kummen, 2016; Shotwell, 2016; Walkerdine, 1997, 2001; Winnicott, 1971/2001), we further demonstrated the ways that acceptance of the notion of childhood innocence can result in harm. Amid a global pandemic during which children's social lives are being reorganized, this chapter has revisited past deconstructions of childhood innocence to show the continued importance of this line of interrogation. Moral panic about threats to innocence and repetitive protective acts to reinforce the cultural value of innocence position purity, in the form of the child, against the corrupting forces of culture (Meiners, 2015). Discourses of childhood innocence position children as being without rich cultures of their own, considering culture as something created by adults, rather than co-constituted by children. If innocence is constituted as an ignorance of adult anxieties and desires, then it is an "empty signifier of adult fantasy"

(Faulkner, 2010, p. 115). Through ascriptions of innocence and purity, children are positioned as passive receivers of adult desire, without agency or desires of their own. By stripping children of the language to articulate their "*own* fears, desires, and questions about their experiences" modern notions of childhood innocence, entrenched through protective rhetoric, paradoxically leave children "ill-equipped to advocate for their own well-being" (Garlen, 2019, p. 64).

Note

1. In an October 14 article for the *New York Times* Parenting section, written by Jessica Grose (2020), Dharushana Muthulingam, a mother whose career has been impacted by the pandemic, is quoted as saying that mothers are "the shock absorbers of our system, and the poorer and more precarious you are, the more shock you're expected to absorb" (para. 13).

References

Berlant, L. (2004). Live sex acts (Parental advisory: Explicit material). In S. Bruhm & N. Hurley (Eds.), *Curiouser: On the queerness of children* (pp. 57–80). University of Minnesota Press.

Bernstein, R. (2011). *Racial innocence: Performing American childhood and race from slavery to civil rights* (Vol. 16). New York University Press.

Black, S. (2020). *Social reproduction and the city: Welfare reform, child care and resistance in neoliberal New York*. University of Georgia Press.

Bloch, M. N. (1987). Becoming scientific and professional: An historical perspective on the aims and effects of early education. In T. S. Popkewitz (Ed.), *The formation of school subjects: The struggle for creating an American institution* (pp. 25–62). Routledge.

Bruhm, S., & Hurley, N. (2004). Curiouser: On the queerness of children. In S. Bruhm & N. Hurley (Eds.), *Curiouser: On the queerness of children* (pp. ix–xxxviii). University of Minnesota Press.

Burman, E. (2017). *Deconstructing developmental psychology* (3rd ed.). Routledge. (Original work published 1994)

Butler, J. (1988). Performative acts and gender constitution: An essay in phenomenology and feminist theory. *Theatre Journal*, 40(4), 519–531. doi:10.2307/3207893

Cannella, G. (1997). *Deconstructing early childhood education: Social justice and revolution*. Peter Lang.

Dyer, H. (2017). Queer futurity and childhood innocence: Beyond the injury of development. *Global Studies of Childhood*, 7(3), 290–302. doi:10.1177/2043610616671056

Dyer, H. (2020). *The queer aesthetics of childhood: Asymmetries of innocence and the cultural politics of child development*. Rutgers University Press.

Edelman, L. (2004). *No future: Queer theory and the death drive*. Duke University Press.

Egan, R. D., & Hawkes, G. L. (2008). Imperiled and perilous: Exploring the history of childhood sexuality. *Journal of Historical Sociology*, 21(4), 355–367. doi:10.1111/j.14676443.2008.00341.x

Eyer, D. E. (1993). *Mother-infant bonding: A scientific fiction*. Yale University Press.

Farley, L. (2009). Radical hope: Or, the problem of uncertainty in history education. *Curriculum Inquiry, 39*(4), 537–554. doi:10.1111/j.1467-873X.2009.00456.x

Farley, L. (2011). Squiggle evidence: The child, the canvas, and the "negative labor" of history. *History & Memory, 23*(2), 5–39. doi:10.2979/histmemo.23.2.5

Farley, L. (2018). *Childhood beyond pathology: A psychoanalytic study of development and diagnosis.* SUNY Press.

Farley, L., & Kennedy, R. M. (2016). A sex of one's own: Childhood and the embodiment of (trans) gender. *Psychoanalysis, Culture & Society, 21*(2), 167–183. doi:10.1057/pcs.2015.59

Faulkner, J. (2010). The innocence fetish: The commodification and sexualisation of children in the media and popular culture. *Media International Australia, 135*(1), 106–117. doi:10.1177/1329878X1013500113

Garlen, J. C. (2019). Interrogating innocence: "Childhood" as exclusionary social practice. *Childhood, 26*(1), 54–67. doi:10.1177/0907568218811484

Gill-Peterson, J. (2018). *Histories of the transgender child.* University of Minnesota Press.

Grose, J. (2020, October 7). Parenting was never meant to be this isolating. *New York Times.* https://www.nytimes.com/2020/10/07/parenting/childcare-history-family.html

Grumet, M. (1988). *Bitter milk: Women and teaching.* University of Massachusetts Press.

James, A., Jenks, C., & Prout, A. (1998). *Theorizing childhood.* Polity Press.

Jenkins, H. (Ed.). (1998). *The children's culture reader.* NYU Press.

Kehily, M. J., & Montgomery, H. (2004). Innocence and experience: A historical approach to childhood and sexuality. In M. J. Kehily (Ed.), *An introduction to childhood studies* (pp. 57–74). Open University Press.

Kincaid, J. R. (1998). *Erotic innocence: The culture of child molesting.* Duke University Press.

Kline, S. (1995). *Out of the garden.* Verso.

McKeon, L. (2016, April 11). What does innocence look like? *New Yorker.* https://www.newyorker.com/culture/photo-booth/what-does-innocence-look-like

Meiners, E. R. (2015). Trouble with the child in the carceral state. *Social Justice, 41*(3), 120–144.

Nxumalo, F., & Cedillo, S. (2017). Decolonizing place in early childhood studies: Thinking with Indigenous onto-epistemologies and Black feminist geographies. *Global Studies of Childhood, 7*(2), 99–112. doi:10.1177/2043610617703831

Pacini-Ketchabaw, V., & Kummen, K. (2016). Shifting temporal frames in children's common worlds in the Anthropocene. *Contemporary Issues in Early Childhood, 17*(4), 431–441. doi:10.1177/1463949116677930

Patton, S. (2014, November 26). In America, Black children don't get to be children. *Washington Post.* https://www.washingtonpost.com/opinions/in-america-black-children-dont-get-to-be-children/2014/11/26/a9e24756-74ee-11e4-a755-e32227229e7b_story.html?utm_term=.3d06a8acd306

Robinson, K. H. (2008). In the name of 'childhood innocence': A discursive exploration of the moral panic associated with childhood and sexuality. *Cultural Studies Review, 14*(2), 113–129. doi:10.5130/csr.v14i2.2075

Robinson, K. H. (2013). *Innocence, knowledge and the construction of childhood: The contradictory nature of sexuality and censorship in children's contemporary lives.* Routledge.

Sedgwick, E. K. (2004). How to bring your kids up gay: The war on effeminate boys. In S. Bruhm & N. Hurley (Eds.), *Curiouser: On the queerness of children* (pp. 139–150). University of Minnesota Press.

Shotwell, A. (2016). *Against purity: Living ethically in compromised times.* University of Minnesota Press.

Silin, J. G. (1987). The early childhood educator's knowledge base: A reconsideration. In L. G. Katz & K. Steiner (Eds.), *Current topics in early childhood education* (pp. 2–27). Ablex Publishing.

Silin, J. G. (1995). *Sex, death, and the education of children: Our passion for ignorance in the age of AIDS*. Teachers College Press.

Stockton, K. B. (2004). Growing sideways, or versions of the queer child: The ghost, the homosexual, the Freudian, the innocent, and the interval of the animal. In S. Bruhm & N. Hurley (Eds.), *Curiouser: On the queerness of children* (pp. 277–316). University of Minnesota Press.

Taylor, A. (2010). Troubling childhood innocence: Reframing the debate over the media sexualisation of children. *Australasian Journal of Early Childhood, 35*(1), 48–57. doi:10.1177/183693911003500108

Walkerdine, V. (1997). *Daddy's girl: Young girls and popular culture*. Harvard University Press.

Walkerdine, V. (2001). Safety and danger: Childhood, sexuality, and space at the end of the millennium. In K. Hultqvist and G. Dalberg (Eds.), *Governing the child in the new millennium* (pp. 15–34). RoutledgeFalmer.

Winnicott, D. W. (2001). *Playing and reality*. Routledge. (Original work published 1971)

Wynter, S. (2003). Unsettling the coloniality of being/power/truth/freedom: Towards the human, after man, its overrepresentation—An argument. *CR: The New Centennial Review, 3*(3), 257–337. doi:10.1353/ncr.2004.0015

CHAPTER 16

Playing With the Politics of Play

Sue Grieshaber and Sally Barnes

As a seemingly 'untouchable' foundation of early childhood education in whatever forms and functions it is conceptualized, the idea of play has generated a number of redoubtable Truths. These include that play should be an essential part of all childhoods, that it is closely connected with learning, and that it is inherently good. Such ideas work to exclude ways of being that are not encompassed by these Truths. Normalized versions of play were contested in the late 20th (e.g., Cannella, 1997) and early parts of the 21st century (e.g., Grieshaber & McArdle, 2010). But little is known of the amount or availability of research that does this work. This scoping review provides an introductory assessment of the extent, scope and nature of research activity in early childhood education (ECE) that conceptualizes play from outside the child development paradigm, that is, research and ideas about play that are Other and Othered. It includes literature that identifiably adopts critical theoretical perspectives (e.g., feminism) including those characterized as post (poststructural, post-developmental, etc.).

The aims are to provide a review of empirical studies and conceptual and policy perspectives of play that are Other and Othered to establish an evidence base for future work and potentially to inform policymakers about this body of evidence. Consistent with Booth et al. (2012), this scoping review provides a "snapshot of a particular topic area" (p. 19) in a specific period (2009–2019). It investigates the extent, scope, and nature of research about a specific topic before summarizing the findings in themes and, in the process, identifies gaps in the extant literature (Arksey & O'Malley, 2005). The method establishes the extent and nature of the literature, and the scope investigates how play is conceptualized from outside the child development paradigm. As part of the scope, this review considers how dominant understandings of play are challenged. The content of the five themes identified in the Findings reflects an understanding of the alternatives available.

Method

The method used to identify the literature followed the approach taken by Fray et al. (2020) in their analysis of the key influences on aspirations for higher education of Australian school students in regional and remote locations. All peer-reviewed articles that met the following criteria were considered for inclusion: (a) Australian and international research, (b) published in English, (c) published during the period from January 2009 to December 2019, and (d) contained the keywords used in the first search (play and early childhood) and at least one of the additional terms used in the second search (play and early childhood and: feminist (e.g., play + early childhood+ feminist and so on for the rest of the following terms: critical theory, poststructural, reconceptualist, postcolonial, post-developmental, posthuman, sociocultural). Publications were limited to refereed journal articles for three reasons. First, our interest is a preliminary assessment of the size and availability of research about play that is Other and Othered that appears in refereed journals rather than edited collections (Brooker et al., 2014). Second is curiosity about where (which journals) this research has been published given the fixation of many universities worldwide with research assessment and performance outputs, often judged by journal quartile rankings, journal impact factors, and such measures. The third reason is to identify absences and silences.

To gather a comprehensive collection of articles, two keyword searches were conducted in four research databases in English: A+ Education, ProQuest Central, ERIC, and AEI. The first search used the keywords play and early childhood; the second combined the keywords used in the first search with the following: play and early childhood and; feminist; critical theory; post-structural; reconceptualist; post-colonial; post-developmental; post-human; socio-cultural. Whilst the keywords used in the first search identified 4027 articles (including duplicates), the second, using the keywords from the first search with additional terms, produced 83. After duplicate articles were removed, 36 titles remained. Abstracts were read and reference lists examined to ensure each article met the criteria. For articles that produced uncertainty about inclusion based on the keywords and title, the abstract was read, a search to identify a conceptual framework (research problem, theory, methodology) was undertaken that included considering the data analysis and conclusion sections, and reference lists were consulted for the names of theorists. Evidence of a conceptual framework resulted in the article being added to the shortlist for consideration in the final list.

Following the process described by Fray et al. (2020) and according to scoping review methodology (Arksey & O'Malley, 2005), a manual search of journals from which three or more articles had been identified in the first search was then conducted. The journals searched in this stage were the *Australasian Journal of Early Childhood, Contemporary Issues in Early Childhood, Children's Geographies* and *Early Child Development and Care*. In addition, a reference list search of all articles identified in the initial search (including a search of theses that were identified in the initial search but excluded from the review as they did not meet the criteria of being a peer-reviewed article) was then conducted. This resulted in an additional 33 articles being identified ($n = 69$). Each of these articles was read, again with a view to identifying the conceptual framework that had been used to analyze the data and discuss the findings of the study. A reference list search for the name of theorists was also undertaken. Following this analysis, 12 of the additional 33 articles were included in the final review ($n = 48$).

In the next stage, full-text articles were retrieved from an online library and read by at least one author. Items included were collated as PDFs, filed by each author's last name and title, and stored in a cloud-based folder for ease of access by the authors. A review template was created that included the following categories: author/s and year of publication; journal title; article title; country of origin of author/s; theoretical perspective/s; research design; participants; data sources; and themes. Themes were added and changed according to detailed reading and assessment of each article. Five final themes emerged: defining or conceptualizing play, play environments, the playing child, the work of teachers in play, and policy mandates.

One of the challenges with this scoping review was the amorphous nature of play in ECE. The topic is fluid and has strands and components everywhere, many of which influence how play is understood in ECE. This ubiquitous nature of play means that it infiltrates almost everything in ways that can be difficult to discern. It is slippery and hard to get a grip on and, in turn, hard to challenge or change because doing so disrupts many things. Another challenge was that during the search, literature identified as new materialist or posthumanist might not have had 'play' in the title; mentioned or referenced play, but it was evident that what was being discussed was play in some form. This was ascertained to be the case because rethinking relationships about space and place in ECE necessarily involves thinking about play.

Findings

Of the 48 items, play or its derivatives (e.g., playing) was mentioned in 30 of the article titles, with one title mentioning play three times. In what follows, we first describe the nature of the research by reporting specific characteristics of the items. These include the location of authors, changes over time, publication sources, theoretical perspectives, and research methodologies and methods. Then the five themes are presented, highlighting key challenges and alternatives. A discussion follows, and the chapter ends with a short conclusion.

Nature of the Research: Characteristics of the Items

Author Locations

Authors came from 10 countries which included Australia, Canada, Finland, Indonesia, New Zealand, Norway, Pakistan, Sweden, the United Kingdom, and the United States. 'Data' were not always drawn from the country of the author (e.g., Malone, 2016). Fifteen items had authors from the United States, 11 from Australia, and six from the United Kingdom. Norway was represented by four items, Canada three, and Sweden two. Five items had authors from more than one country, which included Finland and the United Kingdom (Huuki & Renold, 2016; Rautio & Winston, 2015), Pakistan and Canada (Pardhan & Pelletier, 2017), Sweden and Indonesia (Warin & Adriany, 2017), and the United States, Australia, and New Zealand (Adair et al., 2017). Using the country of origin of the first author, 16 items were published by authors in the United States, 12 by authors in Australia, and six by authors in the United Kingdom.

Changes over Time

Over the 11-year span (January 2009–December 2019), the highest number of publications was recorded in 2017 ($n = 19$), followed by 2014 and 2016 with five each and 2019 when four articles were published (Table 16.1).

Table 16.1. Items Published According to Year

Year	Number of Items Published
2009	1
2010	1
2011	3
2012	2
2013	2
2014	5
2015	3
2016	5
2017	19
2018	3
2019	4
Total	48

Publication Sources

The three journals in which most items were published were *Contemporary Issues in Early Childhood* (n = 12), *Children's Geographies* (n = 4), and *Early Child Development and Care* (n = 12). Apart from these, one journal published three items (*Discourse: Studies in the Cultural Politics of Education*), and four journals published two articles each in the span (*Australasian Journal of Early Childhood*; the *Journal of Early Childhood Literacy*; the *International Journal of Early Years Education*; *Teachers College Record*). Nine journals published one article each, making a total of 17 journals in which the 48 items were published.

Theoretical Perspectives

The ways in which the theoretical resources were identified were inconsistent in that some authors named theorists (e.g., Barad, Foucault), and others named theoretical perspectives (e.g., posthumanism, poststructuralism). Others used secondary sources only (e.g., did not cite original theorists), with the latter reflecting a compromise in rigor in our view. As might be expected, some items used a combination of theorists, theoretical perspectives, and secondary sources. Many items named several theorists and/or theoretical perspectives. Nearly half (n = 23) of the authors either named posthumanism or those associated closely with this perspective, either as a theorist (e.g., Barad, Haraway) or secondary sources, such as authors using this theoretical approach. Poststructuralism and theorists associated with the perspective (e.g., Butler, Foucault), as well as authors drawing on poststructuralism and feminist poststructuralism, were mentioned in 20 items. At times, theorists associated with both posthumanism and poststructuralism were drawn on in the one item (e.g., Bone, 2010). Critical theory or associated theorists (e.g., Arendt, Bakhtin) were used in 10 items. There were some uncommon combinations of theoretical perspectives that included feminist poststructuralism and ecological systems theory (Pardhan & Pelleiter, 2017) and poststructural theory and sociocultural theory (Wood, 2014).

Research Methodologies and Methods

Methodologies and methods are understood as follows: methodology or methodological approach (e.g., survey, ethnography as per Creswell, 2019), methods of data collection (e.g., survey questionnaire, interviews), and tools used for data analysis (e.g., thematic, discourse analysis). Nine items did not name a discernible methodology, which is a weakness regarding overall research quality. For some items, identifying the methodology was challenging as there was little or no distinction between methodology and methods (e.g., Sandvik, 2012, p. 200, referred to "Deleuze as method"). The most common methodology was ethnography (n = 14), which included a range of variants such as longitudinal, and multisensory and multispecies ethnographies. Eight items named case study and four named intra-active/diffractive as the methodology. Three items referred to naturalistic or interpretive methodological approaches and two named 'post qualitative' (Jones et al., 2016; Rautio & Winston, 2015) as the methodology. Four items drew on survey data from other studies undertaken by the authors or used surveys as part of the data gathering methods (Campbell et al., 2017; Harwood & Collier, 2017; Nicholson et al., 2015; Shimpi & Nicholson, 2014). The most commonly used method for gathering data was the interview (all types), with half of the items ($n = 24$) using this approach. Observation (participant, nonparticipant, self) was used in 22 studies, photographs in 21, and field notes and videos were used in 20 studies each. Most items used more than one source to generate data.

Participants

The participants included children from the age of 15 months to 15 years, educators, teaching assistants, and preservice teachers. Researchers worked in a range of countries and settings including preschools and kindergartens, family day care and home environments, nature, and outdoor settings.

Five Themes

All items challenged notions of play informed by child development theories or contested something about what the field currently understands play to be, or should be. Authors sought to expand present understandings of play, address aspects of play differently, or identify features of play that are unrecognized in discourses of child development. Thematic analysis of the 48 items produced five categories:

1. Defining/conceptualizing play (8)
2. Play environments (12)
3. The playing child (15)
4. The work of teachers in play (9)
5. Policy mandates (4)

Theme 3, 'the playing child', yielded the most items with 15, followed by 12 in the 'play environments' category. The 'policy mandates' theme had the least with four items. Each is now discussed.

Defining/Conceptualizing Play (8 items)

This theme is about the 'idea' of play and presents conceptions of play framed by perspectives outside child development theories.

In this theme, items adopting posthumanist theoretical approaches focused on de-centering the human and showing how this might occur. To this end, Änggård (2016) used the concepts of diffraction and intra-action to analyze how matter is agential and to investigate the entanglement of children, matter, and discourse. In response to questions about the educational relevance of playing, Rautio and Winston (2015) also conceptualized play as intra-active. They saw play as entangled and complex, about much more than solely human activity and a means of development or learning or as an end point of development or learning. The relevance of education to children's lives was also tackled by Taylor et al. (2013), who adopted a worlding approach to learning that involves response-ability. Given the current planetary circumstances and enduring colonial legacies, worlding focuses on "multidirectional human/non-human relationships [and] the need to acknowledge our shared response-abilities and learning *with* all of the others in our more-than-worlds" (Taylor et al., 2013, p. 60). For ECE, this means learning with more than human others rather than learning about things in a human-centric curriculum.

In a novel approach, Bone (2010) used posthumanism and poststructuralism to reconceptualize play as metamorphosis, part of which involved a critique of the nature/culture and human/non-human dichotomies; providing an opening where children could explore "what it might be to move as the Other, to feel as the Other, to touch as the Other, and to share the spirit of the Other" (p. 412). Malone (2016) also contested the highly valued children-in-nature relationship that characterizes much writing about nature play in ECE. She deployed diffraction and intra-action to examine the complexity and entanglement of relationships involved in children's encounters with dogs and, in the process, disrupted some of the accepted universalisms of nature play.

Play was conceptualized by Adair et al. (2017) as the collective action of children in "political time and space" (p. 798). Different from an act, collective action (informed by Arendt and Rancière; see Adair et al., 2017) is doing civic action rather than the development of civic action, meaning that children are political because of how they initiate and respond to initiatives from others. They maintain that play is the "most common (and endangered) time and space in which children act for the collective" (p. 798). Like Adair et al., Shimpi and Nicholson (2014) considered children's play in international and diverse communities. They used poststructuralism and postcolonialism to show the limitations of understanding play through a universalized discourse and the inequitable consequences of the inability to deal with the complexities involved in play. Privileging multiple discourses about play was proposed as a step toward increasing equity. The concept of dark play takes neglected aspects of play into account, which enabled Sinker, Phillips and Rijke (2017) to employ feminist theory and psychoanalysis to interrogate a free online game aimed at young girls. Three perspectives (parental, digital, psychoanalytic) highlighted multiple post-feminist narratives experienced when playing: "sex as gender is compromised and limited; princess beauty myths are replicated; pregnancy is medicalised" (Sinker et al., 2017, p. 176). They suggested that adult fears are less about girls playing online games and more about "games playing with girls" (Sinker et al., 2017, p. 176).

Play Environments (12 items)

Items in this theme questioned what are often assumed to be 'natural' environments in indoor and outdoor early childhood settings and the resources in those settings, including humans.

Outdoors featured mud (Mycock, 2019; Somerville & Powell, 2019), nature environments (Änggård, 2011), puddles (Merewether, 2019), place and space (Jones et al., 2016) and place (Proctor & Hackett, 2017). Gender was the focus of two items about the outdoors, with Änggård (2011) using posthumanism and noting that animal and physical play in nature environments can provide "non-gendered play positions" (p. 5) but that superhero play consisted exclusively of masculine gender stereotypes, while family play included feminine and masculine positioning and opportunities for fluidity. In using mud to learn about the more-than-human, Mycock (2019) showed that when mud is deemed to be dirt, it can also work simultaneously as governance by constructing bodies as clean/dirty and as gendered and class-based identities. Embodied mud appeared to be the difference between governance (i.e., gender and class) and the more-than-human entanglements that are seen to benefit learning. A diffractive reading by Somerville and Powell (2019) about mud's play with children indicated how mud "becomes . . . one of the ways in which the world becomes actively present for young children in their everyday lives and learning" (p. 836). Driven by a quest for alternative modes of writing and inquiry necessary for rethinking relationships "between world and human", Somerville and Powell (2019) suggested becoming "immersed in the emergent worlds of young children's play, and to understand the ways in which seemingly fixed spaces and territories of learning are constantly being territorialised and deterritorialised through this emergent play" (p. 839).

According to Merewether (2019), the value of children's perspectives is an integral part of assemblages, and puddles are one way that adults can "join with and learn from young children's everyday multispecies kin-making" (p. 114). Young children have distinct advantages over "humanist-trained adults", and because they are "less habituated into developmentalist, anthropocentric approaches, they may be offering alternative ways of becoming with matter" (Merewether, 2019, p. 106). As such, Merewether (2019) understands children's multispecies stories to be "important for reconceptualising what 'matters' as 'curriculum'" (p. 115). To Jones et al. (2016), place and space making is a political act that involves children, youth, educators, and educational researchers. They aimed for spatial justice by using childhood geographies and new materialisms as these theories open pedagogical opportunities that are otherwise unavailable. In an innovative approach, Proctor and Hackett (2017) focused on emotion and particularly fear in children's play encounters. They argued for reconceptualizing play through new materialism and the cultural studies of emotion, which involves place, objects and children in ways that go beyond reproducing the "idealised human" (p. 223).

Studies in indoor environments concerned digital technologies, furniture, and gender. Three items investigated digital technologies and cultures, with each adopting different theoretical perspectives. Informed by Bakhtin and Foucault, Huh (2017a) found that the digital game playing of four children aged 3 in public spaces (such as hair salons) served as 'heterotopias', where children were able to resist and remake spaces designed for adult usage. Marsh (2017) emphasized the value of moving beyond an exclusive focus on humanism because young children's play "increasingly connects digital and nondigital domains" (p. 1) and because posthumanist theories can assist understanding about how digital and nondigital domains are connected across time and space. Relatedly, Wohlwend (2017) used mediated discourse analysis to highlight the necessity of critical media literacy because of the increase in children playing in transmedia environments. Such spaces bring together a complex assortment of children's cultures, digital literacies, consumer practices, and corporate agendas, some of which may not be discernible.

As a characteristic marker of ECE environments, the small chair (Bone, 2019) was used to query how it denotes similarities and differences between adult and child bodies and to keep adult bodies in their place. Using a combination of 'new' feminist materialism and hauntology, the small chair was also used to provoke thought about children being "prepared to enter the world of sitting" (Bone, 2019, p. 143). Another piece of furniture featuring an oven and sink was the 'active agent' for learning about human and nonhuman intra-actions (Myhre et al., 2017). The intra-actions or "movements and intermingling ... constitute ... becoming" (p. 308), and Myhre et al. (2017) argued that it is the becoming that provides opportunities for "resisting habitual and sedimented practices" (p. 308). Staying indoors, the Foucauldian analysis undertaken by Børve and Børve (2017) indicated that indoor play environments (rooms, zones) and materials were gendered and that children's play practices reproduced staff ideas about gender.

The Playing Child (15 Items)

There are countless empirical studies in the child development paradigm about how children play and many assumptions about how children should play. Some of these conventions include that children should have opportunities for 'free' play, that learning happens because children play (e.g., that mathematical learning occurs when children play with blocks), the type of 'choices' for play that should be provided (blocks, house play, etc.), and that gunplay is inappropriate, as is play that is too messy, dirty, or risky. Most accept that playing children require some form of adult involvement, with the type and amount varying widely from modest involvement to focused intervention. All 15 items in this theme were empirical studies that contested normalized versions of how children play and/or should play. They presented ideas such as children's bodies as sites of politics (Antonsen, 2018; Stratigos, 2015); resisted adult dominated conventions that rely on what is predetermined, known, and knowable by adults (Haywood-Bird, 2017; Huh, 2017b; Rautio, 2014); challenged deficit constructions of children (Henward & MacGillivray, 2014; Nicholson et al., 2015; Watson, 2019), and contested gender norms and stereotypes (Henward & MacGillivray, 2014; Huuki & Renold, 2016; Madrid, 2013; Pardhan & Pelleiter, 2017; Wohlwend, 2011).

The 15 items used a range of theoretical tools and had the most variation theoretically of the five themes. These studies also reflected the most diverse combinations of theoretical perspectives, with some notable infrequent associations such as feminist poststructuralism and Bakhtin (Henward & MacGillivray, 2014), and feminist poststructuralism and ecological systems theory (Pardhan & Pelletier, 2017). Despite these combinations, items using posthuman perspectives were employed most frequently, accounting for just over one quarter ($n = 4$) of the theoretical tools used.

As depicted in this theme, items identifying other ways to conceptualize *the playing child* have implications for pedagogies used in early childhood contexts. Most items addressed pedagogies, and although this is not always explicit, the underlying presence signified pedagogies as a fundamental part of children's play and incumbent adult involvement in it. Ways in which entrenched pedagogical practices can be contested were identified and alternatives included restorying what "children's bodies can do, think, and be" (Antonsen, 2018, p. 17); looking to Bakhtin, "for a view of learning as a perpetual dialogue with others and ourselves" (Cohen, 2009, p. 340); place as a "contact zone" for creating "place stories" and "children's place literacy" (Hognestad & Bøe, 2012, p. 54); play as a pedagogical site for challenging, exploring, and transforming gender stereotypes in children's media (e.g., princess play; Wohlwend, 2011); and, as several of the posthumanist-oriented items indicated, restorying understandings of matter and its agentic nature. Implicit in some of these items were the pedagogical abilities associated with matter.

The Work of Teachers in Play (9)

Rethinking the work of teachers in play disrupts a number of taken-for-granted assumptions (e.g., the benefits of play for children's learning, observation using developmental categories, curriculum that reflects children's interests). Challenges to accepted ways in which teachers work investigated what is or is not allowed, as well as invented or reinvented practices and pedagogies.

Two items explored gender, with one noting that educators can view play differently and challenge children's understandings of gender norms if made aware of how gender can position children and teachers stereotypically (Chapman, 2016). The other concluded that "gender conscious pedagogues" and a "gender sensitive curriculum" are required to be able to "confront and disrupt gendered performances in children" (Warin & Adrinay, 2017, p. 384). While encouraging, gender in all its forms remains a significant and long-term challenge for the field.

Moving beyond the pedagogical binary of play-based/intentional teaching was a challenge that was confronted using poststructuralism (Thomas et al., 2011). And in combination with comic subjectivity theory, poststructuralism was adopted to investigate how a teacher tried to shape children's pretend violence play into "good" or "productive" play (Delaney, 2017). Findings showed that the agency of children can be limited by rules, yet subversive play that resisted teacher control can be a way to reclaim power. Poststructural theory was also used with Noddings' ethic of care to make a case that teachers need to advocate for children's rights to play due to some schools positioning play as incompatible with children's learning (Nicholson et al., 2014). Relatedly, Sisson and Kroeger (2017) considered the encroachment of formal approaches to curriculum adopted in preschools located on public school sites in the United States. They recognized the contested and somewhat fragile nature of play in these contexts and recommended Bakhtinian dialogue to co-construct understandings of academic readiness that includes play.

In one of the few items that addressed race, Latino/a critical race theory (LatCrit) (Arreguin-Anderson et al., 2018) was used to explore the languaging of children in play environments not regulated by a bilingual education model. It provided a lens to theorize how race and racism pervade educational structures, processes, and discourses. Disrupting the supremacy of English requires educators to confront their understandings of bilingualism before changes in pedagogies can occur. Like others, Sandvik (2012) was concerned with pedagogies, indicating that assemblages have unlimited potential for releasing the complexities involved in pedagogical practices: "Pedagogical potential may be hidden in the invisible and uncontrollable" (p. 207). Letting go teacher control for a "more expectant and uncertain pedagogical practice" (Sandvik, 2012, p. 207) is a rethinking of responsibility, and as Mazzei (2009, cited in Sandvik, 2012) noted, about thinking a new pedagogy.

A posthumanist approach by Blaise, Hamm and Iorio (2017) contested the traditional practices of observation associated with ECE, maintaining that they do not engage with complexity and are lacking ethically and politically. Blaise et al. proposed Haraway's idea of feminist modest witnessing as an alternative. Here observational practices can be reworked into "ethical, political and entangled forms of open-ended dialogue" (p. 41), principally because they do more than traditional forms of observation that represent, document, or narrate.

Policy Mandates (4)

ECE settings are purposefully designed interventions that have specific goals, which vary according to country, region and locality. Policy goals and mandates have intensified due to economic analyses (e.g., Heckman, 2011) that claim quality ECE can reduce current and future risks to education, health, and justice systems. This theme revealed some of the shortcomings of mandated policy documents, including that they were not always about the type of quality expressed in the policies and that economic imperatives can contradict equity aspects of policies. However, what was most striking was the 'lip service' given to structural aspects such as gender, race, ethnicity, and culture and the lack of resources or support to enact policy requirements. This is a specific area that should be addressed by policymakers.

All four items used empirical data, with Campbell et al. (2017) drawing on survey data that focused on gender, revealing that educators understood child-centered curriculum, children's interests and play to be apolitical. The human capital agenda and the focus on learning outcomes overshadowed gender equity work, which when it did occur, was associated with providing materials and equipment such as non-gender-stereotyped books. As noted by MacNevin and Berman (2017), the policy requirement to provide racially and culturally diverse resources is not nearly enough to make a difference in how children act when confronted with racism and other oppressions. Educators are often unaware of children's knowledge of race and how it is used in "play and social interactions" (MacNevin & Berman, 2017, p. 834), which is complicated by the fact that observations of children are undertaken mostly from developmental perspectives and do not consider race and oppression. Mandating the provision of racially and culturally diverse resources is an important step but needs to be supported by a range of other policy mandates.

Few items addressed the assessment of play, with Palaiologou (2017) an exception. Palaiologou argued that the formal assessment of play required in England's Early Years Foundation Stage (EYFS) is incompatible with the tenets of play-oriented research and that assessment of child-initiated play is "impossible" (p. 1267). Assessment should focus on performance instead of outcomes and be contextual rather than abstracted from the "immediate social context" (Palaiologou, 2017, p. 1268). Wood (2014) was also concerned with the limitations of assessment and the EYFS, but her focus was the problematic of free choice and free play, and curriculum-mandated structured approaches. Choice comes with issues about children's agency and power relations involving children and teachers, and children and children, which are often unrecognized by teachers.

Discussion

The section includes a series of bullet points that are drawn from the themes. They include comments about absence, theoretical perspectives, and methodologies pertinent to the field and became evident during the analysis. These points can facilitate thinking aimed at reconceptualizing notions of play as well as related (thought and unthought) constructs, practices, relations, and issues.

Absence, Silence, Room for More

- As far as we can tell, there is an absence of Indigenous and First Nations authors in the literature produced from the search, leaving scope for much greater input and thereby enriching the literature.
- A small number of concepts related to Indigenous ways of knowing, being, and doing have been taken up by some non-Indigenous authors (e.g., Blaise et al., 2017).
- Policy documents that require the provision of racially and culturally diverse play materials are "virtually silent on the topic of how race, ethnicity, culture, and other dimensions of difference should inform teacher-child interactions or the development of curriculum" (MacNevin & Berman, 2017, p. 827). There is much work to do here.
- Many studies indicate why it is time to move from a human-centric focus, but one aspect that could be addressed in greater depth is what the work of teachers involves if intra-action is key to learning.
- Items that dealt with inclusion and/or dis/ability were few, with Watson (2019) an exception.
- Colonialism and postcolonial theoretical constructs were scarce but were used to examine colonial histories and current legacies from a posthuman perspective (Taylor et al., 2013), as well as investigate intergenerational play narratives (Shimpi & Nicholson, 2014).
- There is "collective amnesia about children's interest in horror... horrific images and stories that have historically been associated with childhood (i.e., Grimm's fairy tales)" (Henward & MacGillivray, 2014, p. 727). We wondered if this collective amnesia is an effect of research framed by developmental perspectives.

Theories

- The prevalence of posthumanism and 'new' materialism reflects recent trends in the education literature generally, with an increase in publications informed by these theories.

- The use of uncommon combinations of theorists and theoretical perspectives (e.g., ecological systems theory and feminist poststructuralism) has been noted briefly. Where used, such combinations tended not to be explained or justified. We suggest author/s explain why particular theories, theorists, and concepts were used and how they have been put to work together. This is necessary because of the theoretical incompatibility of, for example, sociocultural theory and poststructuralism, which have different epistemological, ontological, methodological, and axiological foundations. While drawing on specific concepts from different theoretical perspectives is worthwhile, rigor and credibility are enhanced if explanations of why and how are provided. As part of this process, relying only on secondary sources compromises quality whereas using original theorists strengthens reliability and trustworthiness.
- Posthumanist perspectives ($n = 23$) were used more frequently than poststructuralist ($n = 20$) and critical theories ($n = 10$; categorized according to the predominant theory with acknowledgment that theoretical combinations such as posthumanism and poststructuralism occurred). An effect of this theoretical preference meant items dealing with matters such as race, ethnicity, ability, class, socioeconomic circumstances, and colonialization were less common, which also reflected missed opportunities for intersectional analyses.
- Gender was the focus or an aspect of 11 items that included a variety of theoretical perspectives. However, gender remains a festering wound in all dimensions of ECE.
- While we didn't do a frequency count, articles adopting posthumanist perspectives were more inclined to provide examples related to boys than girls (this requires more investigation).
- Items adopting posthumanism tended to rely on similar conceptual tools (e.g., intra-action, diffraction, assemblage). Nevertheless, there were some that used novel means such as witnessing (Blaise et al., 2017) and 'deep hanging out' (Somerville & Powell, 2019). Investigations related to gender tended to draw on concepts of power/knowledge and subjectivity. The preference for certain kinds of conceptual tools raises the question of why some and not others.

Methodologies

- Most items were small-scale studies with small numbers of participants, which used methodologies associated with qualitative research; two named postqualitative approaches. Exceptions included survey questionnaires drawn from other studies (Nicholson et al., 2015; Shimpi & Nicholson, 2014) and a subgroup of survey respondents (Campbell et al., 2017). Small-scale studies are generally not given much credence by policymakers. This potential lack of effect and impact on policy makes it important for authors to explain; justify, be able to apply what has been learned to everyday ECE practice and do so in accessible language for policymakers, practitioners, and stakeholders. Doing these things successfully may also impact policy and beyond, such as pre- and in-service teacher education and future research.

Conclusion

This chapter has provided an overview of the extent, nature and scope of empirical research published in peer-reviewed journals that conceptualizes play from outside the child development paradigm (January 2009–December 2019). In conclusion, we identify one matter that we have been pondering while researching and writing this chapter. Not only did items that drew on posthumanism and new materialism use different discourses to discuss play, but these discourses also did not necessarily involve talk about play, per se. Several items identified the political nature of play and the political nature of what happens in ECE settings. Concepts such as "ethical practices as pedagogies" (Blaise et al., 2017, p. 32) appear to be a rethinking of how some aspects of play are seen in developmental discourses but with theories that include political and ethical dimensions. Here we signal the potential of this rethinking and powerful pedagogical impact, engagement, and learning (by all including educators) that is possible when the agenda changes from framing ECE only through discourses of child development to considering the ethical possibilities of pedagogies based on matters of race, gender, ability, culture, and socioeconomic circumstance, as well as equity, human privilege, and environmental justice.

Acknowledgment

Sincere thanks to the editors for their thoughtful and constructive feedback.

References

Adair, J. K., Phillips, L., Ritchie, J., & Sachdeva, S. (2017). Civic action and play: Examples from Maori, Aboriginal Australian and Latino communities. *Early Child Development and Care*, 187(5–6), 798–811. http://doi.org/10.1080/03004430.2016.1237049

Änggård, E. (2011). Children's gendered and non-gendered play in natural spaces. *Children, Youth and Environments, 21*(2), 5–33.

Änggård, E. (2016). How matter comes to matter in children's nature play: Posthumanist approaches and children's geographies. *Children's Geographies, 14*(1), 77–90. https://doi.org/10.1080/14733285.2015.1004523

Antonsen, C. M. (2018). Restorying the image of the child's body in early childhood education. *Contemporary Issues in Early Childhood, 21*(1), 7–19. https://doi.org/10.1177/1463949118805435

Arksey, H., & O'Malley, L. (2005). Scoping studies: Towards a methodological framework. *International Journal of Social Research Methodology, 8*(1), 19–32.

Arreguín-Anderson, M. G., Salinas-Gonzalez, I., & Alanis, I. (2018). Translingual play that promotes cultural connections, invention, and regulation: A LatCrit perspective. *International Multilingual Research Journal, 12*(4), 273–287. https://doi.org/10.1080/19313152.2018.1470434

Blaise, M., Hamm, C., & Iorio, J. (2017). Modest witness(ing) and lively stories: Paying attention to matters of concern in early childhood. *Pedagogy, Culture & Society, 25*(1), 31–42. https://doi.org/10.1080/14681366.2016.1208265

Bone, J. (2010). Metamorphosis: Play, spirituality and the animal. *Contemporary Issues in Early Childhood, 11*(4), 402–414. http://dx.doi.org/10.2304/ciec.2010.11.4.402

Bone, J. (2019). Ghosts of the material world in early childhood education: Furniture matters. *Contemporary Issues in Early Childhood, 20*(2), 133–145. http://doi.org/10.1177/1463949117749599

Booth, A., Papaioannou, D., & Sutton, A. (2012). *Systematic approaches to a successful literature review*. Sage Publications.

Børve, H., & Børve, E. (2017). Rooms with gender: Physical environment and play culture in kindergarten. *Early Child Development and Care, 187*(5–6), 1069–1081. https://doi.org/10.1080/03004430.2016.1223072

Brooker, E., Blaise, M., & Edwards, S. (Eds.). (2014). *The SAGE handbook of play and learning in early childhood*. Sage Publications.

Campbell, S., Smith, K. A., & Alexander, K. (2017). Spaces for gender equity in Australian early childhood education in/between discourses of human capital and feminism. *Australasian Journal of Early Childhood, 42*(3), 55–62. https://doi.org/10.23965/AJEC.42.3.07

Cannella, G. S. (1997). *Deconstructing early childhood education: Social justice & revolution*. Peter Lang.

Chapman, R. (2016). A case study of gendered play in preschools: How early childhood educators' perceptions of gender influence children's play. *Early Child Development and Care, 186*(8), 1271–1284. https://doi.org/10.1080/03004430.2015.1089435

Cohen, L. E. (2009). The heteroglossic world of preschoolers' pretend play. *Contemporary Issues in Early Childhood, 10*(4), 331–342. http://dx.doi.org/10.2304/ciec.2009.10.4.331

Creswell, J. W. (2019). *Educational research: Planning, conducting, and evaluating quantitative and qualitative research* (6th ed.). Pearson.

Delaney, K. (2017). Playing at violence: Lock-down drills, 'bad guys' and the construction of 'acceptable' play in early childhood. *Early Child Development and Care, 187*(5–6), 878–895. https://doi.org/10.1080/03004430.2016.1219853

Fray, L., Gore, J., Harris, J., & North, B. (2020). Key influences on aspirations for higher education of Australian school students in regional and remote locations: a scoping review of empirical research, 1991–2016. *The Australian Educational Researcher, 47*, 61–93. doi:10.1007/s13384-019-00332-4

Grieshaber, S., & McArdle, F. (2010). *The trouble with play*. Open University Press.

Harwood, D., & Collier, D. R. (2017). The matter of the stick: Storying/(re)storying children's literacies in the forest. *Journal of Early Childhood Literacy, 17*(3), 336–352. https://doi.org/10.1177/1468798417712340

Haywood-Bird, E. (2017). Playing with power: An outdoor classroom exploration. *Early Child Development and Care, 187*(5–6), 1015–1027. https://doi.org/10.1080/03004430.2016.1223070

Heckman, J. J. (2011). The economics of inequality: The value of early childhood education. *American Educator, 35*(1), 31–35.

Henward, A. S., & MacGillivray, L. (2014). Bricoleurs in preschool: Girls poaching horror media and gendered discourses. *Gender and Education, 26*(7), 726–742. https://doi.org/10.1080/09540253.2014.949634

Hognestad, K., & Bøe, M. (2012). 'Place' as conceptual centre: A methodological focus on the bodily relations, movements and expressions of children up to three years of age in kindergarten. *Reconceptualizing Educational Research Methodology, 3*(2), 43–55. http://journals.hioa.no/index.php/rerm

Huh, Y. J. (2017a). Rethinking young children's digital game play outside of the home as a means of coping with modern life. *Early Child Development and Care, 187*(5–6), 1042-1054. https://doi.org/10.1080/03004430.2016.1237512

Huh, Y. J. (2017b). Uncovering young children's transformative digital game play through the exploration of three-year-old children's cases. *Contemporary Issues in Early Childhood, 18*(2), 179–195. https://doi.org/10.1177/146394911714080

Huuki, T., & Renold, E. (2016). Crush: Mapping historical, material and affective force relations in young children's hetero-sexual playground play. *Discourse: Studies in the Cultural Politics of Education, 37*(5), 754–769. https://doi.org/10.1080/01596306.2015.1075730

Jones, S., Thiel, J. J., Dávila, D., Pittard, E., Woglam, J. F., Zhou, X., Brown, T., & Snow, M. (2016). Childhood geographies and spatial justice: Making sense of place and space-making as political acts in education. *American Educational Research Journal, 53*(4), 1126–1158. https://doi.org/10.3102/0002831216655221

MacNevin, M., & Berman, R. (2017). The Black baby doll doesn't fit the disconnect between early childhood diversity policy, early childhood educator practice, and children's play. *Early Child Development and Care, 187*(5–6), 827–839. https://doi.org/10.1080/03004430.2016.1223065

Madrid, S. (2013). Playing aggression: The social construction of the 'sassy girl' in a peer culture play routine. *Contemporary Issues in Early Childhood, 14*(3), 241–254. http://dx.doi.org/10.2304/ciec.2013.14.3.241

Malone, K. (2016). Theorizing a child–dog encounter in the slums of La Paz using post-humanistic approaches in order to disrupt universalisms in current 'child in nature' debates. *Children's Geographies, 14*(4), 390–407. https://doi.org/10.1080/14733285.2015.1077369

Marsh, J. (2017). The internet of toys: A posthuman and multimodal analysis of connected play. *Teachers College Record, 119*(12), 1–32.

Merewether, J. (2019). New materialisms and children's outdoor environments: Murmurative diffractions. *Children's Geographies, 17*(1), 105–117. https://doi.org/10.1080/14733285.2018.1471449

Mycock, K. (2019). Playing with mud- becoming stuck, becoming free? . . . The negotiation of gendered/class identities when learning outdoors. *Children's Geographies, 17*(4), 454–466. https://doi.org/10.1080/14733285.2018.1546379

Myhre, C. O., Myrvold, H. B., Joramo, U., & Thoresen, M. (2017). Stumbling into the 'kitchen island': Becoming through intra-actions with objects and theories. *Contemporary Issues in Early Childhood, 18*(3), 308–321. https://doi.org/10.1177/1463949117731024

Nicholson, J., Kurnik, J., Jevjovik, M., & Ufoegbune, V. (2015). Deconstructing adults' and children's discourse on children's play: Listening to children's voices to destabilise deficit narratives. *Early Child Development and Care, 185*(10), 1569–1586. https://doi.org/10.1080/03004430.2015.1011149

Nicholson, J., Shimpi, P. M., & Rabin, C. (2014). 'If I am not doing my own playing then I am not able to truly share the gift of play with children': Using poststructuralism and care ethics to examine future early childhood educators' relationships with play in adulthood. *Early Child Development and Care, 184*(8), 1192–1210. https://doi.org/10.1080/03004430.2013.856894

Palaiologou, I. (2017). Assessing children's play: Reality or illusion? The case of early years foundation stage in England. *Early Child Development and Care, 187*(8), 1259–1272. https://doi.org/10.1080/03004430.2017.1295233

Pardhan, A., & Pelletier, J. (2017). Pakistani pre-primary teachers' perceptions and practices related to gender in young children. *International Journal of Early Years Education, 25*(1), 51–71. https://doi.org/10.1080/09669760.2016.1263938

Proctor, L., & Hackett, A. (2017). Playing with place in early childhood: An analysis of dark emotion and materiality in children's play. *Contemporary Issues in Early Childhood, 18*(2), 213–226. http://doi.org/10.1177/1463949117714082

Rautio, P. (2014). Mingling and imitating in producing spaces for knowing and being: Insights from a Finnish study of child–matter intra-action. *Childhood, 21*(4), 461–474. https://doi.org/10.1177/0907568213496653

Rautio, P., & Winston, J. (2015). Things and children in play – improvisation with language and matter. *Discourse: Studies in the Cultural Politics of Education, 36*(1), 15–26. https://doi.org/10.1080/01596306.2013.830806

Sandvik, N. (2012). Rethinking the idea/ideal of pedagogical control: Assemblages of de/stabilisation. *Contemporary Issues in Early Childhood, 13*(3), 200–209. http://dx.doi.org/10.2304/ciec.2012.13.3.200

Shimpi, P., & Nicholson, J. (2014). Using cross-cultural, intergenerational play narratives to explore issues of social justice and equity in discourse on children's play. *Early Child Development and Care, 184*(5), 719–732. https://doi.org/10.1080/03004430.2013.813847

Sinker, R., Phillips, M., & Rijke, V. (2017). Playing in the dark with online games for girls. *Contemporary Issues in Early Childhood, 18*(2), 162–178. https://doi.org/10.1177/1463949117714079

Sisson, J. H., & Kroeger, J. (2017). 'They get enough of play at home': A Bakhtinian interpretation of the dialogic space of public school preschool. *Early Child Development and Care, 187*(5–6), 812–826. https://doi.org/10.1080/03004430.2016.1252533

Somerville, M., & Powell, S. J. (2019). Thinking posthuman with mud: and children of the Anthropocene. *Educational Philosophy and Theory, 51*(8), 829–840. http://doi.org/10.1080/00131857.2018.1516138

Stratigos, T. (2015). Assemblages of desire: Infants, bear caves and belonging in early childhood education and care. *Contemporary Issues in Early Childhood, 16*(1), 42–54. https://doi.org/10.1177/1463949114566757

Taylor, A., Blaise, M. & Giugni, M. (2013). Haraway's 'bag lady story-telling': Relocating childhood and learning within a 'post-human landscape'. *Discourse: Studies in the Cultural Politics of Education, 34*(1), 48–62. https://doi.org/10.1080/01596306.2012.698863

Thomas, L., Warren, E., & DeVries, E. (2011). Play-based learning and intentional teaching in early childhood contexts. *Australasian Journal of Early Childhood, 36*(4), 69–75.

Warin, J., & Adriany, V. (2017). Gender flexible pedagogy in early childhood education. *Journal of Gender Studies, 26*(4), 375–386. http://doi.org/10.1080/09589236.2015.1105738

Watson, K. (2019). 'We are all friends': Disrupting friendship play discourses in inclusive early childhood education. *Contemporary Issues in Early Childhood, 20*(3), 253–264. http://doi.org/10.1177/1463949118772575

Wohlwend, K. (2011). 'Are you guys girls?': Boys, identity texts, and Disney Princess play. *Journal of Early Childhood Literacy, 12*(1), 3–23. https://doi.org/10.1177/1468798411416787

Wohlwend, K. (2017). Monster High as a virtual dollhouse: Tracking play practices across converging transmedia and social media. *Teachers College Record, 119*(11), 1–20.

Wood, E. (2014). Free choice and free play in early childhood education: Troubling the discourse. *International Journal of Early Years Education, 22*(1), 4–18. http://doi.org/10.1080/09669760.2013.830562

CHAPTER 17

Becoming Convivial With Child: Dismantling the Race/Child/Learning/Human Assemblage

Maria Kromidas

"THE TREE IS watching me play! We look at each other! The tree never closes its eye.... I saw that! I will sit beside the tree to watch more!" So pronounces a kindergarten child, engaged in what can be equally described as play and learning (Icsarescu, 2020). Serendipitously, I encountered this tidbit shared by nature-educator Stef Icsarescu soon after I read Natasha Myers's "Are the Trees Watching Us?" "Indeed, they are watching us!" she proclaims, explaining how the Plant Studies Collaboratory's "repatriated ethnobotany" necessarily entails unlearning "colonial common sense" (2020, n.d.). The direct link between Myers's call to decolonize our current episteme and Indigenous knowledge systems, both within and outside of academia, is clear. Just as interesting yet largely concealed is the deep resonance of the child's pronouncement with Indigenous pedagogies centering land. The child has discovered, and articulates in their own way, the already existing relation between tree and self in an affectively loaded act of learning that one engages *with* human and nonhuman others that represents a radically different—both loving and caring—way of being and relating in the world that transforms both self and world. The child is "becoming-with" trees (Haraway, 2008). That my linkage of these ways of knowing, being, and becoming-with might be perceived as dismissive to Indigenous knowledge systems only underlines how children's contributions to knowledge and ethical life have been dismissed in our current order. In our Western hierarchical system of knowledge that privileges rational, cognitive, value-free, objective, and distanced ways of knowing, children's knowledge and knowing are positioned as lower, automatic, instinctual. Learning (or its parallel in development) is, in fact, presumed to be the process that connects child to adult as fully realized human.

This chapter demonstrates how this race/child/learning/human assemblage is a key aspect of the modern episteme where race functions as the master signifier designating human and not-fully-human, one that institutes the individualized hierarchical subject of the capitalist totality. I argue that dismantling this assemblage is a necessary task to challenge injustice by rethinking justice itself in more liberatory ways through children's contributions. Drawing on developments in various disciplinary and interdisciplinary fields (anthropology, childhood studies, Black studies, Indigenous studies, posthuman, and reconceptualist educational studies), I explore how critiques and rearticulations of race, child, learning, and human explicitly and implicitly redefine the other terms within this knot. For instance, the Black studies critique of race entails new possibilities for narrating the human and, hence, as the antipode to the human, the child. Integrating these insights entails an epistemic break that allows us to retrieve children's radical subjectivities and perspectives in liberatory projects of being and becoming human. I propose centering learning as one productive path of such projects. I propose a formulation of learning as a continual process of being and becoming-convivial-with-the child, a political more than pedagogical formulation that incorporates children into the rewriting, reimagining, and enacting of justice and the good life in ways heretofore unseen.

Black Studies: From Race to Human to Child

The material and existential planetary crises of continuing war, state, and extrajudicial murder of Black and Brown people, mounting inequalities, rise of fascisms, and impending environmental destruction have spurred scholarly developments across various fields that call for radical reorganization of knowledge and ways of knowing that can help bring about new ways of being and relating amongst humans. This scholarship has focused increasing critique on the reigning conception of the Human—the rational, autonomous individual, known in various circles as *Homo economicus*, the Western conception of the person, the liberal humanist subject or, simply, Man. While Foucault's (2008) critique of the liberal humanist subject as *Homo economicus* is perhaps the most well known, Black Studies scholars demonstrate how Foucault and other critical posthuman theorists unwittingly reproduce it by failing to contend with the racial hierarchy that lies at the heart of the human (Jackson, 2015; King, 2017; Weheliye, 2014).

Through their critique of the organizing principles that produce the empirical and existential conditions of being Black in an anti-Black world, Black studies scholars have targeted the white supremacist, settler-colonial, bourgeois origins of this conception of the Human. Sylvia Wynter's work is exceptional in showing how the figure of

"Man-overrepresented-as-human" constructs particular types of subjects that are key to reproducing the hierarchical order. Wynter demonstrates how race as a "purely biocentric grouping and ranking of humanity" is the "status organizing principle" of the global Western order, a "fictional symbolic code of 'White supremacy/perfection/normalcy' versus 'non white' and, most totally, 'Black inferiority/imperfection/deviance'" that enshrines whiteness as fully-human (Wynter, as cited in Ambroise, 2020, pp. 2–4). Every genre of human contains a defining feature or "descriptive statement," a principle governing causality that encodes subjects—telling them who they are and who they should aspire to be (Wynter, 2003, p. 318; 2006, pp. 162, 164n3; 2015, pp. 199–200). Wynter identified biocentrism as the key descriptive statement of Man, whereby the question of who is fully human and who is less than fully human are defined by biology (Eudell, 2015, pp. 33, 45).[1] With biology as the defining feature of Man's species being, the small slice of the global population that are the selected or the normative and are justified as being the winners of the Spencerian survival of the fittest because of their purported natural talents, abilities, and intelligence.

Black studies' critique of the Human as defined by a biocentric order of knowledge has clear intersections with childhood studies' project of reconceiving the child. Childhood studies scholars have convincingly demonstrated how the child as representative of nature and less-than-fully human that is dominant today was foundational to the origins of modern childhood studies in Darwinian theory (Burman, 2017; Cannella & Viruru, 2004, p. 90). Although less-than-human, the normative, that is, to say White child, was the only one expected to reach the heights of full humanhood (Bernstein, 2011; Butler, 2018; Nxumalo & Cedillo, 2017; Pacini-Ketchabaw et al., 2011; Rollo, 2018). The developing child (figured as incrementally progressing in identifiable stages along a unilinear path toward adulthood) continues to reign in fields with regulatory effects on children's lives—education, medicine, psychology (Burman, 2017; Pacini-Ketchabaw, Kummen & Thompson, 2010).

The child's positioning as the very antithesis of the human, however obfuscated by protectionism and fetishization, instantiates a profound misopedy that naturalizes, reproduces, and legitimizes the irreducible power relations between child and adult (Rollo, 2018). As I have argued elsewhere (Kromidas, 2014, 2016, 2019a, 2019b), a critical genealogy of the way the child has been interwoven with the ontologies of race and the human in the projects of modernity is a necessary task in achieving justice for those cast outside the boundaries of the human. Refusing Man that subjects, rules, and disassembles humans is refusing the hierarchy of humanness that is its edifice, a hierarchy in which the White Western liberal bourgeois subject is universal, pinnacle, and the normative figure against which all others are measured and found to lack or be in excess. The child as less-than-fully-human was integral to the biocentric conception of the human as well as the hardening and biologizing of race in the 19th century. The conjoined origin stories of child, race, and human in a biocentric knot underlines the first premises of childhood studies—the construction of the child is profoundly unjust that produces anti-childism as a taken-for-granted feature of the world, it is a tool of an order of whose knowledge productions' singular goal has been the domination and subordination of those cast out of its narrow definition of human.

The critique from Black studies underlines the fact that while all children are situated outside the boundaries of the fully-human, the construct of the child is particularly devastating for non-White and non-middle-class children (Bernstein, 2011; Evans-Winters & Girls for Gender Equity, 2017; Hill, 2018; Owens, Callier, Robinson & Garner, 2017; Winn, 2011). The characteristics that are thought to define the child (e.g., innocence, sensitivity) are not extended to Black and Brown children in a way that routinely denies them justice (Meiners, 2016; Sharpe, 2014; Silver, 2020). Rather than trying to include excluded children into this fold, critical childhood scholars explore how children are never innocent but imbricated in the categorical imperatives of the settler-colonial racial capitalist structure to see, experience, identify with, relate to, and justify the hierarchies of human (Burman, 2017; Kromidas 2016, 2020).

Refusing the normative white child also opens up a space for voices that were refused in order to craft new constructs of both child and adult. It recuperates Black, Brown, and non-Western children and childhoods outside the lack, outside the pathologizing when measured against the white Western middle-class child. This makes visible instead how institutions and their categories, standards, norms, and references pathologize Black and Brown children and childhoods. As Ruth Nicole Brown (2013) writes of the emergent field of Black girlhood studies, "affirm[ing] Black girls and those who love them can make possible new questions, offer alternative explanations, and provide usable knowledge that improves upon Black girls' freedom and the greater emancipatory possibility their lives hold for us all" (p. 229). That is, Black studies implicitly urge the questions: What can we learn about being human from Black and Brown children? How might we bring about a more just convivial order by becoming-with them?

The repercussions of Black Studies call to overturn the order of knowledge for conceptualizing childhood and learning are perhaps best illuminated when counterposed to Black Studies' emancipatory figuration of the human that is yet to come. Black scholars and activists have articulated the most capacious and urgent calls for reimagining the human (Ambroise, 2020). By blasting through the universalist figure of the human through its constitutive anti-humanness, "different modalities of the human come to light," those ways of being that are imagined and lived by subjects outside its domain (Weheliye, 2014, p. 8). Wynter referred to this figure as *Homo narrans*, where we recognize our origins and continual becoming through storytelling and symbols (narrans) and our kinness with humanity, whereby being human is always unfinished praxis. Freeing ourselves from biocentric modes of knowledge production to enact a "new mode of experiencing ourselves in which every mode of being human, every form of life that has ever been ever enacted, is a part of us. We, a part of them" involves committing heresy (Wynter in Scott 2000, p. 197; Wynter 2015). The heretic leaps to imagine the "relational ontological totality of the human," as "interconnected existences that are in constant motion" (Weheliye, 2014, p.5, p.13) necessarily entail *learning*, conceptualized as a becoming-with-the-Other. It is not only the most productive, but the most *just* way to begin to "think of being human anew" with those that have been "cast out as impoverished and colonized and undesirable and lacking reason" (McKittrick, 2015, p. 3). In fact, it is those very qualities by which those that have been cast that we can begin to recuperate a humanism worth its name.

The new figure of the child, freed from its mooring in biology and its slow and steady progress toward Man, has enormous implications for reconceptualizing learning as a continually unfinished process extending into adulthood. Indeed, Wynter puts the onus on the "Western educated" elites—it is they that need to be "radically re-educated" (Gagne, 2007, p. 258). For autopoiesis and sociogenesis (a perpetual becoming human) are processes that characterize childhood but are not confined to this stage. Through their critique of how the universalized figure of Man masquerading as human oppresses Black girls in public spaces, Black girlhood studies have opened up a space to rethink children and childhood and their innovative forms of knowledge in a way that allows actual children, "if we listened, to change the world" (Owens et al., 2017, p. 117). The project of the human yet to come must unlearn hierarchization by which it was formed, and realize itself in relation, a pedagogical and political project of becoming-convivial with the child. Black studies is an indispensable resource to disassemble the tragic race/child/human knot and center learning as becoming-convivial with the child in a way that takes accounts of the force of history and power, and the open-ended possibilities for just futures.

Indigenous Studies: From Human to Learning to Child

Much like Black studies, Indigenous studies contend with the foundational dehumanizing force of the liberal humanist subject and has much to offer a project of centering learning as becoming-convivial-with-the-child. Indigenous studies and Red pedagogies have made the link most explicitly between learning and bringing into being forms of life.[2] Sandy Grande's (2015) *Red Pedagogy* targets settler colonial ways of knowing, systematized and disseminated in institutional schooling, as eroding "relations of mutuality" where life takes priority (p. xvii). Schooling is the primary site for the reproduction of settler colonial logics and "modern consciousness" not through explicit curriculum but by "habituating" children to "specific forms of social organization and behavioral patterns:" independence, achievement, humanism, detachment from sources of local and personal knowledge and detachment from nature (Grande, 2015, pp. 100–101). Grande (2015) acknowledges the near universality of shaping children's "biology and consciousness" but argues that modern societies do so in ways that are "profoundly destructive and unsustainable" (p. 100). The hierarchies and erasures of settler colonialism are so deeply embedded in our epistemic system that they also lurk within critical theories and pedagogies. Indigenous demands for sovereignty cannot easily be collapsed in Marxian terms in which "the end game remains human liberation: a profoundly anthropocentric notion, rooted in a humanist tradition that presumes the superiority of human beings over the rest of nature" (Grande, 2015, p. 31). While Grande's intervention is rooted in the specific experiences of Indigenous students who have been seen through schools' prism of the so-called Indian problem, demands for Indigenous sovereignty and decolonization function as a crucial resource in reconceptualizing child, adult, and their relations for affirming a radically reconceived relationality.

The radical possibilities entailed by Indigenous demands for sovereignty for reconceiving both child and adult are most poetically illustrated by Leanne Betasamosake Simpson's recounting of a traditional Nishnaabeg story of a young girl, Kwezens, who discovers maple syrup after observing and imitating a squirrel, who then shares her knowledge with her family and community. The story frames Simpson's (2014, p. 6) critique of institutionalized schooling:

> No one ever asked me what I was interested in nor did they ask for my consent to participate in their system. My experience of education was one of continually being measured against a set of principles that required surrender to an assimilative colonial agenda in order to fulfill those principles.

Both story and critique serve as a prolegomena to articulating the fundamental principles of Indigenous "land as pedagogy" that center the conditions rather than the content of learning. Kwezens's discovery certainly represents a learner-led self-actualization, the validity of her lived experience, and meaning-making, yet all these aspects are ultimately tied to the well-being of the collectivity. Simpson takes care to warn her audience of the ever-present danger of recasting freedom and autonomy within settler-colonial logics. It is decidedly not the rugged child-learner coming to know a set curriculum through exploration as an individual intellectual pursuit represented by some progressive pedagogies like Montessori and Waldorf schools. The radical nature of the story of Kwezens and Simpson's articulation of "land as pedagogy" is its "reproduction of a loving web of Nishnaabeg networks." As Simpson underlines the fundamental principles for enacting this system—the child as a valued part of the community—a different conception of the child and adult emerges. This child is not coerced into learning, this child has a path into the community, and their individual contributions enrich the larger whole. Simpson (2014) offers us a different term to replace learning—a "coming into wisdom"—a process that "generates generations of living, creative, innovative, self-determining, inter-dependent and self-regulating community minded individuals" (p. 7).

Although calls to "decolonize" education have been routinized and mainstreamed (Tuck & Yang, 2012), the radical demands of centering loving relations with humans and more-than-human others while keeping coloniality in view have inspired scholars decolonizing environmental and place-based education. Scholars working in the

Common Worlds Research Collective have demonstrated the foundational settler colonial and anti-Blackness in environmental and place-based discourses that ignore children's real attachments to place and littered with liberal humanist assumptions of human/nonhuman and nature/culture divides and children's innocence (Nxumalo, 2020; Nxumalo & Cedillo, 2017; Pacini-Ketchabaw & Nxumalo, 2016). In "pedagogista" mode (a model of teacher educator as mentor adopted from Reggio Emilia preschools), they have worked in collaboration with children, childhood educators, and Indigenous organizations in projects that allow children to explore and deepen their relations with more-than-human Others—both living (deer, ants, worms, walking sticks, raccoons) to nonliving (water, clay, rocks, everyday classroom objects; Nxumalo, 2020; Nxumalo & Pacini-Ketchabaw, 2017; Pacini-Ketchabaw & Clark, 2016; Pacini-Ketchabaw & Nxumalo, 2016; Taylor & Pacini-Ketchabaw, 2015, 2019). By nurturing children's loving relations with land, these interventions help bring forth values that "seek and sustain life" (Cajete in Grande, 2014, p. 122), that teach us to be "real human beings" (Jacob, 2018). These different ways of knowing the world entail relations of learning, where desire, joy, and consent are integral aspects of it.

Learning as "radical relationality and reciprocity" entails "onto-epistemological shifts" (Nxumalo, 2020, p. 35). It is no coincidence that many working within CRWC have come to reciprocal relationality through a critique of the developing child that dominates in the educational field. They affirm that the current epistemic system continually repudiates children's embodied and affective ways of knowing and that these are necessary contributions to confront our current planetary crises. While not meant to collapse the incommensurability of Indigenous critiques of the various ways settler colonialism manifests itself in our world to erase Indigenous life (Tuck & Yang, 2012), it forms an important conceptual resource for rethinking and remaking humanness if Indigenous life and knowledge are kept in the center. It opens up a view of human becoming as a convivial entanglement with human and more-than-human beings, a continual pedagogical project that necessarily includes children.

Posthuman Transformations Challenge to the Dominant Order: From Human to Child to Learning

Western modernity's human as the sovereign autonomous (white, male able-bodied adult) figure standing outside and above nature has been critiqued under the banner of posthumanism (Banerji & Paranjape, 2016; Barad, 2007; Braidiotii, 2008; Wolfe, 2010). The posthuman critique targets the mode of knowing consecrated by humanism—a rational, detached, and cognitive process that disavows embodied, affective, intuitive, contextual modes of knowledge creation (Kromidas, 2014). Furthermore, posthumanists argue that defining the human through specific qualities or an "essence," invariably draws boundaries around this figure that polices and excludes Others (Anderson, 2007).

Defining the human instead as a continually shifting and ambiguous figure directs us to the remainders of the human (those who have been heretofore excluded) and how we can become-human in relation with them. That is, it is by incorporating precisely those qualities that have cast specific categories of people outside of the human that can help us reimagine more liberatory ways of enacting justice and being human itself. In the case of children and childhood, how might their fantastical, playful, anarchic, and embodied ways of knowing shift our frames on justice? While such unique qualities of children have long been recognized by observers and educators of children, in this section, I focus on work that suggests, implicitly or explicitly that those very qualities that make children, children, those whom adults have disavowed, have the potential to bring about more liberatory ways of being human.

Anthropology has taken up the posthuman through the concept of sociality, most concisely "the dynamic matrix of human relations" in a way that helps topple and dethrone the reigning figure of the human yet retain what is most distinctive about being human (Long & Moore, 2012, p. 43). These and related conversations have implications for rethinking childhood and learning in ways that emphasize continual becoming for a more just world. Long and Moore (2012) define sociality as "a dynamic relational matrix that constitutes the life of persons," at the center of being human for "human subjects are constantly interacting in ways that are co-productive, continually plastic and malleable, and through which they *come to know the world* they live in and find their purpose and meaning within it" (2012, p. 41, emphasis added). Because relational matrices are always "shot through with inequalities of resources and capacities, and with theories and ideas about those differentials," ontological questions are "irreducibly ethico-political" (Long & Moore, 2012, p. 43). Sociality collapses the dualisms that define how we think about life and the human subject—nature/culture, individual/society, humans/the world, information/material, continuity/change—and, in doing so, operationalize an ethico-political stance. For underlying the notion of "radical relationality" is the requirement of entering into "relations with multiple others . . . 'the minoritarian,' the 'other-than,' women, gays, ethnic and racialized others, the natural, animal and environmental others—all that has been excluded from the rational, humanist subject" (Moore, 2012, p. 51).

Christina Toren's contributions to sociality emerge through her career-long engagement with children and childhood. In her "unified theory of mind," she argues that no aspect of human development can be seen as outside of sociality. It is a radically different conception of development than offered by psychology, for it elevates intersubjectivity as "the context and fundamental condition" for human being and becoming, the fundamental form of sociality for human beings, "newborn babies and geriatric patients included" (Toren, 2012, p. 64). Sociality itself is not uniquely human—animals have this fundamental autopoietic condition of transformation of their life cycles but rather the specific form of sociality in intersubjectivity, unfolding in specific time and place, and so fully social and historical (Toren, 2012, p. 68). This figuration of anthropos bring children into the folds not by making them commensurable but by allowing children to orient us toward open-ended possibilities with social transformation. Toren (2012) argues that children, because of their unique social positioning and biological fact of having spent fewer years alive, are potentially *more* likely to effect change through their learning in the world: "The processes of mind are subject to change and continuity, but as we grow older they become progressively less subject to *radical* change precisely because they are already highly developed" (p. 29, emphasis in the original).

Sociality centers dynamic social process of continually becoming as the constitutive feature of all humans. So long have children been defined and maligned for their becoming that childhood scholars have repudiated this particular quality to the point of recapitulating an over-agentic beingness "often reappearing as the solution to the problem it poses" (Spryrou et al., 2018, p. 1). Admittedly, development's perpetual becoming child is unilinear, with the known endpoint of complete adult adapted to an already existing world. Sociality refigures this perpetual becoming: without a known end point, unpredictable, open to various potentialities, unruly. Moving children from margins to the center of being human, such critiques ask adults to take seriously children's defamiliarizations of accepted meanings and relations that uphold the current order. It is a call to recognize that culture is never replicated in transmission, and children's unique, fantastical, playful, and critical perspectives are necessary to enact convivial relations with living and nonliving beings.

Within the field of education, scholars have explicitly or implicitly been inspired by centering relations with children and opened up vistas to reimaging being human and learning as becoming-with children. What unites these scholars are their insistence that children's knowledge and meaning-making are not only unique and worthy of being heard but that learning and subjectivity are "relational fields" that transform adults and children (Olsson, 2009, p. 20). Emerging from their critiques of the developing child that inaugurates the "pedagogic epic" in which teachers measure, catalogue and oversee children's becoming into adult rationality (Steedman, 1995; see also Baker, 1999; Burman, 2017, p. 16; Farley & Garlen, 2016), these scholars demonstrate how neoliberal subjects are created within the everyday practices we have come to associate with industrial schooling (De Lissovoy, 2015; Moss, 2013; Olsson, 2012). Inspired by posthuman and postmodern approaches, reconceptualist educational theorists have refused narratives of despair within the neoliberal educational assemblage to allow children space to move, create, play, make art, and philosophical pronouncements that challenge established ways of knowing (see Davies, 2014; Moss, 2014, 2018; Olsson, 2009, 2012, 2013).

Rather than presuming to know what learning is, reconceptualist education scholars follow children's lead to underline the embodied and affect-laden qualities that children bring to knowledge-making, processes that are unique and have revolutionary potential vis-à-vis dismantling and rewriting the dominant order of knowledge. Olsson's experiments-qua-pedagogical projects with children go so far as to challenge meaning-making as the central goal of learning, to put forth "intensity, movement, energy" (Dahlberg

& Moss, 2009, p. xxii). Karen Murris (2017) writes that a posthuman education for "doing subjectivity differently" requires ontological shifts so that both teachers and students dissolve in the encounter of "educational intra-relationality." Murris (2020) deconstructs child and human by showing what they share: "Individuals human and nonhuman bodies (of whatever age) materialize and come into being through relationships; and so does meaning" (p. 18). Yet adults must be open to how children differ in ways that overturn the valuation of children and their modes of knowledge. It is precisely those qualities—"children's embodied ways of knowing," "their playfulness and use of fantasy and imagination" in which the human as currently narrated is impoverished, a factor that inhibits becoming-convivial (Murris, 2013, p. 254).

Indeed, Murris (2013) insists that learning "with children could possibly be a life changing transformation for the adults involved" that requires epistemic as well as ethico-political leaps (p. 248). Analyzing a classroom video in which a teacher utilizes the philosophy-for-children approach (Daniel & Auriac 2011; Lipman, 1982), Murris shows how the children, in dialogue with their teacher and each other, "crack open" even our most cherished concepts like peace, life, and death and put forth heretofore unimagined utopias.[3] She admits that sharing this video with teacher-educators that are respectful of children's unique contributions still provokes laughter, a kind of sentimental endearment to their "child-ishness" that not only is condescending but also prevents adults from truly allowing children to turn our vision of the world upside-down (Murris, 2013). For children's thinking is dangerous to the current order, and allowing ourselves to becoming-with them entails ceding adult authority and control over children's lives.

Becoming-Convivial-with-Child

The current planetary crises in which we find ourselves have much to do with how we understand ourselves as a species, the stories we tell ourselves about ourselves. Children as the antithesis of the fully human is one of the foundations of the modern episteme, infecting the knotted conceptions of race, how we become human through learning, and forms the basis of children's continued marginalization and oppression. The child is a powerful site of affective politics that forms adults as subjects. The conceptual resources summarized in this chapter underline the liberatory potential of including children's ways of knowing, being, and relating in the world into our quest to remake a just world where life can flourish.

When considering the heretical epistemic leaps that are necessary for including children in the project of rewriting knowledge to transform the world, I am reminded of Leonard McCombe's (1948) photograph of a group of Navajo children in various stages of what appears to be a sneeze. A White headmistress crouches, sternly inspecting and disapproving one child's sneeze. The photograph was included in an old anthropology textbook (Hoebel, 1959) and captioned "The transmission of culture and the standardization of behavior. Navahos learning to use handkerchief," as the visual prototype for culture-ing, the act of taming nature, in the chapter "The Nature of Culture". The insights of postcolonial criticism have taught us to recognize seemingly benign acts of "culture" as violent impositions. But the violence that should be evoked by the subjects' colonial status as Native is veiled by the subjects' second, less apparent quasi-colonial status as children. "Cultural imperialism" and "cultural domination" seem excessive when children are the objects of the forceful imposition of arbitrary knowledge, because knowledge is imposed on a supposed blank slate that has no value, "nature." The biocentric child as ground zero, the antithesis of the fully formed adult human daily obfuscates the epistemic violence enacted against children.

Dismantling the race/child/human/learning assemblage opens up cracks for children to defamiliarize the most taken-for-granted injustices of the world. As the collective uprisings against police violence against Black people in the last year have shown, justice—as narrated—is inadequate (Brand, 2017). The voices and stories of Black Lives Matter and #SayHerName movements challenge us to rethink and go beyond established notions of justice, by listening and centering the stories of those affected by police brutality (Panaram, 2020). In parallel fashion, children's daily cries of "It's not fair!" have the potential to reformulate the justice of a profoundly unjust order. Yet adults respond to children with platitudes that naturalize the dehumanizing brutalities of business as usual: "That's the way the world works"; "You will understand when you are older"; "It's better you learn this now." If adults succumb to the incessant demands of children to be heard and their incessant demands for a different way to live, adults can then admit to the child within themselves, not just those whimsical qualities of play, humor, and surreal imagination but also the "unbearable (terror, agony, and impossible loss)" (Gailbraith, 2001, p. 194) as well as the righteous anger and fury of children like Toni Cade Bambara's (1972) narrator Hazel, who burns down a movie theater in an act of restorative justice (Kromidas, 2019b). It is only in the ember of the ashes of the world as we know it can the political project of learning as knowledge-making, as becoming-convivial-with-children for liberation, be born.

Notes

1. Wynter outlines how the biocentric principle of Man crystallized by Darwinian science in the 19th century replaced secular rationality that defined post–Renaissance Man. She argues that this shift was decisive for inaugurating racial difference to function as the principal organizer of the human (Wynter, 1984; 2003, pp. 309–311; 2015, pp. 187–189).
2. Much like Black studies, Indigenous studies must contend with the foundational dehumanization of the liberal humanist subject. While the demands of each project (abolition and decolonization) are varied and cannot be collapsed into one another, important parallels exist. As King (2019) writes, both "Black abolition and Native decolonization as projects frustrate liberal (and other) modes of humanism offer new forms of sociality and futurity" (p. xii).

3. While I highlight the potential liberatory qualities of children's play, imagined utopias, and dialogues, this does not negate the always lurking possibility of reifying structured inequalities of race, gender, sexuality, class, and even anthropocentrism. Yet I maintain that the world-making possibilities inherent in play depend on riskiness and danger, outweigh those risks. I thank Tim Kinard for bringing this to my attention.

References

Ambroise, J. (2020). "LET US BREATHE!" Notes on the re-examination, the reckoning and the rewriting of knowledge. In A. F. Ball, H. Sewer, & K. T. McNair (Eds.), *The 2020 project* (pp. 17–21). African and African American Studies.

Anderson, K. (2007). *Race and the crisis of humanism*. Routledge.

Bambara, T. C. (1972). Gorilla, my love. In *Gorilla, my love* (pp. 11–20). Vintage Books.

Banerji, D., & Paranjape, M. R. (Eds.). (2016). *Critical posthumanism and planetary futures*. Springer.

Barad, K. (2007). *Meeting the universe halfway: Quantum physics and the entanglement of matter and meaning*. Duke University Press.

Baker, B. (1999). The dangerous and the good? Developmentalism, progress, and public schooling. *American Educational Research Journal*, 36(4), 797–834.

Bernstein, R. (2011). *Racial innocence: Performing American childhood and race from slavery to civil rights*. New York University Press.

Braidotti, R. (2013). *The posthuman*. Polity Press.

Brand, D. (2017, April 20). *Writing against tyranny and towards liberation* [Paper presentation]. The Barnard Center for Research on Women, New York, NY, United States.

Brown, R. N. (2013). *Hear our truths: The creative potential of Black girlhood*. University of Illinois Press.

Burman, E. (2017). *Deconstructing developmental psychology* (3rd ed.). Routledge.

Butler, T. T. (2018). Black girl cartography: Black girlhood and place-making in education research. *Review of Research in Education*, 42(1), 28–45.

Cannella, G. S., & Viruru, R. (2004). *Childhood and postcolonization: Power, education, and contemporary practice*. RoutledgeFalmer.

Dahlberg, G. & Moss, P. (2009) Foreword. In L.M. Olsson. *Movement and experimentation in young children's learning: Deleuze and Guattari in early childhood education*, (pp. xiii-xxviii). Routledge.

Daniel, M., & Auriac, E. (2011). Philosophy, critical thinking and philosophy for children. *Educational Philosophy and Theory*, 43(5), 415–435.

Davies, B. (2014). *Listening to children: Being and becoming*. Routledge.

De Lissovoy, N. (2015). *Education and emancipation in the neoliberal era: Being, teaching, and power*. Palgrave MacMillan.

Eudell, D. L. (2015). 'Come on kid, let's go get the thing!' The sociogenic principle and the being of being Black/human. In J. R. Ambroise & S. Broeck (Eds.), *Black knowledges/Black struggles: Essays in critical epistemology* (pp. 21–43). Liverpool University Press.

Evans-Winters, V. E., & Girls for Gender Equity. (2017). Flipping the script: The dangerous bodies of girls of color. *Cultural Studies↔Critical Methodologies*, 17(5), 415–423.

Farley, L., & Garlen, J. C. (2016). The child in question: Childhood texts, cultures, and curricula. *Curriculum Inquiry*, 46(3), 221–229.

Foucault, M. (2008). *The birth of biopolitics: Lectures at the Collège de France, 1978–79*. Palgrave Macmillan.

Gagne, K. M. (2007). On the obsolescence of the disciplines: Frantz Fanon and Sylvia Wynter propose a new mode of being human. *Human Architecture: Journal of the Sociology of Self-Knowledge, 5*, 251–263.

Galbraith, M. (2001). Hear my cry: A manifesto for an emancipatory childhood studies approach to children's literature. *The Lion and the Unicorn, 25*(2), 187–205.

Grande, S. (2015). *Red pedagogy: Native American social and political thought*. Rowman & Littlefield.

Haraway, D. (2008). *When species meet*. University of Minnesota Press.

Hill, D. (2018). Black girl pedagogies: Layered lessons on reliability. *Curriculum Inquiry, 48*(3), 383-405.

Hoebel, E. A. (1958). *Man in the primitive world: An introduction to social anthropology*. McGraw Hill.

Icsarescu, S. [@Ics_Stef] (2020, September 26). Child's voice: The tree is watching me play! [Tweet]. https://twitter.com/Ics_Stef/status/1309910685271420934?s=20

Jackson, Z. (2013). Animal: New directions in the theorization of race and posthumanism. *Feminist Studies, 39*(1), 669–685.

Jacob, M. M. (2018). Indigenous studies speaks to American sociology: The need for individual and social transformations of Indigenous education in the USA. *Social Sciences, 7*(1), 1–10.

King, T. L. (2019). *The Black shoals: Offshore formations of Black and Native studies*. Duke University Press.

Kromidas, M. (2014). The "savage" child and the nature of race: Posthuman interventions from New York City. *Anthropological Theory, 14*(4), 422–441.

Kromidas, M. (2016). *City kids: Transforming racial baggage*. Rutgers University Press.

Kromidas, M. (2019a). Toward the human, after the child of Man: Seeing the child differently in teacher education. *Curriculum Inquiry, 49*(1), 65–89.

Kromidas, M. (2019b). "Agent of revolutionary thought:" Bambara and Black girlhood for a poetics of being and becoming human. *Jeunesse: Young People, Texts, Cultures, 11*(1), 19–37.

Kromidas, M. (2020). Learning hierarchy and displacing conviviality: time and subjectivity in the neoliberal kindergarten. *Pedagogy, Culture & Society*. Advanced online publication. https://doi.org/10.1080/14681336.2020.1817972

Lipman, M. (1982). Philosophy for children. *Thinking: The Journal of Philosophy for Children 3*(3/4), 35–44.

Long, N. J., & Moore, H. L. (2012). Sociality revisited: setting a new agenda. *The Cambridge Journal of Anthropology, 30*(1), 40–47.

McCombe, L. (1948). *Navajo schoolchildren get a lesson in nose blowing from their white teacher*. The LIFE Images Collection. https://www.icp.org/browse/archive/objects/navajo-schoolchildren-get-a-lesson-in-nose-blowing-from-a-white-teacher

McKittrick, K. (2015). Yours in the intellectual struggle: Sylvia Wynter and the realization of the living. In K. McKittrick (Ed.), *Sylvia Wynter: On being human as praxis* (pp. 1–8). Duke University Press.

Meiners, E. R. (2016). *For the children? Protecting innocence in a carceral state*. University of Minnesota Press.

Moore, H. L. (2012). Avatars and robots: The imaginary present and the socialities of the inorganic. *The Cambridge Journal of Anthropology, 30*(1), 48–63.

Moss, P. (2013). The relationship between early childhood and compulsory education: A properly political question. In P. Moss (Ed.), *Early childhood and compulsory education: Reconceptualising the relationship* (pp. 2–49). Routledge.

Moss, P. (2018). *Alternative narratives in early childhood: An introduction for students and practitioners*. Routledge.

Murris, K. (2013). The epistemic challenge of hearing child's voice. *Studies in Philosophy and Education, 32*(3), 245–259.

Murris, K. (2017). Reconfiguring educational relationality in education: the educator as pregnant stingray. *Journal of Education (University of KwaZulu-Natal), 69*, 117–138.

Murris K. (2020) Posthuman child and the diffractive teacher: Decolonizing the nature/culture binary. In: A. Cutter-Mackenzie-Knowles, K. Malone, & E. Barratt Hacking(Eds.) *Research handbook on childhoodnature* (pp. 1-25). Springer.

Myers, N. (2020, Autumn). Are the trees watching us? *Spike Art Magazine, 65*. https://www.spikeartmagazine.com/articles/qa-natasha-myers

Myers. N. (n.d.). Research. https://natashamyers.wordpress.com/

Nxumalo, F. (2020). Place-based disruptions of humanism, coloniality and anti-Blackness in early childhood education. *Critical Studies in Teaching and Learning (CriSTaL), 8*, 34–49.

Nxumalo, F., & Cedillo, S. (2017). Decolonizing place in early childhood studies: Thinking with Indigenous onto-epistemologies and Black feminist geographies. *Global Studies of Childhood, 7*(2), 99–112.

Nxumalo, F., & Pacini-Ketchabaw, V. (2017). "Staying with the trouble": In child-insect-educator common worlds. *Environmental Education Research, 23*(10), 1414–1426.

Olsson, L. M. (2009). *Movement and experimentation in young children's learning: Deleuze and Guattari in early childhood education*. Routledge.

Olsson, L. M. (2012). Eventicizing curriculum: Learning to read and write through becoming a citizen of the world. *Journal of Curriculum Theorizing, 28*(1), 88–107.

Olsson, L. M. (2013). Taking children's questions seriously: The need for creative thought. *Global Studies of Childhood, 3*(3), 230–253.

Owens, T. C., Callier, D. M., Robinson, J. L., & Garner, P. R. (2017). Towards an interdisciplinary field of Black girlhood studies. *Departures in Critical Qualitative Research, 6*(3), 116–132.

Pacini-Ketchabaw, V., Kummen, K., & Thompson, D. (2010). Becoming intimate with developmental knowledge: Pedagogical explorations with collective biography. *Alberta Journal of Educational Research, 56*(3), 335–354.

Pacini-Ketchabaw, V., Nxumalo, F., & Rowan, C. (2011). Nomadic research practices in early childhood education: Interrupting racisms and colonialisms. *Reconceptualizing Educational Research Methodology, 1*(1), 19–33.

Pacini-Ketchabaw, V., & Clark, V. (2016). Following watery relations in early childhood pedagogies. *Journal of Early Childhood Research, 14*(1), 98–111.

Pacini-Ketchabaw, V., & Nxumalo, F. (2016). Unruly raccoons and troubled educators: Nature/culture divides in a childcare centre. *Environmental Humanities, 7*(1), 151–168.

Panaram, S.A. (2020). #SayHerName: Seeking justice for Breonna Taylor. *Black Perspectives*. https://www.aaihs.org/sayhername-seeking-justice-for-breonna-taylor/

Rollo, T. (2018). The color of childhood: The role of the child/human binary in the production of anti-Black racism. *Journal of Black Studies, 49*(4), 307–329.

Scott, D. (2000). The re-enchantment of humanism: An interview with Sylvia Wynter. *Small Axe, 8*, 119–207.

Sharpe, C. (2014). Black studies: In the wake. *The Black Scholar: Journal of Black Studies and Research, 44*(2), 59–69.

Silver, L. J. (2020). Transformative childhood studies–a remix in inquiry, justice, and love. *Children's Geographies, 18*(2), 176–190.

Simpson, L. B. (2014). Land as pedagogy: Nishnaabeg intelligence and rebellious transformation. *Decolonization: Indigeneity, Education & Society, 3*(3), 1-25.

Spyrou, S., Rosen, R., & Cook, D. T. (2018). Introduction: Reimagining childhood studies: Connectivities... relationalities... linkage... In S. Spyrou, R. L. Rosen, & D. T. Cook (Eds.), *Reimagining childhood studies* (pp. 1–20). Bloomsbury Publishing.

Steedman, C. (1995). *Strange dislocations: Childhood and the idea of human interiority 1780-1930.* Harvard University Press.

Taylor, A., & Pacini-Ketchabaw, V. (2015). Learning with children, ants, and worms in the Anthropocene: Towards a common world pedagogy of multispecies vulnerability. *Pedagogy, Culture & Society, 23*(4), 507–529.

Toren, C. (2012). Anthropology and psychology. In R. Faldon & O. Harris (Eds.), *The SAGE handbook of social anthropology* (pp. 27–41). Sage Publications.

Tuck, E., & Yang, K. W. (2012). Decolonization is not a metaphor. *Decolonization: Indigeneity, Education & Society, 1*(1), 1–40.

Weheliye, A. G. (2014). *Habeas viscus: Racializing assemblages, biopolitics, and Black feminist theories of the human.* Duke University Press.

Winn, M. T. (2019). *Girl time: Literacy, justice, and the school-to-prison pipeline.* Teachers College Press.

Wolfe, C. (2010). *What is posthumanism?* University of Minnesota Press.

Wynter, S. (2003). Unsettling the coloniality of being/power/truth/freedom: Towards the human, after Man, its overrepresentation—An argument. *CR: The New Centennial Review, 3*(3), 257–337.

Wynter, S. (2006). On how we mistook the map for the territory, and reimprisoned ourselves in our unbearable wrongness of being, of Desêtre: Black studies toward the human project. In L. Gordon & J. A. Gordon (Eds.), *Not only the master's tools: African American studies in theory and practice* (pp. 107–169). Paradigm Press.

Wynter, S. (2015). "The ceremony found": Towards the autopoetic turn/overturn, its autonomy of human agency and extraterritoriality of (self-)sognition. In J. R. Ambroise & S. Broeck (Eds.), *Black knowledges/Black struggles: Essays in critical epistemology* (pp. 184–252). Liverpool University Press.

About the Authors

Editor Authors

GAILE S. CANNELLA (EdD, University of Georgia) is an independent scholar who has served as a tenured full professor at Texas A&M University–College Station and at Arizona State University–Tempe, as well as the Velma Schmidt Endowed Chair of Education at the University of North Texas. She is also a former early-years and elementary school teacher. Her doctoral students have received outstanding dissertation awards from the American Educational Research Association and have, in some cases, published their dissertations as complete volumes. Dr. Cannella's scholarship focuses on diverse constructions of critical qualitative inquiry, reconceptualist childhood studies/care/education, and justice broadly, including related to environmental studies and posthumanism. Dr. Cannella's work has appeared in a range of journals and volumes, including *Qualitative Inquiry, Cultural Studies ↔ Critical Methodologies*, and the *International Review of Qualitative Research*. She was first recognized as the author of *Deconstructing Early Childhood Education: Social Justice and Revolution* (1997) and, with Radhika Viruru, for *Childhood and Postcolonialism* (2004). Her most recent books are *Critical Qualitative Research Reader* (2012) with Shirley Steinberg, *Reconceptualizing Early Childhood Care and Education* (2014; 2nd ed., 2018) with Marianne Bloch and Beth Swadener, *Critical Qualitative Inquiry: Foundations and Futures* (2015) with Michelle Pérez and Penny Pasque, and *Critical Examinations of Quality in Childhood Education and Care* (2016) with Michelle Pérez and I-Fang Lee. Dr. Cannella just completed special journal issues on "Racism and Qualitative Inquiry" and "Justice Matters(ings)" for publication in 2022 and is currently working on research projects that include critical qualitative inquiry as an avenue for increased justice through poststructural genealogical method, multispecies justice and posthumanism, and traditionally marginalized knowledges. Dr. Cannella received the 2017 Reconceptualizing Early Childhood Education and Care Bloch Career Award.

TIM KINARD is an associate professor of early learning in the Department of Curriculum & Instruction at Texas State University in San Marcos, Texas, where his work as a researcher is entangled with his work as a teacher. A unique collaboration with the local public school district in San Marcos has created a space where Tim and his colleagues engage with a community of practitioners, administrators, students, and local families while designing curricula and teaching with/in a public prekindergarten as engagement with complicated conversations about conquest and curriculum, theory, and practice. This ongoing research collaboration and teaching opportunity were created to explore the promises and perils of play-based, place-based multilingual curriculum and pedagogy. Publications emerging from this collaboration have appeared in a range of journals including *New Educator, Theory into Practice, Young Children*, and the *International Journal of Qualitative Studies in Education*, as well as in a book he coauthored with Jesse Gainer and Mary Esther Huerta titled *Power play: Explorando y empujando fronteras en Tejas Through Theory Building and Storytelling in a Multilingual Play-Based Early Learning Curriculum*.

Authors

SALLY BARNES has worked in early childhood education for more than 30 years. She has experience as an early childhood teacher and director, curriculum policy officer, compliance officer, consultant, and academic. As a curriculum writer and developer, Sally has been involved in the development of national and state-based curriculum frameworks, including the Early Years Learning Framework, Australia's first national learning framework for the prior to school early childhood sector. Sally has worked in remote, rural, and metropolitan settings in South Australia and in a variety of early years settings in the United Kingdom.

DAVID (DAVE) P. BARRY is an assistant professor in the Department of Early and Middle Grades Education at West Chester University. Prior to receiving his PhD in curriculum and instruction (early childhood education) at the University of Texas at Austin, Dave taught kindergarten in the Boston Public Schools for 10 years and was a teaching fellow at the Harvard Graduate School of Education for 5 years. His scholarly interests include preservice early childhood teacher education, teacher and preservice teacher self-care and self-compassion, and supporting educators in developing trauma-informed teaching practices.

MINDY BLAISE is a Vice Chancellor's Professorial Research Fellow and a co-director of the Centre for People, Place & Planet at Edith Cowan University, Western Australia. Dr. Blaise is also a cofounder of the Common Worlds Research Collective. Her transdisciplinary and postdevelopmental research with the more-than-human uses emergent, affect-focused, and creative methods to rework a humanist ontology. She is interested in how the more-than-human and feminist speculative research practices activate new meanings about childhood that sit outside the narrow confines of developmentalism.

CHRISTOPHER P. BROWN is a former preschool, kindergarten, and first-grade teacher. He is also an award-winning researcher, teacher educator, and professor of early childhood education in the Education Policy and Planning Program of the Department of Educational Leadership and Policy at the University of Texas at Austin. His research centers on how education stakeholders across a range of political and educational contexts make sense of and respond to policy makers' reforms. He has looked at these issues using multiple theoretical and practitioner-based perspectives that span the fields of early childhood and elementary education, curriculum and instruction, teacher education, and policy analysis.

RENATA DE ASSIS is an MA in clinical psychologist and a parent–infant psychotherapist from Columbia University. She holds an undergraduate degree from Pontificia Universidade Catolica do Rio de Janeiro in Clinical Psychology and Economics. She is a PhD candidate in clinical psychology at Adelphi University. Renata's primary research interest is on early childhood mental health. Additionally, she was trained in Pikler Early Childhood Pedagogy from Emmi Pikler Institute in Budapest. Previously, she has had her private practice with children and adolescents in Brazil.

HANNAH DYER is an associate professor of Child and Youth Studies at Brock University. She is a cultural theorist of childhood with a concentration in art/aesthetics, social conflict, queer theory, and sexuality studies. She is interested in how aesthetic and expressive cultures of childhood reframe relationships to political crises, historical traumas, and social debates about belonging. Her book *The Queer Aesthetics of Childhood: Asymmetries of Innocence and the Cultural Politics of Child Development* extends these lines of analysis.

SUE GRIESHABER is a professor of early childhood education and director of research in the School of Education at La Trobe University, Melbourne, Australia. Her research interests are informed by a range of critical, feminist, and feminist poststructural theories that address social justice and equity and include early childhood curriculum, policy, pedagogies, and assessment. She is foundation coeditor of the internationally known journal *Contemporary Issues in Early Childhood*.

JOSÉ MARTÍNEZ HINESTROZA, PhD, is an assistant professor in elementary mathematics education in the Department of Curriculum and Instruction at Texas State University. A former kindergarten and elementary school teacher, he engages in classroom-based participatory research to explore mathematics teaching and learning in bilingual elementary classrooms. He focuses on how students, teachers, and researchers come together to develop classroom cultures that are inclusive of children's multiple ways of participating. His interdisciplinary research has been published in both research and practitioner-oriented early childhood, mathematics education, and teacher education peer-reviewed journals and edited books.

MLADO IVANOVIC is an assistant professor at the Department of Philosophy at Northern Michigan University. His research focuses on moral, epistemic, political, and environmental challenges tied with the forceful displacement and migration of people, particularly by examining both the sociohistorical and political contexts of human vulnerability and exclusion. Mlado has published work on humanitarianism, refugees, epistemic violence, social and global justice, and human rights and the media. Dr. Ivanovic is also engaged with humanitarian nonprofit and nongovernment communities in Serbia, Greece, and Turkey and serves as an advisor for various student organizations in Michigan that deal with humanitarianism and social justice.

MARIA KROMIDAS is an associate professor of anthropology at William Paterson University in New Jersey. Her work explores how race, schooling, learning, and human being can be rethought through the critical perspectives of children and childhood. Dr. Kromidas has published in the journals *Anthropological Theory, Childhood, Critique of Anthropology, Curriculum Inquiry*, the *Harvard Educational Review, Jeunesse, Pedagogy Culture & Society*, and *Subjectivity*. She is the author of *City Kids: Transforming Racial Baggage* (Rutgers University Press). Maria's current work explores how the mother's labors for the child are a key site where race, class, and gendered subjectivities and inequalities are produced and transformed.

DA HEI KU is a PhD candidate at the University of Texas at Austin in the Department of Curriculum and Instruction, specializing in early childhood. Her research focuses on how gentrification has affected the early childhood education landscape in general and communities, teachers, and policy in particular. Before graduate school, she taught as a bilingual PreK teacher in Chicago.

I-FANG LEE is an associate professor in the School of Education, University of Newcastle. Dr. Lee's teaching, research trajectories, and scholarly publications have focused on contemporary issues relating to equity and justice in the field of early childhood care and education to unpack what is taken for granted in research, policy, curriculum, and pedagogical practices related to childhoods, families, and programs. Her intercultural teaching and research projects are strongly nested across multiple geopolitical locations, including East Asia, Australia, and the United States. She engages in interdisciplinary collaborations to advocate the local and global importance of inclusive and holistic education for all.

ABOUT THE AUTHORS

THEODORA LIGHTFOOT is retired after teaching at the University of Illinois, Chicago, and National Louis University. Although her interests are diverse, she has had a particular focus on identifying and unpacking the societal metaphors that shape our understandings of immigration—particularly in the context of the United States—and of immigrant children in our schools and in popular imagination. She applies methodologies drawn from humanities traditions to social science questions. In her work, she draws on poststructuralist theory, metaphor theory, and, more recently, posthumanist theory.

THERESE LINDGREN has a PhD in pedagogy and works as a lecturer in early childhood education at the Department of Childhood, Education and Society, Malmö University, Sweden. Lindgren's research interests concern historical, cultural, and political perspectives on education at large and the making of the educable child in the intersection among early childhood education research, policy development, and educational practice in particular. She is theoretically versed in poststructural and posthumanist theories and methodologically in policy and discourse analysis.

LUZ A. MURILLO, an associate professor in the Bilingual/Biliteracy Education Program at Texas State University, is an educational anthropologist who studies the biliteracy development of indigenous, immigrant, and Latinx children, families, and teachers. Dr. Murillo earned her doctoral degree in language, reading, and Culture at the University of Arizona and has taught courses in reading/writing/literacy, language and culture, and ethnography for bilingual educators at universities in the United States, Mexico, and Colombia. Her research has been published in English, Spanish, and Tex-Mex in journals including *Anthropology & Education Quarterly, Language Arts,* and the *Journal of Adolescent and Adult Literacy.*

EMILY L. MURPHY is a PhD candidate in the Department of Child and Youth Studies at Brock University. She is primarily interested in the affective remains of childhood and aesthetic modes of survival, whereby music, media, and visual arts act as means to elaborate psychic injury and envisage different worlds. Their work incorporates elements of queer theory, cultural studies, affect theory, psychoanalysis, and sound studies. Emily is a graduate student affiliate of the Posthumanism Research Institute and a cofounder of SOAK, a collective aimed at supporting people of marginalized genders in experimental music.

CASEY MYERS, PhD, is a founding partner of Watershed Early Years, a group dedicated to progressive early education, community-driven professional development, and reconceptualized research with young children. Her research focuses on new materialist and postqualitative inquiries into the everyday life of early-years classrooms. Her teaching focuses on (post)humanities in the early years and theories of childhood. She was named a 2020 recipient of the Emerging Scholar Award from the American Educational

Research Association. She currently lives and works in northeastern Ohio, USA, with her partner and son.

CLAIRE O'CALLAGHAN is completing a master's degree as a higher degree by research student at Edith Cowan University, Western Australia, in the area of early childhood education. Her current research focuses on paying attention to human and more-than-human relations, with a specific focus on water and children. She currently works as an educator in the field of early childhood education and draws from her field experience and applies it to her research and writing.

MICHAEL O'LOUGHLIN is a professor in the College of Education and Health Sciences and Derner School of Psychology at Adelphi University, New York. Since 2018 he has been coeditor of the journal *Psychoanalysis* and *Culture and Society*, and he is coeditor of the book series *Critical Childhood & Youth Studies* (Lexington Books). He directs the Adelphi Asylum project to train doctoral students in asylum evaluation. He is coeditor of the forthcoming book *Childhood Predicaments: Precarity, Desire, Loss, Liminality, (Im)possibility*. He has a private practice for psychotherapy and psychoanalysis on Long Island, New York. Website: michaeloloughlinphd.com

MANDY PIERLEJEWSKI is a senior lecturer in early childhood education at Leeds Beckett University, UK. She leads a teacher education degree focusing on the 3–7 age range. She is also a final-year doctoral candidate at the University of Manchester. Her recent research has been a participatory action research project focusing on improving the educational experiences of Roma Gypsy children in a school in the north of England. Her previous writing has focused on the impact of datafication on child and teacher subjectivity. Prior to becoming an academic, Mandy was an early-years teacher for 14 years.

JENNY RITCHIE has been involved in the early childhood care and education sector since the 1970s, as a childcare worker, kindergarten teacher, parent, teacher educator, education researcher, and grandparent. Dr. Ritchie is an associate professor in Te Puna Akopai, the School of Education, at Te Herenga Waka Victoria University of Wellington, Aotearoa New Zealand. Her research and teaching focus on social, cultural, and ecological justice in early childhood care and education; pedagogies that affirm and support children's cultural, spiritual, and emotional well-being and citizenship enactment; and exploring how applying Māori conceptualizations can enhance pedagogies that protect and care for our planet.

MERE SKERRETT, an associate professor, is the head of the School of Education, Te Herenga Waka, Victoria University. Much of her earlier career included the establishment phase and working in Kōhanga Reo and Kura Kaupapa Māori. She is also interested in equity issues as they relate to Māori as Tāngata Whenua, women's issues, children's rights, and social and ecological justice. Mere hails from tribal groupings in both the North and South Islands of Aotearoa New Zealand. She has five multilingual children, and her research interests have been focused on Indigenous language/s revitalization, and the relationship of Māori language to Māori knowledge, identity, culture, and worldview/s creation.

KYLIE SMITH is an associate professor in early childhood at the University of Melbourne's Melbourne Graduate School of Education. Her research focus is on supporting more equitable and socially just human and more-than-human worlds. She draws on feminist theories to rethink epistemologies, ontologies, and methodologies and disrupt the taken-for-granted truths entangled within the discourses that she navigates in her life.

MAREK TESAR is an associate professor, an associate dean international, and an academic head designate of the Faculty of Education and Social Work, University of Auckland. His expertise is in early childhood education in New Zealand and cross-country contexts, focusing on educational policy, philosophy, pedagogy, methodology, and curriculum. He draws on a qualified teacher background, as well as extensive knowledge of international education systems. He is the editor in chief of *Policy Futures in Education* (Sage Publications), coeditor of the book series *Children: Global Posthumanist Perspectives and Materialist Theories* (Springer), the president of the Philosophy of Education Society of Australasia, and the chairperson of the Steering Committee of the Reconceptualising Early Childhood Education Society.

GYULA VAMOSI is a Roma activist, the first in his community to earn a university degree. He has worked as a Roma language consultant for more than 30 years. He was a personal advisor on Roma issues to two past presidents of the World Bank and to Neelie Kroes, former vice president of the European Commission. In 2010, Gyula built KaskoSan, the first global Roma brand. He is also a film producer. His films, produced for the BBC and Channel 4, have earned millions of views. Gyula works closely with a primary school in the north of England to improve the educational attainment of Eastern European Roma children.

Index

#SayHerName, 289
1951 Convention Relating to the Status of Refugees, 34
1951 Refugee Convention (UNHCR), 22
1968 Commission on Nursery Provision, 230
1989 Convention on the Rights of the Child (OHCRC), 22, 34

A

A+ Education, 260
Abbas, M.S., 58, 67
ABC News, 217–18
Abraham, N., 14
Accelerated Reader, 164–65
Adair, J.K., 103, 109, 111, 113, 265
Adelphi Asylum Project, 5
Adrinay, V., 269
AEI, 260
Agamben, G., 5, 6
agency, 137–38, 185, 194
    critical, 142
    in critical mathematics education, 141–43, 143–47
    individual initiative, intentionality and, 145
    possession, manifestation, and development of, 142–43
    poststructuralist conceptualization of, 146
    role of available discourses, 144
    as transgressing discourses, 143–47, 147–51
    Also see critical mathematics education

Against Purity, 247
Agevall, L., 232
Ahuriri-Driscoll, A., 72
Alaimo, S., 194
Alba, R., 178
Alcock, S., 80
Alim, H.S., 103, 113, 160, 162, 169
Allmänna förlag, 230
Alvarez, A., 12
Ambroise, J., 281, 282
American Federation of Teachers, 91–92
Anaru, N.A., 61, 62, 64
Anđelković, I., 27, 30, 31
Anderson, K., 285
Andersson, A., 141
Änggård, E., 265, 266
Anti-Defamation League, 161
Antonsen, C.M., 268
Antony, M.G., 12
Aotearoa New Zealand, growth, development and consumerism in, 214–17
Apfelbaum, E., 14
Apple, M.W., 104, 107, 109, 110, 113
après coup, 4
Arendt, H., 6, 7
Argyris, C., 106, 107
Arksey, H., 259, 261
Arnold, S., 34
Arnott, L., 81
Aronson, B.A., 184
Aronson, M., 81
Arreguin-Anderson, M.G., 269
Art Gallery of Western Australia (AGWA), 202
Artiles, A.J., 47

Asante, M.K., 184
Ashford-Hanserd, S., 177
Ashton-Warner, S., 72, 75–77, 80
Aslan Tutak, F., 139
assemblages, 215–16
Atkinson, J., 4
Auerhahn, N., 5
Auriac, E., 288
Aurini, J., 108
Australia, growth, development and consumerism in, 210–13
Australaisian Journal of Early Childhood, 261, 263
Avineri, N., 162

B

Baker, B., 287
Bakhtin, M., 267, 268
Baldridge, B.J., 109, 110
Baldy, C.R., 195
Balestra, A., 176
Ball, S.J., 105
Bambara, T.C., 289
Banerji, D., 285
Banner, S., 57
bare life, 5, 6, 14
Barad, K., 123, 125, 192, 193, 194, 198, 216, 285
Bar-Haim, S., 74, 75
Barlow, M.R., 13
barnkrubba, 225
Barnomsorg och skolakommittén, 231, 232, 233
Barry, D.P., 104, 107, 108, 113
Barwell, R., 144
Beatty, B., 103
Becker, G.S., 105
Becker, M., 209
becoming, 177, 179–80
becoming-convivial-with-child, 288–89
becoming-with-the-Other, 283
becoming-with trees, 279
becoming-with water, 192, 195–96, 196–203
Beighton, C., 187
Belmore, R., 201
Belonging, Being & Becoming, 212

Bennett, J., 41, 45, 194
Benson, J., 106, 107
Bereiter, C., 160
Berlant, L., 244
Berliner, D.C., 107, 110
Berman, R., 270, 271
Bernstein, R., 244, 246, 250, 251, 281, 282
Berry, A., 195, 198
Betts, A., 24, 30
Bhabha, J., 7–9, 111
Bialostok, S.M., 81
Biddle, B.J., 107, 110
Biestra, G., 235
bigger nurseries, 227, 228
bilingual children, teaching literacy to, 155–56, 168–70
    Accelerated Reader and, 164
    capitalism and, 164–67
    cultural and linguistic deficiencies, 160–61
    dominant forms of literacy instuction for, 164–67
    emergent bilingual, 178
    kidwatching, teacherwatching and, 167–68
    literature regarding, 158–63
    racist linguistic practices and, 160–63
    radical hope and, 156, 170–71
    science of reading and, 164–67
    Vancouver Conference and, 158–60
bilingualism, 88, 91, 97
Binder, J., 93, 94, 95
Bissex, G., 158
BlackCrit, 184
Black girlhood studies, 282
Black Lives Matter, 289
Black PlayCrit, 182–84
Black, S., 245
Black students, brilliance of, 185
Black Studies, 280–83
Blackmore, J., 209
Blaise, M., 113, 202, 269, 271, 272, 273
Bland, S., 183
Bloch, M.N., 244
Bloome, D., 171
Blue, L., 202

Blum, S., 162
Boaler, J., 141, 145
Bøe, M., 268
Bone, J., 263, 265, 267
Bonilla-Silva, E., 56
Boochani, B., 10
Booth, A., 259
Børve, E., 267
Børve, H., 267
Boutte, G., 183
Bowlby, J., 252
Boxville, 181
Bradbury, A., 175
Bragin, M., 5
Braidotti, R., 214, 285
Brand, D., 289
Brantlinger, A., 139, 140
Breitbart News, 92, 93
Brembeck, H., 232
Britain's Forgotten Slave Owners, 58
Brooker, E., 260
Brown, C., 250–51
Brown, C.P., 103, 104, 106, 108, 109, 110, 111, 112, 113
Brown, K., 112
Brown, R.N., 282
Bruhm, S., 247, 251
Bruner, J., 159
Bryan, N., 176, 182, 183, 184
Buchanan, B., 199
Buckingham, D., 209
Burchinal, M., 108
Burman, E., 48, 244, 246, 254, 281, 282, 287
Burns, J., 166
Bush, G.W., 106
bush kindergarten, 212
Busby, J., 57, 58
Butler, A., 112
Butler, J., 8, 249
Butler, T.T., 281
Byrne, C., 209

C

Cahill, B., 108, 109, 111
Callier, D.M., 282
Came, H.A., 71
Campbell, A.E., 72, 74

Campbell, S., 264, 270, 273
Canavan, M., 217–18
Cannella, G., 40, 48, 103, 107, 111, 112, 183, 193, 198, 207, 244, 246, 254, 259, 281
cannibalizing technologies, 208
capitalism, 164–67
Carneiro, R., 235
Castañeda, C., 224, 235, 236
Castro, J., 99
Cave (Plato), 63
Ceder, S., 216
Cedillo, S., 112, 177, 247, 248, 249, 250, 254, 281, 285
Center for the Economics of Human Development, 105
Century of the Child, The, 225
Chan, A., 112
Chancellor, B., 212
Chao, T., 142, 143
Chaparro, S., 156, 162, 163
Chapman, R., 269
Charters, C., 61
Chávez, K.R., 144
Cheruvu, R., 107
child migration, 3–5, 23–24
    challenges of caring for, 11–13
    dangers of refugee camps, 27–32
    forceful migration of, 21–23, 25–27
    global structures of vulnerability, 24–27
    humanitarian spaces and, 27–32
    legal precarity and, 7–9
    solutions for, 34–36
    statistics about, 23
    subaltern subjectivity and, 13–15
    subjectivities in danger, 11–13
    Western response to, 32–33
Child Migration and Human Rights in a Global Age, 7
childhoods
    environmental justice and, 207–8
        bush kindergarten and, 212
        toys and, 208
        water assemblages and, 215
    forest schools and, 249
    innocence and, 244–45, 246,

247–48, 248–50, 250–52, 254–55, 285
neoliberalism and, 207–8
    edu-capitalism and, 208, 209
    neoliberal toys, 208
politics of, 121–22
    Generation α and, 127
    Generation Z and, 127
    in Hong Kong, 128
    individual responsibility and, 126, 135
    lifeworlds in the 21st century and, 127
    macro politics in Hong Kong, 130–31
    macro politics in Taiwan, 129
    micro politics in Hong Kong, 130
    micro politics in Taiwan, 129–30
    nationalism and, 133–34
    neoliberalism and, 131–33
    personal/family choices and, 126, 135
    rhizomatic, 123–25
    timespacemattering and, 123, 125–26
    troubling the politics of, 131–34
purity and, 247–48, 254–55
children agency paradox, 138
Children's Culture Reader, The, 244
Children's Geographies, 261, 263
Children's Response to Literate Environments, 158
Chu, C.M., 44
Citrin, J., 97
Clark, V., 197, 201, 285
Cliffe, J., 80, 81
Cochran-Smith, C., 166
Cohen, L.E., 268
Cole, M., 159
Cole, T., 184
Colegrove, K.S.S., 110
Colenso, W., 66
collaboration, 193, 196–98
collective trauma, 4
Collier, D.R., 264
Collier, P., 24, 30
Common Worlds Research Collective, 192, 194, 197, 203, 285
Compton-Lilly, C., 159, 163, 169

Constructive Play Lab, 177, 179
Contemporary Issues in Early Childhood, 261, 263
Conversations With Rain, 202
Cook, D.T., 209
Coral Way bilingual school, 90
CRC, 34
creativity, 193, 202–3
Crisis in the Population Question, 228
critical childhood studies, 246, 248
critical consciousness, 139, 140
critical mathematics education, 137–38
    agency as transgressing discourses, 143–47
    classroom examples of, 147–51
    critical agency and, 142
    guiding principles of, 140
    poststructuralist conceptualization of agency in, 146
    tracing the critical in, 138–39
    Also see agency
critical melancholia, 14
critical pedagogy, 139
critical race theory (CRT), 175, 185, 187
    Black PlayCrit and, 183–84
critical theory, 139
Cuban, L., 105
cultural domination, 289
cultural imperialism, 289
culture bomb, 62, 67
culture of poverty, 160
curriculum
    Blackness settler colonization and, 184
    curriculum-becoming, 185
    curriculum-becoming-store, 181
Curry, T., 171

D

da Silva, S., 71
Dahlberg, G., 105, 231, 233, 287
Dahlgren, L., 228, 232, 233
Daniel, M., 288
Davies, B., 55, 68, 141, 144, 145, 287
Davies, D., 178, 180
Davies, S., 108
Davis, K., 183, 184

Davoine, F., 3
de Freitas, E., 141, 145
De Lissovoy, N., 103, 104, 107, 108, 109, 111, 112, 113, 287
De Moed, S.T., 104, 111
de Saxe, J., 161
deficit language, 87
deficits, 178
Delaney, K., 269
Deleuze, G., 123, 134–35, 177, 187, 199, 215
DeLoache, J., 48
Demas, E., 104
Dencik, L., 228
Department of Education and Training, 212
Derrida, J., 7, 14
Derrington, C., 41
Despret, V., 199, 200
Development Matters, 48
Devlin, K., 97
Dewaele, J.-M., 150
Diaz, E., 156
difference, 68
DiGangi, J., 209
Discourse: Studies in the Cultural Politics of Education, 263
discourses, 143–47
discovery, 61
disenfranchisement, 26–27
Do Nascimento, A., 197
Dombey, H., 169
Dombkowski, K., 103
Douglas, M., 193
Drożdek, B., 5, 12, 13
Drudge Report, 92
Duhn, I., 200
Dumas, M.J., 182, 183
Dyer, H., 244, 249, 251, 254
Dyson, A.H., 156, 161, 163, 166, 167, 169

E

Early Child Development and Care, 261, 263
early childhood education (ECE), 103, 110–13
    brilliance of children of color and, 183
    children becoming-with water and, 191–93, 195–96, 196–203
    children in Sweden, 223–24
        bigger nurseries and, 227, 228
        child at risk and, 230–31
        competent child and, 231–32, 233
        figuration and, 224
        independent preschools, 232–36
        "orphans" and, 235–36
        Reggio Emilia and, 233, 235, 236
        Swedish preschool model and, 229–32
        vulnerable child and, 230–31
        welfare state and, 224–27
    high-stakes testing and, 106
    return on investment in, 105–6
    Also see school readiness
Early Education, 48
Early Years Foundation Stage (EYFS), 270
Easter, A., 80
Echautegui, M., 98
Edelman, L., 244
edu-capitalism, 208, 209
Edelman, L., 251
Edelsky, C., 161, 163, 164, 165, 169
Education Review Office, 79
Egan, R.D., 244
Eizadirad, A., 112
Elfström, I., 233
Elliott, S., 212
Émile, 226
encampments, 28
Engelmann, S.., 161
epistemic disobedience, 157
ERIC, 260
Erikson, K., 3
Eriksson, E.H., 230
Erueti, A., 61
Erueti, A.K., 61
Erwin, K., 127
Escobar, A., 192
Eteläpelto, A., 143
ethico-onto-epistemologies, 193, 198–99
Eudell, D.L., 281
Europe 2020, 234
Evans, K., 110
Evans-Winter, V.E., 282

Evison, H., 59, 60, 63, 66
exclusion, 26–27
experimental empiricism, 199
experimentation, 193, 199–201
Eyer, D.E., 252

F

Farley, L., 248, 251, 252, 253, 287
Fassin, D., 5
Faulkner, J., 255
Favela, A., 161
Fazili, H., 10
fear of breakdown, 4
Feine, R., 108
Felli, R., 211
Ferreiro, E., 155, 156, 158, 159, 169, 171
Fiore, E., 216
Flores, N., 144, 156, 157, 161, 162, 163
Floyd, G., 184
Foley, D., 156, 160
Fonseca, I., 40
forceful migration. *See* child migration
Foreshore and Seabed Act 2004, 61
forest schools, 249
Foster, B., 41
Foster, R.M.P., 12
Foucault, M., 88, 144, 267, 280
Fountain, 201
Fox News, 92, 96
frames/framing, 89, 94–96, 96–97
Frankenstein, M., 138, 139
Frankfurt School, 138
Fray, L., 261
Freeman, N., 210
Fregoso Bailón, R.O., 111, 112
Freire, P., 77, 113, 139
Freud, S., 4, 252
Freyd, J.J., 13
Fröbel, F., 225
Fröbel Institute, 227
Fröbel Kindergarten, 225, 233
Funds of Knowledge, 160

G

gadji, 39
gadjikano, 44

gadjo, 44
Gagne, K.M., 283
Gailbraith, M., 289
Galvez, S., 200
Garan, E., 163, 165, 171
García, O., 156, 178
Garlen, J.C., 244, 245, 246, 247, 248, 249, 250, 251, 253, 254, 255, 287
Garner, P.R., 282
Gaudillière, J.-M., 4
Gee, J.P., 163, 164, 166
generation, concept of, 127
Genishi, C., 156, 163, 166, 167, 169
Gesell, A., 227
Gibson, K., 192
Gibson, M., 207
Gillborn, D., 108
Gillispie, C., 108
Gill-Peterson, J., 251
Girls for Gender Equity, 282
Goelman, H., 158
Goldsmith, R.E., 13
Gomez, R.E., 104
González, N., 160
good-enough mother, 247, 252–54
Goodman, Y., 167
Gottlieb, A., 48
Grace, G.W., 182
Grace, M., 127
Gramsci, A., 164
Grande, S., 112, 283–84, 285
Graue, M.E., 110
Greeno, J.G., 141
Greidel, M., 168
Gresalfi, M., 143
Grieshaber, S., 259
Grose, J., 243–44, 245
Grosz, E., 180, 187
Grumet, M., 252
Guattari, F., 123, 134–35, 177, 187, 199, 215
Gullo, D.F., 103
Gutiérrez, R., 140, 145
Gutstein, E., 138, 139, 140
Guzzonato, A., 209
Gypsy Holocaust, 40
Gypsy Laws, 44
Gypsy, Roma and Travellers (GRT), 40

H

Hackett, A., 266, 267
Haggerty, M., 80
Halldén, G., 232, 233, 235
Hamm, C., 269
Hammarlund, K.G., 227, 229
Hancock, I.F., 40
Haraway, D.J., 175, 176, 187, 192, 198, 199, 202, 269, 279
Harrell-Bond, B., 29
Harrison, L., 80
Harte, H.M., 71, 72
Harvey, D., 104, 106
Harwood, D, 264
Hatem, N., 11, 13
Hawkes, G.L., 244
Hawkins, G., 193
Haywood-Bird, E., 268
He Māpuna Te Tamaiti, 79
He Whakaputanga o te Rangatiratanga o Nu Tireni, 57–58
Heath, S.B., 159, 160
Heckman, J.J., 105
Hackman, S., 194
Heckman, J.J., 234, 270
Hector, J., 63
Heilbroner, D., 183, 184
hierarchical thinking, 194
Held, D., 139
Henward, A.S., 268, 271
Herman, J., 5
Heyman, J., 13
Hill, D., 282
Hird, M.J., 191
Histories of the Transgender Child, 251
Hobson, W., 59
Hoebel, E.A., 288
Hoffman, E., 12
Hoffman, J.V., 165, 171
Hognestad, K., 268
homo sacer, 5, 6
Homo Sacer, 5
Hong, S.L.S., 108
How to Bring Your Kids Up Gay, 251
Howell, J., 184
Howlett, C., 175
Hsueh, Y., 81
Hu, G., 110
Huh, Y.L., 267, 268
Hultman, K., 180, 185, 186
Hultqvist, K., 226, 227, 228, 232, 233
Human, 280, 281
human capital theory, 105
human exceptionalism, 194
human-waste relations, 192, 193–94
humanitarian spaces, 27–32
humanitarian sustainability, 35
Humphris, R., 9
Hurley, N., 247, 251
Hursh, D., 106
Huuki, T., 268
hydro-logics, 201

I

Icsarescu, S., 279
'Illegal' Traveller, 9
immigrant children, 87–88
    deficit language about, 87
    in need of help, 90–92
    strong work ethic among, 98
immigrants/immigration, 87–88
    bilingualism and, 91, 97
    deficit language about, 87
    framing and, 96–97
    good side of, 90
    in need of help, 90–92
    productive conversations about, 97–99
    violence and, 95–96
Incredible Years, 79
Indigenous Māori
    British colonialism and, 57–60, 60–61, 62–63, 67–68
    customary rights and, 60
    Enclosure Acts and, 59
    imperialism, colonial powers and, 60–61
    Indigenous histories and, 56
    language and, 56
    language shift through colonization, 61–62, 64–65
    political independence and, 65–66
    racial domination of, 56
    silences, erasures and, 62–63

slavery and, 58, 63, 67
Also see Māori children
Indigenous pedagogies/studies, 112, 280, 283–85
individual agency, 143
Info Park, 27
Ingraham, C., 96
innocence. *See* childhoods
Institute for Advanced Instruction, 161
International Journal of Early Years Education, 263
International Roma Day, 51
Iorio, J.M., 110, 269
Isaacs, S., 72, 74–75, 80

J

Jackson, A.Y., 145, 150, 176, 182
Jackson, Z., 280
James, A., 144, 145, 214, 231, 233, 244, 246
JanMohamed, A., 13
Jenkins, H., 244
Jenkins, K., 71, 72
Jenks, C., 231, 244
Johansson, B., 232
Johnson, L.L., 183, 184
Johnson, M., 89
Jones, A., 72
Jones, D., 142, 143
Jones, S., 264, 266
Journal of Early Childhood Literacy, 263
Juelskjær, M., 125, 126

K

Kampmann, J., 229, 231, 232
Kane, N., 103
Kant, I., 7
Kaplan, L., 5
Kassabova, K., 3
Katz, C., 45
Kawharu, I., 73
Kehily, M.J., 246
Kendi, I.X., 176
Kennedy, R.M., 251
Key, E., 225
Key Vocabulary, 76
Khanna, R., 5, 6, 14
Khosravi, S., 9–11

kidwatching, 156, 167–68
Kinard, T., 177, 181
Kincheloe, J.L., 139
Kindergarten Readiness Tests, 108, 111
Kincaid, J.R., 244
King, B., 183
King, T.L., 280
King Tāwhiao, 65
Kīngitanga, 65
Klaus, S., 41
Kleifgen, J.A., 156
Klein, N., 107
Kline, S., 246
Korpi, M., 223
Korsvold, T., 208
Kövecses, Z., 89
Kozol, J., 162
Krause, G., 110
Kristjánsson, B., 223
Kroeger, J., 269
Kromidas, M., 281, 282, 285, 289
Ku, D., 113
Kummen, K., 197, 248, 249, 254, 281
Kwaymullina, A., 192
Kyuchukov, H., 41

L

Labov, W., 159
Lacan, J., 4
Lachal, C., 12
Ladson-Billings, G., 104, 109, 112, 113, 162
Lakoff, G., 89, 95, 96, 110
Lalueza, J., 41
Lan, Y.C., 109, 110
Land, N., 197
land as pedagogy, 284
Lane, T.M., 112
Langer-Osuna, J., 148
Latinidad, 185
Latino immigrants
    differing descriptions of, 94–96
    difficulty in learning English, 95
    English and, 97–98
    framing and, 94
    low-wage labor and, 98
    poverty and, 95
    right-wing discourses about, 92–94

Latino students
    brilliance of, 185
    extra school funding for, 91
Latino/a critical race theory (LatCrit), 269
Latour, B., 185, 198, 215
Lawler, B.R., 140, 141
Lawrence, P., 176
Lear, J., 156, 157, 171
Leavy, P., 202
Lee, I.F., 107, 113, 126, 128, 134
Leggio, D.V., 42
Lemke, T., 105
Lenz Taguchi, H., 176, 180, 185, 186, 192, 198, 233
Leonardo, Z., 110, 113
Leva, A., 93–94
Lewis, O., 160
Lightfoot, T., 87, 90, 91, 94
Limbu, B., 7
Limited English Proficient (LEP) classes, 92
Lindgren, A.-L., 225, 226, 229
Lindgren, T., 223, 234, 235
linguafaction, 62
Lipman, M., 288
Literacy Before Schooling, 159
Lloro-Bidart, T., 194
Loh, J., 110
Long, N.J., 286
Long Dispute, The, 59
Lopez, M., 98
Louie, N., 142, 143, 144
Love, B.L., 184
Lubeck, S., 109, 110, 111
Lyiscott, J.J., 171
Lyttleton Times, 63

M

Ma, X., 109
MacGillivray, L., 268, 271
Macias-Gomez-Estern, B., 41
Mackey, W., 90
MacNevin, M., 270, 271
Madrid, S., 268
Makareti, 71, 72
Makoni, S., 168
Malone, K., 214, 215, 262, 265
Malting House, 74

Maminachvili, C., 13
Mana Whenua, 57
Manning, E., 180, 181, 182, 184, 187
Manuelito, K.D., 112
Māori. *See* Indigenous Māori
Māori children, 55–57, 71–72
    colonization of emotion among, 73–74
    emotion in current early childhood pedagogies and, 78–79
    emotion in progressive education and, 74–77
    raising of, 66, 71–72
    revalidating and re-visibilising emotion and, 80–81
    Also see Indigenous Māori
Marsh, A., 41
Marsh, J., 267
Martin, D.B., 141, 143
Martin, J.P., 234
Martin Korpi, B., 231, 233
Martínez Hinestroza, J., 150
Martínez, J.M., 141, 143, 145
Martinez-Lozano, V., 41
Marx, K., 59
Masterov, D.V., 234
mātauranga Māori, 63
Material Encounters, 192, 194
Matias, C.E., 71
Matras, Y., 40, 42
May, T., 202
Maxouris, C., 184
May, C., 92
Mazzei, L.A., 145, 150, 175, 182, 269
Mbembe, A., 6–7
McArdle, F., 259
McCombe, L., 288
McDonald, G., 75
McKeon, L., 251
McKittrick, K., 283
McNiff, S., 202
medically necessary abortion, 96
Meiners, E.R., 244, 247, 248, 250, 251, 254, 282
Melamed, J., 109
Merewether, J., 266
metaphors, 89

Metge, J., 72, 79
Meyer, R., 163
Michelle Malkin Blog, 92
Middleton, S., 72, 74
Mignolo, W., 157, 167, 168
migrants, 24
    definition of, 25
    refugees and, 32
Mika, C., 217
Miller, E., 252
Miller, L.L., 110
Miller, R.J., 61
Mincer, J., 105
Moberg, E., 227
Moberg, M., 227
Moll, L.C., 109, 110, 111, 113, 157, 160
Montgomery, H., 246
Monzó, L.M., 162
Moore, H.L., 286
Morantz, G., 13
Morris, M., 40
Morrison, S., 218
Moss, P., 105, 109, 287, 288
Motion Law, 88
Moustafa, M., 166, 169
multiculturalism, 88
Murillo, L.A., 162
Murris, K., 288
Mutu, M., 57
Mycock, K., 266
Myers, N., 279
Myers, Y.C., 207, 208
Myhre, C.O., 267
Myrdal, A., 227, 228, 236
Myrdal, G., 228

N

Nachträglichkeit, 4
Nannup, N., 192, 195
Natalicio, D., 90
Natalicio, L., 90
Nation at Risk, A, 106
National Commission in Excellence on Education, 106
National Education Goals Panel, 106, 108
National Institute of Education, 105
National Women's Law Center, 243
nationalism, 133–34
nationality, 6
nativity, 6
necropolitics, 6, 10, 14
Neimanis, A., 195, 197, 201
Nelson, J.D., 183
Nelson, N., 197
Nelson, R., 244
neoliberal education reforms, 106
neoliberalism, 131–33
New Education Foundation/Fellowship, 72, 74, 75
new materialism, 175
new truth, 126
New York Times, 243
New Zealand Department of Education, 74
New Zealand Ministry of Social Development, 73
Ní Raghallaigh, M., 13
Nicholson, J., 264, 265, 268, 269, 271, 273
No Child Left Behind (NCLB), 106, 110
Noddings, N., 269
Noguerón-Liu, S., 163
Nōpera Panakareao, 59
Norén, E., 141
Nuttal, J., 113
Nxumalo, F., 103, 109, 111, 112, 113, 175, 177, 178, 179, 186, 195, 198, 211, 213, 247, 248, 249, 250, 254, 281, 285

O

Oberg, A.A., 158
O'Brien, G., 89
O'Callaghan, C., 199–200
Ocasio Cortez, A., 99
O'Day, J.A., 106
Office of the Children's Commissioner, 73
OHCRC, 34
Ojala, M., 81
Oliver, K., 24
O'Loughlin, M., 4, 5, 14
Olsson, L.M., 287
O'Malley, L., 259, 261
onto-epistemological diversity, 123
Orange, C., 59, 72
organic reading, 76

Organisation for Economic Co-operation and Development (OECD), 234
Otheguy, R., 156
Other/Otherness, 14, 40, 122, 135, 178, 259, 260, 265, 283, 285
othermothering, 45
Owen, D., 24
Owens, T.C., 282, 283
Owocki, G., 167

P

Pachiv, 46
Pacini-Ketchabaw, V., 112, 175, 179, 192, 194, 201, 203, 213, 248, 249, 254, 281, 285
Palaiologou, I., 270
Panakaraeo, 68
Panaram, S.A., 289
Papastergiadis, N., 7
Paranjape, M.R., 285
Pardhan, A., 263, 268
Parekh, S., 24
parenting, 243–47, 254–55
Parenting Was Never Meant to Be This Isolating, 243
Paris, D., 113, 162, 169
Parks, A.N., 144
Parnell, W., 110
partial birth abortion, 96
Patton, S., 250, 251
Paulson, S., 175
Peckham, K., 48
Peirce, B.N., 144
Pelleiter, J., 263, 268
Penfold, M., 40
Pennycook, A., 88, 89, 168
Pere, R.R., 72
Pérez, M.S., 103, 104, 107, 108, 109, 111, 112, 113, 123, 183, 207
Perpetual Peace, 7
persistent organic pollutants (POPs), 209
Persson, S., 224, 228, 230
Pestalozzi, H., 226
Petrón, M.A., 171
Phillips, M., 265
Phoenix, A., 41, 45
Piaget, J., 75, 159, 230

Pianta, R.C., 108
Pickering, A., 145
Pihama, L., 72, 73, 74
Plant Studies Collaboratory, 279
Plato, 64
play, politics of, 259–60
    absence of themes in literature, 271
    findings in literature about, 261–62, 262–64
    five themes from literature, 264–70
    identification of literature about, 260–61
    learning and, 279
    methodologies within literature about, 272–73
    Other and, 259, 260, 265
    theories within literature about, 271–72
Playing and Reality, 252
Play-Not, 183
Plumwood, V., 192
Pojman, L., 64
Positive Foundations for Learning, 79
posthumanist theory, 175
Pōtatau Te WheroWhero, 65
Powell, A.B., 141, 143, 145
Powell, S.J., 266, 272
Prelinger, C., 5
Preventing Reading Difficulties in Young Children, 166
Proctor, L., 266, 267
Programme for International Student Assessment (PISA), 235
Project Head Start, 103, 104, 105
ProQuest, 260
Prout, A., 231, 233, 244
psychogenesis, 159
Pugh, A.J., 209
Puig de la Bellacasa, M., 202, 203
purism, 193
purity. *See* childhoods

Q

Quality Matters in Early Childhood Education and Care, 235
Quality Rating and Improvement Systems (QRIS), 108, 111

R

race, 175
Race to the Top–Early Learning Challenge (RTT–ELC), 108
race/child/learning/human assemblage, 279–80
    becoming-convivial-with-child, 288–89
    Black Studies and, 280–83
    Indigenous Studies and, 283–85
    posthuman transformations challenge to, 285–88
racial capital, 109
racial grammar, 56, 61, 63
raciolinguistic ideologies, 156, 162
racioliteracy ideologies, 156
radical hope, 156, 170–71
Raining on Kurtal, 202
Ramanathan, V., 178
Ramírez, L., 141, 143, 145
Ramos, R.A., 176
Rangatiratanga, 60–61
Rao, N., 132
Rau, C., 112
Rautio, P., 264, 265, 268
Razek, R., 184
recognition, 55, 68, 179, 182
    Black play and, 183
    collaboration and, 178–79
    critical race theory and, 185
Red Pedagogy, 283
refugees, 24
    Western response to, 32–33
refugee children, 24
    migrants and, 32
    Also see child migration
Reggio Emilia, 233, 235, 236, 285
Reich, R.B., 164
Reitano, T., 30
relata, 216
Remnants of Auschwitz, 5
Rendon, T., 104
Renold, E., 268
residential school syndrome, 4
Reynolds, A.J., 105
rhizome, 123–25, 134–35, 187
    death in a, 182–84

Rice, T., 182
Rijke, V., 265
Ristić, S., 27, 30, 31
Ritchie, J., 78, 79, 112, 216, 217
Rivas, A., 111
Rivera Cusicanqui, S., 168
RNZ, 80
Robertson, M., 210
Robinson, J.L., 282
Robinson, K.H., 193, 198, 244, 251
Rocha, M., 176
Rogers, A., 5
Rogoff, B., 50
Rohan, T., 79
Rollo, T., 281
rom, 39
Roma
    description of, 40
    othermothering and, 45
    parenthood among, 43–44
    Pachiv and, 46
    Romanipen/Romanipe and, 46
    Also see Roma children
Roma children, English preschool education of, 39–40
    code of conduct among, 46–47, 47–49
    construct of play among, 49–50
    developing intercultural understanding about, 51
    educators' expectations about, 45–46
    literature about, 41
    research project to support, 42
    role in family, 44–45
    special education and, 47
    transition to school, 43–44
Romanipen/Romanipe, 46
Rosa, J., 156, 162, 163
Rose, D.B., 74, 192, 195
Rose, E., 103
Rose, N., 105
Rosenbaum, B., 12, 13
Rosenberg, M., 81
Röttger-Rössler, B., 79
Rousseau, C., 13
Rousseau, J.J., 226

Rua, M.R., 72, 73
Rueda, R., 162
Ruíz, R., 144

S

Saavedra, C.M., 109, 111, 113, 123, 183
Sabol, T.J., 108
Salamon, A., 80, 81
Saldivar, E., 162
Salmond, A., 59, 64, 66, 72
Sanders, K., 58
Sandvik, N., 263, 269
Santos, B.d.S., 111
Scheff, T., 72, 79
schizo-mathematics-learner, 142
Schon, D.A., 106, 107
Schneider, D., 210
school readiness, 103
    current crisis of, 108–10
    framed as a crisis, 106–8
    neoliberal education reforms and, 106
    rise of neoliberalism and, 104–6
science of reading, 164–67
Schweinhart, L.J., 105
Schwennesen, N., 125, 126
Scott, D., 282
Scott, P., 58
Scribner, S., 159
Sedgwick, E.K., 247, 251
Seemiller, C., 127
Sellers, M., 177, 183
settler colonialism, 177
Shankar, A., 200
Sharman, F.A., 60
Sharpe, C., 282
Shatto, B., 127
Shields, R., 178
Shimpi, P., 264, 265, 271, 273
Shotwell, A., 193, 247–48, 249, 254
Sigona, N., 9
Silin, J.G., 193, 244, 251
Silva, J., 141, 143
Silver, L.J., 282
Simpson, L.B., 284
Simon, J.A., 56
Sims, M., 207

Sinclair, N., 141, 145
Sinker, R., 265, 266
Sisson, J.H., 269
Sjöstrand Öhrfelt, M., 223, 234, 235
Skerrett, M., 62, 216, 217
Skolverket, 223, 232, 234, 235
Skovsmose, O., 138, 139, 140
Skutnabb-Kangas, T., 56
Slater, G.B., 103, 104, 106, 107, 108, 109, 110, 111
Smith, A., 105
Smith, F., 158, 159, 160, 163, 165
Smith, K., 207, 209
Smith, L.T., 72
Smith, P.H., 162
Smith, T., 41
Snow, C.E., 166
Söderlind, I., 225, 226, 229
Solvason, C., 80, 81
Somerville, M., 266, 272
Sono, D., 106, 107
Sosnowski, J., 162
Soto, L.D., 104, 111
Sotomayor, S., 99
Sound of Rain, 202
Souto-Manning, M., 111, 112
spectrality, 14
spirit murder, 184
Spivak, G.C., 111
Spryrou, S., 287
Stadsbard, 227
Starting Strong report, 234
State of Exception, 5
states of exception, 5
Steedman, C., 287
Stockton, K.B., 251
storbarnkammere, 227, 228
Store, The, 177, 179, 181
St. Pierre, E.A., 144, 182, 187
Strakova, J., 209
Stratigos, T., 268
Styfo, S.J., 103, 104
Suárez-Orozco, C., 12
Suárez-Orozco, M., 12
subaltern subjectivity, 13–15
Sumsion, J., 80
surface metaphors, 89

Swadener, B.B., 109, 110, 111, 178
Sweden. *See* early childhood education
systemas de escritura en el Desarrollo del niño, Los, 159

T

Tabb, W.K., 104
Tallberg Broman, I., 224, 226, 227, 232
Tawhiwhirangi, D.I., 77
Taylor, A., 191, 193, 194, 213, 244, 246, 265, 271, 285
Taylor, R., 59
Te Rauparaha, 60
Te Tiriti o Waitangi, 58, 73
Te Whāriki, 78
Te Wherowhero, 58
Teachers College Record, 263
teacherwatching, 156, 167–68
Teberosky, A., 156, 159, 169
Teja, J.L., 176
Tefft, P., 156
Tesar, M., 216, 217
theory of action, 106, 107
things, 185
Thiong'o, N.W., 62, 67
Thomas, L., 269
Thomas, R.J., 12
Thompson, D., 281
Thrupp, M., 80
Thunberg, G., 217
timespacemattering, 123, 125–26
Tinti, P., 30
Tobin, J., 81, 193
Toren, C., 286–87
Torok, M., 14
Towne, S.D. Jr., 109
toys, 208–10
Traffic Stop, 184
transgressions, 143–47, 147–51
trauma trails, 4
Treaty of Waitangi, 61, 216
Trouble with the Child in the Carceral State, 250
Trump, D., 88, 89
truth, 88
Tseng, C.L., 128
Tuck, E., 284, 285

Turner, E.E., 141, 142, 143, 145

U

UNICEF, 21, 34, 127, 234
United Nations, 127
United Nations Convention on the Rights of Children, 81, 232
United Nations Environment Programme, 209
United Nations High Commission for Refugees (UNHCR), 11, 21, 23, 25, 28, 29, 30
University of Haifa, 97
Unlocking Imagination, Conversations With Rain, 202
Urban, L., 111
Urwin, C., 12

V

Vaca, N., 99
Valencia, R.R., 104, 109
Valero, P., 142, 148, 151
Varvin, S., 12, 13
Vaughn, L., 64
Villanueva, M.T., 195, 198
Viruru, R., 40, 111, 112, 281
Von Nieda, B., 90
Von Spakovsky, H., 96

W

Waitangi Tribunal, 73
Walker, R., 61, 72, 73
Walkerdine, V., 244, 246, 254
Walsh, C., 167, 168
Walsh, O., 4
Walton, J., 66
Wane, N.N., 45
Waniganayake, M., 207
War on Poverty, 104
Warin, J., 269
Washington Post, 95
Watkins, E., 164
Watson, K., 268, 271
Webb, D., 58
Weheliye, A.G., 280, 282, 283
Wei, L., 178

Weikart, D.P., 105
Weisenfeld, G.G., 108
Weizeman, E., 24
Westinghouse Learning Corporation, 105
whāngai, 66
White Savior Industrial Complex, 184
Whitty, P., 134
Wi Parata, 61
Wilkin, A., 41
Wilson, J., 5, 12, 13
Winnicott, D.W., 4, 247, 252, 253, 254
Winston, J., 264, 265
Wintoneak, V., 202
Wohlwend, K., 267, 268
Wolfe, C., 285
Wolff, K., 183
Wong, J.M., 132
Wood, E., 263, 270
World Bank, 103
World Health Organization, 209
Wray, A., 182
Wright, A., 105
Wynter, S., 249, 280–81, 282, 283

Y

Yang, K.W., 284, 285
Yazzie, M.K., 195
Yelland, N., 126, 134
Yosso, T.J., 112, 113
Young, D., 214

Z

Zellman, G.L., 108
Zembylas, M., 71
Zigler, E., 103, 104
Zurn, P., 200